Syndicalism in France

Syndicalism in France
A Study of Ideas

Jeremy Jennings
Lecturer in French Political Thought and Government
University College, Swansea

St. Martin's Press   New York

First published in the United States of America in 1990

Printed in Great Britain

Library of Congress Cataloging-in-Publication Data
Jennings, Jeremy, 1952–
Syndicalism in France: A Study of Ideas/Jeremy Jennings.
   p. cm.
Includes bibliographical references.
ISBN 0–312–04027–X
1. Syndicalism–France–History.   I. Title
HD6684.J46 1990
335′.82′0944–dc20

89–24114
CIP

To the memory of
my grandfather,
Ernest Frederick Leek

Contents

Acknowledgements

I am grateful to the British Academy for funding the extended periods of research in France required to complete this project and to the University College, Swansea, not only for granting me a year's sabbatical leave, but also for making available to me the limited research monies at its disposal.

My thanks go also to my colleague Julian Jackson for companionship and support during two successive summers spent together in the Avenue Reille and to those in Paris who from our first meeting have displayed friendship, encouragement and hospitality: Gisèle Piner, Willy Gianinazzi, Françoise Blum, Christophe Prochasson, Varda and Shlomo Sand, Michel Prat, Marie-Laurence Netter and Jacques Julliard. I am, however, indebted above all to Colette Chambelland for her ceaseless help and generosity and for sharing with me her unrivalled personal knowledge of the people and ideas that made up the syndicalist movement in France.

1 Introduction

On the opposite side of the *Parc Montsouris* from what is now the *Cité universitaire* in Paris' fourteenth *arrondissement* lies the Avenue Reille. It is by no means one of Paris' most famous streets — its place in French history seemingly limited to a mysterious and bizarre roadside meeting between the German spy Esterhazy and two members of the French army implicated in the case against Captain Dreyfus: Félix Gribelin and the Commandant du Paty de Clam — and today, if it is known at all, it is for a fine piece of domestic architecture by Le Corbusier. Yet between 1903 and 1907, at the very height of the 'heroic epoch' of French syndicalism, it was the location for meetings between the members of one of Paris' most secretive circles. Approximately once a month on Sunday afternoons an attentive observer would have seen the leaders of the *Confédération générale du travail* (CGT) making their way towards number 30. The destination of Victor Griffuelhes, Emile Pouget, Alphonse Merrheim and Paul Delesalle was the apartment of Hubert Lagardelle, editor of *Le Mouvement socialiste*: the other people present would have included Georges Sorel, the 'metaphysician' of syndicalism, Edouard Berth, Robert Louzon, middle-class intellectuals such as Ernest Lafont and André Morizet, as well as foreign visitors passing through Paris, for example Robert Michels and Arturo Labriola.[1] The existence of these gatherings on its own destroys a fiction carefully nurtured by the leaders of the CGT themselves: namely that the theoreticians of revolutionary syndicalism and its practitioners were virtually unknown to each other. 'I read only Dumas', Griffuelhes was fond of repeating.[2] Other evidence suggests that the image of a stark divide between the philosophers of the *nouvelle école* of socialism and the militants of the CGT cannot be sustained. Griffuelhes, Pouget and Merrheim were themselves regular contributors to Lagardelle's *Le Mouvement socialiste* and it was here, for example, that the first versions of Sorel's *Réflexions sur la violence* and *Les Illusions du progrès* were published. It is hard to believe that they did not read a periodical in which they were leading participants. Berth and Lagardelle in turn were both to collaborate with the CGT leadership on such syndicalist papers as *L'Avant-garde, L'Action directe* and *La Révolution* and when, for example, the syndicalist movement needed to respond to criticisms over the issue of patriotism and the class struggle it was Lagardelle and Pouget who together took on Durkheim in public debate.[3] We also know from Sorel's letters to Lagardelle that Griffuelhes, Delesalle and Yvetot, the general secretary of the *bourses du travail* section of the CGT, received complimentary copies of *Réflexions sur la violence*:[4] moreover, it was Sorel who wrote the preface to Griffuelhes' *Les Objectifs de nos luttes de classe*.[5]

1

Griffuelhes too, it seems, occasionally figured as an expert on Sorel. On 15 January 1910 *La Démocratie sociale* published an interview with Griffuelhes on the subject of Paul Bourget's controversial play *La Barricade* wherein the dramatist had claimed to draw his conception of the class struggle from *Réflexions sur la violence*. Having seen the play, Griffuelhes commented, 'I can state . . . that M. Bourget has in no way profited from his reading of Sorel'.[6]

Why then were the participants at Lagardelle's apartment so eager to preserve the secrecy of their meetings? The answer lies in the *ouvriérisme*, coupled with an attendant anti-intellectualism, that came increasingly to characterise the French labour movement. But even here the position of the CGT leaders, despite their frequent (and correct) assertion that syndicalism was above all a movement of practice, was more nuanced than has generally been acknowledged. The debate about the relationship of intellectuals to the proletariat began in earnest in France with the publication in 1895 of Karl Kautsky's 'Le Socialisme et les carrières libérales' in *Le Devenir social* (although somewhat ironically in view of its later prominence in French discourse the editors were obliged to point out that there existed no French equivalent of the word '*Intelligenz*' and hence the German original was retained throughout).[7] The whole issue quickly became entwined with the dramatic events associated with the Dreyfus Affair (the publication by the Dreyfusards of the 'Manifesto of the Intellectuals' in 1898 and Barrès' characterisation of intellectuals as 'a band of arrogant madmen' being two of its most significant moments), and through it the appearance of a cluster of intellectuals who came to socialism, as Pierre Monatte was to recall in 1952, 'without any sentiment of class . . . without freeing themselves from their own sense of superiority'.[8] The position of Griffuelhes and his colleagues, given their belief in the primary of the producer, was not only that no valid distinction could be drawn between 'manual' and 'intellectual' labour (a view which found its most eloquent echo throughout the vast corpus of Sorel's work) but also that in a movement which emphasised the centrality of the self-emancipation of the proletariat the intrusion of bourgeois ideas would be corrosive. Their primary objection, therefore, was against the intellectual as 'parasite', the self-seeking exploiter of the working class in search of a position of political power and eminence. Yet collaboration of sorts was possible. 'At *L'Avant-garde* and *Le Mouvement socialiste*', Hubert Lagardelle wrote in 1905, 'where the "worker" members are more numerous than the "intellectual" members, we are only the interpreters of a real movement, which is exterior to us, which we do not create, and of which we only translate its principal expressions'.[9] Intellectuals, in short, could play a useful role if, as supporters of the proletariat, they remained external to the movement.

None of this, of course, is to imply that former cobblers such as Griffuelhes were ever entirely to overcome their antipathy for the *habitués* of the Latin Quarter. In a letter to Berth written in 1912, for example, Sorel was to suggest that Pelloutier had never been able to attain his rightful place in syndicalist circles because as a *'déclassé . . .* the revolutionaries always had the feeling that they had a stranger in their midst'.[10] Similarly, Pierre Monatte was convinced that the former artillery officer Charles Guieysse, editor of *Pages libres* and one of the framers of the Charter of Amiens,[11] was always to exist on the margins of the CGT due to his bourgeois origins.[12] Nor, in reverse, did this mean that the intellectuals who conversed with the CGT leadership in Lagardelle's apartment were at ease in a trade union meeting: Sorel, for all his *militantisme de plume*,[13] was temperamentally suited to the library, not the strike committee. Least of all is it to suggest either that the militants and theoreticians of the movement were in total accord in their analysis of the significance of syndicalism[14] or that works such as *Réflexions sur la violence* had a wide readership and influence amongst the rank-and-file membership of the CGT.[15] What it definitely does do, however, is demonstrate the importance in Paris at the turn of the century of the review (in this case Lagardelle's *Le Mouvement socialiste*) as a *lieu de sociabilité*, a meeting place and point of conviviality, in which ideas were expounded and contacts made, friendships established.[16] It is this that explains the glowing personal tribute to Griffuelhes which appeared in Edouard Berth's article 'Marchands, Intellectuels et Politiciens'.[17]

Moreover, it provides us with a convenient starting point for the examination of the controversial and ambiguous doctrine which at the beginning of the twentieth century came to be known as syndicalism. To date (and this applies not only to the literature in English), interest in this doctrine amongst historians of ideas has been confined for the most part to the study of Sorel (Jacques Julliard's monograph on Fernand Pelloutier being a conspicuous exception), with the result that not only have certain important figures — most notably Edouard Berth and Pierre Monatte — been consigned to virtual oblivion but also attention has been restricted almost exclusively to the ten years prior to the First World War. When this limited perspective has been transcended, as in the case of two recent books by Zeev Sternhell,[18] it has been mistakenly to characterise syndicalist ideas and its principal exponents *primarily* as aspects of the rise of fascist ideology. What in fact emerged out of pre-existing working-class practice at the turn of the century was the beginnings of a tradition which, held together if not by a key text then by a set of common reference points and a complicated series of inter-personal relationships, was to constitute a distinctive, occasionally powerful, and always evolving voice in French life for over 60 years.

The people who met in Lagardelle's apartment were, in a sense, emblematic of this whole process. Brought together for a matter of a few years, they afterwards followed contrasting and sometimes conflicting routes, in turns and at times abandoning or re-interpreting revolutionary syndicalism for differing reasons and in a variety of ways; and it is because of this that they, along with two others known to them, Fernand Pelloutier and Pierre Monatte, make up the core of this analysis of syndicalist ideas in France. By examining the contrasting reactions of a group of individuals caught up in the same historical situations — amongst their many qualities was in some cases a remarkable longevity — one can, through loosely-connected and often separate narratives, not only follow the evolution (and ultimately disintegration) of the syndicalist vision but also perceive how, with the failure of the syndicalist movement to secure its objectives, that vision was transposed into a range of dissimilar practices and possibilities. If that range was not to exclude an admiration for Mussolini, so it was to include an accommodation with nationalism, reformism, Catholicism and bolshevism as well as (and this should not be forgotten) the attempt, against the odds, to preserve intact the original idea and to re-establish its relevance. In twentieth-century French syndicalism tragedy and bathos are found side-by-side.

Finally, a word about the structure of this book. It is not a history of the syndicalist movement as such but takes as its primary vehicle of elucidation the lives and ideas of a group of individuals who were for the most part associates or close friends. The exception to this is to be found in its treatment of the reformist syndicalists, especially Auguste Keufer. The justification for this is two-fold. Firstly, the role of a positivism derived directly from Auguste Comte in the development of syndicalist thought and practice has been almost totally ignored; secondly, much of the debate within the syndicalist movement between 1900 and 1920 is incomprehensible while ever this remains so. Thus, beyond the satisfaction of a legitimate curiosity, the reformist syndicalists act as an essential backdrop to the main issues and personalities under examination here. That they were also to provide a final home for at least one of the participants at the gatherings in the Avenue Reille is just one aspect of a wider irony associated with the history of syndicalism.

II

'As citizens they were courted, as producers they were ignored': in this way Jacques Julliard summarises the political integration and social marginalisation that characterised the position of the French working class in the first decades of the Third Republic.[19] Accorded the right to vote, all male workers at least were full members of a parliamentary democracy and, in alliance with a progressive bourgeoisie, were part of a coalition committed to the eradication of aristocratic and clerical power. Military

service and the State school, the supreme symbols of republican accultur-
ation, were to wed the people to the nation.[20] Yet, as Christophe Charle
has shown in meticulous detail, for all its egalitarian rhetoric the conquest
of power by the republicans brought the creation of new élites drawn
almost exclusively from the upper echelons of the Parisian bourgeoisie.[21]
Trade unions – *syndicats* — remained illegal until 1884 and even after this
a majority of employers refused to recognise their right to negotiate whilst
the State itself would not permit trade union membership for its own
employees. In terms of legislation designed to protect workers from economic malpractice and exploitation France lagged far behind her European
neighbours.

At one level the syndicalist movement can be interpreted as a recognition and willing acceptance of this social and economic segregation
experienced by the proletariat. By seeking to transform a marginalisation
inflicted upon the working class into a self-conscious sense of autonomy,
exclusion into secession, it made a virtue out of necessity. Separateness,
to quote Julliard again, came to be seen as 'a special richness, an aspect
of the proletariat's patrimony'.[22] Yet equally, this sentiment of internal
exile, and with it a certain apoliticism, predated the emergence of syndicalism as a distinct form of working-class practice. In two recent analyses of
French labour in the nineteenth century both William H. Sewell and
Bernard H. Moss[23] have been inclined to see its origin in the associationist
and co-operative trade socialism that emerged during the July Monarchy
and the heady days of the 1848 revolution. Certainly the failure of the
Second Republic (1848–52) had a deep impact upon the proletariat's
perception of the effectiveness of political action and this, coupled with its
subsequent banishment from politics during the Second Empire (1852–70),
meant, as Tony Judt has argued, that 'by the time the French Left re-
emerged as an unrestricted participant in bourgeois politics it had a very
different account to offer of the prospects for integration and improvement'.[24] This conclusion is confirmed by Michelle Perrot's analysis of the
language used by labour leaders during strikes in the early days of the
Third Republic. 'Politics', she writes, 'did not enjoy a good reputation . . .
[it] corrupted and divided, as opposed to economic or social concerns
which united'.[25] Nevertheless, the workers continued to vote in the main
for the advanced republicans.

The first significant signs of renewed working-class militancy after the
defeat of the Paris Commune came in 1876 when, with the ending of the
state of siege, the inaugural *Congrès ouvrier de France* was held. Under the
influence of the Marxist Jules Guesde subsequent congresses — notably
Marseilles in 1879 — were to push workers' movement towards an acceptance of collectivism and political action but divisions between those committed to a variety of revolutionary, moderate and non-electoral strategies
were not slow to emerge. The Guesdist position, embodied in the *Parti*

ouvrier français (POF), was that industrial action should always be subordinated to political ends and therefore with the legalisation of trade unions
in 1884 and the creation of the *Fédération Nationale des Syndicats* two
years later they sought to ensure, through their own ascendency, that the
syndicats would operate as appendages to the socialist party.[26] This stance
not only brought the Guesdists into conflict with the groupings on the
Left more sympathetic to the idea of syndicalist autonomy — for example
the Blanquists led by Edouard Vaillant and the Allemanists — but also
with those for whom the road to proletarian emancipation lay exclusively
in economic means. The latter group was to gain in strength as between
1870 and 1890 the potential of strike action was re-assessed.

The first attempts to foster trade unionism during the Third Republic
aimed to create reformist organisations designed primarily for mutual
assistance and in line with this, as Michelle Perrot has shown, during the
years from 1871 to 1879 considerable efforts were made to avoid strikes
on both ethical and strategic grounds. Strikes, it was thought, were costly,
usually ended in defeat, and when victorious secured only ephemeral and
illusory gains. Disapproval, however, did not prevent the occurrence of
strikes and although, as we shall see, some of these reservations (especially
with regard to individual or 'partial' strikes) continued into the 1890s, it
was largely as a result of widespread (and relatively successful) strike
activity between 1878–80 that they came increasingly to be seen as a
legitimate and concrete expression of proletarian discontent. The strike
tactic was debated at all the key congresses of the workers' movement in
the 1880s, with the result that in 1894 at Nantes a majority of delegates
at the *Fédération Nationale des Syndicats* endorsed the principle of the
general strike. At the same conference the non-Guesdist majority also
resolved to create a new organisation, the *Confédération générale du
travail* (CGT). It should be noted that the practice of the strike precedes
its elevation to a position of centrality in syndicalist theory.[27]

The second challenge to Guesdist dominance of the French labour
movement came in the form of the *bourses du travail* movement. The first
bourse du travail was opened in Paris in 1887 and by the time that the
constituent congress of the *Fédération des Bourses du Travail* took place
in 1892 they numbered fourteen: by 1908 there were as many as 157
scattered throughout the whole of France. The brain-child of the liberal
economist Gustave de Molinari and the less well-known Auguste Leullier,
the *bourses du travail* were designed as employment exchanges intended
primarily to facilitate the movement of labour but as each *bourse* also
acted as a meeting place for all the *syndicats* of a particular town or locality
they quickly became centres of trade union activity and propaganda.
Furthermore, from the outset the *bourses du travail* movement adopted a
strategy of abstention from political activity.[28]

Thus by the time of the first congress of the CGT in 1895 there came into existence a nationwide organisation that had not only succeeded in breaking the hold of the Guesdists over the *syndicats* but that had also established a pattern of trade union independence from political control. Equally, autonomy entailed decentralisation and a confusion of competing constituencies, with *syndicats* joined horizontally through the *bourses du travail* and vertically through separate federations for each industry. Only in 1902 did the *Fédération des Bourses du Travail* properly merge with the CGT and it took another decade for something like a co-ordinated structure to emerge. Furthermore, by no means did every trade union join the CGT nor was every worker a member of a *syndicat*. As late as the eve of the First World War, after years of expansion, CGT membership stood only at around 600 000.[29]

Nevertheless, for all its administrative frailty and numerical weakness, it was the CGT which between 1902 and 1908 unleashed a wave of spectacular and lengthy strikes, grabbing the public's (as well as the Ministry of the Interior's) attention and spreading fear amongst the bourgeoisie. In 1904 there were 1026 stoppages with almost 4 000 000 days of lost production; and two years later the figure stood at 1309 strikes with a record number of 438 500 participants. It was at this moment, at Amiens in October 1906, that by 834 votes to eight delegates to the CGT congress provided the most succinct definition of the methods and goals of the syndicalist movement. 'The CGT', the Charter of Amiens declared, 'brings together, outside every political school of thought, all those workers conscious of the struggle necessary to obtain the disappearance of wage-earners and employers'.[30]

Attempts to explain why a significant proportion, if not a majority, of the French working class were prepared to endorse and engage in this mode of action have varied.[31] In part it can be attributed to the long-established tradition of working-class autonomy, although it is not clear what role, if any, was played by the incoherent set of ideas associated with Proudhonism.[32] Guesde's own authoritarian leadership of the POF, combined with a generally weak penetration of Marxist ideas in France, also had an impact, as did the parlous state of the divided and factionalised political wing of the socialist movement. But why did direct action syndicalism specifically experience a dramatic upsurge in the first decade of the twentieth century? Without question, a period of economic growth and prosperity gave great encouragement to worker militancy and to this can be added a broader disillusionment with the republican régime and political process after the deceptions of the Dreyfus Affair.

What, finally, was the significance and potential of this period of heightened syndicalist activity? Here we touch upon issues discussed at length by the personalities who make up the subject of our inquiry and it clearly would be inappropriate to prejudge and possibly undermine their own conclusions. Suffice to say that neither amongst themselves nor amongst their contemporaries was there general agreement upon these questions. Emile Durkheim, for example, voiced a series of criticisms against revolutionary syndicalism. The syndicalists, he argued, were wrong to suggest that the growth of large-scale industry demanded the removal of existing society. Man could adapt to the new economic order. Nor were the syndicalists right to assert that the worker could be seen exclusively as *homo oeconomicus*. More seriously, to destroy society was to invite a return to 'barbarism'. 'It is not', Durkheim wrote, 'the sun of a new society that will rise, all resplendent with light, over the ruins of the old: instead man will enter into a period of darkness'.[33] For the socialist leader and syndicalism's *bête noire*, Jean Jaurès, the error was to believe that solely through the general strike a determined, active and conscious *minority* could overturn the capitalist system. 'No surprise weapon', he wrote, 'can exempt socialism from winning over the majority of the nation through propaganda and legal means'.[34] And so on: virtually every group or shade of opinion, from the anarchist Jean Grave to Pierre Bietry, leader of the 'yellow unions', from supporters of Christian syndicalism to campaigners against alcoholism, had their say.[35] It is, however, worth dwelling upon three specific analyses — one voiced during the 'heroic epoch', two provided by later historians of the movement — of the possibilities inherent to syndicalism.

Robert Michels was, as we already know, an occasional visitor to the gatherings held at Hubert Lagardelle's apartment. He was also for some years a regular contributor to *Le Mouvement socialiste*. Michels began his public life as a straightforward socialist, moving around 1905 towards syndicalism, and then via élite theory to an allegiance to the Italian nation.[36] Central to this personal trajectory was an analysis of the oligarchical tendencies of political parties, for which his primary evidence was provided by the German Social Democratic Party (SPD). It was acquaintance with the *syndicats*, however, that pushed simple disillusionment with the SPD into a wider recognition that oligarchy was endemic to all organisations. That conclusion first surfaced in Michels' response to an article by Edouard Berth in which the latter, reviewing Michels' own analysis of the Italian social party, had concluded that the *syndicats*, as instruments of direct action by the proletariat, were immune from the perils and treason associated with the *political* representation of the working class. Berth, Michels replied, 'has not thought through his thesis: instead of saying the party engenders *embourgeoisement*, he should have said *organisation* engenders *embourgeoisement* and deviation. And the principle of organisation embraces equally the party and the *syndicat*'.[37] Six years later Michels responded in identical fashion to Lagardelle's long review of his now-classic study, *Zur Sociologie des Parteiwesens in der Modernen Democratie*. 'It is', he commented, 'a curious pretention to maintain that the *syndicat* alone should be exempt from the general laws of sociology'.[38] In short, Michels' claim was that the syndicalist movement was subject to the same corrupting tendencies as all other analogous movements and moreover that as a consequence its intention to establish a classless society through the self-emancipation of the proletariat was without foundation.

The second analysis concentrates upon what are seen as the consequences of the ambiguous origins and 'double character' of the *bourses du travail*. Far from providing the institutional foundations of the new society (as Pelloutier in particular believed) they were, according to Peter Schöttler, part of the 'ideological apparatus of the State'.[39] Each *bourse*, Schöttler emphasises, was set up and in part funded by the local municipality, thus minimising its capacity for independent action and obliging it, out of prudence, to act not as an organisation of 'combat' but as a semi-official vehicle of bourgeois social policy. The libraries of the *bourses du travail*, themselves the subject of a euphoric account by Pelloutier, were in the main, for example, stocked with technical and scientific texts leaving little room for the socialist classics. The *bourses du travail* were, in other words, structured by an internal ideology that made it impossible for them to pursue the '*contre-politique*' required to overturn a hegemonic bourgeoisie.

Even if one does not follow the severe Althusserian logic of Schöttler's argument, his assessment of the *bourses du travail* does serve to highlight the paucity of revolutionary means at the disposal of the syndicalist movement and it is this dimension (although from an altogether different perspective) that is at the centre of Peter Stearns' treatment of syndicalism as 'a cause without rebels'.[40] What Stearns chooses to stress is the *moderation* of French workers as reflected in both their strike demands and tactics and their preference, where possible, always to obtain a negotiated settlement to a dispute. Certainly — and in marked contrast to the image presented by Sorel's *Réflexions sur la violence* — where violence did occur during strikes it was normally far from extensive and when the period of strike activity (1870–90) studied by Michelle Perrot is compared to the period supposedly dominated by revolutionary syndicalism it can be seen that beyond an increase in the number of strikes and strikers there was no significant change in strike patterns.

Each of these three assessments of syndicalism, therefore, focuses upon its limitations and upon the gap which existed between the grandiose rhetoric and expectations of some of those involved directly or indirectly with it and the reality of actual possibilities and results obtained. At bottom, each maintains with some justice that the ideology of revolutionary syndicalism had little impact upon either events or institutions. Yet at the same time each deals with a caricature of the syndicalist movement. As a movement it never laid claim to pursue exclusively revolutionary goals by exclusively revolutionary means (as the Charter of Amiens eloquently testifies). Nor was it a static entity resolutely united behind a common programme of fixed demands: it evolved, pushed forward by experience and the vigorous disagreements that were always such a feature of its congresses. Moreover, through them we cannot grasp the movement's central paradox and dilemma: at one and the same time it was committed both to the eradication of the condition of proletarian and its elevation, through a celebration of the dignity of labour and the virtues of social exclusion, into an exemplary status.

2 Fernand Pelloutier and Revolutionary Syndicalism

Fernand Pelloutier can, in the words of Pierre Monatte, be 'justly regarded as the father of revolutionary syndicalism'.[1] Born in 1867, Pelloutier came to syndicalism via provincial radical republicanism and then orthodox Marxism. By profession a journalist, his break with Guesdism took place in 1892 when he, along with Aristide Briand, jointly defended the use of the general strike. As secretary of the *Fédération des bourses du travail* from 1895 (at the age of only 27) until his death in 1901 he went part of the way towards creating the organisational basis of an autonomous working-class movement and in his books and numerous articles he outlined the rudiments of syndicalism as a distinct ideology. He also provided the syndicalist movement with an example of dedication and commitment that few, if any, were subsequently to surpass.[2]

The key to Pelloutier's thought is to be found in his analysis of the workings of the economic system. 'Can you deny', he wrote in 1894, 'that at the source of all disorder, of bad politics and bad morals, of greed and cruelty, of egoism and envy, one always finds money. Money is the beginning and end of everything'.[3] Specifically, Pelloutier located the cause of the ills of society in a perversion of the system of exchange, the substitution by capitalism of exchange value for use value. The law of supply and demand ensured that products were priced not according to their intrinsic value but in line with the dictates of the market. Inevitably, Pelloutier argued, such a system operated in the interests of those who possessed capital, the manipulators of the system of exchange, and contrary to the interests of the consumer and producer, whose labour benefited only 'the parasite, the rentier and the financier'. 'To the extent that one can say that a man is rich', Pelloutier observed, 'the less he has worked: his useful production is inversely proportionate to his wealth'.[4] Here, in essence, was 'the origin of the modern social system in its entirety'.[5]

The result of this economic inequality was the division of humanity into two classes, the vast majority condemned to a life of labour, servitude and grinding poverty and an idle élite who, in Pelloutier's view, served no useful function and were superfluous to society's requirements. The operation of the law of supply and demand led firstly to the emergence of a class of intermediaries, merchants, who, in the act of purchase and sale, extracted surplus value from the product, and thereby deprived the worker of the full fruits of his labour. In turn, those enriched by the process, fearing the demands and actions of the dispossessed and the loss of their wealth and power, created the instruments of the State to protect their interests. As a result another group of non-producers, the employees of the State — the army, the police, the magistrature, the officials of government — was created and, as the producers directly bore the cost, their poverty was further accentuated. The consequence of the law of supply and demand therefore was the economic impoverishment of the producers and their political enslavement.

Pelloutier was equally critical of the deleterious effects of this economic system. It had created a society of fraud and corruption, based upon competition, rivalry and violence. Little or no thought was given to the common good. The vast majority of the population were condemned to squalor and deprivation. Individual happiness was not attained through the enhancement of the well-being of others but the product of self-gratification and self-aggrandisement. Outwardly respectable, bourgeois society was a society of cant and hypocrisy, of philistine art and sexual depravity. It was also, as Pelloutier repeatedly proclaimed, a society doomed to decay and ultimate destruction.

The objective pursued by Pelloutier was the replacement of this iniquitous social and economic system by one which would re-establish 'the rational functioning of humanity'.[6] Clearly, for Pelloutier this implied the suppression of exchange value, the abolition of its product, capital, and an end to economic inequality. The goal of the new society should be 'to ensure for every man a portion of those fruits of the earth which he has shared in producing, equal to his needs, notwithstanding those physical and intellectual inequalities which distinguish him from other members of the collective'.[7] This, Pelloutier believed, could be achieved by creating an economic system that ensured that only goods of equal value could be exchanged, attained by giving to each product an invariable price. It followed that if the producer was to receive a reward appropriate to his labour then all non-productive intermediaries or functionaries — 'the economic and political parasites of the present social system'[8] — should be eradicated. 'Social life', Pelloutier argued, 'can be reduced to the organisation of production'.[9] Freed from poverty and social and political oppression, the workers would develop a completely new morality. Competition and envy would be replaced by co-operation and a sense of social duty. The 'society of the future' would, above all, be characterised by 'the voluntary and free association of producers'.[10]

The central question faced by Pelloutier was: how could such a society be brought into existence? The socialist and republican traditions in France offered a range of alternatives. Pelloutier rejected them all and set about developing his own strategy for the emancipation of the working class.

In his early articles as editor for the Saint-Nazaire based *La Démocratie de l'Ouest* Pelloutier's suspicions of the parliamentary process can be discerned quite clearly. Initially he limited himself to calling for a closer and tighter relationship between the electorate and their elected representatives, describing 'the perfect representation' of the constituents' views as 'the very essence of universal suffrage'.[11] With time — and noticeably after the Panama scandal[12] — Pelloutier became positively critical of the entire process of election within parliamentary democracy. Elections appeared to be little more than a lottery, the people giving their vote to the candidate 'who lies most, puts up the largest number of posters, eloquently flatters popular vanity'.[13] Parliament was a vehicle for the social advancement of the incompetent and the ambitious. From the perspective of Pelloutier's future society, universal suffrage was a complete irrelevance: the prevailing social conditions and the development of human faculties would ensure that men directed their own affairs.[14]

Pelloutier's disillusionment, not unexpectedly, also extended to the Republic. Again this can be discerned in his articles in *La Démocratie de l'Ouest* where he repeatedly returns to the theme that the Republic, despite its democratic façade, had failed to satisfy the hopes of the working class. In an article entitled 'L'Oeuvre de 1789'[15] published in 1892 Pelloutier was led to ask: 'whether man was more free under the Republic than he had been under the *ancien régime*?'. 'Free to die of hunger, certainly . . . Free to resist oppression? Just let the workers try to make use of their liberty!' was his reply. Likewise the political and civil liberties granted to the proletariat were simply abused by the bourgeoisie. The political Republic, as Pelloutier frequently asserted, needed to be replaced by the 'social Republic'.

This critique of Republican democracy was subsequently extended to include all attempts at reform within the present political and economic system. The interests of the State, Pelloutier argued, were inextricably linked to those of the possessing classes. The *raison d'être* of the State, he wrote, is 'to protect superfluous or harmful political interests'. It made little sense, therefore, to expect an institution based upon wealth to attack the privileges and power of the rich.[16]

This conclusion was confirmed by the experience of legislation purportedly designed to improve the conditions of the working class. Pelloutier was emphatic that the long list of legislation designed to ameliorate working conditions, reduce the working hours of women and children, provide insurance in the case of accident, and so on, had either remained inoperative or had been counterproductive. The capitalist class had had little difficulty in either evading the obligations of the (usually poorly formulated) law or in devising new forms of oppression that had further aggravated the misery of the workers. In addition, it was the workers themselves, through higher taxes, who bore the cost of this legislation. 'Legislative action', Pelloutier concluded, 'is at one and the same time useless and dangerous'.[17]

The way forward, therefore, lay not through piecemeal reform but through the root and branch eradication of capitalism and its political instrument, the State. Unless this were achieved all attempts to secure change by the 'Fourth Estate' would be futile and illusory: the capitalist class would simply claw back what had been given to the proletariat. The power of money had to be destroyed.[18]

If these considerations quickly disabused Pelloutier of the republicanism that had characterised his journalistic writings prior to his move to Paris in 1893, so too did they distance him from the reformist socialism that was gaining ground in France during the 1890s. Not only, according to Pelloutier, had the attainment of socialism by purely legal and parliamentary means never been part of official socialist policy (as defined by the International) but it also distracted socialists from their ultimate goal. Socialism could not be reduced to the possession of political power, a change of political personnel, or a majority of votes for the socialist parties. The State was not a 'simple instrument of social organisation', an institution that could be 'purified' or 'moralised', as some socialists believed. Rather, from within Pelloutier's perspective, it appeared to operate as a means of demoralisation, corruption and temptation, inducing socialists to revere power and authority, a training ground for future authoritarians. The net result of the reformist strategy was the intrusion of the ambitious and the mediocre into the socialist movement and the virtual exclusion of the working class whose role was reduced to that of providing the votes required to keep their leaders in power. Everything indicated, however, that the working class itself, disillusioned by the repeated failures and disappointments of reformism, as coming to realise that only a complete economic and political revolution could secure the establishment of an equitable society. They, if not their socialist deputies in parliament, appreciated that the interests of capital and labour were irreconcilable and that the class struggle was an inevitable reality.[19]

Yet, for all Pelloutier's commitment to the complete and revolutionary transformation of society, his attitude to the Republic and the parliamentary process was not entirely without ambiguity. At times he seemed to concede the propaganda value and potential of elections (on the condition that socialists did not lose sight of their ultimate goal) and he also accepted the utility and desirability of a limited number of reforms: a reduction in working hours, the establishment of a minimum wage, the nomination by the *syndicats* of factory inspectors. Again, however, Pelloutier added the qualification that only those reforms secured directly by the proletariat itself were liable to be effective and durable. It is also evident that Pelloutier, unlike many later syndicalists, was not entirely indifferent to the fate of the Republic. Jacques Julliard has written that Pelloutier viewed the Republic as the régime that 'provided an opening' for socialism and it is certainly true that Pelloutier believed that the Republic provided the socialist movement with far greater opportunities for development than previous régimes. Yet, so too, Pelloutier was of the opinion that there existed 'no essential difference between the spirit of monarchical governments and that of democratic governments'. In the first case, public authority was held by 'one individual'; under a republic popular sovereignty was delegated by 'a plutocratic minority' to 'a few hundred men who enact laws for everybody in the name of everybody'. The overriding impression is that Pelloutier viewed the Republic as a venal and unprincipled system and it is clear that there would be little room for its institutions and parliamentary practices in his new society.[20]

Pelloutier's critique of the parliamentary and statist routes to socialism was plainly applicable not only to reformist socialism but also to those 'revolutionary' parties — notably Guesde's *Parti Ouvrier Français* — committed to a programme that entailed the seizure of political power, by either parliamentary or revolutionary means, prior to the economic expropriation of the capitalist class. This was amply demonstrated in the exchange of open letters between Pelloutier and Jules Guesde in 1892, in which Pelloutier asserted that Guesdist tactics implied the indefinite postponement of socialism.[21] Further, Pelloutier specifically extended his criticisms to include the tactic, associated with the French revolutionary tradition and then part of Guesdist rhetoric, of the *insurrectionary* seizure of State power.

Pelloutier's objections to this revolutionary strategy were two-fold. He argued that the beneficiaries of past revolutions had always been the bourgeoisie and the leaders of the insurgents. The proletariat had paid the cost through the loss of their lives. Secondly, the advance of military technology, the improvement in communications, the rebuilding and modernisation of cities had rendered unfeasible the seizure of power by a determined revolutionary minority: henceforth all the advantages, most notably fire-power, lay with the forces of the State. Here Pelloutier's concern reflected a growing awareness amongst the socialist movement that perhaps the days of street-fighting were over.[22]

Finally, Pelloutier rejected the anarchist tactic of 'propaganda by the deed', direct acts of violence against bourgeois society and the bourgeois State, at their height between 1892 and 1894. Pelloutier's reasoning was simple. He could not support a method that involved 'the sacrifice of innocent victims'.[23]

Simultaneously with this critique of parliamentary reformism and of Guesdist and anarchist revolutionary violence Pelloutier commenced the formulation and elucidation of what he hoped would be a more fruitful and effective means of working-class emancipation: the general strike. Pelloutier first turned his thoughts to the idea of the general strike during a lengthy period of convalescence in 1890–91. From 1892 onwards, after his return to public life, he became its tireless advocate, refining his ideas on the subject in his polemic with the Guesdists and completing the process with the publication in 1895 of 'Qu'est-ce que la grève générale?'.[24]

In his first open letter to Guesde in 1892 Pelloutier referred to the general strike as being both 'peaceful and legal'. What he meant by this is best disclosed in a document entitled 'De la révolution par la grève générale', written jointly by Pelloutier and Aristide Briand.[25]

The authors demonstrate the 'legality' of the strike in curious fashion: by appealing to bourgeois principles of law. Drawing upon the distinction between *possession*, the natural right to use a thing and *property*, the civil right to use and to dispose of or misuse a thing, they conclude that a man's 'muscular energy' must be his property. Therefore he has absolute rights over it and can make use of it in any way he chooses, even if that includes 'abusing' it in the form of strike action. Further, Pelloutier and Briand argue, recent legislation — the 1864 act on the right to strike and the 1884 act legalising *Syndicats* — implicitly recognised this fact: hence strike action was both legal and legitimate.

The exposition of the 'peaceful' character of the general strike fully betrays both the optimism and the naiveté of the authors. Their basic assumption is that the social and economic order could not withstand a strike lasting longer than 15 days. Therefore they recommend that the workers set about creating a fund that could sustain them through such a strike. The required sum (Pelloutier and Briand estimate 400 million francs) could be collected within five years and this would provide each worker with 40 francs a day for the duration of the strike. Food for the strikers would be supplied by 'cooperative societies' which would have established 'vast warehouses' full of provisions. At the appropriate moment the workers would simply stay at home and the system, without their labour, would collapse around them. The revolution would be accomplished 'smoothly, without the spilling of blood, solely by the combination of rest'. Even if, by some unlikely misfortune, the strike were not entirely successful, the workers would be in a position to extract major concessions from the powers that be. The most likely outcome, however, would be the destruction of those very powers.

Pelloutier's conception of the general strike and his thoughts on the utility of strike action changed significantly in the next few years. Firstly, he came out strongly against 'grèves partielles', individual strikes aimed at securing improvements for one particular group of workers. To fully understand this we need to make reference to one of the central beliefs about the working of the capitalist economic system current amongst labour leaders of the period. There existed, Pelloutier believed (following Ferdinand Lassalle), an 'iron law' which ensured that all wage increases were inevitably matched by price increases. At best there existed only a momentary time lag in which wages surged ahead. It followed that an individual strike could only produce a temporary benefit for the workers concerned and would positively harm the interests of those workers who had not been able to secure a wage increase. Moreover, Pelloutier felt that the loss of income sustained during the strike only rarely made strike activity worthwhile and that the meagre results obtained only depressed and disillusioned the workers, encouraging lethargy and inertia. The 'iron law' could only be broken by breaking the economic system.[26]

Secondly, Pelloutier concluded that a general strike, to be successful, need not necessarily involve all of the workers in all trades. Only the strategically important sectors of the economy needed to be brought to a standstill: transport, gas, electricity, major industries, food supplies. The division of labour, for so long a source of capitalism's strength, was to be exploited by the strikers as its principal point of vulnerability.[27]

In addition, Pelloutier now argued against the lengthy preparation of the general strike and specifically criticised his earlier view that the workers should establish vast stores of provisions. The new scenario postulated a general strike of no more than *eight* days duration. If the workers were committed to the strike they would have no difficulty securing food and resources for this short period; if they were not, no amount of preparation would ensure victory. Subsequently, in a review of de Rousiers' *Le Trade-Unionisme en Angleterre*, Pelloutier extended this argument, asserting that excessive organisation and the establishment of union funds could actually engender an unwillingness to go on strike. Many later syndicalists in France were to echo this view.[28]

It is also clear that Pelloutier realised that a general strike would not be confined, as he had earlier believed, to a passive refusal to work and that it would necessarily involve some violence. The bourgeoisie would not meekly accept the demands of the workers or its own defeat and would therefore go on to the offensive. The attraction of the general strike, however, was precisely that it avoided the pitfalls of a revolutionary insurrection. While the army could be deployed against 30 000 insurgents, it was ineffective against a revolution that was both 'everywhere and nowhere', that was diffuse and widespread. The army, quite simply, could not protect every factory or every railway line.[29]

What is evident, above all, is that for Pelloutier the general strike was not perceived as a prelude to the revolution but as the revolution itself. During the strike the workers would take possession of the instruments of production, street by street, district by district. There would be no reliance upon the State or the political party. 'We wish to emancipate ourselves, to free ourselves', Pelloutier wrote, 'but we do not wish to carry out a revolution, to risk our skin, to put Pierre the socialist in the place of Paul the radical'.[30] The movement would be built around the *syndicat* and the *bourse du travail*, with the aim of creating 'the free association of each group of bakers in each bakery, of each group of locksmiths in each factory of locksmiths; in a word, free production'.[31]

We are again at the heart of Pelloutier's vision of society as an association of free producers. 'One dreams', he wrote in 1896, 'of free workshops where authority will have been replaced by the personal sentiment of duty'.[32] The merit of the general strike was precisely that it appeared to offer the definite possibility of establishing this libertarian order. It eschewed the corruption and the temptations of political activity, provided the means of making a revolution without recourse to either political leaders or parties and signified the destruction of hierarchical State authority. Conversely, the general strike operated on a premise that Pelloutier took to be incontrovertible: the priority of the productive process in social life.

Further, with the general strike there was, most crucially, a perfect correspondence between means and ends. If the end pursued was the emancipation of the proletariat, the general strike was a means of self-emancipation. 'We wish', Pelloutier wrote, 'that the emancipation of the people might be the work of the people themselves'.[33]

But were the workers capable of self-emancipation? In Pelloutier's view, any attempted revolution which did not rely upon the direct action of the workers themselves would inevitably lead to the re-establishment of hierarchical and authoritarian structures that would in turn once again enslave the proletariat. The question was whether the proletariat either possessed or could develop the intellectual, moral and technical skills and abilities required not only to carry out successfully the revolution but also to provide the basis of a new and regenerated future society. How could the workers prepare themselves for the revolution that would inevitably come? From 1894 onwards this issue became Pelloutier's abiding preoccupation.

What needs to be stressed is that Pelloutier did not believe that the revolution could either be left to chance or that it would be the result of a spontaneous and instinctive revolt on the part of the working class (a view often misleadingly associated with syndicalist theory in general). For Pelloutier the foundations of the future social and economic order would be laid within present society. The workers could not transform and transcend a debasing society in which they were denied the opportunity of directing their own lives without prior preparation both as individuals and as a class. Without that preparation any attempted revolution would simply be 'a waste of energy'. The lesson to be drawn, therefore, was crystal clear: *instruire pour révolter*.[34]

Pelloutier's efforts to encourage and further the education of the working class in the remaining years of his life took a variety of forms. Since his schooldays Pelloutier had been drawn to journalism and from 1893 onwards he became associated with numerous newspapers and journals, amongst which were Maurice Barrès' *La Cocarde*, Jean Grave's *Les Temps nouveaux*, Bernard Lazare's *L'Action* and Sebastien Faure's *Le Journal du peuple*. For the greater part Pelloutier's articles in these papers consisted either of attempts to further the acceptance of the tactic of the general strike or in accounts of working-class conferences and congresses which were designed to promote an understanding of the proletarian movement. Pelloutier's most significant journalistic enterprise, however, was his own paper, *L'Ouvrier des deux mondes*, which he produced almost single-handedly from February 1897 until June 1899.[35] It was here that Pelloutier sought to exploit to the full what he took to be the educational possibilities of journalism. *L'Ouvrier des deux mondes* was to be neither 'a doctrinaire review' nor 'a polemical journal'. It was, in the words of Pelloutier, to be 'exclusively a medium for economic and industrial documentation', taking as its subjects 'problems of production and consumption . . . working conditions and the situation of the working class, the means employed by the international proletariat to suppress the capitalist régime'.[36]

The logic of Pelloutier's position was clear. If the proletariat was to emancipate itself from economic exploitation it needed first of all to be aware of the nature of that exploitation. What it lacked was an understanding of 'the science of its misery'.[37] In line with this a substantial proportion of Pelloutier's articles in *L'Ouvrier des deux mondes* was devoted to a sombre and detailed account of the conditions of working-class life in France. These studies, written in collaboration with Maurice Pelloutier, were to re-appear as part of a larger scale work, *La Vie ouvrière en France*.[38]

The text reveals Pelloutier's commitment to a meticulous empirical investigation of the conditions of working-class life and work. While the underlying theme is plain — the capitalist system is the root-cause of all the proletariat's ills — the account is relatively free from polemic. In turn are examined the length of the working day, wage rates, the conditions of work for women and children, accident and mortality rates at work, the standard of living of the working class, death rates, and finally alcoholism which is described as 'a consequence of the excessive work to which the working class is subjected'.[39] The overall conclusion of the enquiry is summarised in this way: 'Men forced every day to carry out hard and often dangerous work in unhealthy workshops, reduced to feeding themselves on insufficient and unwholesome food, confined to districts and dwellings that drain them; women condemned to the same labour as that of men and rivals by necessity of their companions in misery; children delivered at an early age to occupations which exceed their strength: such are the general conditions of working-class existence under the régime of industrial "liberty" '.[40] Not even before death, Pelloutier remarks, are the members of the proletariat the equals of their exploiters.

Pelloutier's efforts to enlighten the working class on the nature and causes of their misery were not limited to these empirical enquiries. One cherished project — never realised — was the setting up of *Musées du travail*, museums designed to put before the workers 'the products and history' of their labour. The intention was to offer the people 'the means of observing social phenomena for themselves', the exhibits were to be displayed 'in such a way that the very sight of the products might familiarise the visitors with economic science'. As a means of education, according to Pelloutier, this was more effective than any amount of revolutionary oratory.[41]

Art, too, did not escape Pelloutier's attention. In a pamphlet entitled *L'Art et la révolte*[42] Pelloutier outlined what he took to be the role of art in the revolutionary process. His objection to contemporary art was that it stupefied the proletariat and acted as 'the servant, the accomplice of bourgeois society'. It did more, he asserted, to preserve the capitalist regime than any other social force. Similarly, revolutionary art had a crucial role in liberating the minds of the proletariat: 'Unveiling falsehoods, explaining how and why religions were created and the patriotic cult was invented, why the family was constructed on the model of government and why masters were thought necessary: such ought to be the objective of revolutionary art'.

Pelloutier's own artistic endeavours were a reflection of this aspiration. The poems of Pelloutier, published under the pseudonym Jean Réflec, are frequently to be found amongst the pages of *L'Ouvrier des deux mondes* and were to be reprinted in book form with the melancholic title *De la colère, de l'amour, de la haine*.[43] Pelloutier's conception of what he took to be good art can perhaps therefore best be disclosed by citing one of his own poems entitled *Amour Libre*.[44]

Ils allaient tous les deux dans la splendeur du soir
Très tendres, se disant une foule de choses
De ces gais riens qui font les pommettes plus roses
Plongeant en leurs regards ainsi qu'en un miroir

Tourmenté d'un ennui dont j'ignorais les causes
Je les suivais, bercé de ce fragile espoir
Que leur bonheur ferait trêve aux pensées moroses
Qui m'obsédaient l'esprit et m'ôteraient tout vouloir

Or, je les vis s'etendre, elle et lui, sur la mousse
Et ce fut près de moi l'extase pleine et douce
Qui fit mon coeur plus calme et mon souci moins lourd

A leurs libres transports, à leurs libres étreintes
Moi, dont l'être répugné à toutes les contraintes
Je pensai: voilà bien le vrai, l'unique amour.

Amongst the writers that Pelloutier himself admired were Zola, Anatole France and Ibsen.

Inevitably the preoccupation with the intellectual enlightenment of the proletariat engendered an interest in pedagogical reform. Above all, Pelloutier wished to see an education that was directed towards the real needs of the child. It was to be an 'integral' education, developing the intellectual capacity of the pupil whilst avoiding a reliance upon the use of memory and a concentration upon narrow specialisms. Such an education, Pelloutier contended, could never be provided by the State in whose interest it was to use the educational system solely as a means of control and indoctrination.[45] Only the workers themselves, in Pelloutier's view, could provide both the 'professional' and 'eclectic' education required to destroy 'the dominant tendency of modern industry to reduce the child to a physical action, the unconscious tool of the machine'.[46] The workers were to introduce themselves and their children 'to the discoveries of the human spirit'.[47] The institution within which this was to be achieved was the *bourse du travail*.

Pelloutier attributed the *bourses* with four primary functions: the provision of mutual benefits, education, propaganda and resistance.[48] Mutuality involved payment to members of a form of unemployment pay and accident insurance. In addition members were eligible for receipt of the so-called *viaticum*, a subvention paid to workers travelling the country in search of employment. The *bourses* were also intended to act as labour exchanges, locating jobs for the unemployed. The educational services of the *bourses* were to range from the setting up of libraries (each *bourse* was to have its own library), the establishment of *Musées du travail* and the provision of a technical education for the workers as well as a general education in the *bourses'* own schools for the workers' children.

The propaganda activities of the *bourses* were to take various forms. Pelloutier hoped that the *bourses* would operate as information offices, collecting statistics on the working of the economic system and disseminating this information to the various proletarian organisations. They were, if possible, to publish their own newspapers (as many actually did). Beyond this, the *bourses* were to aid and encourage previously unorganised workers, especially those working on the land or at sea, to establish their own *syndicats*. One favourite project was the setting up of sailors' homes.

Pelloutier also hoped that the *bourses* would be responsible for the creation of co-operatives. Like many syndicalists after him, Pelloutier had an ambivalent attitude towards co-operatives. He doubted their capacity to operate successfully within the capitalist system and feared that they might encourage workers to exploit their own comrades. They were, however, of value to the extent that they provided workers with an opportunity to direct their own affairs and as a means of propagating the idea of co-operative production.[49]

Finally, Pelloutier assumed that the immediate task of the *bourses* would be that of co-ordinating and organising working-class resistance to the exploitation imposed upon them by capitalism.

In short, for Pelloutier the *bourses du travail* were to become the very centre of working-class life. Despite his acceptance of municipal funding for the *bourses* it was always Pelloutier's intention that they should be financed and run by the workers themselves.[50] They were the incarnation of Pelloutier's desire to secure the moral and technical education of the proletariat. The workers were able to acquire the administrative and organisational skills necessary if they were to free themselves from the hierarchical structures imposed upon them by capitalism and, in the process, transcend a narrow egoism through an appreciation of the virtues of co-operative effort. The task of the *bourses* was to turn 'workers into proud and free men'.[51]

Furthermore, the *bourses du travail* were to be the nuclei, the cells, around which the future society was to be created. 'The ambition', Pelloutier wrote, was 'to constitute within the bourgeois State a veritable socialist (economic and anarchic) State'.[52]

Pelloutier's conception of that future society and the place occupied within it by the *bourses du travail* was in part derived from his views on the organisational structure of the syndicalist movement. Pelloutier consistently argued that the *bourses du travail* and the trade based *syndicats* should co-exist as distinct entities pursuing different goals but with a common purpose.[53] This separation was to be maintained and combined with a corresponding division of function. Each *syndicat* was to be responsible for a particular sector of production. Pelloutier specifically mentions, for example, housing and the supply of provisions. The *bourses*, in effect, were to co-ordinate production, collecting and circulating information on productive capacity and consumers' needs.[54]

What the *bourses du travail* and the producers' *syndicats* were definitely not intended to become was an embryonic centralised State. The *bourses* were to act only as intermediaries, possessing no executive authority whilst the *syndicats* were to be 'libertarian organisations', controlling production and directing their own affairs 'with the free consent of their members'.[55] The model appealed to by Pelloutier was the federalism he associated primarily with Proudhon and also with Bakunin.

The affinities of Pelloutier's ideas to anarchism are clear and unmistakeable. He shared, for example, many of the traditional anarchist suspicions of the State. The State was inherently dictatorial and despotic. It was the cause of war. The inflexibility of its laws took no account of the diversity of human nature.[56] It is not therefore surprising to find Pelloutier from 1895 onwards arguing that anarchists should enter the *syndicats*. The libertarian organisation of the *syndicats* and their hostility to piecemeal reform and parliamentary action ensured that anarchists had nothing to fear from entering the *syndicats* and that the independence they cherished would not be threatened. In turn, the anarchists would teach the workers that they must learn to direct their own lives and that a future revolution must entail the permanent destruction of all hierarchical structures. The anarchists would act as the libertarian conscience of the *syndicats*.[57]

The end pursued by Pelloutier never varied therefore: it was the creation of a 'society of free men'.[58] There exists, he wrote, 'in the heart of men not a puerile sentiment of insubordination . . . but the noble and haughty desire to affirm his strength, his intelligence, the best part of himself — his personality'.[59] That personality, Pelloutier asserted, could only flourish and develop in a society shorn of hierarchy and inequality. Men were no longer prepared to be treated as machines and tools; they wished to be 'creators' and 'inventors' of their works. Given responsibility and freedom, Pelloutier argued, men would work more efficiently and produce more with a resulting material prosperity that would enable men to develop themselves intellectually and to live a life that accorded with their natural instincts and aspirations. The task that Pelloutier set himself was that of creating the institutions that would provide 'the moral, administrative and technical education' required to render such a society viable.[60]

Pelloutier consistently and intentionally remained vague about the detailed structure of that future society but the guiding principles are clearly discernible: the control by the workers themselves of the productive process, the rational organisation and utilisation of production for the common good, and the distribution of resources according to need. 'What are we demanding?' Pelloutier asked: 'the perfecting of society, the utilisation of these marvellous resources it offers to human endeavour . . . and, at the same time, the suppression of the means by which it authorises the individual appropriation of common resources: Money and Authority'.[61]

Pelloutier's contribution to syndicalist theory was fundamental. In his writings can be discerned a set of ideas that form the rudiments of a distinct and distinctive ideology. At its core was the conviction that the emancipation of the working class must be self-emancipation and that this emancipation was to be attained through the creation of institutions which the workers themselves were to control and organise and in which they would obtain the moral and technical education appropriate to a future society without masters. The workers were to shun the bourgeoisie, avoid assimilation, and concentrate upon the creation of a self-consciously proletarian society within bourgeois society. The culmination of this educative process was to be the destruction of the capitalist order and the seizure of the means of production via the general strike.

In addition the tone of Pelloutier's writings was to be so typical of syndicalist thought. Pelloutier's struggle on behalf of the working class was sustained by a powerful sense of moral indignation, an awareness of the decadence and hypocrisy of contemporary society. This manifested itself in a variety of ways: criticism of the self-indulgence he associated with modern art, scorn for the sexual morals of the bourgeoisie and, in particular, condemnation of the non-producers, the 'parasites', be they capitalists or politicians. In turn, Pelloutier saw the productive process and those who worked it, the proletariat, as the source not only of society's wealth but also of all true values.

Pelloutier's particular genius — as so many of his contemporaries appreciated — was to be found in his meticulous examination of the exploitation suffered by the proletariat and in his determination to build a set of institutions — most notably the *bourses du travail* — which would allow the workers to free themselves from their enslavement. Syndicalists of subsequent generations were unerringly to turn to his example of selfless dedication in pursuit of this task for inspiration.

II

With the death of Pelloutier in March 1901 Georges Yvetot became general secretary of the *Fédération des bourses du travail*. Paul Delesalle was to be his assistant. In the same year Victor Griffuelhes was elected general-secretary of the CGT. Emile Pouget, the editor of the CGT's *Voix du peuple* since its creation in 1900, was chosen as his deputy. With the merger of the two organisations in 1902 these four men became the effective leaders of the syndicalist movement and through a variety of newspapers and pamphlets were to be its principal publicists. With the exception of Griffuelhes, who in his early years had been a supporter of Blanqui, each came to syndicalism from anarchism.

Anarchists in France began to turn their attention towards the *syndicats* in 1894 when the era of propaganda by the deed effectively came to an end.[62] In October of that year Pouget published an article entitled 'A roublard, roublard et demi' in his journal *Le Père Peinard* in which he argued that the *syndicats* could provide '*les anarchos*' with fertile terrain for their activities.[63] The following year Pelloutier continued the theme with an article entitled 'L'Anarchisme et les syndicats ouvriers' in Jean Grave's anarchist *Les Temps nouveaux*.[64] Shortly afterwards Paul Delesalle began a regular column under the rubric of 'Mouvement ouvrier' in the same paper. Yvetot's contribution to the debate came later in the pages of Sebastien Faure's *Le Libertaire*.

The central issue posed for the anarchists by the *syndicats* was the extent to which the *syndicats* were organisations capable of effecting revolutionary change.[65] For those anarchists opposed to entry into the syndicalist movement, the *syndicats* gave rise to profound misgivings. The *syndicats*, they argued, were by their very nature reformist organisations operating within the capitalist system to secure piecemeal improvements in conditions of work and thus were incapable of generating a radical transformation of society. André Lorulet, a columnist in *Le Libertaire* and founder member of the anti-syndicalist *L'Anarchie*, argued, for example, that the *syndicats* by 'sanctioning' the existence of the employers and the wage-earners actually prolonged 'the life of the existing social structure'.[66] For Lorulet, the capitalist system could only be destroyed, not reformed. Secondly, for individualist anarchists the *syndicats* as *organisations* represented a positive threat to the liberty of the individual. 'When the workers have become conscious', Lorulet wrote, 'they will flee the *syndicats* because they will see that these authoritarian organisations are barriers to the extension of their personality and their action'.[67] Further, those anarchists opposed to syndicalism argued that it was incorrect to assume that the interests of organised labour were necessarily identical to those of all the oppressed and exploited. Preferring to talk of individuals rather than classes they were deeply sceptical of appeals to working-class solidarity. 'All those lacking in consciousness', Lorulet stated, 'are our adversaries'.[68] This category included those workers who had been integrated into and rewarded by the capitalist system. For the individualist anarchist, therefore, the chosen field of action was the affinity group ('*groupe d'affinité*'), a loosely structured assembly of like-minded individuals.[69] 'A combative anarchist', Max Pélerin wrote, dismissing the utility of the *syndicats*, 'will always find a field of action where he will be able to assert himself and carry out propaganda'.[70] The revolution would be the work not of the 'aristocracy of labour' but of what was described by Ernest Girault as the 'black mass': the unemployed, the disinherited, those who remained outside the system and who felt the full force of its exploitative power.[71]

For those anarchists prepared to endorse the suitability of the *syndicats* for their purposes another question arose. If the *syndicats* were useful means to bring about the revolution what role, if any, would they have in the ideal libertarian society of the future? A communist anarchist pamphlet entitled *Les Anarchistes et les syndicats* published in 1898[72] which sought to criticise 'the repugnance felt by certain anarchists towards entering into the *syndicats*' nevertheless concluded that while the *syndicat* was of value as 'an instrument of struggle' it was not to be seen as 'the model of the future society'. After the revolution, it argued, the *syndicat* 'must disappear or be modified to make way for free associations for production'.[73] The fear was that the *syndicat* could establish itself as a new form of political and social authority.

In his writings from 1894 onwards Emile Pouget sought to challenge and dispel these 'prejudices'.[74] For Pouget it was clear that the anarchists needed to change their tactics. In the wake of the repression that constituted the response of the State to propaganda by the deed the anarchist movement in France had been virtually destroyed. For Pouget the creation of '*groupes d'affinité*' appeared to be an inadequate response to this new situation. Lacking 'roots in the masses' such groups would find it difficult to recruit new adherents. The dilemma facing anarchists was thus easily articulated. 'I am', Pouget wrote, 'an anarchist; I wish to sow my ideas: what is the land where they will germinate the best? I already have the factory, the bar . . . I would like something better, a place where I would find workers beginning to understand the exploitation that we are suffering and racking their brains to find a remedy. Does that place exist?'[75] Pouget was in no doubt about the answer. Having long believed that the workers must carry out the revolution themselves a period of enforced exile in London had familiarised him with the growing trade union movement in Britain and had further convinced him that the anarchists had much to gain from entry into these organisations. In contrast to the '*groupe d'affinité*' the *syndicat* was the natural meeting place of those workers who were discontented with their 'sad lot'.[76] Surrounded by his comrades the 'prolo' would begin his 'intellectual education'. Politicians would be kept away; the workers, through strike activity, would learn that the government was always on the side of the bosses and that nothing could be expected from the capitalist system. Pouget was equally clear about the function of the *syndicat*. Firstly it must 'watch' the employer, prevent him from 'reducing' salaries and from carrying out similar 'dirty tricks (*crapuleries*)'. Beyond this 'everyday task', the *syndicat* would prepare the revolution of the future. Thus the *syndicat* was both an instrument of resistance and a vehicle of revolution. The task of the anarchists, Pouget argued, was to ensure that the *syndicats* performed both of these functions. If in 'A roublard, roublard et demi' Pouget did not refer explicitly to the place of the *syndicat* in a libertarian society, this omission was rectified in later articles. In 'Action corporative et duperie politique',[77] published in January 1898, Pouget stated clearly that the *syndicat* must be seen as 'the embryo of the future society', capable of organising 'communist production'.

The arguments deployed by Delesalle and Yvetot to justify anarchist involvement in the *syndicats* were of a similar character. In *L'Action syndicale et les anarchistes*,[78] for example, Delesalle, after having underlined the importance of the *syndicat* as 'the group which best represents the exploited class in the struggle against the avidity of the class which exploits', argued that the role of the anarchists within the *syndicats* was twofold: to demonstrate the futility of reforms and to push the *syndicats* towards the pursuit of revolutionary goals. For both Delesalle and Yvetot little could be expected from what Delesalle described as 'the army of the unemployed, vagabonds and *déclassé* elements'.[79] 'The beggar', Yvetot wrote, 'commits suicide or allows himself to die of hunger whilst the worker fights through the strike or otherwise and if he dies it is because he has been killed and not because he has committed suicide'.[80] It was therefore a matter of being practical. Whilst the ideal might well be the 'exclusively revolutionary group', if the anarchists wished seriously to destroy the iniquitous society in which they lived, the 'ivory tower' had to be abandoned. The *syndicat* offered the most direct and efficient means through which the anarchists could influence 'the great mass of the exploited'.[81] 'Pure theory', Delesalle wrote, 'has too often absorbed us: it is time to know if we wish to return to action'.[82]

Where the libertarian beliefs of men such as Pouget and Delesalle were much in evidence was in their conception of the appropriate organisational structure of the syndicalist movement. As anarchists they were intimately aware that libertarian ends could only be achieved through libertarian means and were thus consistent critics of what they saw as the tactics and practices of 'Marxist authoritarianism'.[83] Moreover they realised that the *syndicats*, if allowed to ossify and to develop bureaucratic and centralised systems of control, could themselves become autocratic and authoritarian. This concern was reflected in a variety of different arguments. Responding to the charge that belonging to the *syndicat* meant an 'annihilation of one's individuality', Delesalle replied that the CGT was not 'a directing committee nor a workers' Senate but a simple correspondence bureau intended to put organisations in contact with each other'.[84] Elsewhere he described the CGT as a 'registering office'.[85] This, in turn, was an echo of Pouget's remark that the central committee of the CGT should be seen as 'a kind of switchboard'.[86] The idea was that the CGT would lack any executive authority. Each *syndicat*, each *bourse du travail*, would be autonomous. Instead of centralisation there would be 'the most absolute federalism'.[87] Such was Delesalle's opposition to centralisation within the syndicalist movement that he opposed the merger of the CGT and the *bourses du travail* in 1902. In a polemic with one of its supporters, Louis Niel, he argued that 'unity' would mean that the proletariat would be in the hands of 'a single committee charged with presiding over the destiny of the working class'. As the CGT and the *bourses du travail* performed different functions they should remain separate organisations. 'In opposition to "unitary" centralisation', Delesalle wrote, 'I propose decentralisation . . . the greatest number of directing groups'.[88] Delesalle subsequently changed his opinion on this issue but only when convinced that the CGT was not a 'centralising organism'.[89]

Pouget was equally adamant that membership of a *syndicat* did not and should not entail a loss of individual autonomy.[90] As a member of the *syndicat*, Pouget wrote, the worker entered into a contract with his comrades but this contract was 'revocable' at any moment and did not entail the 'suspension or abdication of the personality which distinguishes and characterises political votes'. The worker did not delegate authority or grant an unlimited mandate to a set of elected representatives. The division of labour within the *syndicat* was purely administrative: hence the liberty of the member of the *syndicat* was safe-guarded. 'Autonomous he was', Pouget wrote, 'autonomous he remains'. Further, it was precisely in the *syndicat* that the worker could develop his personality to the full. The *syndicat* was a 'school of the will'.

Yvetot and Delesalle as general and assistant secretaries of the *Fédération des bourses du travail* also let it be known that they regretted Pelloutier's original decision to accept subventions from municipal authorities as funding for the *bourses du travail*. An 'autonomous life' as befitted the 'dignity' of the workers, Delesalle remarked, demanded that the *bourses du travail* should be free of all 'financial and political tutelage'.[91]

For those anarchists prepared to enter into the *syndicats*, therefore, the aim was to utilise and exploit the opportunities provided by the syndicalist movement. Whilst for Pouget and Yvetot the *syndicat* was not the ideal means to achieve the emancipation of the proletariat they, nevertheless, believed that, under their own impetus, the *syndicats* and the *bourses du travail* were capable of bringing about revolutionary change and in a manner compatible with their own libertarian beliefs. It was, as Yvetot remarked, a case of 'pushing syndicalism to the extreme limits of its logic'.[92]

This should not, however, be taken to mean that the syndicalist movement as it functioned in the first decade of the twentieth century was the product of anarchist theory. As Victor Griffuelhes remarked, it was rather 'the result of a long practice created more by events than by this or that man'.[93] In effect, the anarchists and the syndicalist movement converged. At the very moment that men like Delesalle were seeking a new terrain for their activities the *syndicats* were distancing themselves and were being distanced from the political parties of the Left.[94]

Victor Griffuelhes had little difficulty co-operating with his anarchist colleagues. Born in 1874 of working-class parents Griffuelhes had left school at the age of fourteen to become a shoemaker. Drawn to socialism by the 'numerous hardships' he had suffered, in 1896 he joined the Blanquist movement. Blanquism, as Edouard Dolléans commented, 'was more a temperament than a political doctrine':[95] by the middle of the 1890s it had all but abandoned the conspiratorial and insurrectional socialism of its founder. Loyal to the memory (and the myth) of the Paris Commune — Patrick Hutton has described Blanquism as 'the politics of anniversary remembrance'[96] — the Blanquists opposed the doctrinaire socialism of Jules Guesde and defended the independence of groups and individuals within the socialist movement.

Griffuelhes was thus as determined in his defence of the autonomy of the syndicalist movement as were the anarchists.[97] He was equally aware of the dangers posed by an undue emphasis and reliance upon organisational structures. One recurring topic of discussion amongst syndicalists was the low subscriptions paid by members and, it was argued, the inefficiency and poverty of the *syndicats* which followed as a consequence. French unions were frequently compared unfavourably with their British and German counterparts. Griffuelhes saw little need for change. What the French *syndicats* lacked in money, he argued, they made up for in 'enthusiasm, energy, the sentiment of sacrifice and the sense of battle'.[98] Did the immense financial and human resources of the German electricians' union, he asked, save it from defeat? It was 'the vigour of the combattants', not a strong organisation, that mattered.[99]

Griffuelhes, significantly, made much of the comparison between the differing characteristics of the trade union movement in France and Germany. Drawing upon his own experience of dealing with German labour leaders and the views expressed by Robert Michels, Griffuelhes concluded that organisation itself was a hindrance to action. The 'immoderate love of moderation' displayed by the Germans could be explained by their desire to avoid any action which might possibly 'endanger the vast but fragile edifice of their organisation'.[100] Superimposed upon this account of the conservatism of the German unions was what amounted to a classification by racial types. Whilst the first reaction of the German worker was to obey, that of the French worker was to revolt, to resist, to protest, to respond by immediate action. 'The German worker', Griffuelhes wrote, 'is unfamiliar with the free and irreverent (*frondeur*) spirit that is our distinctive trademark and is always gripped by fear and dread.[101] Vestiges of Blanquist revolutionary nationalism, these sentiments were to have an important impact upon the actions of Griffuelhes in later years.

These four men then were the principal exponents of revolutionary syndicalism in the first decade of the twentieth century. In numerous pamphlets, newspaper and journal articles, and at CGT conferences, they set forth what amounted to a relatively consistent and coherent statement of their position. What they lacked in theoretical sophistication they made up for in courage and conviction: Delesalle alone amongst them managed to avoid a stay in prison. Their purpose — as befitted what they saw as their role as revolutionary journalists — was not to engage in intellectual debate (although they undoubtedly did this) but to inspire the working class to action. As Delesalle remarked, in Pouget's articles in *La Voix du peuple* 'it was the whole working class which fought through his pen'.[102]

What undoubtedly was missing from their writings was any detailed economic analysis of the working of the capitalist system. For each alike capitalism was perceived in simple terms: it was an iniquitous system which enslaved the worker. Paul Delesalle, for example, in a pamphlet entitled *Aux travailleurs — la grève*,[103] after having argued that the cause of exploitation lay in the seizure of the means of production by the 'strongest, craftiest and most intelligent', concluded that the person 'who has only his labour is the slave of he who owns'. For Pouget capitalism had produced a sharp divide. On the one side were the 'thieves, the masters', those who had appropriated the fruits of the labour of others; on the other side were the 'robbed, the enslaved', those who lived at the mercy of their employers.[104] Both argued that the situation of the worker was little better than that of the feudal serf: ownership of the machine meant ownership of the man. The proletarian, Griffuelhes argued, lived a life of insecurity and hardship whilst the non-producer, the capitalist, enjoyed an excess of consumption.[105] The capitalist system was thus institutionalised robbery: class war was inevitable. The goal of the syndicalist movement, therefore, could be nothing less than the complete disappearance of the categories of wage-earner and employer and the creation of a society based upon communist principles.[106]

Delesalle and his colleagues offered nothing comparable to the detailed studies of capitalism that were such a feature of orthodox Marxism and it was not until Alphonse Merrheim produced his richly documented account of the metallurgical industry and its pattern of organisation that anyone within the CGT sought to provide an analysis of how the capitalist system actually worked. This is not difficult to understand. None of the four men under discussion had more than a knowledge of the rudiments of economic theory. Furthermore, if following Pelloutier the emphasis was to be placed upon the education of the workers, in the heady days of syndicalist expansion and increased militancy it seemed sufficient that the workers recognised that the capitalist system had to be eradicated, not reformed, and that liberty would only exist when private property had been abolished. The revolution did not depend upon the evolution of capitalism or even knowledge of its evolution: it was primarily to be the result of an act of will on the part of the workers themselves. Hence there was little need to do more than expose the injustices of the system. Merrheim's awareness of the power of the steelowners led him to a different conclusion.[107]

At the heart of revolutionary syndicalist doctrine lay the conception of the syndicalist movement as *'le parti du travail'*.[108] The *syndicat*, it was argued, by its very nature united workers according to their economic interests and it was assumed that these interests were more real and permanent than any other considerations or opinions that an individual might entertain. The *syndicat*, Delesalle wrote, 'groups together and could only group together men having common and identical interests and pursuing the same end'.[109] Common needs, which themselves were the product of an identical economic position, would give rise to a concordance of views. It was therefore argued, by Pouget for example, that all the members of the working class, irrespective of how 'baroque' their philosophical, political or religious beliefs might be, were welcome to join the *syndicats*. It was simply required that these views were not introduced into the activities of the CGT. 'The *syndicat*', Pouget wrote, 'groups together those who work against those who live by human exploitation: it brings together interests and not opinions'.[110]

By implication the *syndicats* could only be open to members of the working class. There was, Delesalle wrote, 'no place for alliances or compromises with the bourgeoisie or the intermediary classes . . . whose immediate interests are in conflict with those of the workers'.[111] If this meant opposition to the class described by Pouget as '*les souteneurs*', the 'parasites' who defended the capitalist system, it also entailed the exclusion of middle-class intellectuals and politicians from the syndicalist movement. The working class, Yvetot wrote, 'is right to mistrust people who, not having suffered the same misery, have not received the same education'.[112] Moreover, in Pouget's view, the *syndicat* did not, in any case, provide an environment in which such people could satisfy their personal ambitions: anyone pursuing a 'selfish or private end' would quickly realise that the *syndicats* could not offer rewards or positions of prominence and thus would 'exclude themselves voluntarily' from the movement.[113] It also meant hostility to the very idea of *syndicats* composed exclusively of members of the liberal professions. It made no sense, Griffuelhes argued, to consider doctors as wage-earners.[114]

The class-based nature of the *syndicat* was deemed to be in marked contrast to the pattern of support and membership of all political parties. What distinguished the political party (including those of the Left) was precisely that it grouped people according to opinions and not interests — parties, Pouget wrote, 'were an incoherent mish-mash of men whose interests were in opposition'[115] — and, therefore, at best the political party could only possess a fragile unity which was easily broken when a conflict of economic interests arose.[116] In addition, political parties, given their goal of the conquest of the apparatus of the State, were fertile ground for middle-class opportunists.

Hubert Lagardelle was subsequently to give the distinction between party and *syndicat* greater force by extending it into a full-scale critique of the theoretical postulates of democratic theory but in the hands of the leaders of the CGT the point was a simple one: the *syndicat*, not the political party, was the natural expression of the real needs and aspirations of the producers and for as long as it grouped together only producers it could not be deflected from seeking the end of the exploitation created by capitalism.[117] 'In opposition to the present society which only knows the *citizen*', Pouget wrote, 'stands from now on the *producer*'.[118]

What was less evident was the concern that '*le parti du travail*' should be composed only of the *conscious* producers. Yvetot, for example, displayed an open contempt for '*la foule*', the crowd. The masses, he argued, were 'stupefied by work and alcohol, by the prejudices of the family, the school and the barracks'.[119] In an article contrasting the revolutionary syndicalists with '*les jaunes*', Yvetot condemned the members of the yellow unions (which sought to cooperate with the employers) for being 'ignorant, unconscious individuals, lacking dignity'. The 'reds', in comparison, were 'men who had not left their virility in the confessional, their human dignity in the barracks and who had not drowned their reason and will in alcohol'.[120]

Further, the distinction between the conscious and unconscious producer was also utilised to justify the predominance of the revolutionary syndicalists within the CGT itself. In 1904 at the Congress of Bourges the debate about the appropriate manner of selection and representation for the syndicalist movement came to a climax. The reformists, including Auguste Keufer, favoured proportional representation, a system which distributed votes according to the numbers of members belonging to each *syndicat* and hence which favoured the largest unions, whilst the revolutionaries believed that each *syndicat*, irrespective of size, should have the same vote. The opponents of proportional representation carried the day.[121] The issue was in part a question of tactics (proportional representation would almost certainly have brought the ascendency of the revolutionaries to an end) but it was also a reflection of a genuine disagreement about the prerogatives of what was normally referred to as '*la minorité agissante*'. In a commentary upon the Congress of Bourges, for example, Pouget argued that the adoption of proportional representation 'would permit the numerous and ponderous masses to paralyse the conscious minorities and hence would be an instrument of reaction'.[122]

The hostility to proportional representation derived to a large extent from the general aversion to the ballot box and to what Pouget described as '*l'idée démocratique vulgaire*'. Voting was regarded as an abdication of the self: it taught the people nothing and encouraged them to rely upon the actions and ideas of others. 'One is an elector', Pouget wrote, 'on condition that one is simple enough to wish to be one'. After having voted, he argued, one became again the slave of the representative, 'the servant of the successful candidate'.[123] The electoral system also encouraged the workers to believe the promises of politicians. 'Accustomed to being intoxicated by hollow phrases', Delesalle wrote, 'the masses have marched behind words'.[124] They had thus come to abdicate responsibility for their own emancipation to what Yvetot described as 'a miserable piece of paper which carries the name of a dangerous third-rate actor politician'.[125] The principal objection to the voting process, however, drew upon an elitist characterisation of the individual voter as an unreflecting and compliant slave and of the majority as docile sheep.[126] It was this argument that was used to maximum effect and with no attempt at concealment in the debate about proportional representation within the syndicalist movement.

'Universal suffrage', Pouget argued, 'gives power to unconscious and inactive individuals (or better to their representatives) and suffocates the minority who carry the future within themselves'.[127] Applied to the *syndi-cats* this 'democratic system' would mean that control would be in the hands of an 'inert' mass which 'enjoys economic slavery'. The conscious minority, Pouget believed, were alone 'called upon to decide and to act' and were furthermore under an 'inexorable obligation' to do so 'without taking into account the refractory mass'. The '*zéros humains*' who consti-tuted the 'amorphous and numerous mass' could have little complaint with this arrangement. The majority would benefit from the actions of the minority whilst the minority would suffer the hardships of 'the battle'. Moreover, Pouget assumed that the conscious minority would always act in the interests of the majority. Syndicalist activity, no matter how small the militant minority, never pursued an 'individual and particularist aim'.[128] For the revolutionaries, therefore, little could be expected of the majority and of an electoral system which gave them power. Exhausted by work and in the grip of ignorance the majority would enjoy only moments of lucidity and this thanks to the endeavours of the revolutionary minority. The task ahead was thus one of creating a minority strong enough to overthrow the class which owned and controlled the capitalist system. '*Minorité contre minorité*' was the watchword.[129]

This argument was itself a reflection of a wider and deeper rejection of politics and the political process as they existed in the Third Republic. The articles written by Pouget for *Le Père Peinard* during the 1890s, for example, made constant reference to the corruption and duplicity of politi-cal life and to the fraudulent and unscrupulous nature of the Republic. Marianne, the female symbol of the Republic and of its virtue, was described as a slut, '*une salope*'. 'In place of the Marianne of their dreams', Pouget wrote, 'the people have seen a horrible seductress saving her embraces for upper-class swine'.[130] The people, he argued, had believed that the Republic would bring them liberty and well-being, '*le bricheton assuré*': in reality, nothing had changed except the 'façade' of the regime. The only beneficiaries of the Republic were the 'swindlers': bankers, clergymen and judges, with Rothschild and his family as the 'king of kings'.[131] The Republic, Pouget commented, has 'created a new royalty, that of gold, more rapacious and murderous than the former one'.

The activity of politics was seen as being inherently corrupting and corrupt. For anarchists such as Pouget this was no more than a self-evident truth that was daily confirmed by the numerous scandals that rocked and afflicted the régime and its political establishment. 'Parliament', Pouget wrote, 'is a bazaar where entry is not free and where those who enter seek not to educate themselves but to dupe their fellows'.[132] This, in Pouget's opinion, was true not only of the defenders of the regime but also of those who, in theory, sought its overthrow. In *Variations guesdistes* Pouget delighted in exposing what he saw as the 'bad faith' of Jules Guesde and his followers.[133] Tracing Guesde's path from that of an anarchist who sought to prevent Marx from dominating the International to that of leader of a socialist party which only sought success within 'the four walls of the Chamber of Deputies', Pouget concluded that the Guesdists were 'politicians without scruple or conscience, changing their views according to the interests of the moment and subordinating everything to personal ambition'.[134] The pursuit of power and their 'shabby envy for bourgeois and aristocratic pleasure' led them to abandon all principles in the need to attract votes. 'The vote! the vote!', he wrote elsewhere, 'for them, there is no more than that: this crap (*couillonnade*) has become their sole obsession (*dada*)'.[135]

This critical assessment of Republican democracy was forcefully put to the test by the Dreyfus Affair. If the events and agitation that surrounded the campaign to release Dreyfus posed dilemmas for socialists — should they defend a bourgeois regime? — then the issues raised for anarchists were even more acute — should they even co-operate with their bourgeois enemies and, above all, should they lend their support to the defence of a system of government?[136]

Initially Pouget, like nearly everyone else in France, did not doubt that Dreyfus was guilty. Further, in line with most of the anarchist press, he claimed to be indifferent to the fate of someone who as a bourgeois army officer was by definition an enemy of the people. This position was re-affirmed by Pouget immediately after the publication of Zola's '*J'accuse*' in an article entitled 'Soyons nous-mêmes! ni dreyfusiens ni esterhaziens'.[137] 'Between these two bands of swindlers', he wrote with a characteristic turn of phrase, 'we should not take sides'.

The position of the anarchists, with the notable exception of Jean Grave, began noticeably to change early in 1898. Sebastien Faure, the editor of *Le Libertaire*, canvassed anarchist involvement in the Dreyfusard move-ment as a means of exposing the secrecy of government. Pouget was at first critical of this position but during 1898 his views were slowly to change and when Faure launched the pro-Dreyfus *Journal du peuple* in February 1899 Pouget was to be found amongst its contributors.

At issue in the Dreyfus Affair, Pouget argued, was not primarily the fate of Dreyfus as an individual but the struggle between the forces of reaction and revolution.[138] 'Are we to fall', he wrote, 'more completely than ever under the yoke of the Army and the Church?'. The alternative was that the people should profit by the events of the Dreyfus Affair in order to break the bonds that constrained them and thence 'conquer the well-being and liberty that the Republic had been incapable of realising'.[139] Dreyfus, Pouget argued, was the victim of the Jesuits and the 'top brass' of the army and he was their victim precisely because he was a symbol of the Jew. Their aim was not to destroy Dreyfus in person but through him to attack his race. Dreyfus, Pouget repeatedly stressed, could expect little help from the legal system.[140] Victory over the Jesuits could only be secured by 'the arms of the people', '*les biceps populaires*'. 'It is to the people', he wrote, concluding his most considered statement on the significance of the Affair, 'that falls the task of routing the Jesuit-military Reaction. It is to the people that belongs the role of securing the revision of the trial of Dreyfus — not by the ordinary route but by the revolutionary route'.[141] In 1899 Pouget optimistically believed that as a result of the Dreyfus Affair the people would take that path. His willingness to countenance anarchist involvement in the agitation to release Dreyfus did not therefore entail his reconciliation with the Republican régime.

Paul Delesalle was to display a more positive and less doctrinaire response to anarchist involvement in the Dreyfusard movement and, in contrast to Pouget, he was to feel deep concern for the fate of Dreyfus as an individual. In the early stages of the fight to release Dreyfus anarchists in France frequently argued that the injustices inflicted upon this bourgeois army officer were not unique. 'We too', Delesalle wrote, 'have our innocents in prison'.[142] This was unquestionably true. The '*lois scélérates*' of 1894, outlawing anarchist propaganda in the aftermath of the bomb outrages had been used indiscriminately to persecute all anarchists. For Delesalle the Dreyfus case provided an opportunity for anarchists to denounce the iniquity of the '*lois scélérates*' and, further, in collaboration with their 'temporary allies' to campaign against all violations of justice and liberty. 'Imbued with the true spirit of justice and truth', Delesalle wrote, 'we shall attack the modern Bastilles'. The anarchists, in their rightful place amongst the 'sincere men' who fought against the forces of reaction, would participate in an alliance that 'could only be to the profit of the whole of humanity'.

During 1899 Delesalle translated these words into action. He travelled to Versailles to protect the Dreyfusards at the trial of Emile Zola and on the 11 June he was present at the republican demonstration at Longchamp called as a response to the nationalist demonstration at Auteuil of the previous week. In August he was to be found at Rennes for the re-trial of Dreyfus, there to safeguard the life of Colonel Picquart, one of the first men to become convinced of Dreyfus' innocence. In letters written to his wife from Rennes Delesalle recorded his impressions of the momentous events that were taking place. 'The entry of Dreyfus into the room', he wrote, 'was not without greatness and despite the profound scorn I feel for army officers I felt my throat tighten when I saw advancing, opposite me, his head high but without conceit, the man who had returned from Devil's Island'.[143] Delesalle's views on the trial were made public in three articles published in the *Journal du peuple* in September 1899.[144] Nevertheless Delesalle remained convinced that the Dreyfus Affair would above all serve to disgrace the bourgeois Republic and show it to be nothing more than a 'simple grouping of electoral interests'.[145]

If, with varying degrees of enthusiasm, Pouget and Delesalle were prepared to endorse anarchist involvement in the Dreyfusard movement, both men were unreservedly critical of the socialist deputy Millerand's entry into government and of the legislation he introduced as Minister of Commerce. Delesalle, for example, was not moved by talk of the Republic in danger: 'big words', he wrote, 'which do not convince even the most credulous of people'.[146] Once in power, he contended, Millerand behaved in exactly the same manner as his bourgeois predecessors.[147] This was not difficult to understand. Millerand, as Pouget explained, had become the 'prisoner of Capital'. No matter how well intentioned he might be, Pouget argued, Millerand 'could not break the mould; he is only a cog in the machine of oppression and whether he wishes it or not he must, as minister, participate in the job of crushing the proletariat'.[148]

Millerand was responsible for the introduction of two important pieces of legislation: a law designed to limit the working hours of women and children in factories to ten hours per day and, more controversially, a law which established compulsory arbitration in industrial disputes. Delesalle articulated the response to the first measure. The effect of restricting the working week of women and children, he argued, would be to force women to work for the manufacturer within their own homes, to take on out-work which was even more exploited than labour in the factory. 'The law on the working hours of women and children', Delesalle wrote, 'has worsened the situation of those that it wished properly to protect, since their work has become more arduous, longer and less well-paid'.[149]

Millerand's second measure was seen as nothing less than an attempt to subordinate the workers' movement to the State and thus prolong the life of the capitalist system.[150] Pouget, in a series of articles entitled 'L'Etranglement des grèves',[151] argued strongly that the aim of the law was to constrain the workers, reduce the power of the *syndicats* 'to zero', and prevent any moves towards a general strike. The workers, he commented, had now even lost the right to die of hunger. For Delesalle, the aim of Millerand's law was clear. The numerous restrictions upon the right to strike, including the inability of the workers to go on strike at a moment of their own choosing, were designed primarily to ensure that 'the employers avoided the risk entailed in strikes'.[152]

For the leaders of the syndicalist movement Millerand was not to be the only socialist who, on becoming a minister, betrayed the workers' movement. During the first decade of the twentieth century René Viviani and Aristide Briand were to follow Millerand's example. Briand's treason was, in many respects, the most spectacular. A former advocate of the general strike and friend of Pelloutier, in 1910 as Minister of the Interior he broke a general strike of railwaymen by the use of the most draconian methods. Having declared a military emergency he threatened all strikers with court martial.

By the time of these events the disillusionment felt towards the Republic by many syndicalists was complete. To a certain extent syndicalist hostility towards the Republic derived from straightforward theoretical premises. As an anarchist it made sense for Yvetot to comment that a republic was no different from a monarchy. All governments were the same: 'it is only the name and the personnel which change'.[153] But this was not the case for all syndicalists: for others it was the Republic in action that was decisive in shaping their views. In an article entitled 'Le Fond et la forme'[154] Griffuelhes argued that the workers wanted the substance of emancipation, '*le fond*', and not just its form, the Republic, and that the interests of the workers must not be sacrificed to the form of the regime. The German Empire, he contended, had done more for the people than the French Republic. Why was it, he asked in 'Monarchie et République'[155] that in republican France retired workers were helped by the State at seventy whilst under the Danish monarchy it was at the age of sixty? The nature of the regime, he concluded, was not the cause of progress for the working class: what mattered most was the extent to which the proletariat was prepared to assert and defend its own interests.

It was, however, the manner in which the Republic responded to the demands of the workers and in particular to strikes by workers that did most to disabuse revolutionary syndicalists of what residual faith they might have been prepared to place in it. Strike action all too frequently resulted in the use of the army and, in increasing numbers, in the death of workers at the hands of the military.

In 1898 Pouget could be found comparing the Republic to the Second Empire of Napoleon III.[156] After the turn of the century this comparison became a commonplace. Commenting upon the deployment of the army to deal with a strike at Montceau-les-Mines in 1901 Pouget remarked that nothing had changed with the entry of Millerand into government: 'the troops bivouac at Montceau in the same way that under the Empire they bivouaced at Aubin'.[157]

Events gave ample opportunity to re-affirm these sentiments in the years which preceded Briand's defeat of the railwaymen. In October 1905 Delesalle penned an article entitled 'Assez de massacres' in which he drew attention to the fact that every significant labour dispute brought with it the immediate detachment of troops to the area.[158] In 1906 Alphonse Merrheim provided a detailed account in *Le Mouvement socialiste* of a strike which began in May of that year in the Breton town of Hennebont.[159] What Merrheim described was a town under virtual military siege in which the State lent its total support to the employer in an effort to crush the strike and intimidate the workers. The minority that made up the non-strikers — in the name of 'the liberty to work' — received military escorts to and from their place of employment; the leaders of the strike were threatened with imprisonment; the streets were patrolled by cavalrymen 'with drawn swords'. Merrheim concluded from this experience that 'the

Republic is no better than any other social regime' and that if the Republic
had freed the worker from 'moral oppression' it had replaced it by a
ferocious and pitiless 'economic oppression'. The workers, he argued, had
understood that 'the priest, the owner of the château, the director of the
factory, the Republic, in their *mutual complicity*, were in equal measure
the *Masters* that must be removed'.[160] The following year the 'massacre'
of striking peasants near Narbonne produced the publication of the CGT's
broadsheet headed *'Gouvernement d'Assassins'*[161] and this feeling of out-
rage and bitterness towards the Republic was proclaimed with even greater
fervour after the death of strikers in clashes with the army at Draveil-
Vignous and Villeneuve-Saint-Georges in 1908.[162] A cartoon printed in
La Voix du peuple showing Clémenceau, the prime minister of the day,
balancing two scales of blood and which read 'Last year I massacred the
peasants of Narbonne with cavalry from Paris! This year I'm massacring
the workers of Paris with cavalry from the Midi! That's Equality'[163] summarises perfectly the antipathy felt by the revolutionary syndicalists
towards the Republic and what they saw as its hollow and meaningless
principles. In article after article Clémenceau was vilified. He was, Pouget
wrote, 'not only the king of the cops, he is also the emperor of the
informers and the leader of the prison warders'.[164] Of Clémenceau, Griffuelhes asked, 'does he want more corpses?'.[165]

   The combined effect of what was seen as the repeated betrayal of the
workers' movement by socialist ministers and the violent repression meted
out to strikers was to place leaders of the syndicalist movement such as
Pouget in a position where they could, with conviction and authority,
argue that the proletariat should scorn politics and seek to destroy the
State. There could be nothing in common between the people and those
who sought to govern them. To see Millerand, the socialist deputy, by
the side of General Gallifet, who had taken part in the suppression of
the Paris Commune, was to realise that all politicians were unprincipled
careerists. The State, even in the form of the democratic republic, was
not a neutral institution capable of performing a mediating role in class
conflicts: it always sided with the capitalists. Pelloutier's relative indifference towards the Republic was therefore replaced by an increasingly
vociferous denunciation of all it appeared to stand for and, as Clémenceau's policy of repression led to more deaths and the imprisonment of
the syndicalist movement's leaders, few, if any, would have voiced the
opinion that the Republic was worth saving.

   Hostility towards the Republic was reflected in the response of revolutionary syndicalists to the clerical issue. The Republic had sought to
convince the people that the clergy was their principal enemy and that
emancipation would be achieved by an assault upon the power of the
Church and, in particular, by the dissolution of its educational monopoly.
Freedom meant intellectual liberty which, in practice, meant that French-

men were to be taught to think like good republicans. The revolutionary syndicalists agreed that the Church was an enemy of the people but saw it only as a secondary target. Clericalism, Yvetot agreed, was the enemy (as Gambetta had stated) 'but it is not the only enemy'.[166] Getting rid of the clergy would make no difference if the religion of Christ was replaced by the religion of the Republic: 'we do not wish to free ourselves from one', Yvetot wrote, 'only to become the dupes of the other'.[167] The real enemies of the people were those who oppressed and enslaved them and this meant not only the removal of the Church but principally the bourgeois State in the guise of the Republic. 'Down with the church', Yvetot proclaimed, 'and all the filthy vermin of the mind who live in it! Down with the State and all those who support and perpetuate it!'.[168] The relative unimportance attached to the clerical issue by the revolutionary syndicalists is, however, best shown by the fact that, in an age where the republican press delighted in exposing the minor misdemeanours of even the lowliest country priest, the syndicalist press devoted little space to the activities of the Church.

The issue which, by contrast, did receive enormous attention was antimilitarism. It was here that could be seen the true extent of the divide which separated the syndicalists from the Republic. The anti-militarist campaign gathered pace after 1900. By 1906 anti-militarism had been conflated with anti-patriotism and this, in theory at least, meant an unwillingness to go to war to save the French Republic. At a minimum three factors serve to explain the importance that the syndicalists were prepared to attach to this campaign.[169] After the turn of the century, and especially after the Morocco crisis of 1905, a war between the European powers seemed increasingly likely.[170] Secondly, syndicalist leaders in France grew ever more distrustful of their German counterparts and felt that a concerted internationalist campaign was necessary if the German proletariat was to be prevented from lending its support to the Kaiser in the event of war. Griffuelhes for one never forgot the unsympathetic reception he received from German labour leaders in January 1906. But it was, above all, the systematic use of the army to defeat striking workers that raised anti-militarism to its position of prominence.

The army came to be seen as the principal defender of the capitalist system and of the bourgeois Republic. 'The army', Yvetot wrote, 'is the impassable barrier that must be destroyed'.[171] Syndicalists were haunted by the thought of young workers conscripted into the army being used to quell the protests of their former comrades. 'The bourgeoisie', Pouget commented, 'has perfected the system of exploitation. It protects itself by the use of the workers who create its wealth and when the workers in overalls demand a better lot it sends against them the workers in red trousers'.[172] A cartoon in *La Voix du peuple* showed a young soldier returning home to his mother only to discover that he had killed his own father during a labour dispute. Syndicalist propaganda repeatedly called upon soldiers to disobey orders if told by their officers to shoot at members of their own class.

The anti-militarist campaign had several dimensions. It involved, first of all, the frequent description and characterisation of the army as an institution which brutalised and degraded the recruit. Army discipline was designed to dehumanise, to produce a passive and unconscious animal capable of committing the most vicious acts. Life in the barracks corrupted the soldier and introduced him to the perils of sexual excess and perversion. One special object of attack was the system of punishment deployed in army prisons. The army, Yvetot wrote in the *Manuel du soldat*, is 'not only the school of crime; it is also the school of vice, the school of cheating, of idleness, of hypocrisy and of cowardice'.[173]

After the army came an attack upon the very idea of the nation, '*la patrie*'. Republicanism had made much of the supposed virtues of the French nation and of the patriotic duty of all Frenchmen to defend the cultural patrimony of France. For revolutionary syndicalists these words were meaningless.[174] 'I am a stranger', Griffuelhes wrote, 'to everything that constitutes the moral dimension of our nation. I possess nothing; I must sell my labour in order to satisfy even my smallest needs. Therefore nothing which for some people forms a homeland exists for me. I cannot be a patriot'.[175] Why should the worker protect something he did not belong to or own? The only '*patrie*' the worker possessed was where he worked and from this perspective national frontiers were irrelevant. Yvetot agreed. If, he wrote, the worker, 'starving, without a home, without affection in the land of his birth, crosses the border in order to find an agreeable and easy life, to have friends, to start a family, he forgets his homeland'.[176] Only someone with the temperament of a well-trained dog, he argued, could be a patriot. Nor did they set much store by the democratic liberties granted to every French citizen. As Delesalle pointed out, his own experience had been one of constant persecution and intimidation. Was France really superior in this respect to the other nations of Europe?[177] Overall their general point was that the real division was not between nations but between the exploited and the exploiters. As Yvetot subsequently commented, for the workers the lost provinces were not called Alsace and Lorraine but Life and Liberty.[178]

Faced with the phenomenon of militarism and the threat of war soldiers and workers were called upon to respond.[179] Yvetot, in particular, counselled the conscript to disobey orders or desert.[180] Delesalle recommended those not wishing to join the army to go to prison rather than act against their will.[181] Soldiers were encouraged to turn their barracks into 'schools of revolt', to make contact with the workers in the local *bourse du travail* and to propagandise the syndicalist message among their colleagues.

Above all, the conscript was to be reminded that after his two years in the army he would rejoin the ranks of the proletariat.

In the event of war Pouget and his colleagues had one answer: the general strike.[182] Scorning the schemes for international arbitration advocated by Jaurès and the revolutionary patriotism associated with the French Left the workers were to be exhorted to turn the declaration of war into a social revolution that would bring an end to the exploitation of man by man.[183] But even in 1906, before the syndicalist movement faced the difficult task of attempting to put these ideas into practice, these sentiments were qualified. 'I would excuse', Yvetot wrote, 'French workers or the workers of a nation politically analagous to our own who agreed to go to war in order to resist the invasion of Russian despotism or Turkish barbarism'.[184] The clear implication was that, if in the eyes of the revolutionary syndicalists there was little to choose between the French Republic and the political systems of its often monarchical neighbours, this argument certainly did not apply to Czarist Russia and the Ottoman Empire.

Anti-patriotism clearly did not imply pacifism. Indeed, Charles Guieysse, the editor of *Pages libres* and one of the most perceptive commentators upon the syndicalist movement, pointed out that there existed profound similarities in the ethos typical of a bellicose patriotism and a doctrine which endorsed the class war. 'In revolutionary action', he wrote, 'one finds exactly the same qualities as in patriotic action: the sacrifice of individuals to the collectivity, the use of force for a task which is greater than the individual interest and which appears just'.[185] Moreover, it was accepted that the workers were not yet ready for such a grandiose gesture as a general strike in the event of war. The state of readiness could only be attained as a result of incessant propaganda and a lengthy process of education. 'In order to kill militarism', Yvetot wrote, 'it is necessary as a preliminary to kill the spirit of it'.[186]

Syndicalists were therefore obliged to consider how this end could be achieved and this led them inevitably to reflect not only upon the general question of how the workers attained a level of revolutionary consciousness but also upon the need for educational reform.[187] The general view was that the workers learnt primarily through action. 'In the *syndicats*', Pouget wrote, 'we philosophise little. We do better than that: we act'.[188] Griffuelhes provided two lengthy accounts which appeared to support this argument: *Voyage révolutionnaire* and *La Grève des délaineurs de Mazzamet*.[189] In *Voyage révolutionnaire* he showed how the vast majority of both rural and industrial workers, untouched by the agitation and propaganda of the syndicalist movement, remained in a position of passive submission and obedience. A similar state of affairs existed amongst the sheep-shearers of Mazzamet until the outbreak of a strike. A previously quiescent group of workers, 'hypnotised' by the Church and immune from 'modern ideas', sustained a strike for four months and, in Griffuelhes' view, in the process emancipated themselves from their deferential beliefs. 'What no theory has been able to achieve, what no oral or written propaganda can bring about', Griffuelhes wrote, 'is attained as a result of conflict'.[190] Action, he concluded, was creative: it opened the mind and the eyes.

Nevertheless, it was also recognised that a major obstacle to the intellectual liberation of the proletariat lay in the repressive State educational system.[191] That system, it was generally felt, was an instrument designed to secure the domination of the bourgeoisie. The State school taught the virtues of order, hierarchy and discipline, and respect for the prerogatives of property. The education it offered did not relate to the needs of working-class children: it was centralised and abstract, was imposed upon children in a uniform manner. Above all, it sought to provide the Republic with conscientious and submissive citizens. It was even argued that the real aim of the Republican system of education was to supplement the decadent élite of the bourgeoisie with a new élite drawn from the ranks of the working class. All too frequently, it was recognised, the educated worker deserted his own class.[192]

At the outset it should be noted that the reform of the educational system posed a particular problem for the revolutionary syndicalists: how were they to respond to the desire of State teachers to enter the *bourses du travail* and thus participate in the workers' movement?[193] The dilemma posed for the syndicalists was a simple one. While they sympathised with the desire of the teachers to free themselves from the tutelage of the State, the teachers were nevertheless perceived as a privileged middle-class group. If they had a right to defend their own moral and material interests, as '*fonctionnaires*' those interests were different from those of the producers. Delesalle, in particular, itemised what he took to be the likely consequences of the intrusion of the teaching profession. As 'semi-intellectuals' possessing a superior education and speaking skills they would quickly come to dominate their former pupils and would prevent the workers from obtaining the administrative education offered by their own institutions. As employees of the State, Delesalle asked, could the teachers be trusted to put the interests of the *syndicat* before their own livelihood? Crucially, if it was agreed that the State monopoly of education had to be opposed the syndicalists had little desire to hand over its provision to the teaching profession. The workers were to educate themselves.[194]

For the syndicalists the restructuring of education had several dimensions.[195] There was firstly the question of pedagogical reform. What was to be taught and how? Secondly, there was the problem of its location. Where was that education to take place and who were to be the teachers? By common consent the view was that education should be adapted to meet the needs of the working-class child. 'The educational ideal for us', Yvetot wrote, 'would be to secure the complete preparation of the child for every type of activity'. [196] Physically, intellectually and morally the child was to be made ready to meet the demands of life and work. Both Yvetot and Pouget provided an outline of this envisaged education in practice.[197]

There was to be no distinction between the sexes. Children were to be treated as ends in themselves, as beings in the process of development. Parents were to be denied control over their children's minds. Lessons were to be short, 'with demonstrations and exciting experiences'. There was to be an emphasis upon sport and physical culture; children were to play 'healthy and instructive games' and were to be taught to sing and to laugh. Academic studies were to be practical, not abstract. Children, Yvetot commented, were not to be taught grammar before they had learnt to speak. This applied to all disciplines, including mathematics, geometry and the natural sciences.[198] Children were to learn from observation and their own personal experiences. The natural world was to be studied not in the classroom but in the fields. By making the learning process as agreeable as possible the intention was always to foster the child's insatiable curiosity.

Given the antipathy felt towards the schools of the Republic the aspiration was to create schools that the workers would themselves run and control. In line with the principles set out by Pelloutier and inspired by the example of the model schools established by anarchists such as Jean Grave, the hope was that the workers' children could be given an education within the walls of the *bourse du travail*. Independent '*écoles syndicales*' were to be established. Yvetot, in particular, believed that this was a practical and feasible project.[199]

An integral part of the education received by the working-class child was to be a training in a trade or craft for which the child, by temperament and ability, was most suited. Again, it was argued that this training should be provided by the workers themselves and not by the State. 'It is', Delesalle wrote, 'in the workshop, the worksite, the factory, in the area of modern production, amidst the progress which every day is realised in each industry, that the apprentice of today, the worker of tomorrow, can learn the trade which will enable him to earn his livelihood and contribute his labour to the community'.[200] Beneath this vision, however, lay the realisation that the *syndicats* would only be able to provide an education suited to the intellectual and technical needs of the free producers of the future when they themselves had seized control of the means of production. With this we reach the heart of the syndicalist project.

Debate about the precise nature and detail of the appropriate tactics to be employed by the proletariat continued to flourish after the turn of the century (and after Pelloutier's death) as syndicalists sought both to advocate new strategies and to learn from their recent experiences. Significantly, and despite the fact that Delesalle could provide a virtual restatement of Pelloutier's account of the functions of the *bourses du travail*,[201] with the unification of the movement in 1902 it was the *syndicat* which came increasingly to occupy a position of centrality. Co-operatives, despite the educational opportunities they provided for workers, were deemed to possess only limited potential. 'The primordial error', Delesalle wrote, 'is to believe that it is possible within capitalist society to organise the systems of production and exchange of the future society'.[202] There was, however, an awareness that the peasant, and not just the industrial worker, should be a vital element of the syndicalist movement. Indeed, Pouget went so far as to assert that co-operation between the two groups was indispensable for the success of the revolution.[203]

Jacques Julliard has written that the originality of French syndicalism lies not in the goals it pursued but in the methods it sought to employ.[204] Hostility to the State and the political process combined with a recognition of the primacy of class interests meant that the emancipation of the proletariat had of necessity to be self-emancipation. This formula became known as *direct action* and, as defined by Pouget, amounted to 'the putting into operation, directly, without intermediaries, without intervention from outside, of the strength which lies within the working class'.[205] The emphasis fell upon autonomy of action and the utilisation of means that the workers themselves employed and controlled. Direct action was action freed from what were regarded as impurities. The working class was to take its destiny into its own hands and to free itself from a faith in a providential State (and a providential God) and the dominance of middle-class politicians this implied.[206] Further, in the minds of men like Pouget, direct action was an explicit rejection of the policies of social peace, a pure and undisguised expression of class war. Direct action was also a manifestation of vitality, initiative and human personality: through it the worker learnt 'to reflect, to decide, to act'.

Direct action took several forms and it would, Yvetot argued, vary according to the circumstances and needs of the moment.[207] Given that the system of law was a bourgeois creation designed to protect the established order the legality or otherwise of a particular act was not viewed as a relevant consideration.[208] One of the qualities of direct action was precisely that it extracted concessions from the employers and the State by engendering a sense of fear and duress. Included in the category of direct action were various types of consumer boycott, the award of a label of approval to employers who had met workers' demands and agitation in the streets as a means of exerting external pressure, but in the hands of the revolutionaries its principal manifestations were in the use of sabotage and in strike activity.

Sabotage was first discussed by the CGT when Paul Delesalle presented a report advocating its adoption at the Toulouse Congress of 1897.[209] Emile Pouget had already recommended its use to the readers of *Le Père Peinard* and *La Sociale* and over the next decade was to be its principal supporter.[210] The tactic of sabotage was also unequivocally endorsed by Yvetot and Griffuelhes and, in addition, received support from other syndicalist militants.[211] By contrast, it should be noted, it was not popular amongst the theoreticians of the movement and was unreservedly criticised by Hubert Lagardelle and Georges Sorel.[212]

Sabotage was defined broadly by Pouget as poor work for poor pay. It included go-slows, working to rule (*obstructionnisme*), the improvement of the quality of goods produced so as to reduce the employer's profit margins, and, in certain circumstances, the destruction of machinery. The existence of two irreconcilable economic classes and, therefore, of two distinct moral codes meant that proletarian acts of sabotage could not be judged by bourgeois values. 'It is necessary', Pouget wrote, 'that the capitalists recognise that the worker will respect the machine only on the day when for him it has become a friend and not, as it is today, an enemy'.[213] The vindication of the use of sabotage lay solely in its efficacy as a means of resisting exploitation and of fulfilling the goals pursued by the working class. Sabotage meant that the proletariat, even in the most difficult and unfavourable circumstances, could always respond to the actions of its enemies. To the charge (voiced by Jaurès and Sorel) that sabotage diminished the technical proficiency of the worker and thus undermined the syndicalist vision of the future society, Pouget responded that this argument amounted to a negation of the class struggle. The skills possessed by the workers should not be sold cheaply and moreover, he implied, far from inculcating bad habits sabotage actually increased the initiative and combative qualities of the proletariat.

By far the most controversial aspect of the defence of sabotage was the acceptance of the legitimacy of acts of physical damage in the form of such activities as machine breaking. In Delesalle's submission to the Toulouse Congress it was pacific forms of sabotage that were emphasised but both Pouget and Yvetot made little effort to disguise the fact that, in their view, sabotage also entailed acts of physical violence against machines and property (although not persons).[214] This form of sabotage, Pouget argued, aided the success of strikes. In the first place, it was likely that the strikers would only comprise a minority of the workforce and, in this context, sabotage served to impede 'the desertion of the masses' by making a return to work impossible. Likewise broken machinery prevented the army from strike breaking. Sabotage also served to bring a strike to a speedy conclusion. 'To demonstrate and tighten one's belt for months on end', Yvetot wrote, 'are absurd tactics'.[215] Sabotage received one final justification from Pouget. In his opinion, sabotage in the form of a whole series of industrial and commercial malpractices which daily impoverished and threatened the lives of the people was the essence of the capitalist system. 'Capitalist sabotage', he wrote, 'is a means of intensive exploitation'. It was the expression of a rapacious greed. In contrast, the sabotage employed by the working class was both generous and altruistic in spirit and intention. By freeing the masses from exploitation 'it was a ferment for a radiant and better future'.[216]

In *Aux travailleurs — la grève* Paul Delesalle argued that strikes were the 'logical consequence of the state of war which brought capital and labour into conflict'. Each side — in the shape of either surplus value or salary — sought to maximise its share of the wealth generated by the productive process. Was this, therefore, to suggest, Delesalle asked, that individual strikes (*grèves partielles*) could bring about an amelioration of the position of the working class? The answer was in the negative. Holding true to the 'law of salaries' that had underpinned Pelloutier's analysis of capitalism Delesalle argued that the employer would either recoup his losses at the earliest opportunity or that, if this did not occur, a general price increase would nullify the benefits of a higher salary. The strike, therefore, was best seen as 'the skirmish which prepared the way for the revolution'.[217] Nevertheless, only three years later Delesalle was to comment that 'to represent us as the enemies of all reform is to present the supporters of revolutionary syndicalism in a false light . . . We know, for example, that there is not a worker who, for the same salary, would not prefer to work for eight hours rather than ten hours'.[218] Yet, according to the 'law of salaries' previously endorsed by Delesalle such a reform was impossible to achieve under capitalism.

Delesalle's change of position was a reflection of a broader dilemma that arose from a genuine uncertainty about the goals and purposes of strikes. In stark terms, at issue was the question of the place of the pursuit of reforms within a movement which sought to secure revolutionary change through the eventual destruction of the capitalist system. Were the revolutionary syndicalists to oppose on theoretical and practical grounds any amelioration within bourgeois society of the condition of the working class? Was all hope, as Delesalle implied in *Aux travailleurs — la grève*, to be placed in the revolution in the form of the general strike? What is clear is that the hostility to '*grèves partielles*' was gradually replaced by a more realistic appraisal of the moral and material benefits that accrued from a successful strike. Integral to that process, of necessity, was the ditching of the 'law of salaries'.[219]

There was little disagreement about the merits of strikes as a form of direct action. Strikes, Griffuelhes argued, were the best means for the wage-earner to show his strength and to demonstrate that without his labour society could not survive. Strikes also represented the most straightforward and unambiguous method by which the worker could attack the capitalist and thus symbolised 'the rupture by which the proletarian dared defend his rights and interests'. The worker, through strike action, was fighting upon his own terrain. He was using the only weapon at his disposal: the withdrawal of his own labour.[220]

The changing perspective through which individual strikes (and hence reforms) were viewed is best illustrated by reference to Pouget's *L'Action directe* and Griffuelhes' article 'Romantisme révolutionnaire'.[221] Pouget argued that the final goal of general expropriation could not be separated from the daily struggle for piecemeal improvements. The folly of the all-or-nothing tactic, he argued, was that it failed to realise that each minor gain constituted a partial expropriation of the privileges held by the capitalists and thus opened up the way for greater demands on the part of the workers. To defend that position, and the necessity for proletarian action it involved, he argued against what he termed the 'catastrophic miracle', the view that the revolution would be brought about mechanically and fatally at some future date, and dismissed the veracity of the 'law of salaries'. Both entailed resignation and passivity: all effort, apart from that of the final struggle, was vain. By contrast, Pouget wanted to argue that the vigorous and energetic action of the proletariat could break the link between salaries and prices. This could be supported by appeal to the empirical evidence provided by countries which had short working hours and high salaries. There life was less expensive than in countries with long hours and low salaries. Further, Pouget also disputed the claim that misery acted as a ferment of revolt. Poverty and long hours, he argued, destroyed the worker both mentally and physically. Better conditions, on the other hand, did not mollify the worker. As they were inevitably the result of successful struggle they served to raise the dignity, consciousness and combativeness of the working class.[222]

Griffuelhes' article sought to dissociate revolutionary syndicalism from what he saw as a romantic and mystical faith in the redemptive qualities of the general strike. Recognising that the days of street fighting and barricades were over, the earliest supporters of the idea of the general strike, he argued, had nevertheless retained their belief that capitalism would be overthrown in one short and not-too-distant act of defiance. The vocabulary had changed — guns had been replaced by the sudden stoppage of production — but the vision, Griffuelhes wrote, had remained the same. Everything had now to be directed towards the general strike. Within this framework a strike which sought only to attain gradualist goals was viewed as a harmful waste and weakening of the strength of the working class. Griffuelhes' point in distancing himself from this view was to stress that it was precisely through the daily struggle that the revolution was prepared and organised. 'The day is not far away', he wrote, 'when every militant will recognise that *truly revolutionary action* is that which, practised every day, increases and augments the revolutionary value of the proletariat'.[223]

On this view, therefore, the pursuit of reforms in the shape, for example, of higher salaries and better working conditions was a feasible and desirable project and Pouget, in particular, vigorously denied the claim that the revolutionaries were not interested in securing such goals. 'To be a revolutionary', he wrote, 'in no way implies a disdain for day to day improvements'.[224] Nevertheless, it was their opinion that the only reforms worth having were those which the proletariat had secured through direct action. 'We know', Delesalle commented, 'that if we have been able to impose them, we are also capable of holding on to them'.[225] Furthermore, as Griffuelhes' remarks made clear, each individual strike had to be seen as part of a broader process of preparation and education leading to the expropriation of the capitalists through the general strike. Pouget, Griffuelhes, Yvetot and Delesalle persistently and frequently referred to strikes aimed at securing piecemeal improvements in terms of metaphors which evoked the image of training and mobilisation. The strike was *'une salutaire gymnastique'*, *'une gymnastique d'entraînement'*, *'une grande manoeuvre'*.

It was within this overall context that revolutionary syndicalists welcomed the campaign for the eight-hour-day launched by the CGT at the Congress of Bourges in 1904 and whose centrepiece was to be a series of one day strikes concentrated upon May Day.[226] Pouget, for example, saw this campaign as *'une machine de guerre'*. Through it the workers would secure not only material gains but a greater sense of what the revolution entailed. They would flex their muscles and improve their state of readiness.[227] Delesalle argued that the campaign would bring about shorter working hours, no loss in salaries, and a general decrease in unemployment. He also argued that it was long hours that induced resignation and exhaustion and which prevented the workers from pursuing their general emancipation.[228] These sentiments were echoed in CGT propaganda which, in general, sought to stress the physical and moral benefits accruing from the campaign while at the same time emphasising that the conquest of the eight-hour-day was part of the revolutionary process.[229]

Underpinning this defence of *'grèves partielles'*, however, was the realisation that no matter how short the working day might become, how high salaries might be, and how much the hygiene and conditions of factories might be improved, the continued existence of the categories of employer and wage-earner ensured that economic conflict between the classes would persist. And, in Pouget's opinion, this struggle would continue to grow in scale and bitterness as the workers grew in strength and came to appreciate their true value. The oppressed would voice their demands with ever increasing persistence and force until the moment when they were prepared for the decisive conflict. This final rupture would be 'direct action raised to its highest possible magnitude: the general strike'.[230]

The general strike was defined by Griffuelhes as 'the refusal of the producers to work for the pleasure and satisfaction of the non-producers'.[231] It was to be more than a mere withdrawal of labour. As the logical conclusion of the struggle of the proletariat to secure its emancipation the general strike was also to entail the seizure of the means of production. This much was agreed upon. Views differed about the likelihood of the use of violence. Griffuelhes was of an open mind. 'The general strike or revolution', he wrote, 'will be violent or peaceful depending upon the resistance to be overcome'.[232] Yvetot, on the other hand, was in doubt that the use of violence would be an integral part of any successful general strike. An attempt by the workers to take possession of the means of production, he argued, would meet an immediate response from a government determined to save the bourgeois social order. Faced by repression and what Yvetot referred to as 'the establishment of terror' the proletariat would of necessity need to respond or accept defeat.[233] The violent suppression of a general strike in Spain and the failure of a pacific general strike in Sweden appeared to confirm this prognosis.[234] Pouget, in non-visionary mood, commented that, whilst it was impossible to foresee the conditions under which a general strike would occur, it was certain that the general strike would be preceded 'by frictions, blows and contacts of a more or less brusque nature'.[235]

Opinions also varied about the significance to be attached to the use of violence. Yvetot, whilst he saw force primarily as a means to secure a desirable end,[236] also frequently characterised the use of violence as being appropriate to the activist temperament of the French working class. 'Our own method', he wrote, contrasting the French with the moderate and unexcitable Swedes, 'corresponds to a prompt, energetic, violent and supreme act'.[237] Pouget, by contrast, argued that the people did not have violent instincts. If they had, he commented, they would not submit for a day longer to the misery and privation inflicted upon them. The people, he wrote, 'have nothing of the endemic violence which characterises the ruling classes and which is the bedrock of their domination'.[238] If the general strike did involve violence, therefore, the responsibility for it would not belong to the proletariat. Significantly, neither Griffuelhes, Pouget, Yvetot or Delesalle provided anything like a systematic defense of the morally regenerative and creative qualities of violence.

It was also not clear who the participants in the general strike were to be. Delesalle, in his description of the general strike as the 'complete, unanimous and simultaneous stoppage of production', clearly assumed that *all* the workers in 'common accord' would leave their places of work only to return when the goal of general emancipation had been attained.[239] This fitted uneasily with the revolutionary syndicalist emphasis upon active minorities and with the ambivalent attitude adopted by Yvetot and Griffuelhes. Griffuelhes, for example, was of the opinion that the revolution would not be accepted by everyone and therefore that it would be the work of a minority 'which our incessant efforts at propaganda and action tend to enlarge'.[240] This, in turn, raised the issue of the likely pattern and structure of the general strike. Was it to be decreed by the CGT? How, if at all, was it to be organised? None of the militants under discussion provided clear and adequate answers to these questions. This was partly by design. 'I have no desire', Griffuelhes wrote, 'to play the role of prophet by outlining a plan which would assign to every man the role that he would occupy'.[241] Griffuelhes himself, however, did not appear to discount the need for some organisation and co-ordination of effort.[242] But the accepted view seems to have been that the general strike would itself evolve almost naturally out of a strike within an individual sector of the economy. Certainly the articles by Yvetot and Pouget in *La Voix du peuple* covering strikes leave the reader in no doubt that a strike, for example, by railwaymen, peasants or shopworkers, if it were taken up by workers in other trades, was capable of creating a revolutionary situation. This also seemed to be the intention behind the massive May Day demonstrations. In such a situation of almost spontaneous revolt the role of the CGT would be a minimal one.

When, finally, would the general strike take place? Again the leaders of the movement would not be drawn. 'We do not intend', Griffuelhes wrote, 'to fix either the day or the time when the wage-earners and the owners come into conflict'.[243] Was the general strike, therefore, 'a Utopia, a dream'?[244] Events, even if a completely successful general strike had not occurred, proved the contrary. The Russian Revolution of 1905 in particular indicated that a general strike could be brought to a successful conclusion and this example, along with other lesser cases, showed that far from being a dream the general strike was a living reality.[245] The Utopia, Yvetot countered, was to 'believe it to be impossible to realise the idea of the general strike'.[246]

Pouget, however, in *Comment nous ferons la révolution*, written in collaboration with the leader of the electricity workers Emile Pataud, was prepared to offer an account of the general strike in fictional form. Griffuelhes dismissed this work as a piece 'of literary and imaginative fantasy' but Pouget, in his reply to the criticisms voiced by Jaurès, seemed to suggest that even the most far-fetched aspects of the tale — such as the '*aéroplanes télé-mécaniques*' designed to defend the revolution — should be taken seriously.[247] What Pouget and Pataud's depiction emphasises is the manner in which a revolutionary climate is steadily created and how this situation is set aflame by one incident, the 'massacre' of workers. A general strike, at first spontaneous, later more organised, follows. As the conflict, replete with demonstrations, power black-outs and acts of sabotage, spreads from Paris to the provinces and the countryside discipline within the army breaks down and the troops side with the strikers. Inspired by an '*élan magnifique*' the workers storm parliament and simultaneously begin the task of the dissolution of the bourgeois State and the capitalist system. Gradually, through a process of 'rational requisitions', the new society comes into existence.[248]

Yet arguably the most significant aspect of Pouget and Pataud's account is the description they provide of the envisaged future society. In theory this was deemed to be impossible. Griffuelhes, scorning the role of prophet once more, argued that just as it had been impossible for the bourgeoisie of the eighteenth century to outline in advance the structure of the society they were subsequently to create, so equally the syndicalists were unable to describe the form of a free society.[249] However, syndicalists inevitably turned their attention to this topic and Griffuelhes himself was to be responsible for the launching of a general enquiry which invited participants to reflect upon the organisation of society in the wake of a triumphant general strike.[250] Listed amongst the seven questions asked were specific queries relating to the organisation and distribution of production, the transport of goods, and relations between industries. Syndicalists, in effect, were asked to consider how the *syndicat* might be transformed from an instrument of struggle into the key component of a new type of community. The often detailed replies were discussed at the Congress of Montpellier in 1902 and were published in *La Voix du peuple*. Furthermore, the response of Amadée Bourchet (taken sufficiently seriously to be appended to the report of the proceedings of the Montepellier Congress, published in *La Voix du peuple*, and reprinted in pamphlet form with the title of *Au Lendemain de la grève générale*[251]) was, despite its brevity, in all essentials identical to the sketch provided in *Comment nous ferons la révolution*.

Pouget had, in fact, published earlier projections of the future, most notably 'Faramineuse consultation sur l'avenir' printed in the *Almanach du Père Peinard* in 1896.[252] The libertarian communist ethos of this piece is much in evidence in *Comment nous ferons la révolution* and, in truth, the later fiction only filled out in greater detail the initial vision. At the heart of this vision was a conception of a 'decentralised, federative society where the human being would be able to develop in complete autonomy'.[253] To achieve that end the centralised machinery of the State would be demolished and replaced by a system of communal ownership and control. The *syndicats* would organise production whilst the *bourses du travail* would act as co-ordinating agencies — a 'vast telephone network' — providing statistical information necessary to ensure that the distribution of goods was carried out efficiently and the needs of consumers met. The transport of merchandise and people would be free of charge, the workers within the railway industry receiving '*carnets de consommation*' as payment for their services. With the abolition of private property agricultural production would become a cooperative enterprise; the village would become a 'large family' and the uprooted who had migrated to the towns would return to the land. There would be no uniform pattern of production: large-scale and artisanal enterprises would exist side-by-side. Everyone would be entitled to equal remuneration. This, it was argued, would be a system superior to capitalism capable of securing efficient production, the satisfaction of all real needs and free from human drudgery.[254]

In addition, reflection upon the future allowed Pouget to consider issues not normally found in syndicalist discourse. With the advent of the new society the prisons would be emptied but this did not mean that 'society would be put to the mercy of brigandage and idleness'.[255] In the first place, those who refused to accept the new conditions of life would be escorted to the country's borders and banished from its territory. Faced with the phenomenon of crime, it was argued that those cases (formerly the greater proportion of offences) deriving from inequality and misery or caused by the baneful effects of the environment would cease to exist in a society characterised by equitable harmony. Crimes that remained could be dealt with in a variety of ways. One expedient amounted to public censure. Each offender would be judged by his peers. If he was ajudged to be ill, he would be given treatment; if not, he would receive not physical punishment but a 'moral chastisement in the form of shunning or scorn'.[256] This 'quarantine' would be ended when it was felt that the offender had mended his ways. More serious crimes — child molestation and rape are cited specifically — evoked an altogether different response.[257] Such behaviour on occasion would be subject 'to acts of summary justice'. The perpetrator would be 'executed without pity', the victim of the legitimate 'indignation' of the populace. For all its cruelty, it was argued, this was better than the cold-blooded punishment meted out by the magistrates.[258]

The standing army would be abolished: the people, in the form of the *syndicats*, would 'arm themselves in order to protect liberty'. As for the liberal professions and intellectuals in general, the assumption was that they would, broadly speaking, welcome the revolution. Freed from the need to sell their knowledge and experience their occupation would be transformed into social functions performed in a spirit of moral and professional obligation. These groups would receive no special treatment or favours: their reward would derive from the privilege of performing their task. On the broader issues of intellectual and religious freedom, complete liberty was to be proclaimed. In the press, for example, there would be no limit to criticism. The Church would be stripped of its power although everyone would be free, if they so desired, to be a 'Christian, Buddhist or theosophist' as one's religion was a purely private affair. This tolerance, however, rested upon the presumption that with an improvement in material conditions the incidence of religious faith would gradually decline. The best examples of Church architecture were to be preserved. Art would become the possession of the people. The producers of luxury goods would use their skills to adorn public buildings. Literature and the theatre would become forums for free expression.

Social life would also change. The bar and the café would be replaced by the library and the discussion group. Alcoholism — always a major issue of concern for syndicalists — would be eradicated, as the workers were freed from the deleterious effects of overwork and exhaustion. With free and improved transport the people would move out of the squalid cities and would enjoy a 'semi-rural' existence. Women, too, would be emancipated. The sensible use of new inventions would transform domestic life and thus allow women to escape Proudhon's brutal dilemma of 'housewife or prostitute'. Public laundries and kitchens would exist. Children could be brought up in communal care. 'The first effect of this moral and material independence of women', it was argued, would be 'to purify and ennoble sexual relations'.[259]

Where Pouget and Pataud's account bordered upon the bizarre was in their discussion of the international repercussions of the revolution and the manner in which it was envisaged that external attacks would be repulsed.[260] The point of reference was the revolution of 1789. Events in France, it was argued, would engender enthusiasm and support among the peoples of Europe but their governments would try to kill the revolution at birth. The revolution would be protected not by the reconstitution of the army — this would entail a return to the *ancien régime* — but by the development and employment of highly sophisticated weapons of destruction which would not only crush the enemy but also effectively put an end to war. What all this indicates (apart from a prescient awareness on the part of the authors of the ability of technology to alter the character of war) is the realisation that a revolution, if it is to survive, must at a minimum be able to defend itself from its foreign enemies. Unfortunately, if revolutionary syndicalists paid little attention to the organisational and strategic aspects of the general strike, they showed even less interest in this dimension of their struggle.

Comment nous ferons la révolution, for all its faults, is of interest because not only does it provide an insight into the wilder and incautious hopes and aspirations of its authors but also because it discloses the rudiments of an ethical theory which, for all its simplicity, was at the basis of much syndicalist writing. Man would be transformed by his environment — the text refers to man's 'plasticity' — from '*la bête humaine*' of capitalism into a 'sociable human being'. Rivalry, discord and struggle would be replaced by 'understanding, cordiality and mutual aid'. The only battle that would remain would be between man and the forces of nature.[261] In short, by a process of enlightenment man would come to perceive that, in a system of communal ownership and mutual obligation, there would exist no conflict between private and public interest. Man's natural sociability — restored in the new society — meant that each person's liberty would not be restricted but extended by the liberty of others.[262]

It is when we consider the question of how man's natural sociability is to be restored that we return to Pelloutier's central preoccupation of the creation of the free producers of the future. Maxime Leroy, in a work entitled *La Coutume ouvrière*[263] published in 1913, pointed out that the syndicalist movement was in the process of developing a 'new juridical system' that was 'exclusively proletarian'. The *syndicats*, through a series of rules, sanctions and punishments, sought to enforce a new code of behaviour which took as its central principle the obligation of all workers to act in accordance with the dictates of proletarian solidarity. The individual's liberty was not abandoned or alienated but was rather enhanced and extended by participation in the decision-making process of the *syndicat* itself. The relative simplicity of this procedure and the absence, in the main, of a sense of constraint derived from the homogeneity of the economic interests of a group of workers employed in the same occupation. Nevertheless, a 'tradition' or pattern of working-class behaviour — with a whole set of verbal and written obligations — was being self-consciously initiated.[264]

The mistake, therefore, is to believe that Pouget and his colleagues — for all their libertarian credentials — sought to establish a society characterised by untrammelled freedom. The future, in effect, was to be the *syndicats* and the CGT writ large. The Republic, the State, capitalism, the bourgeois legal system, the army and bureaucratic administration[265] were to be abolished and in their place was to be an arrangement of interrelated but independent producers' organisations. The supposition was that in this new situation the individual would be markedly freer than he had been before but there were also discernible limits to freedom of action. An individual, upon the basis of precepts embodied by the *syndicats*, would not be free, it can be assumed, to be idle or, for example, to act in a manner contrary to the productive endeavours of his colleagues. If, in the new society, such an individual would not be imprisoned he would certainly feel the full force of society's moral opprobrium. Freedom, when it clashed with sociability, could be restricted in the interests of the superior claims of reciprocal duty towards the community. What the workers were being offered was, indeed, greater liberty but individual autonomy, when defined in terms of an extension of personality and capacity, was compatible with an element of restraint.[266]

The primacy of the *syndicat* for all syndicalists derived from the centrality of the productive process, and hence of the producer, in social life. In the years that immediately followed Pelloutier's death the effective leaders of the CGT — Griffuelhes, Pouget, Yvetot and Delesalle — sought to develop a strategy that would enable the workers to capitalise upon this seemingly undeniable and inescapable truth. If Pelloutier's concern to further the education and preparation of the proletariat remained, his efforts to explore the nature of capitalist exploitation were superceded by a frequently and stridently repeated call for proletarian action. Pelloutier's distrust of politics was systematised into a coherent attack upon the Republic, the State and the political order. As the likelihood of war increased, anti-militarism and anti-patriotism were raised into central features of syndicalist doctrine. Most significantly, syndicalist theory discarded the law of salaries and thereby made possible a re-evaluation of the purposes and goals of strikes. Reform and revolution were no longer incompatible. But what remained untouched and with equal conviction was the core of Pelloutier's thought: the emancipation of the proletariat must be self-emancipation and the means to secure that end lay in the creation of exclusively working-class organisations which, ultimately, would bring down the capitalist system and its institutional and cultural superstructure by means of a general strike. In the hands of men of greater erudition and sophistication these ideas were to form part of a broader attack upon the theoretical premises of democratic society but when expressed in the pages of *La Voix du peuple* and at CGT congresses they were designed to inspire and guide a movement which, it was hoped, in the not-too-distant future would destroy the iniquitous system of capitalism and its repressive institutions. The tragedy was that by 1909 for Griffuelhes, Pouget, Delesalle and Yvetot these hopes had all but disappeared.

3 Georges Sorel and the Nouvelle Ecole

In 1899, after a direct appeal on his behalf by Jean Jaurès to the minister of commerce Alexandre Millerand, an impoverished Fernand Pelloutier took up temporary employment at the *Office du Travail*, his task to complete a statistical enquiry on trade unions in France. The unlikely intermediary between Pelloutier and these two representatives of reformist socialism was Georges Sorel.

Sorel first became acquainted with Pelloutier through *L'Ouvrier des deux mondes* for which he produced three substantial articles[1] and subsequently he wrote the preface for Pelloutier's *Histoire des bourses du travail*. Sorel was unambiguous in his assessment of Pelloutier's achievements. This 'great servant of the people' had spurned the role of socialist theoretician and intellectual in order 'to convince the workers that they would easily find amongst themselves men capable of directing their own institutions'. In his efforts to secure that end Pelloutier had created, in the *bourses du travail*, a set of institutions that embodied 'a conception of socialist life'.[2]

Sorel's own route to syndicalism was less direct than that taken by Pelloutier. Born in 1847 of middle-class parents and educated in Paris, first at the Collège Rollin and then at the prestigious Ecole Polytechnique, Sorel spent the greater part of his working life employed as an engineer in the *Ministère des Ponts et des Chaussées*. He remained throughout his entire life outwardly conventional, the epitome of bourgeois respectability and sobriety. The bookshops of Charles Péguy and Paul Delesalle, rather than a trade union meeting, were his chosen field of action. Yet it was in that environment — as Boris Souvarine recently testified[3] — that Sorel exercised enormous influence, moulding the thoughts of a new generation of Parisian Left Bank inhabitants and fostering — primarily in the forms of Hubert Lagardelle and Edouard Berth — what he himself was to describe as the *'nouvelle école'* of socialism. The *'nouvelle école'*, Sorel wrote, was 'Marxist, syndicalist and revolutionary' and its function was to purge traditional Marxism of all that was not specifically Marxist in order to preserve the 'heart' of the doctrine: the notion of class struggle. Marxism was no longer to be seen as a *'philosophie de tête'* but as a *'philosophie de bras'* and its principal physical manifestation, as *the* instrument of social war, was to be the *syndicat*.

I

The first products of Sorel's prodigious intellectual energy began to appear in 1886, whilst Sorel was stationed in the southern town of Perpignan. Until his death in 1922 there followed a regular stream of books, articles and book reviews encompassing the principal political, philosophical, religious and scientific issues of the day.[4] Amongst his earliest writings those that touched upon politics display no interest in socialism but they do, nevertheless, betray the sentiments of an outsider, disenchanted with the official Parisian culture and *mores* of the Third Republic. *Le Procès de Socrate*, published in 1889, directed its fire against the intellectual and political élite of French society, castigating its vulgarity and opportunism and its lack of moral seriousness. Beneath lay Sorel's sense of the moral decay of contemporary France, rooted in his acceptance of the traditional values of rural, Catholic France and articulated by constant reference to Proudhon, not as anarchist but as the defender of an austere moral code.

Sorel first turned his attention to socialism in general and Marxism in particular in 1892, the year of his retirement from government service and his move to Paris. He initially saw Marxism as a science, a doctrine capable of providing an objective understanding of both society and economic activity and hence of putting an end to the moral and philosophical uncertainties of his day. Sorel quickly distanced himself, however, from the 'orthodox' interpretation of Marxism as a science capable of providing predictive knowledge of future societal development and from 1896 onwards began a fundamental re-interpretation of Marxism that was to lead eventually to his espousal of syndicalism.

In his re-reading of Marx, Sorel sought to make a return to the 'spirit' of the original texts. Accordingly he denied the scientific validity of the so-called laws of capitalist development (deployed by Marxists to justify their belief in the imminent demise of capitalism) and endeavoured to disencumber Marxism of the accretions associated with Engels, most notably the dialectic. Having thus deprived the Marxist movement of the certitude of its ultimate victory Sorel contended that Marxism should be properly seen as an ethical doctrine. The vision of the 'catastrophic' collapse of capitalism derived from the 'orthodox' postulates of the immiserisation of labour and the increasing ferocity of capitalist crises was replaced by that of a moral struggle in which an ethically vigorous working class would overturn the values of bourgeois society. Socialism, Sorel wrote, 'stands before the bourgeois world as an irreconcilable adversary threatening it with moral catastrophe'.[5]

For Marx, Sorel asserted, the class struggle was not simply a clash of material interests. It was a conflict about rights, about principles of social and economic organisation. The workers sought not only their economic emancipation but also the abolition of class distinctions and the achieve-

ment of an honourable life for all men. They protested in the name of
the oppressed invoking 'their birthright against historical superiorities'.[6]
Marx, Sorel wrote, 'never failed to highlight the juridical aspects of social
welfare'.[7]

Sorel was here concerned primarily to disabuse Marxists of their belief
in the inevitability of the collapse of the capitalist system (and thus of the
emergence of a socialist society). He was obliged therefore, in the context
of Marxist debate in the 1890s, either to abandon Marxism or redefine its
status. By specifying that the 'mission of the proletariat' was 'essentially
moral'[8] he adopted the latter course. In the process he relied upon a loose
amalgam of ideas derived to a large extent from his earlier reading of
Proudhon and Vico[9] and only indirectly from Marx. The key notion was
that of a juridical conscience.

Throughout his life Sorel was haunted by a sense of the moral decline
and decay of the society in which he lived. Firmly Proudhonian in moral
outlook, he revered the values of the land: hard work, personal responsibility and the family.[10] All around him he saw an urban culture glutted
by excess, frivolity and sexual indecency. The development of a juridical
conscience within the proletariat was seen by Sorel as a means by which
the decadence and purely utilitarian ethics of his day could be put to an
end. By juridical conscience Sorel meant an internal moral discipline
guided by reason, duty and right. 'There is nothing more important for
the future of a country', Sorel wrote, 'than the progress of the juridical
education of the people. The workers must understand that there are
duties before which the feelings must give way and that it is not necessarily
a good thing to destroy every obstacle that restrains them'.[11] This notion
was grafted by Sorel onto the more overtly Marxist perspective which
stipulated that the working class acquire the skills and capacities required
to run a highly complex and sophisticated industrial economy, thus leaving
Sorel with a definition of socialism which postulated the moral and technical education of the proletariat as the necessary prerequisite of a future
socialist society.

Sorel was convinced both that this education would not be produced
spontaneously and that it could not be imposed upon the proletariat. It
had of necessity to be 'the product of a long evolution' within the proletariat itself undertaken *prior* to the emergence of a socialist society.
Accordingly the various tactics and practices (both institutional and political) adopted by the socialist movement had to be assessed from the point
of view of the 'preparation' of the working class and judged in terms of
their capacity to further that education.[12] 'It is not a question', Sorel wrote
in 1898, 'of knowing what is the best morality, but only of determining if
there exists a mechanism capable of guaranteeing the development of
morality'.[13]

Two points may be made by way of clarification. Sorel specifically rejected the 'official' Marxist view which saw ethics as a simple reflection of the economic base. For Sorel institutions acted as vital mediators between that base, the working practices required by it, and the ethical consciousness of the proletariat. 'Institutions', he wrote, 'exercise a powerful educational force and from this point of view their importance cannot be overstated'.[14] Sorel therefore considered it to be self-evident that the new code of morality, the new juridical conscience, would arise out of one or more of the various working-class institutions and organisations.

Likewise Sorel disputed the widely-held belief that modern industry generated standardised production methods. In Sorel's view advanced technology would not reduce the worker to an automaton but would require great skill and technical sophistication for its operation. The future would demand 'a superior worker, capable of very qualified work, able to follow the fastest and most difficult movements of a machine and who uses skill rather than strength'.[15] Sorel sought to discover the institutional framework most appropriate to secure the required level of technical expertise.

Sorel's strongest criticisms were directed against the German Social Democratic Party, at the time the very essence of a socialist party and the largest organisation of its kind.[16] The SPD, Sorel contended, was a bureaucratic and autocratic party run in the interests of its predominantly bourgeois leadership. In organisational terms it reproduced the hierarchical structures of the State and effectively excluded the working class from its decision-making processes. The workers were intentionally kept in ignorance and were controlled and directed in almost military fashion by their leaders. The SPD's reliance upon a strategy that defined the future revolution as a simple transfer of political power was designed, Sorel felt, to secure the continuing dominance of the party leadership. The SPD, Sorel wrote, 'is, in the last analysis, an organisation of workers under the direction of orators; it is an oligarchy of demagogues, governing the working class, providing its reading matter, telling it which candidates to support in elections and living off its profession as directors of the people'.[17]

Sorel's critique of the bourgeois leadership of the SPD extended to intellectuals in general. By intellectuals Sorel meant members of the liberal professions, a class of person who gained their livelihood outside the productive process. Sorel's opposition to the intrusion of intellectuals into the socialist movement derived in part from his perception of them as representatives of the dominant bourgeois culture but arose largely from his assessment of their distinct 'professional interests' which, Sorel asserted, would be jeopardised by a genuine proletarian revolution. 'The true vocation of intellectuals', Sorel wrote, 'is the exploitation of politics . . . Intellectuals wish to convince the workers that it is in their interest to carry them to power and to accept the hierarchy of capacities which puts the workers under the control of politicians'.[18] Moreover, the disenchanted intellectual, spurned and rejected by his own class, saw in the working class the vehicle to express his own hatred and resentment. 'The ferocious jealousy of the impoverished intellectual who wishes to guillotine the rich speculator is an evil passion', Sorel wrote, 'which has nothing to do with socialism'.[19]

Implicit within Sorel's critique of intellectuals was a clear rejection of the view which equated the transformation of society with electoral victory by the socialists. In addition to believing that such a victory would lead only to the domination of 'an oligarchy of intellectual masters' Sorel argued that the belief in the control of the State by the people rested upon a 'fiction'. 'Never', Sorel wrote, 'has anyone tried to justify the singular paradox according to which the vote of a *chaotic majority* leads to the appearance of what Rousseau called a general will which could not err'. Yet this 'fiction' was 'the last word' in democratic theory.[20] Further, in contemporary society (even under universal suffrage) a vote was not an indication of a rational and deliberate choice or decision. It was 'rather an *abdication* by people who recognised their own incompetence and their own incapacity to act'.[21]

Yet this should not be taken to mean that at this stage Sorel disputed the merits of all political activity. It was not in fact until 1903, after the Dreyfus Affair had all but run its course, that Sorel sought to distance the working class from politics completely. However, even at this point, he did wish to confine the political activity of the working class within definite limits. Like Pelloutier, Sorel was not entirely indifferent to the fate of the democratic regime. A parliamentary system, inspired by liberal principles, provided the working class with opportunities to extend their own organisation and education. It was in part for this reason that Sorel lent his support initially to the Dreyfusard movement.[22] Accordingly Sorel thought it legitimate for the working class to engage in political activity in order to secure legislation favourable to its own development. All action which either strengthened the power of the State or augmented the position of political élites was to be avoided. As the aim was to create a new proletarian society the working class was to use the political process to obtain reforms which ultimately would deprive the existing political structure of its functions.[23]

It was but a short step from this largely negative appraisal of the parliamentary route to socialism to a critique of State socialism. It is important to realise that Sorel, upon his own admission and unlike many of his contemporaries in France, did not come to Marxism via Jacobinism.[24] His earliest writings, most notably *Le Procès de Socrate*, display in full his hatred of the Jacobin tradition, its middle-class Parisian adherents and their *penchant* for dictatorial State power. Sorel's reading of Marx and his analysis of the 'bureaucratic State' of the SPD confirmed and strengthened his hostility towards the structure and character of State power. All States rested upon a false dichotomy between producers and non-producers, manual workers and intellectuals, the incompetent and the capable. A socialist State would reproduce this division, spawning a class of functionaries which would decide *for* the proletariat. 'State socialism', Sorel argued, followed as 'a natural consequence': 'since the workers were not capable of governing themselves and needed to be protected from the capitalists, one was obliged to use the State to direct the economy'.[25]

In essence, Sorel's critique of the organisational structure and tactics of political parties, and specifically the SPD, rested upon his conviction that political parties simply reproduced the hierarchical and centralised structures of the capitalist order. The revolution would be carried out for the proletariat but not by the proletariat with the result that the working class would remain in a subordinate position and would receive a new set of masters — the intellectuals. A political revolution, a mere change in personnel leaving existing structures intact, would require no prior education of the proletariat. The working class would continue to embody a 'morality of slaves', not 'the morality of free men', which Sorel took to be the ethical basis of socialism.[26] Moreover, State socialism, the inevitable outcome of the seizure of power by a political party, did not allow the working class to acquire the technical skills required to ensure the superior use and organisation of the means of production developed by capitalism.

Sorel concluded, therefore, that the emancipation of the proletariat should be self-emancipation. 'Remain exclusively working class', he counselled.[27] The route to socialism lay through economics, not politics. The workers should reject the State and its authoritarian traditions, and in their place create their own institutions based upon federal and decentralist principles. 'If', Sorel wrote, 'capitalist society is characterised by uniformity and unity, the workers' movement leads to local diversity'.[28]

Sorel's search for autonomous working-class organisations did not take him directly or immediately to the *syndicats*. In his efforts to establish the correct relationship between the political party and the working-class movement he turned initially to the example of the Belgian socialist party.[29] What impressed him about the socialist movement in Belgium was that it was built upon a loose federal structure of *syndicats*, co-operatives, mutualist societies and political groups in which the political party saw itself as the servant of the other organisations. The party sought 'reform in order to restrain the power of the State, instead of demanding its continued extension'.[30] Sorel also turned his attention to the American Federation of Labour.[31] Again, the attraction was that the AFL did not reproduce the centralised organisational structures of the bourgeois political order.

It was, however, the British trade union movement, as perceived by Sorel through the writings of the conservative sociologist Paul de Rousiers, which provided the model for Sorel's *L'avenir socialiste des syndicats*, published in 1898. This pamphlet, along with two articles in *La Science sociale*, 'Les Grèves' and 'Les divers types de sociétés coopératives',[32] provides the clearest exposition of Sorel's ideas immediately prior to the turn of the century and the earliest indication of his move towards syndicalism.

The trade unions and *syndicats* were judged by Sorel not in terms of their capacity to provide the workers with material benefits but as institutions of 'self-government' and as potential 'mechanisms of moralisation'. What Sorel saw in the British trade unions were institutions created by the working class, which had been able to attract the best members of their trade, and which had exerted a morally beneficial (and sobering) influence upon their members. Through the trade unions, the workers had acquired a personal sense of responsibility and an awareness of their obligations to their fellows. 'In general', Sorel wrote, 'the trade unionists do not pursue selfish ends . . . They seek a general goal to the benefit of all workers, even those who made the struggle more difficult by their apathy or by their laziness'.[33]

Sorel maintained that as purely working-class organisations the *syndicats* enhanced the capacity of the workers to direct their own affairs and were free from the tutelage of intellectuals. In place of the fictitious and illusory equality of political democracy the *syndicats* initiated 'the new political principle of the proletariat': selection from and government by the occupational group. The abstract citizen was to be replaced by the worker, the political arena by the factory.[34]

Furthermore, the *syndicats* sought to invert the existing relationship between capital and labour and in the process they created a new set of juridical principles. Here Sorel specifically cited and highlighted for the first time the activity of strikes. By disputing the claims of the capitalist to sole control of the factory, strikes, according to Sorel, provided the workers with the opportunity to assert their proprietorship of their own labour and their place of work. Moreover, the actual activity of a strike broke down the barriers between individual workers and forged them into an integrated group with a strong sense of solidarity. No one, for example, could abandon their comrades without being considered a traitor.[35]

One further beneficial and indirect result of strike activity was that it enhanced the technical capacity of the proletariat. The pressure exerted by strikes forced the employers to utilise the latest innovations in machine technology. 'The obligation to pay high salaries', Sorel wrote, 'is the stimulus par excellence of contemporary industry'.[36] The workers were thereby able to acquire and master a range of new and sophisticated skills and in consequence, Sorel argued, their attitude towards their work was transformed. 'The inertia, malevolence and thoughtlessness which characterised the worker in the days of starvation wages', Sorel commented, 'is overcome for good'.[37] Whereas the artisan-proprietor persevered in the utilisation of old-fashioned skills the 'modern proletarian', despite his non-ownership of the means of production, 'did not cease to advance and to keep up with the most difficult techniques'.[38] In this context, Sorel voiced the opinion — *contra* Proudhon — that high salaries and a shorter working day were perfectly compatible with technological advance and would not have deleterious consequences upon the proletariat.[39] Strikes, therefore, secured both of the objectives defined by Sorel as the preconditions of a socialist society: the moral and the technical education of the proletariat.

Given Sorel's belief that the highest and most sophisticated levels of factory production would be achieved within capitalist industry it followed that the co-operatives did not offer a general alternative to capitalist production. Nevertheless Sorel recognised that both consumer and producer co-operatives, run according to socialist principles, could perform certain valuable functions. Most obviously, by cutting out intermediaries they provided the workers with material benefits. They were also able to supply the workers with cheaper and better housing. The co-operatives were of pedagogical value to the extent that they taught the workers to direct their own affairs. Of greater significance for Sorel it seemed was the fact that the directors of the co-operatives were selected because of their exceptional abilities and moral probity. It was, Sorel commented, an 'aristocratic' system, which had its faults, 'but which is not exposed to the accidents of demagogic constitutions'.[40]

Sorel stressed in particular the utility of agrarian co-operatives. In addition to improving the productive capacity of the peasant farmer it effected a transformation within the peasant himself. In line with the impact of the strike upon the factory worker, the peasant was educated, transformed, freed from old work practices and routines, made able to work in a more scientific manner and to employ the latest tools. Subsequently, in *Introduction à l'économie moderne*, published in 1903, Sorel was to criticise socialists for their ignorance of the role played by agriculture in securing the progress of production and for their neglect of the qualities and skills engendered by agricultural labour. The factory worker, according to Sorel, had much to learn from the peasant's meticulous care of and attachment to his land.[41]

It was therefore within capitalist society and through the creation of the workers' own institutions, particularly the *syndicat*, that the foundations of a new society would be established. The workers, by their own efforts, would engender and master new productive forces which called for the deployment of the most advanced technical skills. Through the practices of their daily lives a new socialist morality would come into existence. The hierarchical structures of the bourgeois political and economic order would be emptied of significance, rendered irrelevant and ultimately replaced. What is more it seemed that Sorel was of the opinion that this process of transformation would be largely, if not entirely, pacific.

Despite his recognition that each strike was 'a partial manifestation of the revolutionary idea of the general strike'[42] and that the general strike alone was capable of securing the destruction of the traditional institutions of the State and of establishing a purely proletarian system of administration there was little hint of the violence associated with Sorel's later conception of the general strike.[43] Strikes were war-like in the sense that they brought two irreconcilable conceptions of society face to face. Above all, Sorel recognised that the preparation required by the working class had not been completed and concluded that 'it would be criminal to carry out a social revolution that would put in peril the little morality that exists'.[44] Sorel's position, therefore, was that the working class should concentrate its efforts upon seeking piecemeal reforms and upon furthering its own moral and technical education. 'Socialism', Sorel wrote, is realised 'in so far as we are able to conceive what socialist conduct is and know how to direct our institutions and thus to the extent that the socialist ethic is embodied in our conscience and our life'.[45]

Sorel's enthusiasm for British trade unions was not slow in waning. He quickly concluded that the trade based structure of British unions would engender a 'corporatist' spirit amongst their members and hence would hinder the development of a sense of common interests and class solidarity. Undaunted, at the turn of the century he transferred his praise to Pelloutier's *bourse du travail* movement.[46]

Sorel appeared to discern three primary qualities in the *bourses*. The *bourses* were a new type of organisation, unbureaucratic and decentralised, free of the predilection for 'unité gouvernementale', and thus not 'imitations of the bourgeois tradition'. Instead of constituting 'a new authority', Sorel wrote, Pelloutier had ensured that the *Fédération des bourses* operated as 'an administrative bureau, which would serve to put the *bourses* in contact with each other in order that they might share their ideas and experiences'.[47]

Secondly, the horizontal structure of the *bourses* had the merit that it drew upon the strong local ties of the workers. 'The organisation of the *bourses du travail* ', Sorel wrote, 'has as its first condition the existence of relations that arise between workers pursuing different professions but living in the same place'.[48] For Sorel, it seemed obvious that in the great majority of cases 'the workers of the same town have more interests in common than do workers of the same trade living in different towns'.[49] They were united by familial ties, shared the same friends, and had been to school together. A common physical environment ensured that they experienced a similar style and pattern of life whilst their sense of a communal life was enhanced by a complex web of local societies and organisations. These concrete associational ties formed the people into a 'véritable unité' and were the bedrock of the future socialist society.

Finally, Sorel accepted Pelloutier's characterisation of the *bourses* as autonomous organisations capable of providing the workers through their own efforts with a wide range of services. 'The *bourses*', Sorel wrote, 'can easily become the administrative structure of the workers' commune'.[50]

Sorel's praise for the *bourses du travail* was accompanied by overt criticism of their then rival, the CGT which, he felt, was in danger of becoming an adjunct to the State and also by an awareness on Sorel's part of the potential for degeneration within the socialist movement as a whole. The *bourses*, in Sorel's opinion, pursued a course of action that reconciled the demands of the day-to-day practical organisation of the proletariat and the preservation of revolutionary convictions. Sorel's fear was that the socialist movement would either abandon those convictions entirely or preserve them only in the form of idle rhetoric and 'casuistry'. This concern was most clearly expressed in an article entitled 'Qu'est-ce qu'un syndicat?' published in 1903.[51]

Sorel distinguished three distinct 'types' of trade union or syndicalist activity, each inspired by different motives and sentiments. The first 'type' took as its model the example of 'le trade-unionisme anglais'. Here the unions sought primarily to defend the interests of their members. This goal was secured by obtaining higher wages and by offering protection against the competition of other workers (especially cheaper unskilled and female labour). The second 'type' was the 'revolutionary syndicalism' that Sorel specifically associated with Pelloutier, its 'principal theoretician', and with Paul Delesalle and Georges Yvetot. 'Whereas', Sorel wrote, 'according to the previous conception, every dispute between the bosses and the workers tends to take the form of a wrangle between two merchants, here everything is different: it becomes one episode in the irreducible conflict that exists between Capital and Labour'.[52] The revolutionary syndicalists sought the abolition of the wage system itself and with that the end of capitalism. Thirdly, Sorel identified a new form of institutionalised *syndicat*, which, he argued, operated as 'une municipalité de métier'. Modelled on existing political parties these *syndicats* sought to obtain 'material benefits for their clients' and to that end compromised and bartered with the institutions of the State. In essence, they sought to share the spoils of the capitalist system and were the institutional embodiment of social peace. Circa 1903 Sorel believed that this 'protectionnisme ouvrier' was destined to dominate the syndicalist movement.

The causes of Sorel's apparent disillusionment with the syndicalist movement are not difficult to discern. Sorel's reformulation of Marxism, begun in the pages of *Le Devenir social*, led him not only to endorse the political reformism of Edouard Bernstein but also to question the empirical veracity of Marx's account of the social bifurcation, the dichotomous division into capitalists and proletarians, created as a consequence of capitalist accumulation. The middle classes were not disappearing, as Marx had predicted, and they were, consequently, destined still to play an important role in the political evolution of society. One of the tasks of the socialist movement, Sorel wrote in his preface to Merlino's *Formes et essence du socialisme*, was to ensure that this 'intermediary' group aligned itself with the working class and this could be secured if socialism was seen to defend 'every victim' of oppression regardless of their social class.[53] For Sorel this necessarily entailed socialist involvement in the defence of Dreyfus and, by implication, socialist support for a government of 'Republican defence'. Socialism thus was conceived as part of a broader democratic movement designed to safeguard 'the spirit of liberty and to augment the legal guarantees given to man'.[54]

Sorel was subsequently forced to admit that he had completely misjudged the likely consequences of this strategy and it was his disgust with its results that explained his pessimism in 1903. 'La Révolution dreyfusienne',[55] as Sorel termed it, had seen the destruction of 'l'aristocratie républicaine' and the emergence of a group of petit-bourgeois, careerist politicians determined to utilise the Dreyfus Affair to secure their own political supremacy. Their 'new philosophy' of social 'solidarity' was in reality a 'philosophy of hypocritical cowardice'. Terrified by the working class they had sought to pass social legislation designed to improve the conditions of the workers in the hope that the proletariat would lend them their support. This policy appeared to have worked with the result that the socialist movement had lost its autonomy and had become enmeshed in the structures of bourgeois society. If socialism was to be revivified it had, therefore, to free itself from the tutelage of Dreyfusard politicians and distance itself from what Sorel now saw as the corruption and degradation of parliamentary politics. A new tactic was required: by 1905 Sorel had concluded that it must be *revolutionary* syndicalism. In 1906 he produced its classic expression: *Réflexions sur la violence*.[56]

The logic of Sorel's new position was straightforward. If capitalism was to provide the economic foundation of the future socialist society it depended upon the existence of an active and energetic capitalist class which concerned itself solely with securing the advance of industrial production. A 'timorous, humanitarian' capitalist class, imbued with the spirit of social peace, would, in Sorel's opinion, engender economic decline and hence prevent capitalism from attaining its historical perfection. The use of violence by the proletariat was the perfect means of disabusing the capitalists of their paternal concern for the condition of the workers and of ensuring that they would again devote themselves to realising the progress of production. 'To reply by blows to the advances of the propagators of social peace', Sorel wrote, 'is a very practical way of indicating to the bourgeoisie that they should mind their own business and that only'.[57]

If the existence of a weak capitalist class was the first obstacle to the attainment of a socialist society then *parliamentary* socialism, according to Sorel, was the second. 'Politicians', Sorel wrote, 'are people whose wits are singularly sharpened by their voracious appetites and in whom the hunt for fat jobs develops the cunning of Apaches'.[58] Socialist politicians, especially the now loathed and despised Jean Jaurès, were no exception to this rule: they exploited and used the proletariat as 'instruments' to secure their own supremacy. The 'picture' of a revolution led by these socialists, Sorel argued, shows us 'how the State would lose nothing of its force, how the transmission of power would be from one privileged class to another, and how the producers would merely change their masters'.[59] If anything, Sorel commented, the 'new masters' would be less able than their predecessors. They would make 'flowery speeches' but the people would remain 'the passive beast that bears the yoke'.[60]

The alternative was the proletarian general strike which, according to Sorel, embodied 'the chief tenets of Marxism'. In *Réflexions sur la violence* Sorel did, in fact, say remarkably little about the organisational basis and structure of the general strike. First and foremost, he stressed that a general strike, carried out by the proletariat and not under the auspices of their erstwhile bourgeois teachers, was the most vivid and complete expression of the class war. Sorel now argued that the division of society into 'two fundamentally antagonistic groups', of which Marx had spoken, would not arise naturally in capitalist society but could be secured by 'a certain effort of will'. In a general strike, Sorel wrote, 'all parts of the economic-judicial structure reach the summit of their perfection: society is divided into two camps and only two, on the field of battle'.[61] Secondly, the enthusiasm engendered amongst the proletariat by the general strike preserved and enhanced their spirit of revolt. 'The idea of the general strike', Sorel wrote, 'has such force that it drags into the revolutionary track everything it touches'.[62] Under its influence, every conflict between the workers and their employers, however small, was seen as 'an incident in the social war', every strike 'begets the perspective of a total catastrophe', the complete destruction of the capitalist system. Not even the most popular social policies, nor the desertion of comrades into 'the ranks of the bourgeoisie', could 'weaken the fundamental opposition of the class war'.[63] With the general strike, the revolution appeared as 'a revolt, pure and simple'.[64]

Moreover, it was Sorel's contention that the violence employed by the proletariat generated what he termed 'an entirely epic state of mind'.[65] 'Lofty moral convictions', according to Sorel, were not produced by rational argument but depended upon 'a state of war in which men voluntarily participate'. The violence of strike activity led the workers to perceive themselves as 'the army of truth fighting the armies of evil'.[66] They were participants in a struggle that demanded complete dedication and

were engaged in 'serious, formidable and sublime work'. Their use of
violence was sullied neither by the desire for material gain nor by the
sentiment of jealousy but was unselfish, disciplined and heroic. Sorel
perfectly summarised the imagined scenario:

> The proletariat organises itself for battle, separating itself from the
> other parts of the nation, and regarding itself as the great motive power
> of history, all other social considerations being subordinated to that of
> combat: it is clearly conscious of the glory which is attached to its
> historical role and of the heroism of its militant attitude; it longs for
> the final contest in which it will give proof of its valour. Pursuing no
> conquest, it counts on expelling the capitalists from the productive
> domain and on taking their place in the workshop created by
> capitalism.[67]

In *Réflexions sur la violence*, therefore, the emphasis fell upon class
division and confrontation as the means of countering the deleterious
consequences of the doctrines of social peace, parliamentary socialism and
democracy. The workers, through their acts of violence, were to spurn
the advances of bourgeois politicians and philanthropic employers and
were to distance themselves from the corrupt and decadent values of
official 'civilisation'. They were to engage in a relentless and uncompromising struggle and in the process were to bring forward a vigorous and heroic
morality. 'It is', Sorel concluded, 'to violence that socialism owes those
high ethical values by means of which it brings salvation to the modern
world'.[68]

If Sorel's analysis of the Dreyfus Affair and its aftermath gave an added
intensity and fervour to his thought, it would be incorrect to conclude
that his commitment to revolutionary syndicalism amounted solely to an
endorsement of the use of violence by the proletariat. What did not
change — although it tended to be hidden beneath the rhetoric of class
confrontation — was Sorel's stress upon technological advance and the
accompanying 'ethics of the producers'.[69] To believe otherwise leads to
the incorrect conclusion that Sorel admired physical action *per se*, as an
end in itself.

It was Sorel's view that the violence employed by the workers was
compatible with and indispensable for 'the continuous progress of production'. It alone was capable of arousing 'the enthusiasm of the workers'
and of instilling a sense of dedication irrespective of any 'personal,
immediate or proportional reward' without which the advance of industry
was an impossibility. Furthermore, it is clear that for Sorel what differen-
tiated the proletariat from all the other groups who in the past had
displayed an ethic of commitment was that the proletariat and the proletariat alone — once it had acquired the technical skills and moral discipline

required for work in the modern factory — was capable of generating what Sorel described as 'un progrès réel'.[70]

For Sorel science and technology were progressive, objective activities which were deemed to advance to the extent that they were able to impose a man-made order, an 'artificial nature', upon the recalcitrant matter of the natural world. The syndicalist, the embodiment of *homo faber*, through his work in the factory was engaged in a permanent battle with the destructive and unpredictable forces of nature itself. Through his labours — and not through the abstract speculations and utopias of the intellectual — man 'superimposed on nature an ideal workshop formed of mechanisms functioning with a mathematical rigour, aiming to imitate with a close approximation the changes taking place in natural bodies'.[71] Real progress — not the 'illusion of progress' of bourgeois society — was achieved, therefore, through experimental work and technological advance in the modern factory and as a result of the efforts of skilled and dedicated craftsmen.

Sorel's call for the use of violence by the proletariat was accompanied by the equally controversial evocation of the power of 'myth' to inspire action. As an assiduous reader of the works of Max Nordau, Theodore Ribot and Gustave le Bon, as well as Henri Bergson, Sorel had become acutely aware of the non-rational sources of human motivation. Individuals, Sorel wrote, 'do nothing great without the help of warmly coloured and clearly defined images, which absorb the whole of our attention'.[72] A myth, according to Sorel, was a collection of such images which, taken as a whole, comprised 'the strongest inclinations . . . of a class, inclinations which recur to the mind, with the insistence of instincts'.[73] Their value lay in their capacity to inspire action.

Secondly, in the course of his re-reading of Marx, Sorel had successively redefined certain of the key concepts of Marxism as 'metaphysics', then as 'social poetry', and, from 1903 onwards, as 'myths'.[74] Marx, Sorel now argued, 'had always described the revolution in mythical form',[75] in a manner which simultaneously conveyed the essence of socialism and the nature of the future society. In similar vein, Sorel argued that the general strike of syndicalist theory was 'the myth in which socialism is wholly comprised'.[76] It encapsulated the convictions of the proletariat and provided 'a set of images capable of evoking instinctively all the sentiments which correspond to the different manifestations of the war undertaken by socialism against modern society'.[77] It mattered little therefore whether the general strike was a reality or a figment of the popular imagination: it was sufficient that as a myth it gave the syndicalist an 'intuitive' grasp of socialism and served as an expression of the will to act.

Subsequently Sorel was to concede that in *Réflexions sur la violence* he had understated the juridical character of proletarian conflict thus giving the appearance that his stress upon the capacity of myth to provoke action amounted to a relegation of socialism to a product of the blind and irrational will. In reality, Sorel feared nothing more than actions guided by an uninformed and unstructured will. Perhaps, therefore, the most intriguing paradox within his thought lies in the fact that in *Réflexions sur la violence* the language of moral sublimity through action is accompanied by a continued awareness of the role of proletarian institutions, including the family, as a means of moulding and of creating the juridical consciousness of the workers. The action inspired by myth is for Sorel not an end in itself but is rather a means of ensuring the participation by the workers in institutions which in turn will transform them 'into the free producers of tomorrow working in factories where there are no masters'.[78] Violence and myth sustained enthusiasm but the ultimate goal remained the realisation of a socialist society based upon the ethic of the producers.

Sorel undoubtedly provided the most sophisticated and articulate expression of syndicalist theory. His appetite for ideas was unquenchable and he brought to syndicalism the fruits of a lifetime's voracious reading in the fields not only of history, politics and ethics but also religion, science and philosophy. At bottom, however, Sorel's syndicalism drew its inspiration from the belief that French (and more generally European) society had entered a period of decline. From 1889 onwards Sorel sought to locate either a political grouping, a class, or a set of ideas or institutions which would act as a mechanism capable of generating a morality that would bring this state of decadence to an end. Out of a pessimistic view of the present, in which everything is decadent, there arises an aspiration to a life of dignity and honour, an aspiration to a life which is morally the reverse of the present, a life in which everything may be raised to the rank of virtue. Sorel repeatedly presents us therefore with a series of images of the sublime life: the ancient Greeks, the early Christians, the Napoleonic soldier and, of course, the syndicalist worker. Each is sustained by a sense of their own virtue and the dignity of their task. Further, to gain entry into the Sorelian pantheon a group must never be contaminated by the sins of its age. To remain persecuted outside society rather than achieve toleration within it is the means to achieve moral grandeur.

The corollary to this is that the transformation of society will not be secured by adherence to a sceptical and relativistic ethic nor by an ideology characterised by what Sorel regarded as a shallow optimism. It will be obtained only by a supreme act of will, undertaken in the knowledge that it is a task that will require heroic action, discipline and the willingness to endure hardship and sacrifice.

For Sorel the struggle of the proletariat against both the bourgeoisie in capitalist society and the recalcitrant forces of nature through their work in the factory became the supreme symbol of the heroic life. By arguing that 'the warrior of the ancient City has become the worker of the factory, weapons have been replaced by machines'[79] Sorel self-consciously transposed that life from pre-Socratic Greece to a modern industrial setting.

The austere and virtuous life of the Athenian farmer-citizen, evoked by Sorel in *Le Procès de Socrate* as a critique of the Socratic intellectual and indirectly of the self-seeking bourgeoisie and their commercial culture, finds its contemporary equivalent in the efforts of the proletariat to create a socialist society and in their ceaseless struggle to master the forces of nature. In this account socialism was, above all, 'a philosophy of producers'.[80]

At the heart of Sorel's socialism, therefore, was a vision of the industrial workplace as the locality for the development of a new proletarian culture centred upon the activity of production. The factory would exist as the school in which skilled craftsmen, the exemplars of both moral rectitude and technical proficiency, would educate their colleagues in the skills and practices of their labour. Such a conception of socialism is accordingly undermined if it is established that technological innovation leads to the standardisation and routinisation of the productive process, if the artisan is replaced by the amorphous and undifferentiated masses of the modern factory system.

It is not difficult to locate the causes of Sorel's subsequent disillusionment with the syndicalist movement. Sorel repeatedly chose to describe himself as an 'observer' of the workers' movement, yet as Madeleine Rebérioux has pointed out he was its opposite: he saw only what he wanted to see.[81] Few movements, if any, could have lived up to Sorel's expectations. The workers, in practice, sought on the whole to raise the level of their wages and to improve their working conditions. Such material gains were for Sorel no compensation for a loss of moral purity and the abandonment of the strategy of working-class self-emancipation.

Nor is it hard to discern the roots of the ambivalence within Sorel's thought. From the moment of his initial endorsement of socialism Sorel obstinately insisted that his ideas were in perfect accord with the precepts for proletarian action to be drawn from a correct reading of Marx. Yet the central place within his writings of a set of values derived largely from Proudhon is sufficient to indicate both the revolutionary and conservative character of his work and serves to explain in part how in the years after 1909 Sorel could become one of the intellectual heroes of the right-wing critics of liberal democracy.

II

Edouard Berth was, according to Georges Sorel, along with Hubert Lagardelle one of 'the most authoritative representatives of revolutionary syndicalism'. From 1899 to 1909 he published a stream of articles in *Le Mouvement socialiste* and through his column 'Les Revues socialistes allemandes' was a regular commentator upon developments within the German socialist movement. In addition, during this period he published two books, articles in *La Revue socialiste, Pages libres* and *l'Avant-Garde*, and translations from Italian and German. This prolific productivity was all the more remarkable given Berth's unusual professional circumstances.

Born in July 1875 Berth was educated in Douai and Paris, where he proved to be a brilliant student. Nevertheless at the height of the Dreyfus Affair he chose, like his contemporary Charles Péguy, to cease his academic studies. After a brief sojourn in Lille (where he participated for the first time in the socialist movement) and a short-lived job working for a Parisian publisher, he was employed from 1903 onwards, with a break only for military service during the First World War, as a hospital administrator. His writing activities were normally confined to three hours each morning before leaving for his office.[82]

Edouard Berth was, in the words of Pierre Andreu, Georges Sorel's 'closest and staunchest friend'. He first became acquainted with Sorel's ideas in 1898 when as a student at the Sorbonne he read 'L'Ancienne et la nouvelle métaphysique'.[83] Shortly afterwards they became friends and, in contrast to the fate which befell their respective friendships with Hubert Lagardelle, remained so until Sorel's death in 1922.

Few, if any, of Berth's books and articles failed to betray Sorel's influence and it was not uncommon for an article by Berth to be built around a central theme or concept taken from Sorel's writings. Indeed, on occasions an article by Berth would amount to no more than a commentary upon Sorel. Sorel's 'La crise de la pensée catholique', published in the *Revue de métaphysique et de morale* in 1902, for example, engendered Berth's own 'La crise de la pensée catholique', published in *Le Mouvement socialiste* in 1904.[84] Certainly at the time Berth was seen as Sorel's faithful associate and little distinction was made between their ideas.

However, the picture of Berth as Sorel's disciple and of his writings (and actions) as an accurate reflection and application of those of his master, while correct to a point, is also misleading. Firstly, as Pierre Andreu has argued, Sorel's letters to Berth reveal that Sorel in turn was indebted to Berth. This was particularly the case on philosophical issues in which Berth possessed considerable sophistication and erudition and was especially pertinent when Sorel called upon Berth's detailed knowledge of Bergson. It also seems possible that Berth, by drawing out the implications of Sorel's ideas in his own writings, was responsible, in part, for encouraging developments within Sorel's thought. More importantly, Berth's books and articles did not consist solely, or even primarily, of Sorelian exegesis and interpretation. Berth succeeded in producing his own individual interpretation of the significance of syndicalism and did so by drawing overtly not just upon Sorel but upon a *mélange* of ideas and perspectives taken in almost equal measure from Marx, Proudhon, Nietzsche and Bergson. Sorel, for example, made only a handful of references to Nietzsche in the entire corpus of his work: in Berth's writings references to Nietzsche were a commonplace. Likewise Berth made infinitely greater and more constructive use of the ideas of Bergson than did Sorel and perhaps more than anyone else merits the designation of Bergsonian Marxist. Berth, in short, made a distinctive contribution to syndicalist theory and, furthermore, continued to do so until shortly before his death in January 1939.

In 1901 Edouard Berth published *Dialogues socialistes*.[85] As its title suggests, the book consisted of a stylised conversation between four young men of whom one, Edouard Darville,[86] was a 'convinced socialist' whilst the other three, variously described as philosopher, neo-Christian and poet, were, we are told, committed to the view that socialism was a 'materialistic, anti-aesthetic and amoral doctrine'. In refuting this charge Berth produced a eulogy in praise of socialism that displayed an unqualified faith in its properties and its capacity to renovate civilisation.

The basic assumption upon which Berth's belief in socialism was grounded was the view that the class which represented the most advanced economic form, the proletariat, also embodied 'a superior civilisation'.[87] For Berth, the society engendered by capitalism was a society characterised by egoism, conflict, brutality and ugliness and capitalism was deemed to be responsible for all its ills. The 'socialisation' of the economy, combined with the new working methods that this would inevitably entail, would ensure that a harmonious society based upon fraternity and solidarity would come into existence and that the maladies arising from capitalism — anti-semitism, alcoholism, a low birth rate, for example — would be eradicated. The proletarian movement, therefore, was in the process of elaborating 'a new conscience, a new type of man, a new social world'.[88]

Significantly, the vision of the future society presented by Berth was that of a community structured around the activity of work. 'It is not legitimate', he wrote, 'to compare the future socialist civilisation and present bourgeois civilisation respectively to civilisations of laziness and languor and of activity and progress'.[89] By divorcing ownership from production, capitalism had produced a parasitic class with no genuine interest in technical advance. Socialism, by contrast, was imbued with the spirit of technological innovation, would use the most advanced methods of production, and sought, through co-operative endeavour, to unleash the creative energies of the producers.

In response to further questioning by his imaginary fellow conversationalists Berth also showed that his socialism was not that of Guesdist orthodoxy. It was a mistake, he argued, to confuse genuine, proletarian socialism with State control, centralisation and bureaucracy. Socialism, correctly perceived, represented 'the resorption of the State into society; it is society governing and administering itself in an autonomous manner'.[90] Socialism, therefore, entailed political and economic decentralisation and federalism.

The State would exist only as a 'juridical framework' designed to prevent the 'rivalry' between the numerous autonomous working-class organisations from degenerating into capitalist competition. Accordingly, Berth saw no fundamental break in theory between socialism and liberalism.

Summarising his overall position on the prospect held out to man by socialism Berth eloquently concluded: 'in sum, the essential difference between the bourgeois economic order and the socialist economic order is this: today each individual, given the anarchy of production, is in no way sure of the results of his labour . . . Tomorrow, on the contrary . . . production will be organised and each individual is sure of his future from the moment he begins work; remuneration will not depend upon the hazards of competition but will correspond exactly to personal effort'.[91] Virtue, it seems, would receive its due.

Berth's efforts to illustrate the moral dimension of socialism were continued in the final three sections of the book, dealing in turn with religion, art and the role of women.

Like Georges Sorel, Berth was fascinated by the phenomenon of Christianity and its relationship to socialism. His discussion of this issue in *Dialogues socialistes* was, therefore, to be only the first of many such discussions and the conclusions reached were to diverge markedly from the position adopted by Berth in his later writings where he sought to reconcile socialism and Christianity.

In 1901 Berth viewed Christianity as the necessary ideological complement of the division of society into hierarchically structured social classes. The emancipation of the proletariat, therefore, required both its economic and *spiritual* liberation. 'It is a question', Berth wrote, 'of considering as *immanent ends* that which religion has regarded as *transcendent ends*: in a word, we are considering an immense intellectual revolution'.[92] The essential difference between socialism and Christianity, according to Berth, was that whereas Christianity saw the individual as the direct emanation of God, for socialism the individual was 'a product of the City'. Christianity, by emphasising personal salvation, divorced man from the community and destroyed any genuine desire to establish a real social existence. Man was condemned to a spiritual individualism. Socialist morality, by contrast, saw man only in the context of his society, rejected 'mythical egoism' in favour of 'living social cooperation' and sought to construct an ethical code appropriate to this conception of life. 'To make social and individual life richer, more noble and more beautiful: to enhance the collective, material and spiritual wealth of humanity,' Berth wrote, 'that, henceforth, is our Duty'.[93] The proletariat, as the exemplar of human solidarity, was the embodiment of that ethic.

Art, on the other hand, was a legitimate expression of human spirituality. Socialism, having abolished class differences and established social harmony, would generate 'a completely new art' freed from the sterile 'academic taste' of the bourgeoisie. Released from financial dependency upon a particular economic class, the artist would be free to express his own sentiments and the aspirations of the community. Gone would be the divorce between art and nature. The city, the world of men, would be a source of inspiration. Art would act as the mediator between the heart and the intellect. 'With socialism', Berth wrote, 'we will have at last a truly social and truly human art'.[94]

Berth specifically denied that socialism would mean the enslavement of the artist and the imposition of artistic uniformity. Socialism, he believed, was compatible with a 'wide variety of tastes, moods and ideas' and the physical conditions created by socialism — specifically the abolition of class differences – would put an end to 'all dogmatism, all absolutism'. Under socialism, economic activity would be controlled and co-ordinated but 'the mind would be free'. 'The artist', he concluded, 'would be no more than a free man amongst free men'.[95]

In discussing the role of women Berth placed himself upon the side of feminism — referring specifically to 'we feminists'.[96] If socialism meant the existence of free men, so too it aspired to create free women. 'What we assert', Berth wrote, 'is that the juridical, political and social equality of the two sexes is necessary, if woman, like man, is to attain her full physical, moral and intellectual development'.[97] Such an end could only be attained if women were 'economically independent of men' and this, ultimately, was only possible in a socialist society. Under capitalism, Berth argued, 'the poorly-paid female worker is reduced for the most part to prostitution and the social and economic activity of women, in general, far from assuring their independence only delivers them up to the caprice and arbitrary behaviour of men'.[98] Significantly, in the light of his later views, Berth argued that the advent of a socialist society would not mean the reintegration of women into what he described as their 'old domestic servitude' but would rather be a continuation of the trend, begun under capitalism, of women working outside the home. The predicament described (and endorsed) by Proudhon — 'courtesan or housewife' — would be superceded as woman became, for the first time, the 'true companion of man'.

Berth's call for the economic liberation of women was combined with a strident attack upon the hypocrisies of 'bourgeois' marriage and an equally firm denial that female emancipation meant sexual licence. Under socialism, women would cease to be 'instruments of pleasure' or 'humble servants' and the relationship between men and women would be based upon genuine affection, 'a full, deep and superior love'. Berth's later writings on the issue were to continue this strong moral tone but with altogether different conclusions.[99]

Berth's conception of the role of women was given an added (and unorthodox) dimension through the designation of love as a key compon-

ent in the moral transfiguration of man and thus as an indispensable
element in the ethical basis of a socialist society. According to Berth
there were, above all, two forces which 'moralised' man: work and love.
Through the activity of work man acquired both a moral and intellectual
discipline and, in addition, became aware of the social dimension of his
existence. 'In working', Berth wrote, 'man participates in the objective
creation of a social milieu'.[100] It was, however, love — perceived by Berth
as a female emotion in origin — that exalted man and which transformed
work from an acknowledged social obligation into a gift freely given. 'The
most active and progressive peoples', Berth wrote, 'are, in general, those
where woman is most honoured and respected'.[101]

Dialogues socialistes, published when Berth was only 26 years old, was,
therefore, an unequivocal statement of his belief in the capacity of socialism to rebuild society anew. There was no indication of self-doubt nor
perception of the difficulties that the task involved. As such, the book
was a reflection not only of Berth's youth but also of the enthusiasm and
hope for the future engendered by the apparent victory of the Dreyfusard
cause. The mood, then, was one of moral redemption and purification
and within that perspective it was, for Berth, Kant and Hegel as much as
Sorel, Proudhon or Marx who provided the injunction to moral seriousness
and austerity. The Sorbonne student of philosophy was still very visible.
The bases of Berth's syndicalism, for all his comparison of socialism and
liberalism, had, however, been laid. Berth had rejected State-socialism in
favour of a decentralised system of autonomous working-class units. His
objection to capitalism was as much an ethical as an economic one. And,
centrally, the future society envisaged by Berth was to be built around
work in the factory with the proletarian occupying the dual role of producer and moral exemplar. Missing were the key epistemological distinctions which were to be the distinctive feature of his syndicalism.

The most immediate practical manifestation of Berth's endorsement of
socialism was support for socialist participation in the Dreyfusard movement and, initially, a welcoming acceptance of Millerand's participation
in government. Here was an occasion where the specifically class interests
of the proletariat embodied the 'general' or 'human' interests of society
and in which the working class could profitably combine with elements of
the bourgeoisie to defeat a common enemy.[102] In the light of experience
Berth, like Sorel and Lagardelle, was to distance himself in stages from this
position. In the process he was to move towards revolutionary syndicalism.

According to Berth, during the Dreyfus Affair socialism had made the
transition from Utopia to science, by which he meant that the socialist
movement had passed beyond what he termed 'the purely political or
legalistic phase' and had entered the phase of the 'living ethic'.[103] Less
ambiguously he commented: 'the passage from Utopia to science is for
the proletariat the change from a position of tutelage to one of

autonomy . . . it is, at the same time, the move from theory to action, from passivity to reflective, self-conscious and reasoned activity'.[104] In terms of tactics the contrast was between Guesdism and what Berth chose to describe as the 'new method' of Jaurès. Guesde, according to Berth, 'raises into dogmas, into absolute laws, into cast-iron truths, the laws of the capitalist economy and, in the name of Science, forbids all forms of action except one: political action'.[105] The proletariat was seen as a class to be educated and controlled: the socialist movement was both above and external to it. Jaurès, in comparison, was deemed by Berth to believe in the subordination of political to economic activity and thus to wish to extend the possibilities for the 'autonomous development' of the proletariat through its own institutions. Recognition of the need for the latter, according to Berth, was the central lesson to be derived by socialists from the Dreyfus Affair.

Underpinning this analysis was a broader philosophical perspective. The triumph of Jaurèsian socialism also symbolised the victory of what Berth termed the 'new materialism' over the 'old materialism'. Historical materialism could now be perceived correctly, as a 'philosophy of action' that recognised that the transformation of society was brought about by the 'reciprocal action' of circumstances and human activity and not as a doctrine which involved a 'fatalistic quietism'.

The concept of the 'new materialism' was to provide the organisational category around which Berth's thought was to be structured. In essence, between 1901 and 1909 he was to use variants of this idea as a means of assessing and criticising a range of different positions — anarchism, orthodox Marxism, social Catholicism, the theoretical postulates of contemporary democratic society — with a view to showing that they were all manifestations of a similar defective mentality and that revolutionary syndicalism alone embodied the new philosophy. Deployed originally to praise Jaurès, the 'new materialism' was ultimately used to disparage all he stood for.

The 'new materialism' represented, according to Berth, a means of surpassing what he termed the 'sterile and futile opposition between idealism and materialism'.[106] Both philosophies were, in truth, only the 'extreme positions' of an 'intellectual and dogmatic attitude' which conceived mind and matter as static and immobile entities. 'If idealism', Berth wrote, 'hypostatises the mind, subjectivity, then the old materialism hypostatises matter, objectivity'.[107] In each case a part of reality had been abstracted to produce either a 'pure intellectualism' in which it was thought possible to change man without changing his environment or a 'brute materialism' which implied a mechanistic determinism. 'Idealism', Berth argued, 'considers the individual as *noumenon* . . . materialism allows him only an existence as *epiphenomenon*'.[108]

In contrast, the 'new materialism' took as its central idea the notion of 'becoming'. It demonstrated, according to Berth, that what until now had been seen from the point of view of speculation, henceforth had to be perceived from 'the point of view of action'. Reality had to be viewed as a process of flux, mobility and movement upon which man acted self-consciously and constructively. Knowledge was not prediction of the future, despite what the 'high priest of modern abstract intellectualism', Comte, might say.[109]

This 'ideological somersault', according to Berth, was a reflection of the impact of capitalism. As long as the economy had remained static, it had been possible to believe in a stable and eternal order, existing independently of and prior to all human effort. Capitalism, and specifically *industrial* capitalism, had opened a 'formidable breach' into this seemingly pre-ordained pattern. Henceforth, nothing was immutable or eternal. Time was invention, creation: the producer was 'the antithesis of the intellectual, the living contradiction of the alexandrian'.[110]

For Berth, the two principal exponents of this new philosophy were Marx and Bergson, the philosophies of whom, when correctly understood, were adjudged by Berth to be complementary to each other.[111] The role attributed by Marx to technical innovation as a means of ensuring the victory of man over nature was identical to that attributed by Bergson to the process by which the bodily organs adapted to the external world. 'The economic system', Berth wrote, 'is for society exactly what the senso-ry-motor system is for an individual organism'.[112] The 'essential point' of similarity, according to Berth, was that in each case what was involved or contemplated was the process through which life, as a result of activity, was progressively disengaged from what Bergson termed 'the rhythm of necessity'.

This, in turn, gave rise to what Berth regarded as a definition of liberty appropriate to the 'men of the twentieth century'. 'To be free is in our eyes', Berth wrote, 'to be oneself, that is an original creative energy'. Liberty, in line with what Bergson had to say, was 'invention', the activity in which temperament, sensibility and intelligence combined to produce a rupture or break with reality as conventionally perceived. Marx's views on the revolutionary character of machine technology pointed to an ident-ical conclusion.[113]

This was Berth's view in 1901 and it was re-affirmed after the publication of Bergson's *L'Evolution créatrice* in 1907. Referring specifically to Berg-son's identification of *homo sapiens* with *home faber* Berth concluded that Bergson, 'like Marx, derives a theory of intelligence from industrial production'. Bergsonian philosophy, he wrote, was 'a philosophy of creation'.[114]

Subsequently Nietzsche and Proudhon were cited as precursors of the new 'realist' position. The dominant idea of Nietzsche's philosophy, Berth argued, was that only those things which made life stronger and more

beautiful were good and true and 'everything that raises any value whatsoever into an absolute, outside and above life, whether it be science, art
or morality, is bad, a sign of exhaustion and decadence'.[115] Nietzsche,
therefore, opposed all forms of abstraction and, for all his aristocratic
condescensions, was an indispensable aid to the syndicalist movement in
its attempts to unmask the 'intellectualist' philosophy.

Berth's debt to Proudhon was wider and deeper but here too emphasis
was placed upon Proudhon's belief that action preceded thought and that
the natural state of matter, and of the world in general, was one of
movement. Life had to be seen as a constant effort to adapt to an ever-
changing reality. Inertia, both mental and physical, meant decay.[116]

In the first instance it was Berth's view that the actions of Jaurès during
the Dreyfus Affair, with their apparent emphasis upon the 'economic
and moral evolution of the proletariat', were an example of the 'new
materialism'. So also, he believed, were the activities of the *syndicats*.
Through their participation in these exclusively working-class institutions,
the proletariat showed that it was no longer 'hypnotised by the static
vision of the future city'. It had distanced itself from a faith in the dialectic
of history and now asked itself what it, the proletariat, could do through
its own actions and institutions to hasten its own development and emancipation.[117] Berth quickly concluded that Jaurèsian socialism was antithetical
to the new syndicalism[118] but it still remained to distance syndicalism from
all other competing ideologies.

In 'Anarchisme individualiste, Marxisme orthodoxe, Syndicalisme révolutionnaire'[119] Berth went part of the way towards achieving that end.
Berth's was a bold thesis. ' "Orthodox Marxism" and traditional individualist anarchism', he wrote, 'are two, divergent but complementary, aspects
of the same, at bottom identical, social psychology whose dominant trait
is an excessive faith in rationalism and science'.[120] They were 'brother
enemies', the products of an intellectual epoch that was about to die.

Individualist anarchism, Berth argued, drew its inspiration from two
central convictions: an extreme love of liberty, with freedom conceived,
according to Berth, in pre-social terms; and a fierce anti-statism that
reflected the hatred of the peasant farmer for a civilisation in which
he was an 'outsider'. Anarchism, Berth believed, had abstracted these
sentiments, producing an ideology that was ultimately self-defeating and,
paradoxically, authoritarian.

The concomittant to the fervent anticlericalism of the anarchist had
been to raise science into a new religion, a 'metaphysical cosmology'.
Science had been transformed into a dogmatic system which claimed to
encompass all of reality in a unitary set of abstract and simple formulae.
Science was the 'one and universal Truth', a complete explanation of the
world. What power it therefore gave to its adherents. All competing truths
could legitimately be 'exterminated' and, in the name of Science, a moral

and social 'unity' could be secured. Anarchism could not escape the 'law' of all intellectualism. 'In the heart of every individualist anarchist', Berth wrote, 'sleeps — and occasionally awakes — an authoritarian'.[121]

Similarly the conception of liberty presented by anarchism was based upon the vision of an abstract individual divorced from any contact with social reality. The individual was seen as 'an absolute, a monad . . . with neither doors nor windows to the outside'.[122] It was impossible for the anarchist to conceive of a social relationship as anything other than a limitation upon individual freedom and thus equally impossible for the anarchist to resolve in a meaningful way the supposed dichotomy between individual and society. Anarchism was the victim of its own abstract logic.

Marxism, according to Berth, was a 'philosophy of action with, as its basis, a *tragic* conception of life'. Orthodoxy — by which Berth usually meant Guesdism — had turned it into an 'intellectualist philosophy'.[123] Science — in this case the belief that Marx had discovered 'social and economic truth' — had been elevated into a cult, with the result that there was no room for dissension. The proletariat was to obey its leaders. Was it any wonder, Berth enquired, that the respective histories of the socialist parties were histories of exclusions and excommunications? Orthodox Marxism, Berth therefore concluded, 'led in practice to the same authoritarianism as individualist anarchism'. In each case we remained in the world of abstraction and were removed from the 'terrain of life and action'.

Berth's own account of the factors which induced such a similar mentality in two apparently markedly different ideologies was itself revealing. Individualist anarchism, according to Berth, was a manifestation of outmoded, pre-capitalist patterns of thought. It was appropriate to the perspective of a peasant farmer. What distinguished that form of life was precisely the absence of innovation, the reliance upon routine. Liberty was conceived negatively: the peasant asked only to live happily and in tranquility upon his land.[124] Orthodox Marxism derived its vision of the future from the hierarchically organised factory of modern capitalism in which the individual worker was deprived of any sense of responsibility and initiative. The State took over the role formerly occupied by the capitalist as the instrument through which the efficient organisation of production was to be achieved. As with anarchism, work was conceived primarily as a form of routine. The purpose of socialism, therefore, was to reduce labour to a minimum, to set man free by providing an unparalleled abundance. We were, Berth wrote, in the presence of what he described as 'a socialism of distribution, a socialism of pleasure . . . a socialism of idleness'.[125]

Syndicalism, by contrast, saw work not only as a necessity which would continue to occupy a major proportion of our lives — poverty, not material plenty, would be the norm — but also as an activity which we would embrace 'with love, with joy, as artists'. 'The factory', Berth wrote, 'is no longer a barracks: it is an association of free workers'.[126] And it was precisely this institution that was to resolve the supposed dichotomy between individual and society that the abstract logics of anarchism and orthodox Marxism had failed to achieve. Through his mastery of new and increasingly sophisticated industrial techniques, the individual worker would retain his individuality and freedom; yet, at the same time, he would willingly accept the obligations imposed upon him by the need to co-ordinate production. 'This discipline', Berth wrote, 'is no longer a military and autocratic discipline involving a totally passive obedience: rather it is what I call an impersonal discipline that only the technical necessities of the division of labour demand'.[127] Liberty and discipline would be reconciled in the world of production, in the world of the 'real'.

At the very end of 'Anarchisme individualiste, Marxisme orthodoxe, Syndicalisme révolutionnaire' Berth extended the range of his criticisms to include a third target: democracy. If, he wrote, anarchism and orthodox Marxism were abstract ideologies which, despite their 'negation of the State', led to authoritarianism, then the same thing could be said of democracy which had itself elevated State power to the status of an absolute. This critique of democracy was ultimately given fullest expression in Berth's article 'Marchands, Intellectuels et Politiciens'[128] but it had its origins in his analysis of the victory of the Dreyfusards.

In 1903 Berth began his article 'Socialisme ou étatisme'[129] by stating categorically that 'today liberty is gravely threatened'. The threat to liberty that he had in mind was posed not by the forces of reaction but primarily by the victorious democrats. A year earlier, in 'La Politique anticléricale et le socialisme'[130] he had voiced similar fears. Initially Berth had believed that the Dreyfus Affair had brought two divergent conceptions of society into conflict: the democratic and socialist vision of 'an organic unity . . . where individuals co-operate freely and voluntarily' was locked in combat with the clerical and militarist conception of society as 'a mechanic and external unity'.[131] In 1902 he again argued that the socialist movement was right to combat the Church as it was the supreme representative of 'the spirit of domination and the opposition to free enquiry'[132] but questioned whether what he termed 'la démocratie unitaire' was a sufficient and correct antidote. In Berth's view, the Dreyfusard cause had represented the 'fearless, heroic and stubborn negation of any notion of raison d'Etat' but once in power the Dreyfusards had sought to destroy the liberty of those who dared to oppose them. 'In all this,' Berth remarked, they had displayed 'no sense of justice, no concern for tolerance, no spirit of liberty'.

The logic that governed the actions of the democrats was simple and clear. All men, as a natural right, had the right to intellectual liberty. In practice, the Church opposed that abstract right: therefore the Church could be destroyed and its power and attributes (for example, the control of education) could, without hesitation, be transferred to the State. 'All our brave idealists', Berth wrote, 'set out to war in the name of Truth, Justice, Reason . . . and Liberty and have nothing else in mind than to oppress those people obtuse enough not to conceive Truth, Justice, Reason and Liberty in the same way'.[133] A Catholic theocracy was to be replaced by a lay and rationalist theocracy, a religious catechism by a civic catechism. The victorious democrats were, therefore, another manifestation of an abstract, idealist and intellectualist movement. When faced with a recalcitrant reality that refused to conform to their ideals there was no alternative, as in all 'idealist revolutions', but to resort to force.

In 'La Politique anticléricale et le socialisme' Berth sought only to warn the socialist movement of the dangers of this mentality and to establish that socialism rested upon entirely different premises. He himself recommended that socialists should pursue the separation of Church and State, a greater element of political and administrative decentralisation, and the implementation of measures which would enhance the capacity of the working class. 'A truly anti-clerical politics', Berth wrote, 'is not a jacobin and pseudo-democratic politics but a liberal and socialist politics'.[134]

'Catholicisme social et socialisme',[135] published in 1903, gave Berth's critique of democracy a further dimension. Drawing specifically upon Sorel's article 'Idées socialistes et faits économiques',[136] Berth sought to demonstrate the analogies betwen Marxism and what he, following Sorel, described as 'Manchesterianism'. By 'Manchesterianism' Berth meant classical liberal economics which, he argued, in its emphasis upon anti-statism, free trade and anti-militarism was identical to Marxism. The only major difference was that whilst the former saw capitalism as an 'eternal economic category', for the Marxist it existed only as an 'historical category', a stage of development which ultimately would be superceded. What Berth wanted to stress above all was that for liberal economists and Marxists alike the relationship between employers and workers was adjudged to be a purely economic one. There were no social or ideological ties. 'Class egoism' was the driving force of the capitalist economy. The prospects for a genuine socialist society were thus threatened by any moves designed to foster social solidarity. If one example of such a strategy was the social Catholicism inspired by Leo XIII's encyclical *Rerum novarum*, another was the glut of social legislation passed in the immediate aftermath of the Dreyfus Affair to pacify the workers. Justified variously in terms of the 'Gospel, Social Science, and the Rights of Man', in each case the ultimate objective was to secure social peace. In contrast, according to Berth, the correct socialist tactic was to deepen and extend class antagonisms. 'Worker democracy', he concluded, 'should follow altogether different rules from those preached to it by either Christian democracy or radical democracy'.[137]

The following year in 'Esprit démocratique et esprit socialiste'[138] Berth produced an altogether different criticism of democracy. Again the idea came from Sorel but upon this occasion the source was Sorel's *Introduction à l'économie moderne*[139] and the contention that socialists should draw inspiration from the practices of contemporary agriculture. Contrasting the austere and dedicated life of the peasant to that of the city-dweller Berth displayed an unconcealed moral indignation to prove that 'democracy is essentially urban', and that by basing itself upon the city socialism was being corrupted. The inhabitants of the city, working in their shops and offices, dreamt only of distractions. 'Eager for news, greedy for excitement, readers of newspapers', the city-dweller 'gets involved in politics, goes to the café, plays games, becomes interested in actors, gives himself the illusion of living, believes himself to be very intelligent, to know everything, knows nothing thoroughly, gossips incessantly'.[140] The city was thus the home of a 'new aristocracy'. It was populated by 'quasi-oisifs', people who above all were consumers, not producers, and democracy, like the Emperors who gave the Roman people bread and games, was there to satisfy their needs. 'Is there a civilisation more frivolous', Berth asked, 'than the civilisation of the salon which our democrats wish to present to us as an ideal civilisation?'[141]

It was, however, in 'Marchands, Intellectuels et Politiciens' that Berth was to produce his most singular and extensive analysis of democracy. Here, if it could be said to exist anywhere, was Berth's syndicalist testament.

Berth chose to focus his attention upon merchants, intellectuals and politicians precisely because these groups were the supreme representatives of bourgeois and democratic society. It was these people who had created the modern State, elevated it into a metaphysical entity, and who had transformed it into an instrument designed to protect their material interests. But the key to Berth's argument was that each group embodied an aspect of bourgeois society which had been originally intended to liberate man but which had become an instrument of his enslavement. There were, Berth argued, profound analogies between what he termed 'the concept, the State and exchange'.[142]

Intellectuals in bourgeois society, Berth contended, relied almost exclusively upon conceptual thinking. Concepts, he argued, were useful means of liberating man from the chaos presented to him by a multitude of conflicting sensations, what he referred to as 'un particularisme sensible', but so too (as Bergson had shown) they trapped man, distanced him from reality, from 'la vie profonde', induced intellectual torpor. Conceptual thinking, bourgeois thinking, had therefore to be transcended, to be replaced by philosophical intuition.

An analysis of the State produced analogous conclusions. What, asked Berth, was the State if not an 'immense simplification, an immense abstraction'? The French Revolution, in creating the modern State, had destroyed the particularisms of the feudal order, had eradicated a multiplicity of local customs and had thus been a 'process of liberation for social life'. But here too the instrument of emancipation had turned into a means of control. The State, elevated into a metaphysical concept, would not tolerate any life that existed independently of it, viewed with intense suspicion all private associations. 'The State-monster', Berth commented, 'devours everything, groups and individuals, and turns itself into an instrument of collective servitude'.[143]

Likewise, the activity of exchange began as a process of liberation. Prior to the existence of the market, every producer was confined within the horizons of his own family, producing not for sale, but for his own consumption. The market had put an end to this 'production particulariste' and thus had removed the restrictions upon man's productive capacity. However, the process of exchange was now controlled by the merchant who had turned it to his own advantage, thus impoverishing the producer. 'Exchange, like the concept and the State', Berth concluded, 'must be transcended'.[144]

This analysis of what Berth clearly took to be the premises of bourgeois and democratic society was then used to demonstrate in an almost indiscriminate fashion that virtually every manifestation of this society represented a corrupt, abstract, consumer mentality, voracious in its desire for physical and sensual satisfaction. Again, Berth stressed that its natural locale was the city, the place in which everything was up for sale and subject to financial speculation at the hands of 'big businessmen, traffickers in ideas and elections' (*brasseurs d'affaires, brasseurs d'idées, brasseurs d'élections*).[145] The housewife was a thing of the past: the prostitute flourished. Even Christianity was characterised as a 'religion of the City, the religion of the merchant bourgeoisie'. As if to summarise this mercantile society completely, the prodigious complexity of the world of production was simply beyond its comprehension.

Socialism, in the specific form of syndicalism, was perceived by Berth as the antithesis of each of these superficially different doctrines. Orthodox Marxism, anarchism, democracy, given the abstract epistemological premises upon which they rested, were inevitably authoritarian in practice and application.

'Socialism', Berth wrote, 'is not a doctrine, a science, a philosophy, a new dogmatism, a new absolute: essentially realist and relativist, it is, in consequence, opposed to all idealism'.[146] Whereas the idealist wished to impose liberty upon the individual in the name of an ethical or scientific truth, for the socialist 'liberty was achieved through a ceaseless contact with reality, life, the movement of things and ideas'.[147] With the demise of the old abstract philosophies the task of each individual would be recognised as being that of extending our grasp of what Berth described as the unknown, but knowable. This, of course, was to be achieved, according to Berth, *primarily* through the activity of production in the modern factory. 'Entrenched within his occupation', Berth wrote, 'the individual creates for himself an original life, becomes an autonomous centre of action, obtains a positive liberty'.[148]

Socialism, therefore, conceived freedom not in terms of absolute rights but in terms of *capacity*. A man became free when he became a worker 'capable of invention'. We tend to forget, Berth wrote, that liberty 'is something that we are obliged to earn and to merit'.[149] Within this perspective the function of the socialist movement became that of creating the environment in which individuals could acquire the technical skills and mental aptitudes required to transform them into autonomous creative beings. Centrally this meant that for the first time the producers must occupy a position of 'social hegemony'.[150]

Berth's assessment of the appropriate means to secure that goal evolved steadily during the first decade of the twentieth century. From the outset he recognised that the *syndicats* had a crucial role to play in helping the workers develop the 'sentiments of free men' and he quickly concluded that politics had the reverse effect. The Millerand 'experiment' taught him that the proletariat must concentrate upon becoming a 'class for itself' and that it must free itself from all 'petit-bourgeois political' influences.[151] In 1904, in an article entitled 'Politique et socialisme',[152] he firmly rejected Ostragorski's recommendations for the replacement of political parties by leagues, arguing that leagues would not overcome the 'fundamental vice' of democracy — the absence of 'public spirit'. Yet in the same article he also argued that it was possible for the proletariat 'to collaborate with democracy and capitalism'.[153]

Berth, in fact, outlined a 'criterion' which he felt would enable socialists to appraise the appropriate form and level of such collaboration and thus allow them to formulate a strategy for the attainment of a socialist society.[154] The key distinction used by Berth had its origin in Proudhon but was derived by Berth specifically from Sorel's *Introduction à l'économie moderne*. Within capitalism, Berth argued, the systems of exchange and production were 'heterogeneous', incommensurable entities. Exchange — the commercial environment in which production took place — could be seen as a 'mechanical apparatus', 'a neutralisable and depersonalised milieu' which could be socialised without challenging private property and thus could be transformed through legislation. The system of production, on the other hand, resembled a 'living organism', it possessed an 'organic and concrete nature', it was not susceptible to partial change. The socialisation of exchange and the socialisation of production could therefore be perceived as distinct moments in the realisation of socialism. As the historic mission of capitalism was to subordinate exchange to production it was perfectly legitimate for the proletariat to collaborate with members

of the bourgeoisie to secure that end and hence to conceive the socialisation of exchange as a preliminary step towards the 'truly revolutionary
act of the socialisation of production'. By pursuing only those reforms
which furthered that process socialists would be engaged in what Berth
described as 'revolutionary reformism'. Berth, however, from 1904
onwards was in no doubt that the final seizure of the means of production
by the proletariat would inevitably be a revolutionary act which would
entail the use of violence.[155] Through the general strike the workers would
themselves bring the reign of the non-producers to an end.

The main thrust of Berth's writings in the first decade of the twentieth
century, therefore, was the attempt to relocate socialism upon the epistemological premises of what he saw as a new realist perspective derived
in large part from the philosophies of Bergson and Marx. Orthodox Marxism (in the form of Guesdist State socialism), anarchism and democracy
were characterised as abstract philosophies which would only enslave the
workers. Syndicalism, by contrast, was seen as the practical embodiment
of the new philosophy. It thus represented, in Berth's opinion, not only
the philosophy of the producers but also the triumph of liberty.

III

In 1895, at the age of 20, Hubert Lagardelle began the publication of a
journal entitled *La Jeunesse socialiste*. Based in Toulouse and jointly
edited by Lagardelle and Joseph Sarraute, it included Georges Sorel
amongst its distinguished contributors.[156] The young Lagardelle simply
solicited Sorel's collaboration by letter; Sorel, ever eager to locate a
publication that would disseminate his ideas, accepted the offer. The
personal contact between Sorel and Lagardelle continued, with only inter-
mittent gaps, until their final quarrel in 1910. Sorel's letters to Lagardelle,
published by Lagardelle himself during the 1930s, are not only testimony
to their professional intimacy during these years but also offer an invaluable insight into both Sorel's character and the development of his
thought.[157] Further, it was Lagardelle who, in the pages of *Le Mouvement
socialiste*, was to publish Sorel's most forthright and controversial articles
in support of revolutionary syndicalism. Not the least of these were the
original drafts of both *Réflexions sur la violence* and *Les Illusions du
progrès*. Sorel, in turn, was not slow to praise Lagardelle for his grasp of
the principles of syndicalism. The immediate cause of their quarrel (the
bitterness of which was to remain with Lagardelle until the end of his life
in 1958) was Sorel's association with certain members of the royalist
movement in France; ironically, Lagardelle himself was to take a circuitous
route that ultimately led to collaboration with the Vichy regime.[158]

Hubert Lagardelle was born on the 8 July 1874 at Le Burgaud (Haute-

Garonne), near Toulouse. The son of well-to-do parents, he joined the *Parti Ouvrier Français* in 1893 and two years later established *La Jeunesse socialiste*.

Lagardelle's initial conception of the status and character of socialism was clearly and vigorously expressed in an article, entitled 'Nos Principes',[159] outlining the editorial position of his new journal. In what was a period of social, economic and intellectual anarchy, science alone, according to Lagardelle, could provide the solution to what he termed the 'social problem'. The advances of science meant that man could for the first time control the forces of nature, and free himself from economic drudgery and slavery: as a consequence an 'infinitely more noble life' was in the process of being created. 'Science', Lagardelle eulogised, 'is the great Redeemer of Humanity, the Messiah that comes to save the world'. Science, no less importantly, also embodied sound method. Scorning metaphysics and abstraction, it utilised experimental observation and reasoning: it was both positive and practical.

Socialism, according to Lagardelle, was a manifestation of science and embodied both its goal and method. Like science, it relied upon 'the impersonality of the experimental method' and therefore correctly refused to describe the future society. Recognising that 'the evolution of human society is determined by the progress of economic phenomena', socialism limited itself to exposing the 'monstrous contradictions' of the present economic order and to establishing that the constitutive elements of a new collectivist society were in the process of maturation. Further, for Lagardelle, knowledge or science and the power it gave to control events was synonymous with liberty. Socialism, as the pinnacle of social science, ensured therefore that the socialist was 'the freest of men', equipped to understand his own society and to nurture and construct the collectivist society of the future.

The final component of this enthusiastic *résumé* of what Lagardelle termed the 'general and elementary ideas' of socialism was the conviction that the proletariat would come to comprehend the revolutionary route to be taken by society and that this knowledge would not be the result of abstract reasoning but would arise out of the daily experiences of the working class. 'It is not only', Lagardelle concluded, 'a question of finding bourgeois society distasteful and of wanting to destroy it: we need to know where we are going'.

Lagardelle's brief editorship of *La Jeunesse socialiste* came to an end when he was called up for military service but in 1897 he was to be found in Paris mixing in the highest circles of the POF. Lagardelle's eagerness to free himself from the intellectual strait-jacket of Guesdism was, however, quickly demonstrated by the publication in 1898 of an article entitled 'La Question agraire et le socialisme'.[160] Here he criticised, by implication, the Guesdists for their adoption of what he termed a 'solution doctrinariste' to the problem posed for socialists by the continued existence of a large agrarian sector in the French economy. As a consequence, Lagardelle argued, they had divorced theory from practice. Lagardelle himself recommended 'la solution scientifique et révolutionnaire', which amounted to saying that while the socialist party could not help the farmers as producers it could concern itself with them as consumers and citizens. The task of the socialist party, Lagardelle argued, was 'to eliminate the painful phenomena that accompanies their disappearance, soften their fall, attenuate the convulsions of death'. Disillusioned with the tactics of the POF and disenchanted with the personal style of Guesde's leadership, Lagardelle set off upon a lengthy tour of Europe (and in particular Germany) with the avowed intention of improving his knowledge of socialist theory and the socialist movement. Upon his return, after due consultation with Georges Sorel, he was to begin publication of *Le Mouvement socialiste*.

The first issue of *Le Mouvement socialiste* appeared on the 15 January 1899 and it remained in existence until 1914. It was, by any standards, a remarkable journal, a forum for the expression of ideas as well as a source of information upon the condition of the working class and socialist movements throughout the world. Lagardelle, typically, succeeded in attracting to it an impressive list of contributors, not only from France but from Europe and beyond. There was, for example, always a strong Italian contribution: a fact which reflected Lagardelle's belief that there existed a special relationship between Italian and French socialism. Robert Michels was a regular commentator upon developments within the German socialist movement. Amongst the many distinguished French participants were Jean Jaurès (given pride of place in the first issue), Charles Péguy, Daniel Halévy, J-B Séverac, Francis de Pressensé, the leadership of the CGT as well as Edouard Berth and, of course, Georges Sorel. Most importantly, *Le Mouvement socialiste* served as the principal vehicle for the expression of Lagardelle's own ideas and the different phases of *Le Mouvement socialiste* itself — from its initial adoption of a strategy of socialist unity to its open espousal of revolutionary syndicalism in 1904 and its later hesitant rapprochement with the socialist party — were a reflection of Lagardelle's own intellectual and political evolution.[161]

In 1899 socialists throughout France were faced with the acute problem of being required to formulate a coherent response to the novel situation created by the Dreyfus Affair and the ensuing 'Cas Millerand'. Lagardelle's own response, like that at the time of Georges Sorel, was initially to endorse socialist involvement in the Dreyfusard cause and, with qualification, to support Millerand's entry into the government of Waldeck-Rousseau.[162]

The Dreyfus Affair, Lagardelle argued, was a decisive stage, after the Boulangist crisis and the Panama scandal, in the battle between the liberal and reactionary elements of the bourgeoisie; while it was not, Lagardelle conceded, the ideal terrain for proletarian action, the socialist movement, he felt, must support the former in their struggle against the reactionary forces that gravitated around the military and the Church. The fact that Dreyfus himself was a class enemy was deemed by Lagardelle to be irrelevant. The socialists needed to defend Dreyfus as an individual, as a member of society, and thus strive to ensure that similar acts of injustice were not wantonly and indiscriminately inflicted upon members of the working class. In the process the bourgeoisie would be deprived of any moral authority that it had previously possessed. Further, the socialist movement should aid the liberal bourgeoisie in their defence of the democratic and republican regime as it alone gave the proletariat the freedom to develop itself both politically and economically. Within this framework Lagardelle justified Millerand's acceptance of a government post in terms of the 'gravity of the situation' and the overriding need to save the Republic.

In general terms Lagardelle argued that the adoption of this policy by the socialists represented the acceptance of a strategy that eschewed both doctrinal dogmatism and simple opportunism. It avoided what Lagardelle regarded as revolutionary verbalism and hence freed the working class from the domination of 'phrases, formulae and persons', whilst at the same time it pursued only those reforms and measures which aided the development of the proletariat as a distinct class. Lagardelle did not therefore see Millerand's entry into government as an end in itself but he did lend his support to the passing of legislation which ameliorated the condition of the working class. For Lagardelle the change of tactics involved in the support of the Dreyfusard cause and the defence of the Republic, coupled with the new 'realism' it entailed, provided the basis for unity within the socialist movement as a whole. 'The last practical lesson that socialism can draw from the Dreyfus Affair', Lagardelle wrote, 'is that unity is realised in the world of deeds, not through doctrinal controversies . . . practical action unites, abstract discussion divides'.[163] For Lagardelle, at this time, Jean Jaurès was the physical embodiment of that aspiration towards unity and a united socialist party was to be the vehicle through which the emancipation of the working class was to be achieved.

Lagardelle's subsequent realisation that he had misjudged both the character and consequences of the Dreyfus Affair was to have a dramatic influence upon the development of his thought and it was the recognition of his own errors combined with an assessment of the impact of 'ministerialism' that, more than anything else, pushed him towards revolutionary syndicalism. Having easily disengaged himself from the theoretical sterility of Guesdism he was now obliged to undergo the painful process of self-criticism. Lagardelle, for example, was candid enough, when reviewing the early editorial policy of *Le Mouvement socialiste* in 1904,[164] to admit that he had believed that the agitation surrounding the Dreyfus Affair would lead to the rejuvenation of socialism and that the formation of a unified socialist party would be sufficient to prevent socialism from being engulfed by reformism. In reality, he conceded, socialism had been virtually destroyed by the experience. 'The humanitarian intervention of Jaurès', Lagardelle wrote, 'opened the doors of socialism to all the old democratic, philanthropic, pacific and governmental ideas which are the negation of the proletarian movement'.[165]

At first Lagardelle moved tentatively towards a reappraisal of his position. As early as the latter half of 1900 he realised that Millerand's continued membership of the government would be a cause of disunity within the socialist movement and hence he called for his resignation. It was, however, the events of 1901 that were to prove decisive. The pardoning of Dreyfus in that year made Lagardelle realise for the first time that by participating in the Dreyfusard movement the socialists had not achieved their goal of discrediting the bourgeois political class and of overturning the military establishment and that the true victors had been the liberal bourgeoisie (previously thought by Lagardelle to be incapable of defending the Republic): 'they have gained power', Lagardelle wrote, 'and they intend to keep it'.[166] Further, these events had shown Lagardelle that the liberal bourgeoisie in France were less attached to democracy and were more reactionary than he had previously supposed. In the same year Millerand's reception of the Russian Czar revealed the true extent of the dangers posed by the participation of socialists in governments of even a supposedly radical character.[167] In two articles, both entitled 'Ministérialisme et Socialisme',[168] Lagardelle now provided a detailed critique of what for the first time he referred to as 'le crétinisme parlementaire'.

In short, Lagardelle argued that the Millerand experiment had produced little of advantage to the working class. The Republic had been saved but the forces of reaction and of militarism had not been challenged. Both internally (in their response to strikes and their persecution of radicals in the universities) and externally (in the shape of the Franco-Russian alliance) the government had lent its support to the policies of repression and order. Worse still, the reformist social and economic policy of the Waldeck-Rousseau Millerand ministry amounted to an extension of 'patronage gouvernemental': the workers were to be taught to look to the State for their salvation. Socialist politicians, in turn, had been corrupted by the pursuit and the fruits of power. Socialism had been 'dislocated, weakened, maimed'.[169]

Underlying this critique of the consequences of socialist participation in the Dreyfusard cause and the self-criticism it entailed there was, nevertheless, a consistent thread to Lagardelle's argument. His assertion of the need to defend the democratic institutions of the Republic had, in part, derived from the belief that these institutions would allow the proletariat to organise as a class and, hence, ultimately to emancipate itself. For example, in 1900 at the very time that he was defending Millerand he had argued that the attainment of socialism depended upon the organisation of the proletariat — 'that is, the class which is in irreducible opposition to the existing capitalist system'[170] — into an autonomous class with common aims and an awareness of its shared class interests. This, he clearly felt, was perfectly compatible with socialist participation in munici- pal elections which, he argued, served to 'enhance the administrative ability of the proletariat'.[171] What occurred was that Lagardelle came to realise that the goal of working-class self-emancipation would not be secured by the participation of the proletariat in what were essentially bourgeois political movements and institutions. 'From the defeat we have just suffered', Lagardelle wrote, 'we can draw this conclusion: socialism will only triumph if it remains true to itself'.[172]

In the years that followed 1901, therefore, Lagardelle sought to expli- cate a strategy for the socialist movement which would make working- class self-emancipation into a reality. Certainly by 1902, in a series of articles entitled 'Socialisme ou Démocratie?',[173] it is possible to discern a new phase in the development of Lagardelle's thought. In opposition to what he termed 'socialisme gouvernemental' he called for the espousal of 'socialisme révolutionnaire'. In 1903 he was to be found advocating 'un retour à Marx'.[174] At this point, however, he still remained convinced that a socialist political party had a crucial role to play in the attainment of a future socialist society. Not until 1904 did he specifically endorse 'un socialisme ouvrier' which gave pride of place to revolutionary syndicalism. Even then, it should be noted, Lagardelle persevered in insisting that a political party, if it possessed a modest and humble conception of its functions, could be of some, if limited, use to the socialist movement.[175]

In 1900 Lagardelle had, in fact, completed a *Thèse de doctorat en droit* entitled *L'Evolution des syndicats ouvriers en France: de l'interdiction à l'obligation*[176] in which he gave a clear indication of what he took to be the potential of the *syndicats* to become the focus of working-class life and organisation. Tracing the evolution of the *syndicats* from the revolution of 1789 onwards Lagardelle showed how the *syndicats* had steadily extended the range of functions that they performed and how, under the pressure of capitalism, they had forged a new level of consciousness amongst the workers. A year later he made favourable reference to the general strike as 'the revolt of the producers'.[177] It took, however, the Congress of Bourges in 1904 to convince Lagardelle that the future of socialism lay with revolutionary syndicalism.[178] Prior to that point it had been possible to believe that the *syndicats* might develop in a reformist direction: the victory of the revolutionary syndicalists proved otherwise. 'The Congress of Bourges', Lagardelle wrote, 'has shown to even the most blind how the *syndicats, when they pursue revolutionary goals*, are the best instrument for

struggle and for the formation of working-class consciousness'.[179] After
the 'révisionnisme réformiste' of the previous years, the way was now
clear for the development of what Lagardelle termed 'le révisionnisme
révolutionnaire'.[180]

The first thing to note about Lagardelle's exposition of revolutionary
syndicalism is that it rarely made reference to the writings and ideas
of other syndicalist and socialist theorists. Sorel (despite their regular
correspondence and close ties) was cited only infrequently and Lagardelle's writings, although they made reference to Marx, reveal only a
superficial knowledge of his ideas. Few other writers were mentioned with
approval. Nor did Lagardelle locate his argument within the framework
of a detailed analysis of the workings of the capitalist system. From the
outset Lagardelle took it to be axiomatic that capitalism was an iniquitous
system and that one day it would be superceded by a socialist society.
The principal evidence drawn upon by Lagardelle was that derived from
his unrivalled knowledge of the evolution and character of the socialist
movement in France and Europe. For this reason Lagardelle's special
contribution to syndicalist theory lay in his meticulous examination of the
relationship between the working-class movement, the political party and
the democratic process.

At the heart of Lagardelle's syndicalism (as one would expect) lay the
conviction that the working class constituted the 'pivotal' point of socialism. Firstly, the interests of the proletariat (unlike those of other classes)
could not be reconciled with the continued existence of the capitalist
system and, secondly, the working class was responsible for the economic
and technical advance upon which the society of the future would be built.
Out of the inevitable class struggle and from within the workers' own
organisations would arise both the industrial and the ethical foundations
of the new society.

From within this perspective Lagardelle made short work of the reformist strategy. Beyond the general charge of corruption, levelled first at
Millerand and from 1906 onwards at Aristide Briand,[181] Lagardelle contended that reformism, by relying upon the State to achieve its goals and
by seeking to transform the socialist party from a class party into a broadly-
based populist party, guaranteed the continued existence of bourgeois and
capitalist society. 'To expect the administrative machinery of bourgeois
society', he argued, 'to create a socialist society is as foolish as expecting
a plum-tree to produce beans or a field of corn to produce hay'.[182] Parliamentary socialism, he concluded not without a hint of irony, was 'Uto-
pian'. A similar argument was deployed by Lagardelle to refute the 'révolutionnarisme électoral'[183] of Guesdism. What Guesde and the other
revolutionary socialists committed to the seizure of power by parliamentary and electoral means failed to realise, according to Lagardelle, was
that participation in the structures of bourgeois democracy and acceptance

of its practices (for example, a willingness to compromise) necessarily thwarted the revolutionary potential of a movement. 'The impossibility of conducting the class war in the world of electoral and parliamentary politics' he wrote, 'is obvious'.

In this Lagardelle said little that could not be found in the writings of other syndicalists but he went on to give the syndicalist critique of democracy a new dimension by exposing what he took to be the theoretical postulates of republican democracy in France. Out of this Lagardelle was to draw what was to be for him — and for other syndicalists — the crucial distinction between *l'homme abstrait* of democratic theory and *l'homme réel* of socialism. This in turn gave rise to a new principle of democratic organisation appropriate to the proletariat and provided Lagardelle with the key categories around which he was to formulate a, largely critical, appraisal of the political party.

Central to Lagardelle's assessment of democracy was the view that democratic theory rested upon a false conception of man and that it chose to ignore or discount the economic realities of capitalist society.[184] 'Democracy', Lagardelle argued, 'considers only the citizen, the "political" man, detached from the social category to which he belongs . . . It disregards the differences between men and between groups of men brought about by material circumstances; it places itself above classes and class conflict'.[185] In emphasising the primacy of the political, at the expense of the economic, it supposed that all men, as they possessed equal political and legal rights, were, in fact, of equal status. Political democracy and democratic theory, therefore, presupposed the actual existence of the abstract man, the classless citizen, freed from the realities imposed upon him by economic necessity.

Lagardelle found fault with the category of *l'homme abstrait* and the assumptions it embodied on several counts. By disregarding the existence of classes with distinct class interests, or at best by believing that their conflicting desires would be reconciled within the framework of capitalism, it sought to establish an imagined community of interests and hence to ensure the continued survival of bourgeois society. To accept its premises was to acquiesce, in reality, to the supremacy of the bourgeoisie. 'Democracy', Lagardelle wrote, 'is conservative'.

In addition, Lagardelle argued that the concept of *l'homme abstrait* did not furnish a valid principle of political organisation. Like Sorel, Lagardelle believed that democracy rested upon a 'necessary fiction', namely that the general will of all the citizens could be said to exist and that it made itself felt in the political process and was, therefore, embodied in a society's laws. Accordingly, it assumed that each citizen possessed an equal capacity to deliberate upon all aspects of a society's life. Once again, democratic theory belied reality. The political activity that arose as a result of taking this unattainable 'fiction' seriously was described by Lagardelle as being 'unstable', 'chaotic', 'lacking in direction'. Government by all the citizens was only possible if the masses were educated and were thus suitably equipped to carry out their duties. Yet, Lagardelle argued, 'the area covered by politics is too vast and the questions it deals with too complicated to allow the masses to be sufficiently educated to play their role effectively'.[186] The masses as abstract citizens could not govern: hence their dependence under the system of parliamentary democracy upon their representatives.

At bottom, however, each criticism of democracy derived from Lagardelle's fundamental objection that the theoretically equal, abstract citizens of democratic theory were engaged in a relentless economic struggle between themselves to secure their very existence. It was this reality — the reality of *real* economic needs and *real* class interests, not abstract similarities — that socialism took as its basis. The proper terrain of socialism, therefore, was not political activity but the economic struggle through which the workers would become aware of the irreducible divisions between themselves and the bourgeoisie. 'The economic organisation of the proletariat', Lagardelle wrote, 'only knows real men (*des hommes réels*), workers who gather together and act together to defend their material and moral interests. We are no longer in the presence of abstract notions but are facing well-defined, concrete relations. There is nothing in common between the political and the proletarian *milieus*'.[187]

Corresponding to the needs of 'real', economic man, and in opposition to *'la démocratie politique'*, socialism posited the establishment of what Lagardelle termed *'la démocratie ouvrière'*. Based upon entirely different premises from those of liberal democracy it took as its organisational structure the autonomous institutions of the working class, and in particular the *syndicat*. It was a new type of democracy in which workers of the same trade, drawn together as an occupational group, would discuss those matters of common interest upon which they possessed some expertise. 'Workers' democracy', Lagardelle observed, 'therefore rests essentially upon the organised groups of the proletariat . . . The conception of abstract equality is replaced by real equality'.[188]

There was a further dimension to workers' democracy. In his *thèse de doctorat en droit* Lagardelle had argued that the *syndicats* were composed of an 'élite' which had the right to 'legislate' for all the members of their trade: 'this government of the élite', he had remarked, 'is the best safeguard of the interests of the mass'.[189] This theme was expanded upon in 'Socialisme ou Démocratie'. Here Lagardelle argued that the defence of the workers' interests naturally and necessarily led to the emergence within the *syndicats* of a hierarchy which would gradually extend its functions and which would be composed of the most competent and able workers in their profession. 'From the moment that we are in the presence of real men, workers who do not have the same qualities or capacities', Lagardelle wrote, 'a necessary differentiation is produced between them'.[190] Everyone is not on the same level because they do not possess the same aptitudes. The new élite, chosen upon the basis of proven competence (not randomly as in political democracy) and selected by their peers, would be the expression of 'true democracy'. It would guarantee the 'efficient organisation' of the *syndicats* and would constitute 'an élite of able administrators who would ensure the success of the proletarian organisations and cover them with glory'.[191]

In Lagardelle's view such a system of organisation would avoid the instability and compromises of parliamentary politics. 'The destinies of the working class', he wrote, 'would be freed from the uncertainties and oscillations of the movements of opinions which are produced in political democracy'.[192] In contrast to its chaos, a workers' democracy would be 'stable' and 'organic'. The 'wise' and 'prudent' administration of the *syndicats* would replace that of 'loquacious politicians'.

The distinction between 'real' and 'artificial' man was also crucial to Lagardelle's critique of the political party and was deployed repeatedly in his efforts to establish the primacy of the economic and hence syndicalist, organisation of the proletariat.[193] For Lagardelle a class was defined by the common economic position and moral values of its members. In the case of the proletariat, a shared working experience had given rise to a sense of solidarity born out of struggle, a distinctive working-class ideology and a set of independent organisations, the *syndicats*. The *syndicat*, Lagardelle therefore argued, 'by definition groups together only workers to the exclusion of members of every other class. And in doing so, it takes the worker as producer, thus capturing his very essence, that which informs his life. From morning to night, the wage-earner is dominated by the activity of production, his whole existence unfolds within the factory, around which gravitate all his preoccupations and his thoughts'.[194] The assumption then was that the activity of work was the most fundamental and real aspect of a person's existence — it was, according to Lagardelle, 'the most marvellous manifestation of human strength'[195] — and that it forged genuine and real bonds between members of the same class. The *syndicat*, the grouping together of producers as producers, was the natural institutional expression of the workers as a distinct class.

The political party, by contrast, took as its constitutive element not the producer, but the citizen, the elector. Sustained by the 'democratic fiction' of social equality, the party was composed of a loose amalgam of individuals, not from a single class but from differing classes and united *only* by shared beliefs. Parties were thus 'artificial agglomerates of men', members of the bourgeoisie, workers, peasants and traders, brought together around a common principle or ideology but lacking a firm footing in the realities of economic life.[196] The interests and views they articulated were 'artificial', 'secondary', 'superficial', touching only the 'surface'. Parties were at best therefore fragile constructions, easily destroyed or broken apart, the expression of an abstract and transient political reality: a class, on the other hand, 'could not lose the members that constitute it'.[197]

The same argument was used by Lagardelle to undermine the position of intellectuals. At the time of the Dreyfus Affair Lagardelle had cautiously welcomed their participation within the socialist movement. Writing in *Les Intellectuels devant le socialisme* he had argued that intellectuals could justifiably fulfil the role of 'journalists, propagandists, deputies' on condition that they recognised that they were to serve, not lead, the people. 'The whole problem', he had written, 'consists in ensuring that there exists an organisation powerful enough to control and direct them'. It was only a weak and fragmented socialist movement that had anything to fear from the intrusion of intellectuals.[198]

Lagardelle's subsequent disenchantment with parliamentary socialism hardened his attitude and led him, in parallel to his distinction between class and party, to juxtapose class and intellectual. Like the political party and in obvious contrast to a class, intellectuals were not united by a set of material interests derived from a common economic experience. 'Lacking a uniform existence and their own ideology', Lagardelle wrote, 'intellectuals defend the interests and ideas of the classes or parties around which they aggregate'. In effect, the accusation was that, in comparison with an economic class which had a real, permanent and tangible existence, the intellectual would support that group or class which enhanced his own personal position.

The ultimate goal of all intellectuals, Lagardelle concluded, was to preserve the distinction between intellectual and manual labour and thus ensure their own domination. Like Sorel, therefore, Lagardelle believed that politics was the 'vocation of intellectuals' and that they had no rightful place within the syndicalist movement.[199]

The final element of Lagardelle's critique of the institutions of bourgeois society entailed an analysis of the character of the State and what he regarded as the related issue of patriotism.[200] Clearly, Lagardelle's hostile and critical assessment of the apparatus and power of the State derived, in large measure, from his appraisal of the consequences of the Dreyfus Affair and his rejection of party politics and the democratic system. Like all syndicalists Lagardelle never tired of repeating that the transformation of society required more than a change of government personnel and that the emancipation of the workers demanded the abolition of *all* hierarchical structures, including the State. 'It is not a question of conquering the State', he wrote, 'but of destroying it, of paralysing it and of divesting it of its functions and attributes'.[201] The State corrupted all those — especially socialists — who came into contact with it.

Beyond this standard syndicalist diatribe against the iniquities of the State Lagardelle located his own criticism within what was a rudimentary account of the State's evolution and development. Moreover by drawing attention to what he took to be the interrelationship between the specific character of the State in France and the phenomenon of patriotism (in its various forms) he was able to highlight a further aspect of his own syndicalism.

For Lagardelle States were the product of wars, and, not surprisingly therefore, in the case of France the revolutionary and Napoleonic wars had had a decisive impact upon the development of the State. 'The State', Lagardelle wrote, 'was organised upon the lines of the Imperial army. It constituted a sovereign power capable of submitting the citizen to an iron rule'.[202] Sustained by an ardent, warlike patriotism *la patrie* had been defended and France had carried war across Europe. Yet, according to Lagardelle, that war-like spirit had been quickly dissipated and the years after 1815 had seen the development of what he termed a 'patriotisme pacifique'. In line with this 'l'Etat guerrier' had been replaced by 'l'Etat protecteur'.[203]

Lagardelle's explanation of this occurrence and his assessment of its significance drew heavily upon a description of French capitalism as essentially timid and non-expansionary and a characterisation of the French bourgeoisie as a class concerned solely with their commercial interests.[204] French industrialists, Lagardelle argued, wanted safe markets for their products combined with security and stability of production. They did not, therefore, want the State to engage in costly and potentially hazardous wars with other major European powers. Rather they demanded protection from foreign competition through the establishment of a colonial Empire and the control of all internal dissent on the part of the workers. 'Against the threats and protests of the working class', Lagardelle wrote, the army 'is the rampart which protects the owners of the means of production'.[205]

The move towards 'economic nationalism' had engendered a further significant development — a new emphasis upon 'national unity' and 'social solidarity', culminating in the emergence of the doctrine of 'social peace' and the stress upon the 'moral unity' of the nation. The doctrine of economic protectionism presumed the existence of a community of economic interests and in this context the task of the State was to reward or punish each class or group within the nation according to its willingness or otherwise to recognise the existence of these shared interests. 'Against the bosses', Lagardelle wrote, the State 'has legal power, against the workers military power'.[206] The overall aim, however, was to replace the national unity associated with heroic patriotism by a spiritual bond which would at one and the same time serve to unite the people and ensure the continued dominance of the bourgeoisie.

Lagardelle drew two central conclusions from the emergence of the paternalistic, yet repressive State. The first was that the idea of 'la patrie' was the supreme symbolic expression of collaboration between classes and that therefore it could only be opposed by those who sought the complete destruction of the State. The concomitants to this were that wars were essentially capitalist affairs and that the army, when used internally, was the instrument of State domination. Anti-patriotism therefore entailed anti-militarism.

Lagardelle's second conclusion revealed a debt to Sorel's moral vision. According to Lagardelle the decline of a warlike patriotism and its replacement by a purely 'commercial' conception of the nation revealed that the bourgeoisie wished, above all, 'to live in peace'. The decline of 'l'esprit guerrier' was indicative of the moral corruption and decadence of bourgeois society and its expression, 'a pacific and State-dominated democracy'. Fortunately, Lagardelle concluded, the qualities associated with the military period of patriotism — 'heroism, courage, sacrifice, dignity' — had not disappeared entirely but were alive in the hearts of 'the true heirs of the warlike spirit', the proletariat. In due course, these sentiments would erupt out of the 'general torpor' of society like a volcano. 'War', Lagardelle wrote, 'will not disappear, it will simply change its form'.[207]

Lagardelle's formulation of the goals and methods of syndicalism, in contrast to his critique of the political practices and institutions of bourgeois society, was fragmentary and largely unoriginal. For example, he paid little attention to the actual workings of the *syndicats* and was content to iterate the tactics expounded by syndicalist activists. The moral fervour he was prepared to attribute to the workers' struggle drew its inspiration from the vision of ethical sublimity propounded by Sorel. It was, for example, Sorel, not Lagardelle, who argued — stealing a phrase from Nietzsche — that socialism denoted a re-evaluation of all values.[208]

In brief, therefore, Lagardelle argued that the class struggle was 'the beginning and end of socialism'[209] and that its goal was to free 'the factory from the authority of the employer and society from the authority of the State',[210] thus establishing 'free work in a free society' (*travail libre dans la société libre*).[211] The vehicle through which that goal was to be secured was primarily the *syndicat* — 'the natural organ of the class struggle' — and the tactics to be employed were those of 'direct action' (in contrast to the 'indirect action' of political parties and parliamentary democracy), culminating in the general strike. Unlike Sorel, Lagardelle appeared to believe that the general strike would actually take place although its occurrence would in all probability be in the distant future. In the meantime, the 'idea' of the general strike would serve to protect the syndicalist movement from lapsing into reformism.

Lagardelle intentionally avoided presenting a detailed picture of the post-general strike society on the grounds that for the syndicalists theory and practice were not distinct and that therefore the future and the present could not be separated. The future society would evolve out of the day-today practice of the *syndicats*: their decentralised, federal and autonomous structure would become the basis of the new order: 'no more suffocating centralism and coercive power', Lagardelle wrote, 'but extensive federalism and complete autonomy . . . a constant appeal to the sentiments of initiative, responsibility and struggle'.[212]

In 1911, at the height of his quarrel with Sorel and Edouard Berth, Lagardelle republished some of his best essays in a volume entitled *Le Socialisme ouvrier*.[213] In the Preface he sought not only to justify his own position and conduct but also to summarise what he took to be the significance of his own work and that of his erstwhile colleagues on *Le Mouvement socialiste*. 'From the first to the last line, in 1900 as in 1910', Lagardelle wrote, 'it has been the same question that I have asked myself: will socialism issue from workers' organisations or political parties?'. He had always, Lagardelle stated, given the same answer: 'socialism was the work of economic organisations, not political clubs'. Upon this, Lagardelle remarked, all of the collaborators of *Le Mouvement socialiste* had been in agreement. Yet, Lagardelle felt, he had made his own specific contribution to syndicalist debate. 'For my part', he wrote, 'I was determined to highlight the antagonism . . . between politics and economics, party and class, citizen and producer, democracy and socialism'. At bottom, he went on, 'this differentiation poses a question about method: the eternal opposition between the abstract and the concrete'.

There can, indeed, be little doubt that despite Lagardelle's slight exaggeration of time scale this was the unifying theme of his writings from 1902 onwards. The truly remarkable thing, as we shall see, is that the distinction between the 'abstract' and the 'real' or the 'concrete' remained the key concept in his writings until his arrest for collaboration in 1944. In the first instance, however, he had to withstand the challenge posed by Edouard Berth's attempted fusion of syndicalism and monarchism.

IV

In 1909 Sorel announced that he would cease to write on syndicalism. Recent events had convinced him that the syndicalist movement had lost the sense of its own originality and that by participating in the procedures of parliamentary democracy it had forfeited its autonomy. As, in his opinion, Hubert Lagardelle had been one of the principal culprits responsible for this decline — against Sorel's advice he had attended the socialist congress at Toulouse — Sorel decided to withdraw his support from *Le Mouvement socialiste*. Edouard Berth quickly followed Sorel's example, publishing his last article in Lagardelle's journal in January 1909. The 'nouvelle école' came to an abrupt and bitter end.

At the same time Sorel decided against participation in several reviews which claimed to continue the tradition of revolutionary syndicalism. *L'Action directe* — amongst whose contributors were Lagardelle, Griffuelhes, Robert Louzon and Pierre Monatte — was described by Sorel in a letter to Paul Delesalle as 'the principal mouthpiece of politicians masquerading as syndicalists'.[214] Although he agreed to aid Pouget in his publication of *La Révolution* — wishing Pouget well in his fight against the 'apaches of politics' — in private he made it clear that he had no such intention.[215] He was also deeply suspicious of Pierre Monatte's *La Vie ouvrière*. Was it 'le monde juif' which was behind Monatte, Sorel wondered? In addition, after the publication of Sorel's *La Révolution dreyfusienne* the friendship between Charles Péguy and Sorel became increasingly strained and it seemed unlikely that Péguy's *Cahiers de la quinzaine* could take the place of *Le Mouvement socialiste*. Disillusioned and displaying psychosomatic symptoms of illness Sorel, momentarily, was without a forum for the expression of his ideas.

There followed what is undoubtedly one of the most controversial episodes in the history of the syndicalist movement.[216] From 1905 onwards members of the royalist movement in France, and specifically its principal organisation *Action française* under the leadership of Charles Maurras, began to show a serious interest in the ideas of revolutionary syndicalism. In their desire to gain a hold amongst the working class, the syndicalists were perceived by the monarchists as allies in the struggle against the common enemy of parliamentary democracy. The task of convincing the syndicalists of this similarity of purpose, and hence of the possibilities for collaborative action, was undertaken primarily by Georges Valois.[217]

Valois' views were most succinctly expressed in *La Révolution sociale ou le roi*, published in 1907, and were restated at greater length in *La Monarchie et la classe ouvrière*.[218] In both studies Valois sought to disabuse syndicalists of their faith in the social revolution and thus lead them to recognise that the only alternative to the despised Republican regime lay in the restoration of the monarchy. Both 'historically' and 'logically', Valois argued, it could be shown that the State was necessary for the preservation of order. By denying this, the syndicalists ran the risk of thrusting society into a state of economic and political chaos in which the only beneficiaries, according to Valois, would be the Jewish financiers who would be able 'to expropriate the French bourgeoisie to the profit of Israel'. The restored monarch alone, Valois contended, was able to protect the interests of the working class. Eschewing the corporatist ideology traditionally associated with monarchism, Valois argued that it was no part of the royalist design to diminish class sentiments. The monarch as 'Roi du travail' would perform the function of sovereign arbiter: acting above the classes, he would free the workers from the tutelage of bourgeois democrats and intellectuals. 'Being royalists', Valois wrote, 'we are syndicalists'.

In 1908 Valois launched an *enquête* on this issue in his journal *La Revue critique des idées et des livres*. Although taken aback by the apparent absurdity of Valois' argument Lagardelle decided to give Robert Louzon the job of replying on behalf of *Le Mouvement socialiste*.[219] According to Louzon it was a republic, not a monarchy, which provided the best terrain for the war between capital and labour.[220] Sorel provided his own reply. The belief held by the working class that the monarchy was responsible for the death of 30 000 Parisians in the fall of the Commune in 1871, Sorel argued, was sufficient to ensure that the restoration of the monarchy was not a serious possibility.[221] Nevertheless, in the immediate aftermath of his withdrawal from *Le Mouvement socialiste* Valois was to be amongst those to whom Sorel turned.

In 1910 Sorel, Berth and Valois in conjunction with two other monarchists, Jean Variot and Pierre Gilbert, made plans to publish a journal entitled *La Cité française*. Beyond the appearance of a forthright prospectus which stated that 'it is absolutely necessary to destroy democratic institutions' little came of the project and it is clear from Sorel's correspondence with Berth that almost from the outset he had doubts about the wisdom of the entire enterprise.[222]

However, in March 1911 Sorel's name figured alongside that of Variot and several other right-wing activists on the editorial board of the review *L'Indépendance*. Amongst its future distinguished contributors were to be Gustave le Bon, Paul Claudel, Maurice Barrès and Vilfredo Pareto. Berth, on the other hand, collaborated with Valois in the formation of the *Cercle Proudhon* and its review, the *Cahiers du Cercle Proudhon*, which appeared intermittently between 1912 and 1914.[223] The *Cercle Proudhon* was never more than an ephemeral organisation grouping together an assortment of young men from the far Left and far Right: the *Cahiers du Cercle Proudhon* failed to secure more than 200 regular subscribers. It was here that Berth, under the pseudonym of Jean Darville, came to endorse a doctrine which sought to combine monarchism and syndicalism.

In 1910 Georges Guy-Grand published a lengthy series of articles entitled 'Le Procès de la démocratie'.[224] The theme of Guy-Grand's articles was that, irrespective of their mutual antipathy towards parliamentary democracy, monarchism and syndicalism could not be reconciled. 'They combat the same adversary', Guy-Grand wrote, 'but for contrary reasons and ends'.[225] The following April Berth produced a reply (published in Valois' *Revue critique des idées et des livres*) and in so doing set the tone for his writings in the period prior to the First World War.[226]

In 'Le Procès de la démocratie' Guy-Grand had argued that syndicalism and democracy were separated by nothing more than a 'metaphysical disagreement': for Berth this disagreement represented a fundamental 'gulf'. Extending the argument of his earlier writings, democracy was described as 'nominalist, subjectivist, individualistic, atomistic'. It was

Cartesian and Socratic, urban and abstract. A 'regime without a memory', it cared neither for the past nor the future, was impatient with the old and the young, lived only for the present. Democracy was hostile to everything that was concrete and real, to all links of 'time and place'. It scorned the bonds of 'blood, race, history, earth [and] profession,'[227] abstracted the individual from all that was 'stable, fixed and permanent'.[228] What united the syndicalists and the members of *Action française*, Berth argued, was their adherence to a 'realist mentality' and thus their defence of those 'national and occupational' realities or institutions that democracy sought to destroy. *Action française* and the syndicalist movement confronted us with what Berth described as a 'réalisme national' and a 'réalisme ouvrier', embodying in turn 'the realism of the *patrie* . . . conceived as a territorial reality' and 'the realism of work and profession conceived as organic realities'.[229] Lumped together as their common enemies were liberal Protestants, Catholic modernists, parliamentary socialists, feminists, Jews, jacobins and free-masons.

A similarly strident, frenzied and rhetorical style, replete with a set of phobias and prejudices directed indiscriminately at what were seen as the representatives of democratic nominalism, was deployed by Berth in the articles he published in the *Cahiers du Cercle Proudhon*. Indeed, the same tone was typical of almost every article that appeared in its pages. A declaration signed by the members of the *Cercle Proudhon* in March 1912, for example, directed its fire at 'l'Etat judéo-républicain' and 'la ploutocratie internationale'.[230] Valois echoed Maurras in condemning Jews, free-masons, Protestants and foreigners for the ruin of France.[231] 'As workers, heads of families and as Frenchmen', Albert Vincent wrote, 'our most pressing obligation is to destroy democratic institutions.'[232] The *Cercle Proudhon* was also firmly nationalist. Proudhon was chosen as its patron, Valois argued, precisely because he belonged to 'the most authentic and oldest French tradition, that which is born and formed in the heart of the French peasant.'[233]

Berth began his contributions to the *Cahiers du Cercle Proudhon* by offering a definition of the significance of Proudhon's thought.[234] Proudhon, he argued, was 'the greatest *French* socialist philosopher'. He was French 'from head to foot', springing from 'the purest French source'. For Berth, therefore, Proudhon was able to combine a love of liberty with a sense for unity and order. He was neither a pacifist nor an optimist. No-one else, Berth wrote, had written such a 'superb panegyric' in defence of war. Proudhon embodied the Christian and classical traditions that had been at the basis of French culture and greatness. Proudhon spoke, Berth concluded, a language that recalled that of 'our greatest moralists, when the tradition of antique wisdom combined with the supernatural virtues of Christianity, formed the substance of the national spirit.' He was thus the very antithesis of the shallow and cynical civilisation that dominated contemporary France.

The same severe and uncompromising vision informed Berth's article 'Satellites de la ploutocratie' but it was here that could be perceived clearly the distance covered by Berth since his departure from *Le Mouvement socialiste*. 'Satellites de la ploutocratie'[235] was inspired by two events: Italy's 'audacity' in beginning the Tripolitan war and the uprising of the Balkan states against the Ottoman Empire. It took as its theme an aphorism to be found in Nietzsche's *Will to Power*: 'a society which rejects, definitively and by *instinct*, war and the spirit of conquest is in decadence: it is ripe for democracy and a government of grocers'. Such, according to Berth, was the condition of France, the 'most plutocratic of modern nations'. Bourgeois pacifism was matched by socialist pacifism. Yet, Berth argued, the true extent of France's decline and decomposition could only be properly appreciated when one considered the rejection of war from 'a purely sentimental, Tolstoyan, bourgeois pacifist point of view' by the syndicalist movement. Even the syndicalists had been so absorbed into the plutocratic system that they had forgotten that 'war, in certain cases, could be a revolutionary event of the first order'.

To defend that statement and the open criticism it implied of syndicalist anti-militarism Berth outlined what he termed a 'revolutionary justification of patriotism'. It was the rich, Berth argued, not the poor who had no country. The 'man of the people' was immersed in his '*patrie*', its language, local customs, national traditions. Rejecting a key canon of syndicalist doctrine, he argued that man was not only a producer: the world could not be reduced solely to the factory. Berth made it clear that he did not regard this as something to be regretted: the sense of belonging to a nation, he argued with Proudhon's defence of war in mind, was a source of inspiration; it could evoke sacrifice and heroism, engender sublime sentiments. Even more striking was his denial of another central aspect of syndicalist faith. In challenging the internationalism of the syndicalist movement Berth questioned the feasibility and desirability of securing the destruction of the State. Was this not naively to assume, Berth argued, the complete disappearance of all antagonisms within the world and the fusion of all countries into one humanity? Did it not also imply 'the end of all movement and of all progress in the world?'

Berth's acceptance of the desirability of the restoration of the monarchy drew upon these points.[236] The rapid degeneration of the syndicalist movement, he argued, showed that democracy was the 'worst terrain' upon which one could engage in a 'true class struggle'. Democracy's lay pacifist theology substituted peace for war: it meant an absence of conviction, a decline into mediocrity. 'Only a return to warlike thought', Berth argued, 'could save the modern world'.[237] It was precisely this possibility that the seemingly opposite but, according to Berth, 'perfectly convergent' movements of *Action française* and syndicalism held out. Further, it was a mistake to believe that democracy entailed a limited State and therefore preserved the autonomy of the working-class movement. Democracy, on the contrary, meant an 'unlimited, excessive State flowing over the whole of society like a raging river'. Given that universal peace between nations was a chimera and thus 'the absolute necessity for the maintenance of the State', there existed only one solution: monarchy. Using the formula of Maurras, Berth wrote: 'I, a syndicalist, see no difficulty in concluding in favour of a traditional, anti-parliamentary, hereditary and de-centralised monarchy.'[238] Here alone could be found a 'neutral State' freed from the intrigues of politicians and sects, embodying the 'most noble and sacred' aspects of the 'national tradition'. Here existed a State which was 'absolute' in its own sphere — the dispensation of justice — but which was 'restricted, confined, divided', surrounded by a network of institutions and groups enjoying a complete autonomy upon the syndicalist model. The king, Berth argued, would be 'the incarnation of the warrior State, the personification of those interests which by their general character are superior to the classes and to their antagonisms'.[239] For the rest, each social and economic class would be free to pursue its own ends, to engage in conflict with its rivals, safe in the knowledge that it would not compromise either 'the national or general social interest.' In this way, class struggle — the 'fundamental condition' necessary for the existence of a 'serious working-class movement' — would exist. The argument (in opposition to that stated by Louzon in *Le Mouvement socialiste*) was that the syndicalist movement, located within the inescapable reality of the nation, would fare better under a monarchy than it would under the parliamentary regime of the Third Republic.

In 1914 Berth published *Les Méfaits des intellectuels*.[240] Wedged between an opening and concluding chapter, which restated his defence of the monarchy, were reprints of two articles — 'Marchands, Intellectuels et Politiciens' and 'Anarchisme individualiste, Marxisme orthodoxe, Syndicalisme révolutionnaire' — previously published in *Le Mouvement socialiste*. Berth himself did not find this to be paradoxical. Whilst he accepted that syndicalism and the nationalism of *Action française* existed as 'antinomies' it was, he argued, out of their opposition that would result a 'new social equilibrium'. To illustrate that point he turned to Nietzsche's famous contrast in his account of the birth of tragedy between the Apollonian and Dionysian spirits. Casting Maurras in the role of Apollo, the spirit of beauty, and Sorel in the role of Dionysus, the spirit of the sublime, Berth contended that, as formerly in ancient Greece, the Apollonian-Dionysian duality was indispensable. 'Dionysus without Apollo', he wrote, 'falls into extravagance and folly; Apollo . . . without Dionysus falls into formalism'.[241]

In July 1909 Georges Sorel published an article entitled 'La disfatta dei "mufles" ' in the Italian syndicalist journal, *Il Divenire sociale*. A month later, under the title 'Socialistes antiparlementaires', it was reprinted in *L'Action française*.[242] The *'mufles'* were the 'louts' that controlled the democratic system and who, according to Sorel, had 'corrupted everything that they have touched in our land'. Contained in this article — alongside an assertion that *Action française* would certainly fail to restore the monarchy — was praise for 'the friends of Maurras' as the 'avant-garde' in the struggle against France's parliamentarians, the *'mufles'*. The following April, *Action française* published Sorel's review of Charles Péguy's *Le Mystère de la charité de Jeanne d'Arc* entitled 'Le Réveil de l'âme française'.[243] Péguy's name, Sorel wrote, would become 'inseparable from the renaissance of French patriotism'. Shortly afterwards the first tentative but ill-fated plans were made to launch *La Cité française*.

Not surprisingly perhaps it was widely assumed that Sorel had been converted to the cause of monarchism. This was not the case and there is no evidence to suggest otherwise. Sorel, for example, counselled Berth against involvement in the *Cercle Proudhon*, advising him not 'to associate with an enterprise which cannot produce good results'.[244] When the *Cercle Proudhon* organised a dinner in his honour at the Café de Flore Sorel refused to attend. Even a whole issue of the *Cahiers du Cercle Proudhon* devoted to an examination of the significance of his thought and in which Henri Lagrange wrote that 'without Georges Sorel the *Cercle Proudhon* would not exist'[245] failed to solicit Sorel's collaboration. Was this not, as Pierre Andreu has suggested, only prudence on Sorel's part?[246] Certainly, if Sorel did not endorse the restoration of the monarchy, he found little difficulty — as his participation in Jean Variot's *L'Indépendance* showed — in finding an element of common ground with members of the royalist movement.

Two statements help us to understand Sorel's actions and the evolution of his thought in the period prior to the First World War. In a note to 'Mes raisons du syndicalisme', published in Italy in 1910, Sorel commented: 'contemporary experience shows that democracy engenders very complex party political structures which tend to limit th autonomy of working-class life; one is entitled to ask whether this autonomy is more easily preserved in aristocratic regimes than in republican ones which are so preoccupied with national solidarity.'[247] After 1909 Sorel became obsessed by what he saw as the power of democratic, republican government to subvert the revolutionary initiatives of the working class and he came to look favourably upon any organisation, including Maurras' *Action française*, which appeared to give back to each class something of its former independence and energy. This did not mean, in Sorel's opinion, that he had abandoned his earlier views. In a letter published in *Terre libre*, for example, he complained bitterly about the suggestion that his thought had recently entered what had been described in the paper as its 'deuxième manière'.[248]

The second remark appeared in Sorel's long review of Urbain Gohier's *Le Réveil*.[249] Gohier, like Sorel, was a former Dreyfusard who had become bitterly disillusioned by the outcome of the Dreyfus Affair. Sorel wrote:

> People who like me are in their sixties cannot read *Le Réveil* without feeling very strong emotions because one finds there, in a language worthy of their nobility, some of the sentiments which inspired the liberalism of the young generation in the last years of the Second Empire. That generation admired, in an intelligent way, French traditions, believed that the greatness of a people was measured by a scale of moral values, despised *parvenus* more than they have ever been despised. It condemned in the existing regime a materialistic order which was cherished by those adventurers who disregarded the opinions of good families and who were hungry for money and swollen with pride. One hated a government which appeared to dishonour France because of its ignorance of the national genius.[250]

In other words, France's republican democracy had descended to the level of the Bonapartist Second Empire. Why did Sorel believe this to be the case and what did this comparison imply? The answers were largely to be found in the final chapter of *La Révolution dreyfusienne*, published in 1909.

'The Dreyfus Affair', Sorel wrote, 'has had the result of precipitating the ruin of the social structure which made possible the tolerable working of the parliamentary regime.'[251] Such a system, if it were not to decline into the rule of demagogues, depended upon the existence of what Sorel termed a 'republican aristocracy', an élite formed around France's old republican families. Deprived of power during the Second Empire, this aristocracy had regarded the Bonapartists as 'political adventurers, stock market swindlers, men without culture and without morality': it had, in contrast, attached great importance to the nobility of birth. During the early years of the Third Republic this republican aristocracy had effectively ruled France. Men of the highest moral standing, they had acted as 'social authorities', embodying all that was sound in the republican tradition. Nevertheless, they had failed to appreciate the limitations of their authority and the significance of the 'Dreyfusard revolution' was precisely that it represented the end of their reign. The formation of Waldeck-Rousseau's government of 1899 and the general corruption it entailed, according to Sorel, represented the seizure of power by a new class of *parvenu* politicians, resembling that which had formerly surrounded Napoleon III. As a consequence, the parliamentary regime was turned into a 'farce': 'the republican aristocracy was only a memory'.

The greater proportion of the articles written by Sorel for Variot's *L'Indépendance* sought to expose the implications of this 'revolution' and the abandonment it involved of what Sorel referred to as 'our old republican principles'.[252] This specifically was the context for three articles which conveyed profoundly anti-semitic sentiments.[253] 'In the Jews who claim to direct our country', Sorel wrote, 'we encounter to an exaggerated degree the faults that were formally criticised so bitterly in the men of Napoleon III'.[254] For people such as Urbain Gohier, Sorel commented, anti-semitism was a 'natural consequence' of their anti-Bonapartism. Only when the socialists were absorbed into the bourgeoisie did they cease to be anti-semites.

If such sentiments were a commonplace amongst members of the extreme Right they were not unknown in the syndicalist movement. In 1906, for example, Robert Louzon had published an article entitled 'La faillite du Dreyfusisme ou le triomphe du parti juif' in *Le Mouvement socialiste*.[255] Responding to the declaration of Dreyfus' innocence by the *Cour de cassation* in July 1906, Louzon had argued that this decision revealed the ascendancy of the 'parti juif' within the French bourgeoisie. 'Around the Jews', Louzon commented, 'there exists a bourgeois caste with its own character, strength and influence'. Sorel had been impressed by this article and had even recommended that Lagardelle should send a copy to Edouard Drumont, the anti-semitic editor of *Libre parole*. As Shlomo Sand has shown, Sorel's own attitude towards Jews — when viewed from the perspective of his work as a whole — is not easily categorised as racist but it was certainly, at times, anti-semitic.[256] This was especially so from 1906 onwards. In private correspondence, for example, Sorel used expressions such as 'youpins' or 'circoncis' to describe Jews. In Sorel's political vocabulary 'Jew' became synonymous with a support of the despised Jean Jaurès. Elsewhere, in contrast, he condemned anti-semitism as a 'doctrine of hatred' and consistently defended Bergson from those detractors who drew attention to his Jewish origins.

The articles in *L'Indépendance* portrayed Jews, and in particular Jewish intellectuals, as the quintessential representatives of the political class which had taken control of France in the immediate aftermath of the Dreyfus Affair. Sorel's loathing of politicians and of bourgeois intellectuals was focused upon the form of the messianic and rootless Jew as the antithesis of everything that had brought greatness to France. Sorel's article on Urbain Gohier therefore concluded with a question: 'Was Urbain Gohier mistaken to maintain that French people should defend their State, their morals and their ideas against the Jewish invaders who wish to dominate everything?[257] 'Quelques prétentions juives' ended in a similarly menacing tone. Having praised Charles Maurras for his 'defence of French culture', Sorel commented: '*Action française* seeks to inculcate its ideas amongst the youth of our universities: if it succeeds in attracting a sizeable minority of students to its cause, the Jewish intellectuals will experience bad times. But perhaps the Jews will be wise enough to gag their intellectuals?'[258] Sorel's objection to the Jews was thus primarily a cultural one. The Jew was perceived as a foreign and corrosive influence upon France.

It was, however, Sorel's antipathy towards *modernisme* that served to unify his writings in the period before 1914. At the end of 1907 Sorel had published an article entitled 'Modernisme dans la religion et dans le socialisme'.[259] Drawing a parallel between the Catholic modernists who wished to bring religious faith into line with what they saw as the discoveries of modern science and the socialist modernists who wished to turn socialism into 'bourgeois literature' by abandoning its 'barbarism', Sorel condemned both groups for their 'equal hatred of the men who had preserved the belief in old principles'. For the Church, Sorel argued, a return to the Bible would be equivalent to a return by socialists to the doctrines of class struggle.

Modernism, as Sorel's articles in *L'Indépendance* showed, took numerous forms. It affected not only politics and religion but art, literature, morality, education and culture in general. The Jewish intellectual was one manifestation of its pervasive influence. The interest amongst young people for 'the Russian novel, neo-Catholicism and anarchism' was another.[260] At issue was a conflict between what Sorel saw as two opposing conceptions of life. On the one hand was the vision of life perceived through the perspectives offered by the Christian and classical traditions. Life took the form of tragedy and demanded an attitude of moral seriousness. The socialism of Marx, Sorel believed, was dominated by this pessimistic spirit. So too was the austere morality of Proudhon. On the other hand there existed what Sorel regarded as the superficial and optimistic mentality of his day. For Sorel this view of life had its origins in the Reformation and reached fruition amongst the *philosophes* of the Enlightenment. The world was seen as a source of pleasure. Progress, irrespective of man's actions, was thought to be inevitable. The individual was thus set free to enjoy a life of indulgence and frivolity.

Prior to 1909 Sorel had believed that the syndicalist movement had embodied the austere and pessimistic world-view and that through its actions the bourgeoisie would come to adopt a similar mentality. Its antithesis had been the parliamentary socialism of Jaurès and the parallel democratic ideology which reduced politics to the search for compromise and the competition for spoils. After 1909 Sorel saw a working class (and a bourgeoisie) which had adopted the attitudes of *modernisme*. He saw workers who through their attendance at the Dreyfusard *universités populaires* had come to despise manual labour.[261] He saw a culture which preferred such non-entities as Henry Bernstein and Charles Seignobos to Corneille, Pascal and Bossuet.[262] France was a country descending rapidly into mediocrity and decay. In *L'Indépendance* Sorel directed his fire against those he regarded as the representatives, both political and cultural, of *modernisme*. Subject to particular venom was the Sorbonne as

the institution primarily responsible for the creation of the lay and rational-
istic ethic which permeated democratic society.[263] Here too was the criticism (echoed by Berth) of all those who were deemed to be the destroyers
and opponents of the traditions of France.

The years immediately before the First World War offered Sorel little
cause for enthusiasm and encouragement. The hopes that he had placed
in the syndicalist movement had come to nothing. There appeared to be
no limits to the destructive impact of parliamentary democracy. Nevertheless the future did not appear to be entirely without promise.

Shortly after the publication of Bergson's *L'Evolution créatrice* in 1908
Sorel published a lengthy and critical review of it in *Le Mouvement socialiste*.[264] At the time it was widely assumed that Sorel's views — and specifically his philosophy of violence — were an application of the biological
vitalism to be found in Bergson's work. Sorel, in fact, at no point used
Bergson's key concept — that of the *élan vital* — as a means of explaining
the enthusiasm generated amongst the workers by the myth of the general
strike and in his review article and subsequent comments on the text
stated his opposition to Bergson's use of biological analogies to explain
social phenomena.[265] Yet Sorel recognised that the publication of Bergson's book was of major importance and, unlike many other commentators
upon *L'Evolution créatrice*, he perceived the direction which Bergson's
thought was taking.

Where Sorel and Bergson were of like minds was in their mutual hostility towards positivism and scientism. For Sorel, the significance of
L'Evolution créatrice was that it openly endorsed a metaphysics which
accepted the reality of the divine and the supernatural. In line with this,
Sorel concluded his article 'Vues sur les problèmes de la philosophie' with
the remark that '*L'Evolution créatrice* is essentially a manifesto signifying
to modern man that the principal preoccupation of philosophy should be
to reflect upon the mysteries of life'.[266] The importance of Bergsonian
philosophy, therefore, lay in its capacity to bring about a spiritual — and in
particular a religious — resurgence. As Sorel commented, in *L'Evolution
créatrice* 'the God of Pascal has defeated the God of Descartes'.[267]

For Sorel (and also for Berth) the idea that Bergsonian philosophy was
capable of engendering an 'intellectual revolution' was the principal source
of comfort in the years before 1914. Bergsonian philosophy could, potentially, create a new sensibility which would denote the end of the sterile
and unproductive rationalism which, in Sorel's view, had dominated western thought and society for three centuries. Man would then be free once
again to adopt an ethic of sublimity. 'I am convinced', Sorel wrote, 'that,
thanks to Bergson, in fifteen or twenty years a new generation — released
from the phantoms constructed by intellectualist philosophies since
Descartes — will only listen to men capable of explaining the theory of
evil'.[268]

The initial reaction of Hubert Lagardelle to the sudden departure of Berth and Sorel from *Le Mouvement socialiste* was one of anger and dismay tinged with incomprehension. Two swallows, he remarked with contempt, did not make a summer.[269] The correspondence between Sorel and Lagardelle continued (and retained its amicable tone) until December 1910 but Sorel made no effort to explain to Lagardelle the new course he was taking. Lagardelle was therefore left with little alternative but to formulate a response to what he took to be the conversion of *both* Sorel and Berth to the cause of *Action française*.

Lagardelle was clearly shaken by the entire episode. Under his editorship *Le Mouvement socialiste* devoted considerable space to an examination of 'la crise du syndicalisme' but Lagardelle's own contribution to the journal declined dramatically. He found a temporary point of equilibrium in the study of the history of the syndicalist movement[270] but in 1912 he resumed his travels, spending a large proportion of the years before the First World War on a succession of lecture tours in the Balkan states. As if to symbolise his own malaise and the distance that separated him from his former colleagues, Lagardelle began in 1913 to publish articles in Jaurès' *L'Humanité*. The irony is that in these years Lagardelle shifted the emphasis within his own writings and thus paved the way for a course which, via regionalism in the 1920s and *planisme* in the 1930s, led to his appointment as Minister of Labour under the Vichy regime.

The essence of Lagardelle's case against Berth and Sorel was that it was quite simply 'monstrous' to believe that syndicalism and monarchism could be reconciled.[271] At its most obvious they were in fundamental disagreement on several substantive points. The monarchist doctrine of corporatism which sought to bring workers and employers together was the antithesis of the syndicalist doctrine of class struggle. The desire of the monarchists to carry out a 'political revolution' had nothing in common with the syndicalist tactic of progressively reducing the power of the State. Syndicalist anti-militarism and religious indifference were in stark contrast to the defence of the Church and Army which, in Lagardelle's view, represented 'the beginning and end of neo-monarchism'.[272] Nor, Lagardelle argued, did the monarchists have the right to turn to Proudhon to support their case. Virtually everything, Lagardelle conceded, could be found in Proudhon — 'except royalism'. 'His whole system', Lagardelle wrote, 'consists in dissolving politics into economics . . . in order to destroy the relics of monarchism'.[273] At the heart of Lagardelle's argument, however, was the belief that the monarchists, including Sorel and Berth, had misrepresented and misunderstood the nature of the syndicalist critique of democracy.

The syndicalists, Lagardelle argued, had criticised democracy not 'in order to abolish it but in order to go beyond it'. For all their objections to what Lagardelle termed 'the superstitious confidence in government' and 'the fetichism of the representative regime' the syndicalists sought not to destroy democracy but to eradicate the faults of the system by limiting the role played by the State and the political parties. 'In putting the accent upon the *syndicat*', Lagardelle wrote, 'we did not wish to deny that the socialist party had a role'. The task of the syndicalist movement was to reduce the domain of politics to what Lagardelle described as 'limited proportions'. Taking up the theme of Louzon's original reply to Valois, Lagardelle stressed repeatedly that democracy provided the best environment in which the syndicalist movement could operate. That this was the case was not difficult to explain. 'Nothing,' Lagardelle wrote, 'is sacred for democracy: it cynically shows us the political machine in all its nakedness. Compare this to monarchy, to even the most modern monarchy, with its quasi-divine conception of authority, its religious respect for the royal family, its fanatical love for traditional institutions'.[274] On this scale, even the worst of democracies was better than the best monarchy.

To a certain extent, Lagardelle's remarks — for all their truth when applied to the initiatives of *Action française* to attract the proletariat — missed their target. Sorel, after all, did not support the return of the monarchy and it was not until 1914 that Berth was formally converted to the idea. What Lagardelle's comments highlighted was their differing appreciations of the nature of parliamentary democracy under the Third Republic and the limited potential that each was now prepared to assign to the syndicalist movement. For Sorel and Berth, democracy had become the root cause of what they saw as a general societal decline and syndicalism no longer seemed able to reverse that process. For Lagardelle, the difficulties experienced by the syndicalist movement — and Lagardelle was as much aware of the movement's problems as were Sorel and Berth — seemed to have convinced him of the need to compromise the grandiose aspirations championed so vigorously in the pages of *Le Mouvement socialiste* in the years 1904–8. Syndicalism now appeared destined only to rectify the faults and imbalances of the democratic system and not to create an entirely new structure that would replace it. That Lagardelle believed that the syndicalist movement was merely one of several factors which, when combined, would eradicate the problems associated with democracy only became evident with the publication of 'La Démocratie en France' in 1912.[275]

The question posed by Lagardelle was how could 'authoritarian democracy' be transformed into what he termed 'liberal democracy'. The French State, he believed, was the prototype of the modern unitary State. All 'intermediary groups' had been eliminated: the isolated and 'parcellised' citizen stood alone before a highly centralised structure which sought to subordinate all individual and collective activity to its will. In parallel to this process, the citizen had been encouraged to see the State as the vehicle of Providence and, in the absence of a monarch or emperor, under the Republic that faith had been transferred onto the institution of parliament. Politicians had thus been able to extend their corrupting activities to cover even the smallest details of individual and national life. 'An artificial France, in false colours, perpetually agitated on the surface', Lagardelle commented, 'has been substituted for the real France of work and order'.[276]

The real France, Lagardelle believed, was now re-asserting itself: the nation was in revolt against the State. In the wake of the disillusionment with the political process that had followed the Dreyfus Affair the excesses of government and the political parties were being challenged. One challenge came from the syndicalist movement, 'the insurrection of work against incompetence and parasitism', but this was only one example of the 'associationist tendency'. Throughout the economy, industrialists, landowners, small businessmen and peasant farmers were turning their backs on the State and were organising their own activities. It was possible, Lagardelle argued, to talk of 'la syndicabilité croissante de la société française'. The growth in the number of leagues — Lagardelle, unlike Berth, saw the value of Ostragorski's observations — was another indication of the re-awakening of 'public spirit' in the French population.[277] The same concern to limit the power of the State and its abuse was also evident in the demands that were being made for the introduction of proportional representation and administrative decentralisation. The latter was characterised by Lagardelle as 'the re-construction of provincial life.'

'The present crisis', Lagardelle wrote, 'arises from the disproportionate place occupied by politics at the expense of economic life and of authority at the expense of liberty'.[278] Each of the movements he had cited, Lagardelle believed, represented the desire to correct that imbalance. The shift in Lagardelle's own position was evident in his assertion that this was a desirable goal — to abolish the State altogether, he argued, was to invite 'a return to the corporative or communal particularism of the Middle Ages' — and therefore that what had to be decided was the correct and respective parameters of political as opposed to social and economic activity. For Lagardelle it seemed clear that there were certain functions that the State and the State alone could perform. The State, he argued, 'expressed the common needs, the common interests of the individuals and groups out of which the nation was formed'[279] and, as such, could legitimately act as the guarantor of certain basic individual rights — Lagardelle specifically cited liberty of the press and of association — and was correctly responsible for external relations with other States. Where the State should not intrude, in Lagardelle's opinion, was in the broader areas of social and economic life. Here the watchword was not to be 'solidarity' but 'antagonism', 'the organisation of variety', 'the struggle between social groups'. In this way vitality would be restored to the nation, France would be freed from the superstitious belief in politics, and the individual would escape from 'his isolation'. The 'new liberalism', Lagardelle concluded, would be *'un libéralisme de groupes . . . un libéralisme organisateur'*.[280]

Missing from Lagardelle's article was any reference to his key distinction between the 'abstract' and the 'concrete' but it should be clear that this was at the heart of his argument. The world of labour remained the 'real France' in contrast to the 'artificial France' reflected in the world of politics; the isolated citizen of 'authoritarian' democracy was to be replaced by the group member of 'liberal' democracy. There were, however, significant innovations. Firstly, Lagardelle had diluted his opposition to the State and to politics in general. He now conceded that in a country such as France it was inconceivable that the State would disappear altogether: the best that could be hoped for was its reform. Secondly, in opposing the absolutist State Lagardelle, for the first time, emphasised the importance of the provinces as separate entities. For Lagardelle, the future now lay not just with the *syndicat* but in the 'autonomous groups' and 'spontaneous associations' which constituted the 'sanctuary of competence, ability and liberty'.[281]

With the outbreak of the First World War *Le Mouvement socialiste* ceased publication. In truth, since the departure of Sorel and Berth it had lost much of its original impetus and direction. The war itself placed new burdens upon each of the former members of the 'nouvelle école'. In 1914 Lagardelle was mobilised. In 1916, after what he himself described as 'a long illness', he was detached to the *Comité d'Action Economique* in his home region around Toulouse. Remarkably he did not return to Paris until 1928.[282] Berth was also called up. Despite his requests he was not to visit the front and spent the entire war in a variety of administrative posts. His willingness to contribute in 1918 to a volume in honour of Charles Maurras and to restate his evocation of the 'fraternal alliance' between the Apollonian and Dionysian spirits would seem to indicate that the experience of war had not changed his views.[283] In 1915 he joined the Roman Catholic church. Sorel did not follow the example of his closest friend. In a letter to Madame Berth he commented: 'the ideas for which I have struggled so hard have been crushed . . . but any gesture which could be interpreted as desertion would be contemptible'.[284] Nor did he display anything but despair and anguish at the outbreak of the war and its probable consequences. Any lingering sympathy he might have had for Maurras (who, along with the *Action française* movement, rallied to the defence of the Republic) disappeared completely. Exiled from Paris, he lapsed into virtual silence. 'I sense', he wrote to Mario Missiroli in September 1914, 'that my time is finished. I cannot write anything that is susceptible of being read usefully by my contemporaries. I am an old man who no longer understands the tendencies of the present day'.[285] It took the events of the Russian Revolution to rekindle Sorel's enthusiasm.

4 Reformist Syndicalism

In an article entitled 'Un Marx inédit!' published in *Le Mouvement social-iste* in 1904 Edouard Berth commented that there existed a 'veritable abyss' separating the positivism of Comte from the historical materialism of Marx. The inspiration behind the two doctrines, he asserted,

> was completely different: the first is essentially conservative, anti-revol-utionary; it puts duty above right, order before justice and to understand this it is sufficient to see in action a positivist like A. Keufer! Is not the moderate, pacific, governmental direction that he would like to impress upon the workers' movement radically opposed to the explicitly revol-utionary direction that the syndicalists — those faithful interpreters of the essential ideas of Marx — wish to give to it?[1]

If it was with some justification that Berth rejected the claim that signifi-cant parallels existed between the thought of Marx and Comte he was undoubtedly mistaken in reserving the designation of syndicalist for those who believed in revolutionary action. The syndicalist movement was nothing if not heterogeneous and whether Berth chose to recognise it or not it contained many people who drew their ideas from Comtean positiv-ism and even more who were not afraid to describe themselves as reformists.[2]

Reformism within the French trade union movement took a variety of forms. For Emile Basly, leader of the miners' union, the *syndicat* was conceived primarily as a pressure group which, in alliance with its own parliamentary representatives, was capable of extracting progressive reforms from the State. Basly himself was a member of the Chamber of Deputies and there were times when the miners' federation (which did not affiliate to the CGT until 1908) seemingly functioned almost exclus-ively with the aim of keeping him in that position.[3] Albert Thomas, former student at the Ecole Normale Supérieure, founder of *La Revue syndicaliste* and future minister for armaments during the First World War, advocated a gradualist strategy entailing collaboration between the socialist party, trade unions and co-operatives which, after the defeat of the railway workers in 1911, emphasised a policy of nationalisations combined with the extension of democracy through worker participation in industry.[4] There were still others who, like Léon Jouhaux, Alphonse Merrheim and Georges Dumoulin,[5] came to pursue a reformist practice whilst clinging to the vestiges of a revolutionary rhetoric. The subject-matter of this chapter, however, is an undisguised and open reformism which was unequivocal in its defence of the absolute autonomy of the syndicalist movement, which saw the *syndicat* as the fundamental instrument of proletarian emancipation and which opposed any moves to subordinate syndicalism to a political goal or movement.

Auguste Keufer, the man maligned by Edouard Berth as the antithesis of all that syndicalism represented, was, for example, a consistent critic of the political process as a vehicle for proletarian emancipation. In an article entitled 'Réfutation nécessaire', published in 1909, he pointed out in his defence that for the past twenty-five years he had consistently counselled the workers to rely upon their own efforts and to steer clear of the State. 'I did not wait for the prophets of modern syndicalism', he commented, 'before drawing attention to the abuses of parliamentarism and the need to protect our organisations from them.'[6] In 1896 at the Congress of London he voted with Pouget and Pelloutier to defend the right to participate of those who did not endorse political action and in 1906 he again demonstrated his hostility to Guesdism by voting against the motion of Victor Renard and for the so-called Charter of Amiens presented by Griffuelhes. In 1910 he rejected the suggestion that the *syndicats* should follow the English example and form their own political party. To Montélimard's argument that the syndicalist movement had been singularly ineffective without parliamentary representation Keufer replied that the formation of such a party would seriously compromise and divide the *syndicats*. In a language similar to that used by his revolutionary colleagues within the CGT he charged that the intrusion of politics would open up the syndicalist movement to 'regrettable ambitions and depressing desertions'.[7] In *L'Humanité* he stated unambiguously: 'We are neither governmental syndicalists nor anti-governmental syndicalists: we are independent syndicalists'.[8]

For all that, Keufer and his associates on the reformist wing of the syndicalist movement were locked in a bitter and often acrimonious struggle with the revolutionary leadership of the CGT throughout the first decade of the twentieth century. In Keufer, Pierre Coupat (of the engineers' union) and Eugène Guérard (of the railwaymen) the reformists had a powerful leadership with considerable numerical support within the CGT. In 1909 their candidate, Louis Niel, replaced Griffuelhes as its general-secretary. From 1905 onwards the reformists, in addition to union papers such as Keufer's *La Typographie française*, had in *La Revue syndicaliste* what amounted to their own journal and in 1909 this was supplemented by *L'Action ouvrière* under the aegis of the reformist *Comité d'union syndicaliste*. They were also able to make their views known through the regular use of the 'tribune syndicale' column in Jaurès' *L'Humanité*.

If, as Félicien Challaye commented in 1909, the reformist syndicalists were less original and paradoxical than their revolutionary counterparts, they nevertheless represented a sizeable body of opinion within the syndicalist movement and they did so with considerable sophistication and energy. Their views were an integral part of any debate which took place within the CGT and so much so that Keufer could accuse Griffuelhes of suffering from what he characterised as 'keuferophobie'. The two sides were in fundamental disagreement upon most of the substantive points of syndicalist doctrine and no CGT conference was complete without the ritual of an ill-tempered quarrel between *each* faction. Where Challaye was mistaken was in his suggestion that the reformists were of only little interest in terms of ideas. The reformists, unlike the revolutionary leadership of the CGT, did not constitute an homogeneous group: they were brought together largely by tactical considerations. Auguste Keufer, as Berth correctly observed, was a positivist and as well as being the general secretary of the printers' union and the first treasurer of the CGT he also occupied the position of President of the *Cercle des prolétaires positivistes* from 1880 onwards. The place of Comtean positivism within the French labour movement has largely been ignored but in Keufer it has arguably its finest representative. Louis Niel, by contrast, gradually evolved towards reformism from an original position which had its inspiration in anarchism. In 1909, at the very moment that he became the champion of the reformist cause, he outlined a rudimentary social theory drawn primarily from Kropotkin's concept of mutual aid. That Sorel should dismiss this work, *Deux principes de vie sociale*, as 'an indication of the stupidity of a worker who believes himself to be clever'[9] not only tells us something about the biting invective used by him to disparage his opponents but also does not necessarily diminish its significance. The reformists, even if they did not attract supporters of the intellectual calibre of the 'nouvelle école' that gravitated around *Le Mouvement socialiste*, were a focal point of debate within syndicalist discourse. That the actual practice of the CGT came increasingly to conform to their ideas only serves to enhance their significance.

I

In the *Cours de philosophie positive* (1830–42) Auguste Comte sought to reduce acquired knowledge to a single body of homogeneous doctrine. By outlining a developmental epistemology of science, constructed around his now famous 'Law of the three stages', he hoped to show that all our intellectual endeavours could henceforth be organised around the principles of positivist science. If this were true of mathematics, astronomy, physics, chemistry and biology, so too it applied to the study of social phenomena in the form of a new discipline described by Comte as 'social physics'. The true purpose of Comte's scheme was revealed in his assertion that the reduction to order of intellectual anarchy, the creation of 'perfect mental harmony', would effectively put an end to moral and political anarchy. The key categories of the new social theory were to be 'order' and 'progress'.

In his later writings, and most notably in the *Système de politique positive* (1848–54) and the *Catéchisme positiviste* (1852), Comte, with considerable controversy, outlined the organisational and religious dimensions of the new social order. The subordination of temporal power in the hands of *les industriels* to the spiritual power legitimately embodied in a class of *savants* was not only to entail the virtual elimination of politics but was also to be crowned by a new 'cult of humanity' replete with its own positivist calendar, priesthood and rituals. Raised to a new religion, positivism symbolised 'the victory of social feeling over self-love'.[10]

Traditionally Comtean positivism has been regarded as an authoritarian and hierarchical doctrine — Charles Maurras, leader of *Action française* was, for example, one of the many right-wing thinkers attracted to Comte's critique of the excesses of individualism[11] — but it was also undoubtedly deeply concerned to improve the condition of the people and in Fabien Magnin, converted to positivism in the 1840s and executor of Comte's will, positivism had its first proletarian disciple.[12] An early example of positivist interest in the condition of labour can be found in the *Rapport à la société positiviste par la commission chargée d'examiner la question du travail* published in 1848 with a preface by Comte himself.[13]

Comte was an opponent of both laissez-faire economics and of socialism and communism. An economics which counselled neutrality before the forces of industry was a heresy to a philosophy which saw knowledge as prediction whilst socialism and communism were to be condemned for seeking political and economic solutions to problems which demanded moral reform. In Comte's view, the anarchy and injustice of industrial life derived not from the existence of private property and its unequal possession but from the abuses associated with its use. It was a mentality, not an institution, that needed to be abolished. Property would be socialised when the capitalists, whose talents Comte believed to be indispensable to the success of industry, recognised that ownership was not a privilege but implied social duty and when egoism had been replaced by altruism. United by a feeling of social solidarity, classes would remain but only in the sense that they would perform different functions.

After the death of Comte his ideas were subject to a wide, and often conflicting, series of interpretations but Fabien Magnin continued to spread the gospel of 'le positivisme ouvrier'.[14] In 1863 he established the *Cercle des prolétaires positivistes* which in 1870 formally affiliated to the First International. With the advent of the Third Republic and the rapid renascence of the workers' movement the positivists developed in greater detail their conception of the role and function of the proletariat. This process, which culminated in positivist opposition to the collectivist resolutions adopted at the Congress of Marseilles in 1879,[15] produced its most complete expression in a document entitled *Le Positivisme au congrès ouvrier* in which Magnin, Emile Laporte and Isidore Finance outlined the major components of the positivist strategy for proletarian emancipation.[16]

In their preface to this volume the authors specifically denied that positivism was 'an oppressive doctrine which . . . seeks to re-establish a past despotism'. Rather, they argued, the doctrine of Comte offered each individual the opportunity of developing their intellectual aptitudes to the full. There would be no castes or circumscribed classes. Positivism did, however, recognise that society would of necessity be divided into 'theoreticians' and 'practitioners' and that the latter group would itself be divided into 'entrepreneurs' and 'workers'. These divisions were an 'essential element' for the progress of society. The goal of positivism, therefore, was to define the precise and proper relationship between each group so as 'to ensure their cooperation for the attainment of the general good whilst preserving their respective independence'.[17]

The concern to safeguard the independence of the workers was reflected in positivist opposition to co-operative societies. Co-operatives were to be avoided not only because they did not work (few workers actually benefited from them) but primarily because they were divisive. Those workers who participated in them were transformed into disguised bosses and adopted a bourgeois mentality. 'The co-operative movement', Isidore Finance concluded, 'has become essentially bourgeois and conservative in the worst sense of the word'.[18]

An identical concern was manifest in Magnin's articulation of the positivist response to the parliamentary representation of the proletariat.[19] Participation in parliamentary politics would deprive the proletariat of its best elements. Further, Magnin characterised parliamentary assemblies as passing phenomena of doubtful and dubious worth. 'The extravagant pretension of our parliamentarians', he wrote, 'which leads them to speak ceaselessly about everything but above all about what they do not understand, contrasts conspicuously with the no less extravagant pretension of preventing the public from discussing things with which it is acquainted, which interest it and for which it is responsible'.[20] Under the influence of a 'few jolly clowns' the most important decisions were made by the ignorant and by what Magnin described as an 'infime minorité d'indécis'. The electoral system ensured that each citizen, regardless of his abilities, was deemed to be of equal worth and that voting – only a temporary activity according to the positivists – was seen as the primary social function. 'Through the vote,' Magnin remarked, 'every new idea is ordinarily thrust aside'.[21]

These sentiments, when voiced by Isidore Finance at the Congress of Marseilles, received enthusiastic applause. The proletarian positivists saw themselves as socialists — Finance talked of the need to develop a 'rational, scientific, positive socialism'[22] — and were of the opinion that they disagreed with the revolutionaries only in terms of means and not ends.[23] This view is only half true. The positivists, like the collectivist majority of Marseilles, sought to improve the lot of the workers and to replace an economic system which they believed to be characterised by exploitation and selfish individualism. They too clearly believed in the autonomy of the working-class movement. The disagreement on means was unambiguous. 'We prefer', Magnin and his colleagues wrote, 'peaceful, enduring, slow but sure changes to dangerous agitation'.[24] But what separated the positivists, above all, from the increasingly radical membership of the workers' movement was their view that in the future society classes would not be suppressed. Faithful to the dictates of Comte's original pronouncements the positivists held to the belief that the social problem did not demand a transfer of wealth or the abolition of property but rather 'the establishment . . . of a set of reciprocal duties between industrial leaders and their employees'.[25] Pierre Laffitte, who was largely responsible for converting Keufer to positivism, went so far as to argue that 'the political direction of societies belongs in the last analysis to the class of bankers'.[26] Education, not violence, was what was needed.

The positivist view of the State was that it should be reformed rather than abolished. Magnin, for example, wrote that 'the central power should divest itself of several unwieldy and useless functions . . . and limit itself to protecting the physical environment, external relations and finances'.[27] In institutional terms this was translated into support for the Republic as the system best suited to allow and make possible the existence of a positivist society. The Republic, Laffitte wrote in 1878, 'is not only necessary, it is also inevitable: it is the indispensable condition for the renovation of the Occident'.[28] In line with this positivists were prepared to participate in the activities of the State and from the 1890s onwards they were to be found in influential positions in consultative bodies such as the *Conseil supérieur du travail* and the *Office du travail*. Designed to facilitate mutual understanding between workers, employers and the State these organisations were the physical embodiment of the solidarist aspiration for social and economic peace. Amongst those involved were Auguste Keufer who became vice-president of the *Conseil supérieur du travail*. The minister of commerce was its president.

Born in Alsace in 1851 Auguste Keufer entered the printing trade in 1871. A year later he joined a union and in 1881 attended the inaugural congress of the *Fédération du livre* whose general-secretary he became in 1884. He remained in this post until 1920. Under his leadership the *Fédération du livre* became a powerful, well-organised and centrally-controlled union whilst the tactics it employed were frequently in marked contrast to those of the other workers' federations.[29] Joint employer-worker *commissions mixtes* were established in 1898 and in 1906 the *Fédération du livre* openly proclaimed that it would seek to implement a nine-hour day

and not the eight-hour day endorsed by the CGT. Keufer himself supported Millerand's entry into government in 1898 (and that of Viviani in
1906) and was frequently to be found in the company of government
ministers and employers. Both his own and his union's actions were, in
Keufer's view, perfectly in accord with the positivism he had adopted as
a young man and which he openly professed throughout his life. An active
participant in the cults and rituals of positivist religion, Keufer's writings
were as likely to be found in the *Revue occidentale* and the *Revue positiviste
internationale* as in *La Voix du peuple*.

Auguste Comte, according to Keufer, 'has taught us that the aim of
existence, the source of happiness, was to live for others'.[30] The history
of humanity, on this view, comprised a constant struggle between the
interests of the individual and the superior claims of the collectivity. The
present epoch was one in which the whole notion of public and private
duties had been abandoned and 'the most sacred general interests' had
therefore been 'subordinated to base egoism' and the 'pursuit of osten-
tatious pleasures'.[31] The special claim of positivism was that, upon the basis
of 'experimental method', it could replace the theological and materialistic
doctrines which had given rise to this situation of social anarchy and
instability and give to man a purely human destiny in which the collective
character of all actions would be recognised and accepted. Positivism,
Keufer wrote, 'has as its goal the purification of our sentiments, the
invigoration of our thoughts, the ordering and stimulation of the actions
of every one of us so that we might all devote our efforts to ensuring that
the social sense, the notion of duty in the carrying out of our respective
functions (from the most humble to the most elevated) always prevails'.[32]

In true Comtean fashion, therefore, Keufer was of the opinion that
what was needed was a mental and moral evolution on the part of all the
individuals who made up society and that the adoption of the positivist
'Religion of Humanity' would be the means through which this would be
obtained. For the positivists, Keufer observed, 'religion, freed from all
theological elements, [was] the necessary complement to education: it
unites men by a common faith and through the constant development of
the most generous sentiments of human nature is the best means of
regulating private and public life'.[33] What that religion would enable us
to appreciate, Keufer believed, was that the material and intellectual
wealth of a society was the product of the labours of successive generations
and that this heritage had been passed on and extended through the
centuries. It followed from this, according to positivist logic, that wealth
was social in origin and therefore that 'it should be equitably shared
between members of the present generation'.[34]

Keufer, however, endorsed Comte's view that the social origin of wealth
did not entail communal ownership. The use to which wealth was put,
Keufer argued, was far more important than its possession and the present

abuses derived not from the existence of private property as the 'revolutionary doctrines' simplistically implied but from the 'distressing phenomenon' of 'the period of individualism that we were passing through'.[35] Private property, Keufer argued following Comte, was a source of initiative, energy and independence and the effect of its complete suppression would be to turn society into a 'vast agglomeration of individual wills living without ties, without direction'.[36]

The implications of this position, as Keufer readily and frequently acknowledged, were profound and its espousal had dramatic consequences. For Keufer, in contrast to the revolutionary leadership of the CGT, the attempt to establish a 'communist society' with producers' associations grouped around the *syndicats* as its basis was a 'chimerical' nonsense. He stated categorically:

I have never believed that this organisation [the *syndicat*] would be sufficient to bring about the material, intellectual and moral transformation of the world, to direct society, to secure the acquisition of materials, the manufacture of products, their planetary distribution: in a word, I have never nursed the hope that through this intermediary a new and perfect order would be set up where complete harmony, goodness and justice would reign for ever.[37]

What the positivists wanted to see was a situation in which the bosses and capitalists would consider themselves as 'managers' of the 'social wealth (la richesse sociale)' which was in their possession.[38] There was no need for what Keufer described as 'the brutal re-distribution of capital'.[39]

There remained, therefore, a series of crucial questions. By what mechanism were the industrialists to be constrained to recognise their responsibility and obligation to utilise their wealth in a manner conducive to the social and general interest? Given that positivism accepted 'the constant development of inequalities between individuals' how was a system which characteristically saw 'the crushing of the weak by the strong' to be replaced?[40] What role, if any, was the proletariat to play in this process and how was it to benefit? More specifically, what function was the *syndicat* to perform and what tactics was it to employ?

Auguste Comte, Keufer wrote, 'deserves the gratitude of the proletariat because he has assigned to it the role that it ought to occupy in modern society'.[41] That role derived from several qualities attributed by positivism to the working class. At one level, the proletariat was perceived, in Keufer's phrase, as 'the powerful trunk which spreads sap throughout the whole of society'.[42] It was, in other words, the source of a society's energies and intelligence, its basic raw material. The proletariat was also, Keufer remarked, the place of return for those members of the bourgeoisie defeated by struggle and misfortune. Less frequently the 'active' proletariat which included both manual and factory workers and inventors

(amongst whom positivism and Keufer placed such luminaries as Guten-
berg and Montgolfier) was accredited with an essential role in the satisfaction of a society's material needs and requirements but, in contrast with
revolutionary syndicalism, little emphasis was placed upon the primacy of
production, and hence of the producer, in social life. For positivism, the
primary function of the proletariat arose not from its economic role but
from what Keufer in 1914 described as its 'habitual unselfishness and social
feeling'. The impartial and generous sentiments traditionally displayed by
the working class coupled with its numerical strength made it the ideal
candidate for the task described by positivists as 'appréciation'. The proletariat was to operate as the constant and permanent judge of the acts of
all those who exercised social, political and economic power. In effect,
the proletariat was to embody an enlightened or 'true public opinion',
which through its intellectual and moral force would be sufficient to ensure
that political authority was not abused and that the owners of capital
would use their wealth to the benefit of society as a whole. The proletariat's 'mission d'appréciation', Keufer argued, would mean that it would
'be able to impose the performance of their social duty upon industrial
leaders, entrepreneurs and the holders of temporal power on pain of
moral stigma and excommunication'.[43]

The positivist diagnosis of the ills of contemporary society recognised
that the proletariat was not as yet mentally equipped to perform such a
function. Left to themselves, existing in a situation of poverty and
'deprived of a positivist education', the workers were a prey to outmoded
metaphysical doctrines and the blandishments of the parliamentary
regime. They were, in short, in need of guidance but the only guidance
they were receiving came from irresponsible journalists and incompetent
intellectuals who, lacking any ideal, threatened to destroy the very basis
of society. What was desperately required, positivist orthodoxy decreed,
was the creation of a 'new spiritual power', a moral authority embodying
the positivist doctrine of social duty, which would act in alliance with the
proletariat. 'Auguste Comte', Keufer wrote, 'foresaw the indispensable
collaboration of a noble idea (*une grande pensée*) which enlightens and a
great force which acts'.[44]

What form was this 'new spiritual power' to take? It was to be composed
of '*savants*', intellectuals, men of the highest general culture, who had
refused to participate in the activities of 'temporal power' and who scorned
the attractions of material wealth. They were to act as 'informed, disinterested and respected' advisers to the proletariat, even to the point of
preventing the workers themselves from committing 'errors' and 'abuses'.
Through their counsel, the proletariat was to be raised above the pressing
and narrowing concerns of daily life to an awareness of its broader social
obligations. At another level, the new spiritual power was to challenge
those who had misled the proletariat. It must, Keufer wrote, 'energetically

censure those who, irresponsibly and without concern for the consequences, waste their abilities . . . in dangerous activities, leading astray
the opinions of the masses or corrupting their feelings and thus pretending
to acquire a reputation for originality and philosophical independence
whilst troubling and perverting the popular conscience and good sense'.[45]

When, however, Keufer referred to the spiritual and moral aid required
by the proletariat he cited not only that to be provided by the new
intellectual priesthood. In line with Comte's later description of women
as 'le sexe aimant' and their elevation in the 'cult of humanity' into semi-
religious objects of veneration and reverence, Keufer spoke of a necessary
coalition between the proletariat, the *savants*, and women who, as 'le sexe
affectif', would reveal to man the power of love and the deeper feelings
of his emotional life. Anyone who had read Comte, Keufer remarked,
'would appreciate the true role that [woman] exercises in the development
of general sentiments not just in children but also in men; they would
appreciate how she contributes to the improvement of general
sociability'.[46]

The positivist vision of the future, therefore, was one in which the
'active' proletariat, guided by both 'the new spiritual power' and a sancti-
fied womanhood, would exercise a permanent and pervasive moral authority over a 'temporal power' composed of a property-owning industrial
class. Social peace, which itself was taken to be a desirable goal, would
only exist when this had been attained and in societal terms this meant
that the proletariat would at last have been fully incorporated into the
society to which it belonged. Keufer was in no doubt about what this
offered the workers. 'The proletarians of both sexes', he wrote, 'ought to
be assured of a normal, full education capable of bringing the classes
together; beyond this they should receive a regular, well-paid job and
possession of a home, thus dispelling the cruel worries of working-class
life'.[47] For the community at large Keufer was equally clear as to its
significance. 'Positivism', he wrote, 'wishes to re-organise society without
god or king through the cult of Humanity'.[48]

If this was the overall positivist framework through which Keufer viewed
the emancipation of the proletariat he nevertheless accepted the necessity
of proletarian organisation in the form of the *syndicat*. The fact of the
matter was that upon Keufer's own admission the proletariat faced a
powerful capitalist class 'lacking any social feeling' which was prepared to
use all the means at its disposal to defend its privileges and thwart the
legitimate aspirations of the working class. To overcome this 'blind resistance' and 'odious egoism', Keufer argued, the proletariat was obliged 'to
act, to defend itself, to fight every day so as to proceed in a *continuous
manner* towards a better and final social order'.[49] No other institution or
'religious doctrine' was as able as the *syndicat* to 'impose' duties upon the
rich and thus put an end to the insecurity which was a consequence of the

present economic disorder. Parliamentarians, Keufer remarked, 'could not perform miracles and the placing of a ballot paper in a ballot box could not transform the social order'. Like his positivist forbears Keufer questioned the efficacy of co-operatives and was left to conclude that it was 'infinitely more safe to act in our *syndicats*'.[50]

Furthermore, Keufer was able to find a crucial place for the *syndicat* in the education of the proletariat. 'What will be', he asked, 'the authoritative and respected educational organ which will teach the young apprentice, then the worker, his duties towards his comrades in the factory?'.[51] With the partial demise of the family Keufer appeared to concede that women were unable to fulfil this role with any great success. Likewise it was unrealistic, given the absence of family ties, to expect its performance by other workers, no matter how dedicated they might be. The task, therefore, fell to the *syndicat*. But in contrast to the revolutionary syndicalists Keufer insisted both that the education provided by the *syndicat* was not sufficient unto itself and that this education was to be of a largely professional character. Citing Pelloutier with approval he argued that sheer numbers were not sufficient to ensure victory to the proletariat and therefore that it was 'important above all else that the members of the *syndicat* acquire a personal value (*une valeur personnelle*), that they pursue steadfastly their intellectual and moral development'.[52] It was to be through the *syndicat* that the worker was to acquire the sentiments of social solidarity and professional obligation which would enable him to combat the 'greed and demands of the bosses'.

Keufer was adamant that broader issues – for example, theories and conceptions relating to property, the family, government and parliament, employers and wage-earners – were not directly the *syndicats'* concern and should be left to what in those writings not dealing explicitly with positivism he described obliquely as 'another organ, another institution'.[53] However, as his revolutionary colleagues appreciated, this fitted uneasily with his assertion that the *syndicats* should, as their 'first obligation', make their members understand 'the necessity for the study of professional and social questions and this because their preoccupations must embrace the whole of the workers' interests'.[54] Where, by contrast, Keufer was in agreement with the leadership of the CGT was in his belief that the general education received by the proletariat should not inculcate the workers with 'excessive ambitions' and a distaste for manual labour or produce 'déclassés'.[55]

To complete this description of the *syndicat* as both an instrument of struggle and of proletarian education Keufer produced a detailed account of what he took to be the appropriate structure and activities of the syndicalist movement. At its heart, and in opposition to the 'méthode révolutionnaire', was a defence of what Keufer termed the 'méthode organique'. Keufer liked to think that this strategy was the outcome of reflection upon his own daily practice but in truth it owed much to a comparison between the British and French trade union movements. If Pouget's knowledge of the British unions convinced him of the revolutionary potential of the *syndicat* Keufer drew a more conventional conclusion. In 1898 Keufer provided a preface to *Les Syndicats ouvriers en Angleterre* written by another proletarian positivist François Fagnot.[56] Fagnot's book was itself largely a commentary upon *The History of Trade Unionism* by Sidney and Beatrice Webb, recently translated into French, and in its writing Fagnot had received assistance from British positivists such as Frederic Harrison and union leader Robert Applegarth. Fagnot's argument was a simple one. If they were to obtain the same commendable results, Fagnot stated, 'the French workers are obliged, by force of circumstance, to organise themselves in the same manner as that adopted by their English comrades'.[57] Keufer concurred. The strength of the British unions, he argued, derived in part from the moderate and 'organic' character of the anglo-saxon population but in the main it was the result of their concentration upon the more immediate and practical goals of the daily struggle, 'la lutte quotidienne'. The British unions, in line with positivism but unlike their French counterparts, recognised that 'the basic foundations of the social order were beyond all attempts at complete overthrow' and therefore that it was 'puerile' to believe that one could destroy, either in an instant or in a series of violent acts, a set of institutions or habits which, in Keufer's phrase, reflected 'the real needs of our nature'.[58] The correct emphasis, as the British unions demonstrated, was upon the gradual and piecemeal improvement of the position and status of the working class.

In the first decade of the twentieth century Keufer frequently restated this conclusion and sketched out its practical implications.[59] On this view, the 'principal mission' or function of the *syndicat* was to determine the conditions of work experienced by each occupational group within the proletariat. The *syndicat's* first and most immediate concern, therefore, was to raise the salaries of its members and, where possible, introduce a reduction in working hours. Referring to the 'sophism' which stated that wage increases were a 'deception', Keufer denied that there existed an exact correspondence between wages and the prices of commodities. Equally desirable was the removal of the numerous unfair restrictions and regulations existing in factories which diminished the independence and dignity of the worker. The *syndicat* also had an important role to play in the supervision and development of industrial apprenticeships, securing better hygiene at work and, where needed, in finding jobs for their members through their 'service de placement'. 'In working-class life', Keufer commented, 'if salary plays an important role, it is no less true that the possession of a job and security for the future constitutes one of the most serious worries'.[60] Like the British unions, Keufer hoped that all the *syndicats* would provide a range of 'secondary' services and benefits to include financial assistance in cases of illness, unemployment, old-age and death. Those services, he believed, were the practical manifestation of 'la solidarité syndicale' and it was through them that the sentiments of loyalty and camaraderie were built up amongst workers in the factory, between members of the same trade, and towards the *syndicat* itself. An element of prudence was also involved. For some years, Keufer commented, he had believed that the workers would come to the *syndicat* for disinterested reasons: disabused of this notion he now recognised that 'it was above all through the bait of certain advantages' that the *syndicats* would attract significant numbers. Keufer also believed that financial support needed to be provided to strikers. Distancing himself from those who believed that *élan* was sufficient to secure victory, he argued that to be successful a strike required more than strong convictions and determination on the part of the participants.

Where Keufer's positivist convictions intruded strongly into his account of the 'méthode organique' was in his assessment of the appropriate response to the problems posed by female labour. Keufer's own union, the *Fédération du livre*, was implacably opposed to the employment of women in the printing industry and this accorded with Keufer's own views. As a positivist, he proclaimed, he saw female labour in factories and offices as 'a social disaster, as a real cause of the plague of alcoholism, the lowering of the moral standards of young people, domestic disharmony and the disintegration of the family'.[61] If women were to fulfil their 'natural' and 'moral' mission as educators of man they needed to be freed from industrial tyranny and exploitation and allowed to stay within the home and the family. Keufer did, however, recognise that for some women — notably those responsible for dependents and those who wished to remain unmarried — this was not a feasible alternative. In this circumstance the responsibility of the *syndicat* was to ensure that the added competition for jobs did not lead to a lowering of wages and that the principle of 'equal work for equal pay' was always observed. Keufer, as the Couriau affair was later to demonstrate clearly, had little time for what he referred to as 'a feminism inspired by a blind vanity'.[62]

Corresponding to this outline of the reformist goals to be pursued by the *syndicats* was an unambiguous statement of what were considered to be the admissible methods of action. For Keufer negotiation and dialogue were always preferable to 'intransigence, threats and struggle to the bitter end'. Only after 'amicable' discussions between the two sides in a dispute had broken down was strike action to be considered. A defender of joint employer-worker commissions, Keufer acknowledged that in certain situations the intervention of outside forces — including municipal officers, prefects, priests, bishops, politicians and 'even ministers' — might have its uses in resolving conflict. 'I realise', Keufer wrote, 'that this method does not suit the supporters of revolutionary action who fear calm on the pretext that it will lead to a lessening of energy and the suffocation of agitation and revolt'.[63]

Similarly Keufer recognised the utility in present conditions of parliamentary legislation. 'Is it necessary', he asked, 'that public opinion should be entirely transformed, that a respected spiritual power should exist, before so many abuses and miseries are remedied?'.[64] If, in other words, the long term goal of positivism remained the 'suppression of the parliamentary regime' and its deceptions and malpractices, in the short term reforms introduced by the State could significantly ameliorate the conditions experienced by many workers who, as yet, were 'incapable of protecting themselves'. If for no other reason, the power of the centralised State was needed to counterbalance the 'no-less centralised' and previously unknown power of industry which, if left unchecked, was capable of committing arbitrary excesses. Keufer, therefore, lent his support to parliamentary legislation specifically criticised by the likes of Pelloutier and Pouget such as that regulating female and child labour and accidents at work and to much more legislation besides.

Nevertheless, Keufer was clear that there were definite limits to the desirability of State action and that, whenever possible, the workers should dispense with the assistance of politicians and intellectuals. For the workers to behave otherwise would be to 'paralyse their initiative and effective intervention in the social struggle'. And, as there were occasions when the employers were not amenable to peaceful negotiation, situations arose when, however reluctantly, the proletariat had to contemplate and, where necessary, resort to strike action.

Every worker, whatever his trade, possessed, in Keufer's view, the right to strike. 'No rule, no order, no force', he stated, 'can remove the individual and collective liberty to withdraw labour when those involved wish it or when they believe it to be of use to defend their interests'.[65] There were, however, appropriate conditions in which this right was to be used and a range of actions associated with it which rendered strikes, in Keufer's eyes, as either legitimate or illegitimate.[66]

Strikes, for Keufer, were 'an extreme means' of defence or attack. They were not to be seen as a normal state of affairs or as part of a 'permanent war between the employees and employers'. A strategy of continuous strikes, leading to a hoped-for revolutionary general strike, was both inexpedient and undesirable. 'I do not believe', Keufer wrote, 'that this ideal society will suddenly appear complete out of the revolutionary chaos, the general disorder for which strikes will have been the prelude, the preparation'.[67] It was, he argued, naive and reckless to imagine that the bourgeoisie and the government would leave themselves defenceless before the revolutionary onslaught. Repeated strikes would provoke concerted resistance and an inevitable reaction in public opinion against the worker's cause. Defeated, the proletariat would be discouraged and exhausted whilst the *syndicats* would lay dismembered and powerless before their united opponents. 'I have nothing to say', Keufer commented, 'on the question of the general strike . . . and I categorically deny its efficacy as a means of effecting the expropriating revolution (*la révolution expropriatrice*), of bringing about the total transformation of society'.[68]

Implicit within this critique of a policy of systematic strike action was a rejection, in principle, of the use of violence in all its forms. Violence against persons could never be seen as 'a normal means of progress' and this view was extended by Keufer to include threats against individuals, what he termed 'manoeuvres frauduleuses' or deceptions and corruption, and unlawful attempts to interfere with liberty at work. On the use of sabotage Keufer was unequivocal. Sabotage, he wrote, is 'a system which lacks morality, courage, dignity and which cannot attain with any certainty the goal for which it was used'.[69] Amongst the morally acceptable and workable tactics to be employed by the workers were '*la résistance passive*' such as go-slows, picketing 'without threat or violence', the use of consumers' boycotts, placing bad employers on an index and granting good ones a seal of approval, 'la marque syndicale'. Keufer could, nevertheless, understand what inspired acts of violence. 'Personally', he wrote, 'on more than one occasion I have felt a sentiment of violent revolt before the intransigence and callousness of the employers. The desire to destroy has taken hold of me'.[70] In *Education syndicale* he remarked that he would have willingly gone to prison as recompense for an act of violence if the gesture had been able to assure success by inflicting a 'just punishment' upon an employer or upon strike-breakers.[71] Force, Keufer acknowledged, could sometimes bring a boss to see reason. But his overall view remained that violence was morally indefensible and of doubtful utility. Direct action could be 'accidentally revolutionary' but it should be 'pacific and organic'.

Keufer was also prepared to place a further restriction upon strike action. 'If this right exists beyond all question', Keufer noted, 'we must not forget that a society cannot live if each citizen claims only his rights without concerning himself with the duties he has to fulfil'.[72] There were circumstances where a strike could have dire consequences and became a 'public calamity'. The suspension of work by workers in key social services relating to hygiene, hospitals, the provision of food and so on would not harm the rich, the capitalists, the bourgeoisie but would adversely affect 'the whole population, even the mass of the people'. For this reason Keufer suggested that these trades could be saved the need for strike action by the establishment of joint committees responsible both for ensuring that employees enjoyed 'honourable conditions of work' and for resolving disputes.[73] It was this suggestion when voiced by Keufer in an interview in *La Petite République* which led Griffuelhes to argue that such no-strike agreements would leave the workers involved in a powerless position.[74]

The final element of the 'méthode organique' was an advocacy of an appropriate organisational structure for the syndicalist movement that differed markedly from that endorsed by anarchists within the CGT. In place of a decentralised and skeletal structure relying heavily upon the personal initiative of *minorités agissantes* and which exuded a distrust of administrators and bureaucracy Keufer sought to create a well-financed, efficient and competent system of administration for the *syndicats*.[75] 'What real force', he commented, 'do those organisations represent which every morning wish to carry out a revolution and which do not even possess the means to pay their modest rent?'.[76] To perform their numerous and complicated functions the *syndicats* needed the requisite financial resources and in order to secure them individual subscriptions, '*cotisations*', had to be substantially increased. Higher membership fees would free the *syndicats* and *bourses du travail* from funding by municipal authorities and thus give genuine substance to what, under the revolutionaries, was only the rhetoric of proletarian independence. Keufer also saw the necessity for a well-trained, permanent staff, free from the worry of frequent re-election, which would be able to guarantee the sound management and running of the *syndicats*. Finally, for Keufer the model *syndicat* was to be composed not of a class-conscious minority but of the mass of the workers in a particular trade. Only if this were the case could durable results be obtained.[77]

To attract the majority of the proletariat to the *syndicats* Keufer consistently argued that they should observe a strict 'neutrality' in all 'philosophical, political and religious matters'. He opposed, as he demonstrated in the key debate at the Congress of Amiens in 1906, the intrusion into the syndicalist movement of a whole series of issues which, in his opinion, had an explicitly political dimension and which were alien to the *syndicats'* purely professional concerns. Foremost in this category were the 'anarchist doctrines' of anti-militarism and anti-patriotism. Everyone should be free to propagate or combat these views, Keufer believed, but 'outside the *syndicats*'.[78]

Keufer's own response to these subjects was again heavily indebted to positivism and served to distance him further from the prevailing mood within the CGT.[79] 'During the first years which followed the war of 1870', Keufer wrote, 'I remained a fervent supporter of revenge, *la revanche*'.[80] A native of Alsace, upon his own testimony it had been positivism which had cured him of this emotion by enabling him to recognise that two nations could not be thrust into a 'horribly bloody and atrocious war' to recover the lost territories. Nevertheless positivism provided Keufer with a framework within which there was a place for an attachment to '*la patrie*'.

The positivist schema saw civilisation passing through three distinct and successive stages. The first phase was 'la période conquérante' in which

peoples and nations were formed. This was followed by 'la période défens-
ive' in which the possibilities of war were daily diminished and culminated
in the third period, the 'pacific and industrial regime', with as its logical
consequence the simultaneous abolition of all armies. Humanity presently
stood at the point of transition between the last two stages. Under the
pressure of greater intellectual, artistic and industrial collaboration
between nations the military spirit was weakening but the world was still
subject to bitter national rivalries that, if no longer inspired by the pursuit
of territorial expansion, had their source in economic competition.

The mission of the proletariat (and also the special mission of France),
Keufer believed, was to push society towards the realisation of a durable
peace but in the present circumstances it was rash and foolish to believe
that armed conflicts were about to disappear before a few demonstrations
against militarism and patriotism. 'The army', Keufer concluded, 'will
remain an organ of defence, the national group will continue to exist and
it ought to preserve all its strength as ought any individual who wishes to
live and to take action'.[81]

According to Comte, Pierre Laffitte wrote, the nation, *la patrie*, was to
be a City confined to the natural limit of the territory sufficient to sustain
it and in which lived families, bound by ties of affection, with a common
past and who worked towards a common future. With the acceptance of
the religion of humanity, it was argued, 'positivism would demand the
political decomposition of France'[82] and the same would be expected of
all other nations.[83] In the new positivist order, the centralised State would
vanish and, shorn of all intermediaries, all that would remain would be
the units of the family, the city and humanity.

In the short term, however, positivists reconciled themselves both to
the State in the form of the Republic (as we have already seen) and to
the notion of France as *la patrie*. The sentiments of altruism and social
solidarity, nurtured in the family, were only gradually to extend beyond
national borders to encompass first the West (hence the frequent reference
to the Occident in positivist discourse) and then to the remainder of the
world, the Orient, presently subject to the 'theocratic regime'. The nation
in the interim acted to enlarge the feeling of sociability between individuals
by making each citizen aware of the general significance and impact of his
actions. 'National loyalty (*le sentiment national*)', Comte wrote, 'becomes
a genuine intermediary between domestic affection and universal love'.[84]

For Keufer, in consequence, 'the collectivity called one's country' was
not an artificial or superficial entity brought into existence by accident but
something which had roots deep in the past. 'It is', he maintained, 'an
aggregate of labour, sorrows, sufferings, intellectual and moral endeavours
formed by the passing of the centuries'.[85] In the nation, people spoke
the same language, observed the same moral code, accepted the same
obligations and were guided by the 'same historic traditions'. This applied

equally to all its members including the workers who, like every citizen, had benefited from 'the social heritage passed on by their ancestors' and who, through the protection afforded by the nation, had themselves been able to develop into men and 'useful' citizens. 'Yes', Keufer replied to *Le Mouvement socialiste's 'enquête'*, 'the worker . . . has a homeland (*patrie*) and he can be a patriot'.[86] What Keufer wanted to see was the emergence of what he referred to as 'a purified patriotism', a love of one's own country without a hatred of other peoples.

Keufer therefore was unable to lend his support to the revolutionary tactic of '*la grève générale militaire*'. There was no evidence, he argued, to suggest that the French example would be followed elsewhere and if employed in France alone it would be with dangerous and deadly consequences. A wiser and more practical procedure was to organise the proletariat at an international level and through it to propagandise for an end to war and the politics of conquest. If simultaneously the *savants* pursued an identical course, the combined efforts to engender a new higher morality would bring into existence 'the final regime of humanity, the pacific regime'. To act, however, as if such a situation already existed was to fall prey to a 'dangerous Utopia'.

On the vexed question of the intervention by the army in strikes, Keufer had some advice for his colleagues. Faced by this abuse of force the *syndicats* needed to campaign for the neutrality of the army in all industrial disputes but in turn the *syndicats* themselves had to use their influence and authority to ensure that during strikes acts of violence were avoided. If order and the security of persons and property were guaranteed, he suggested, the army was less likely to intervene on the side of the capitalists.[87]

In theory, the positivist project was a radical one. The political order was to be progressively dismantled to make way for a new society dominated by a spiritual power in the form of *les savants*. This group was to embody a supreme authority derived solely from its role as the principal representatives and purveyors of the positivist cult of humanity. States and nations were to be disbanded and life itself was to be directed and guided by the all-encompassing concept of social duty. Shorn of its authoritarian and hierarchical trappings, from Magnin onwards positivism found a place for the workers within its overall frame of reference and offered them the prospect of a society in which their efforts and dignity would be properly recognised and rewarded. Part and parcel of this long-term project was by implication the eradication of all conventional forms of political citizenship associated with democratic society.

Nevertheless by holding out the twin objectives of 'order' and 'progress' Comtean positivism displayed an unconcealed desire to secure social stability and this, coupled with the proclivity to locate all issues within a pattern of social development which saw the realisation of the positivist order as a far-distant goal, meant that positivists were easily reconciled to the nation-state, the Republic and a form of economic organisation resting upon inequality and private property.

Keufer's views epitomise this ambivalent position. Drawn to syndicalism by a distaste for the impurities of political activity and the desire to improve the mental and material conditions of the working class he endorsed a reformist strategy which repeatedly placed the attainment of immediate and piecemeal gains before what he acknowledged to be desirable and more fundamental aims. In his hands, syndicalism, as evidenced by the conduct of his own union, was always to favour negotiation, compromise and dialogue with its opponents. A change of heart amongst industrialists was deemed to be more important than the expropriation of their wealth. It was this approach to syndicalist practice which brought him into permanent conflict with the revolutionary leadership of the CGT in the first decade of the twentieth century.

II

In 1910 Louis Niel published an article entitled 'Réflexions sur l'évolution syndicaliste' in the reformist *L'Action ouvrière*[88] in which he argued that the history of the syndicalist movement in France fell into three distinct phases. At their beginning in the early years of the Third Republic the actions of the *syndicats* were little different from those of the political parties. The second phase commenced around 1895 with the rise to prominence of the anarchists. It was, Niel commented, 'a period of enthusiasm, fanaticism, intransigence, verbiage, theoretical assertions and of absolutes'. Nothing was expected from the State, the law, Parliament or even the elector. The third and current phase, in his opinion, was marked by a *rapprochement* between the forces of Left and Right within the movement and represented a maximisation of 'reason, method and practical sense'. There was now, Niel remarked, a near unanimous acceptance of the fact that legal provisions could supplement and complete the activity of the *syndicats*. For all his endorsement of a strategy which derived from these developments, in the same article Niel was candid enough to admit that he himself had once been a 'convinced supporter' of the tactics utilised in the second phase. This was no idle jest.

Louis Niel first came to prominence in the mediterranean city of Montpellier. A former waiter, in 1901 at the age of 28, he became general-secretary of its *bourse du travail* and for some years after this southern and largely agrarian region remained his power base. An article published in *La Voix du peuple* in December 1900 gave a clear indication of his position. Attacking Millerand and supporting the idea of a general strike he called upon the workers 'to cease to be sheep' and to educate themselves so as to be worthy of the Revolution.[89] A year later he took up the cause of syndicalist unity arguing that if the workers were one day to be able to launch a successful general strike it was indispensable in the interests of effective action that the *bourses du travail* should be subordinated to the CGT.[90] His commitment to the revolutionary overthrow of the capitalist system was stated unambiguously in a pamphlet entitled *Les Syndicats et la révolution* published in 1902[91] in which he proclaimed that 'the *syndicats* will be revolutionary or they will not exist' and was confirmed the same year in an article which concluded by observing that 'in the same way that for certain illnesses surgery is better than medicine, so revolution is preferable to reforms. For the social problem we are on the side of the surgeons'.[92] These views were translated into biting attacks upon 'les jaunes',[93] endorsement of the superiority of the tactics of direct action[94] and calls for all syndicalists to recognise the revolutionary potential of the French peasantry.[95] His support for the revolutionary position, however, was best illustrated by his contribution to the debate on proportional representation at the Congress of Bourges in 1904.[96] In order to defend the privileged status of the revolutionary minority Niel utilised an argument which unashamedly drew upon a stereotyped picture of the differences of morals, character, temperament and history to be found in national groups. If the 'cold temperament' of the English, Americans and Germans explained their attraction to the mathematical simplicity and rigour embodied in the principle of proportional representation, 'amongst latins' like the French, Niel argued, it was 'will, intelligence and sentiment' that should guide action.[97] In 1905 he lent his support to the campaign for the immediate implementation of the eight-hour day arguing that the proletariat must 'impose' its demands upon the employers.[98] Here, and in a debate with Delesalle on the consequences of reducing the working day, he affirmed his belief in the veracity of the 'iron law of salaries'.[99]

It was in 1906 that Niel moved discernibly towards reformism. In the September of the previous year he had published an article entitled 'Le Parfait syndicalisme' in *La Voix du peuple* in which he explored what he took to be the relative merits of two very different unions, Keufer's printworkers and Merrheim's metalworkers. In the *Fédération du livre*, Niel argued, was to be found a high level of organisation and a wide range of services but an absence of 'revolutionary spirit' whilst in the *Fédération des métallurgistes* there existed a 'clear awareness of the necessity for a merciless struggle against the employers' combined with an almost total disregard for the material advantages that could accrue to the workers. The ideal was an amalgam of the best elements of both organisations as, in Niel's view, it was perfectly possible for a *syndicat* to provide material benefits to its members 'without weakening the revolutionary flame minus which syndicalism will only be a corpse'.[100]

What this amounted to saying was that the distinction between revol-

utionaries and reformists was a false and unnecessary one and this was to
be the line pursued by Niel in the years which immediately followed.
In 1909, for example, he published an article entitled 'Les Réformes
révolutionnaires'[101] in which he argued that every syndicalist who obtained
a reform which in some way diminished the economic power of the capitalists was accomplishing a revolutionary act.

At the same time, however, he campaigned vigorously for the observ-
ance of a strict political neutrality within the syndicalist movement and it
was this, in particular, that was progressively to distance him from such
men as Griffuelhes. At the Congress of Amiens in 1906 he criticised both
the socialists and the anarchists for what he saw as their desire to undermine the autonomy of the *syndicats*[102] and afterwards he continued to
attack the 'politique oblique' being foisted upon the syndicalist movement
by the rival supporters of parliamentary and anti-parliamentary action
(especially those designated by Niel as the 'hervéo-anarchistes'). Syndicalism, he argued, should not have a colour.[103]

This stance was best illustrated in his response to the issues of anti-
militarism and anti-patriotism. Although Niel acknowledged the logic of
the anti-patriotic argument and the desirability (if not the feasibility) of a
general strike in the event of war, he nevertheless told delegates at the
Congress of Marseilles in 1908 'you have no right to introduce these
questions into the *syndicats*'.[104] If, he argued elsewhere, the workers saw
clearly that the army defended the interests of French capitalists it was
not so certain that they understood that it also safeguarded German
capital. Therefore the *syndicats* were best advised to concentrate their
efforts solely upon anti-militarism which had a direct bearing upon the
daily livelihood of the proletariat and to leave the divisive and contentious
matter of anti-patriotism to one side.[105] Niel's position, as stated at Marseilles, was that the 'essential preoccupation' of syndicalism should be to
protect the purely 'professional and economic' interests of the workers.
As if to symbolise this attitude Niel warmly welcomed the American trade
union leader Samuel Gompers to France in 1909 with the commendation
that 'he regards anti-statism, anti-patriotism and anti-clericalism to be
none of his concern and it is no doubt because of this that he is so
powerful'.[106]

This argument contained a further all-important dimension. At Marseilles Niel argued that the *syndicat* could not alone bring about the emancipation of the proletariat. 'The task of social emancipation', he commented,
'is a complex one. Syndicalism has its role but you would be mistaken in
my eyes in wishing to make it achieve the whole task'.[107] Society, he later
remarked, was too vast and complicated to be amenable to simplistic
solutions[108] and for this reason the *syndicats*, whilst maintaining their
independence and autonomy, should acknowledge the utility of legislative
reform. 'With respect to parties', he argued, 'we ought to observe the

neutral and benevolent attitude that I propose and that was victorious at the 1906 Congress of Amiens: "Neither Alliance nor War" '.[109]

Niel's shift of viewpoint made him briefly the candidate of reformism within the CGT[110] and this coincided with the publication of the two fullest statements of his position. In *La Valeur sociale du syndicalisme*[111] Niel outlined what he took to be the political, economic and moral significance of the syndicalist movement. The roots of syndicalism, he argued, lay indubitably in the economic exploitation suffered by the working class and therefore its primary object lay in securing 'a more just distribution of production, better conditions of work whilst always pursuing as its end the most just distribution of production and the best conditions of work that it is possible to obtain through the suppression of the capitalist class'.[112] Syndicalism was thus to combine the dual functions of 'daily reform' and 'future revolution'. Syndicalism's political value lay in its capacity, through strikes, demonstrations, propaganda and so on, to exert external pressure upon the State so as to hasten the implementation of legal measures of benefit to the proletariat. Rather obliquely Niel also commented that syndicalism revealed the futility and inadequacy of reforms in bourgeois society. Morally, syndicalism raised the dignity of the worker and extended his love of liberty and sense of justice. If, Niel concluded, syndicalism was not sufficient on its own to transform the world it remained 'the most immediate and practical means that the workers could and ought to employ in their struggles'.[113]

Niel's concern to emphasise the moral dimension of syndicalism was made more explicit in *Deux principes de vie sociale*. Before us, Niel argued, lay the choice between two distinct principles of social organisation: 'la lutte pour la vie' and 'l'entente pour la vie'. The former described a bourgeois morality resting upon the existence of private property which itself was the outcome of theft and deception. Behaviour was primarily egoistic and men, viewed as unreflecting animals, were the subject of a Darwinian struggle for survival. By contrast the superior morality of *entr'aide*, mutual aid, drew upon a sense of social solidarity and an awareness that we live in a state of dependence upon other people. 'We have no difficulty in concluding with Kropotkin', Niel wrote, 'that the practice of mutual aid is more natural than that of struggle because if acts of solidarity were not more numerous than those of brutal egoism, life would not be possible and human society would not exist'.[114] The source of this new morality lay in the emerging conditions of work which favoured communal endeavour but nothing, Niel argued, did more to further its development than 'the practice of life in the *syndicats*'. There were, however, clear limits to the feelings of solidarity. It could only operate amongst individuals having interests in common and could not, as a consequence, exist between workers and their bosses. It followed that to attain a higher level of solidarity it would be necessary to remove the principal obstacle to its full attainment: private property, 'the source of struggle, competition and of egoism'. 'L'entente pour la vie', therefore, demanded the existence of common ownership as the basis of a 'new world of well-being and liberty'.[115] In that new society, Niel concluded echoing Sorel and Pouget, the struggle between men would be replaced by the struggle against the elements, against the earth, disease and the causes of death. 'In other words', he stated, 'there is nothing which produces more slavery than the artificial liberty of the *struggle for life* and nothing which produces more liberty than the artificial slavery of *co-operation for life*'.[116]

Niel's position was thus a very different one from that adopted by Keufer. Placed at the time amongst the more revolutionary of the reformists he did not dispute the desirability or ultimate feasibility of the eradication of an economic system based upon private property with all its attendant social ills and injustices.The impression, however, is that he came increasingly to regard the complete and final emancipation of the proletariat as a far-distant goal and that in the interim it was more important for the *syndicats* to pursue the realisation of immediate and piecemeal improvements in the workers' condition. This perspective was bolstered by reference to what was taken to be the unreadiness of the proletariat for the massive task ahead of it and to the numerical weakness of the syndicalist movement itself. To this end the *syndicats* were advised to limit their activities to those issues directly relevant to the professional and economic interests of the proletariat and to leave to one side such extraneous matters as anti-patriotism which, in Niel's view, only served to deter the workers. The *syndicats*, in effect, had to offer the proletariat real and tangible results. 'It is not with symbolic bread' Niel commented, 'that one assuages the hunger of millions of workers who cannot wait'. To work each day towards the realisation of a new reform whilst infusing all reformist action with the broader ideal of justice and an end to economic slavery was, he argued, 'the true *gymnastique révolutionnaire*.'[117] In the eyes of his opponents, however, Niel's roots in the agrarian south, if nothing else, served to explain how he had lost all sight of the final goal of complete emancipation through the destruction of capitalism.

III

Debate between the revolutionary and reformist wings of the syndicalist movement grew apace after the Congress of Montpellier. In 1903 Pouget and Keufer exchanged views in two articles entitled 'Réformes et révolution'.[118] Asserting that no major disagreement existed between the rival factions and that the whole affair was a plot by politicians to divide the syndicalists, Pouget concluded by stating that there was no need for Keufer and he to be enemies just because 'in order to get from Paris to Saint-

Etienne he prefers to go by train and I prefer the automobile'. Keufer's contribution, however, was less conciliatory and pursuing what was to become a familiar theme he immediately castigated the revolutionaries for their intolerance of other people's views. Whilst he was against the entry of politics into the *syndicats*, he argued, 'I have never declared that political action, exercised individually and outside the *syndicats* by their members, was useless'. Keufer's unrestrained tone set the scene for what was to become an increasingly acrimonious dispute.

At the Congress of Bourges in 1904 each issue under discussion turned into a battle between the two groups, with Keufer acting as the central figure opposing the revolutionary leadership. The conference itself had been preceded by the publication by *L'Action directe* (to which Pouget, Griffuelhes and Delesalle were contributors) of a special issue devoted to examining 'le Danger positiviste' and this served to strengthen Keufer's conviction that the statutes of the CGT were being violated and that his own union was being unfairly treated and denigrated by its opponents. 'It is the duty of the Congress', he asserted, 'to affirm the respect for the autonomy of all organisations whatever their method of action'. Keufer (though not Niel) followed this up by an unsuccessful, and heavily defeated, call for the introduction of proportional representation and concluded his contribution to the conference by challenging the wisdom of seeking the immediate implementation of the eight-hour day. For all this, the leadership of the CGT secured easy victories on all the motions discussed and for the first time the Congress committed the syndicalist movement to campaign against militarism and war.[119]

Hostilities were renewed at Amiens in 1906. Having first expressed their support for Esperanto, delegates at the conference moved on to discuss the crucial issue of the relationship between the CGT and the newly unified socialist party (SFIO). The two sides united to defeat the socialist Victor Renard's proposal for closer collaboration but Keufer's own motion stating that the CGT should no longer be 'an instrument of anarchist and anti-militarist agitation' was not even put to the vote. That the official resolution subsequently known as the Charter of Amiens (drawn up, according to Edouard Dolléans, by Griffuelhes, Pouget, Delesalle, Niel and André Morizet in a restaurant) was then adopted by 830 votes to 8 should have been sufficient to indicate to all concerned that it was open to a wide variety of interpretations and this proved, indeed, to be the case. For the reformists, and especially for Louis Niel who raised it into an article of faith, Amiens was an acknowledgement that the CGT was to observe a strict neutrality in all political issues whilst the revolutionaries saw it as a vindication of their defence of direct, revolutionary action. The conference concluded by re-affirming, after the briefest of debates, the need for anti-militarist propaganda thus demonstrating that for the time being it was to be the interpretation of the revolutionaries that was to be observed.[120]

For the next three years the debate continued unabated and with increased bitterness. Whilst the reformists through the pages of *La Revue syndicaliste* continued their fight for what was described as a 'well-organised, absolutely autonomous syndicalism, independent of all political attachments',[121] the revolutionaries, exercising tight editorial control, pressed home their message via *La Voix du peuple*. Keufer, in articles bearing such titles as 'Misérable comédie' and 'Les Justiciers du syndicalisme',[122] complained that he was being blamed 'for all the sins of Israel' and countered by remarking that his union had secured more improvements for the working class than its reputedly more revolutionary rivals. 'The whole argument levelled against me', he commented, 'is demolished by this simple statement'.[123] Niel, in the self-styled role of conciliator, advocated a centrist strategy designed ostensibly to foster 'moral unity' within the syndicalist movement but this concordance of views, as his opponents were aware, was only to be obtained by the effective exclusion of what he referred to as the 'parliamentary and anti-parliamentary camps'.[124] Undaunted, the leadership of the CGT, by its strident rhetoric and actions, pressed on with its policy of confrontation with the employers and the Clemenceau government. During 1907 strikers were killed at Nantes, Narbonne and Roan l'Etape and, to the delight of the revolutionaries, a detachment of troops mutinied en route to the scene of a labour dispute.[125]

1908 saw further dramatic events. At the beginning of August, after two months of turbulent strike activity, Clémenceau responded by imprisoning Griffuelhes, Yvetot, Pouget and other leading members of the CGT's Confederal Committee. The following month the CGT met at Marseilles and, despite the absence of their principal spokesmen, the revolutionaries again carried the day. A motion calling for the introduction of proportional representation was defeated and the Congress re-affirmed its intention, in the event of the declaration of war, to call a 'revolutionary general strike'. The reformists, however, unequivocally blamed the reckless tactics pursued by their colleagues for the fatalities of the previous 18 months.[126]

The CGT's imprisoned leaders were released on 31 October but they proved to be unable to regain their position of ascendency. Following accusations of financial irregularities in the administration of the CGT's new headquarters, the *Maison des Fédérations*, Griffuelhes resigned on 2 February 1909, only to be replaced by Louis Niel who secured election to the position of general-secretary by only one vote. Niel's success was warmly greeted by his supporters. According to Keufer, for example, his election meant a recognition of 'free action for every organisation, courteous discussion of methods, mutual consideration'.[127] Pouget, in contrast, under the scathing title 'Victoire ministérielle' commented: 'our class enemies would be mistaken to claim victory. The election of Niel in no way modifies syndicalist attitudes. The battle will continue as energetically and as vigorously as before'.[128]

Niel himself quickly ran into trouble. In March a strike by post office employees began and after what appeared to be broken government promises the CGT called a general strike of support in May. This call received little response and the post office workers quickly returned to work but the revolutionaries felt able to attribute this humiliating failure to Niel who, on the eve of the strike, had made a speech, the so-called 'Discours de Lens', in which he had commented that in his opinion the workers were neither 'sufficiently strong, conscious nor rebellious to obtain success'.[129] Niel duly resigned on 26 May 1909 to be replaced by Griffuelhes' virtually unknown candidate, Léon Jouhaux. The revolutionaries seemed again to be in control but the situation was such, according to Keufer, that it was only what he described as a 'marriage forcé' which prevented the syndicalist movement from splitting into two.[130]

The level of abuse was such that the issues at stake tended to become hidden behind a welter of personal insults but it should be clear that the open conflict which erupted within the CGT during the first half of 1909 had its roots in profound disagreements on issues of principle and tactics. In March 1909 Niel published an article entitled 'A l'oeuvre tous, pour les résultats' in *La Voix du peuple* which produced a simultaneous (and presumably co-ordinated) response from the revolutionaries in the form of an article by Raymond Péricat entitled 'A l'oeuvre tous, pour la grève générale'.[131] To Niel's arguments that the most urgent and essential task of syndicalism was to secure 'immediate results' and that in this context theory was only divisive, Péricat responded by stating categorically that 'the working class is essentially revolutionary'. Niel continued his call for what he regarded as 'practical action' only to be met by the reply that it was the revolutionaries who were practical and that he had lost sight of the ideals which syndicalism embodied.[132] No sooner did this exchange of views come to an inconclusive end than Yvetot and Keufer clashed on a different issue.

In 'Parlementarisme ou dictature'[133] Keufer took the revolutionaries to task for their apparent indifference to the fate of the Republic. Recognising the faults and abuses of the parliamentary system he questioned whether a 'revolutionary crisis' was the best means of eradicating these ills. As, in his opinion, it was folly to believe that out of such a revolution would arise a proletarian dictatorship the most likely outcome appeared to be either the establishment of a military dictatorship or the restoration of the monarchy or Empire. 'Is this the result', he asked, 'which the anti-parliamentarians who slander the present regime wish to achieve?'. The revolutionaries, in other words, were carrying out the work of the reactionaries with possible dire and incalculable consequences for both themselves and the proletariat. 'Yes', Yvetot replied, 'we are indifferent to all the assaults of the royalist or any other reaction against the Republican reaction' but it was not their aim to bring back to power those who wished to restore their lost privileges. 'Our intentions', he argued, 'are not theirs and theirs, naturally, are not ours'. The proletariat, he remarked optimistically, equipped with a moral, technical and administrative education, would be in a position quickly to overturn a 'State of Monarchical Reaction' should it ever arise.[134]

The conflict of ideas was, however, most easily visible in the discussion which took place at the CGT's Toulouse Congress in 1910 of the events leading up to Niel's resignation.[135] In his defence Niel argued that from the outset he had been incorrectly seen and judged as the candidate of reformism. The virulence of his critics derived in part from their need to cast him as a scapegoat for the defeat of May 1909 and from the fact that his former anarchist comrades were not prepared to forgive him for his abandonment of the libertarian creed. But the key issue highlighted by Niel related to a clear disagreement about the role and function of the *syndicat*. Taking up Pouget's point that the *syndicat* grouped together interests and not opinions and that, in his view, this should be interpreted to mean current and immediate interests Niel again contended that the *syndicats* should restrict themselves to matters touching directly upon the professional and economic concerns of the workers. 'I am not for', he commented, 'this syndicalism of everything (*ce syndicalisme du tout*)'. It was left to Yvetot to articulate the response. If as syndicalists, he argued, the deployment of troops in strikes had to be opposed 'we are obliged as a consequence to propagate anti-patriotism', and, if this was the case, then it followed that the syndicalists must also oppose the parliamentary regime because 'the parliamentarian is forced to be a patriot'. Everything, Yvetot observed, 'is connected'. It was, therefore, a nonsense to believe that syndicalism could achieve its aims without an assault upon both the State and the idea of the nation. 'As anarchists', Yvetot stated, 'we want the complete emancipation of the individual; as syndicalists, we want the complete emancipation of the working class'.[136]

5 From Crisis to Schism

'Assez curieuse année que 1909', Pierre Monatte wrote[1]. The election of Léon Jouhaux, the candidate of the revolutionaries and Griffuelhes' friend, as Louis Niel's successor in July 1909 could not hide the fact that the CGT was isolated, factionalised and uncertain about what direction to take. Only three years after the success of Amiens membership was stagnating and élan and given way to reflective introspection and increased caution. Jouhaux, in the words of his biographers, 'was completely unknown to the majority of workers'[2]. The 'heroic days of syndicalism' appeared to be at an end[3]: the 'crisis' of syndicalism had begun.

Amongst syndicalists themselves, accounts of the nature and causes of this crisis and the remedies proposed for its resolution varied dramatically, as was exemplified by the contrasting and incompatible reactions elicited by an 'enquête' into this issue by *Le Mouvement socialiste*[4]. Successive defeats at the hands of the government quickly produced a re-assessment of syndicalist tactics coupled with dissent from the revolutionary wing of the movement. The situation of internal turmoil was further aggravated by the traumas and deceptions associated with the CGT's failure to organise even the semblance of opposition to the commencement of the First World War. The pro-war 'majority', led by Jouhaux, did its best to silence the anti-war 'minority' and with the cessation of hostilities between the warring nations the acrimony and cries of treason continued as syndicalists divided over their responses to the Russian Revolution. The long-expected schism occurred in 1921 when at the Congress of Lille the pro-Bolshevik minority was effectively forced out of the CGT and in December of that year the dissidents formed the *Confédération générale du travail unifié* (CGTU) which in 1923 adhered to the trade union offshoot of Lenin's Third International in Moscow. It was, moreover, in this period that the coterie of intellectuals and militants who had first met in Lagardelle's apartment went their separate ways.

I

In an article entitled 'La Leçon du passé' published in October 1909[5] Griffuelhes argued that in part the CGT's problems derived from the seduction and corruption of syndicalist leaders by successive government ministers, in particular Millerand and Briand. 'The regime of worker corruption', at its height between 1899 and 1902, had, he argued, been pursued during the previous three years 'discreetly, quietly and without ostentation' but with the intention of turning the working class towards the pursuit of purely material improvements in their standard of life. 'Never', Griffuelhes commented, 'did syndicalism lower itself, never did it walk in the salons, the boudoirs, the corrupt antechambers, the governmental dens that it does today'[6]. Moreover, in 'La leçon du passé' Griffuelhes pinpointed what he clearly took to be a more fundamental cause of syndicalist weakness. Millerand, 'this French Chamberlain', wanted, according to Griffuelhes, to create a country that was 'prosperous, active and enterprising' but this, Griffuelhes argued, needed 'strong, stubborn men', not a weakened and discouraged working class. The truth, as he was to point out in three articles published in *Le Mouvement socialiste*[7], was that there was a direct relationship between economic development and the growth of trade union organisation: France, and therefore the syndicalist movement, suffered from economic stagnation which itself was a reflection of the weakness and inferiority of French capitalism. 'The proletariat', Griffuelhes argued in almost Sorelian fashion, 'does not often enough come face-to-face with an active, audacious *patronat*, whilst for its part the *patronat* finds itself in the presence of a proletariat which is insufficiently organised and which does not understand that well-being is inseparable from economic progress'[8]. By implication, only when the French capitalist class had freed itself from its conservative and unadventurous practices would there exist a sizeable and vigorous syndicalist movement. 'For our part', Griffuelhes stated, 'we ask that French employers be like American employers'[9]. Yvetot's position, in contrast, drew upon his anarchist roots[10]. There was no crisis, he argued, only a *malaise*, fostered by the clash of personalities and ideas that had accompanied the final, controversial months of Griffuelhes' tenure of office. Out of this ordeal, he countered, syndicalism would emerge 'healthier, more alive and active, and more threatening'. Implicitly laying the blame upon the leadership, Yvetot called for what he termed 'démocratisation syndicale': it was for syndicalists at the base to impress upon their officials the need to unite all the exploited within the ranks of the CGT.

The reformists, nor surprisingly, had their own analysis of recent events, articulated most forcefully by Keufer[11]. The root cause of the CGT's disarray and impotence, he argued, lay in the unwillingness of revolutionary activists to respect its political neutrality. 'The Congress of Bourges', he wrote, 'was the first manifestation of a method which consisted of imposing upon the sheep-like mass the conceptions of a clever, active and noisy minority'. The CGT as a consequence had become divided, numerically and morally weakened, and almost destroyed, with the tragic outcome of the strikes at Draveil and Villeneuve-Saint-Georges as its graphic illustration. All these events demonstrated that to secure the support of the workers it was not sufficient to pass motions calling for violent, revolutionary change: 'bluff can succeed occasionally but it cannot be raised into a system of efficient and durable action'. This applied equally to the *bourses du travail* which, for all the grandiose plans of replacing the bourgeois State, had failed almost totally to perform any of the functions attributed to them by Pelloutier. The error lay in the attachment to 'absolute, extremist, sectarian principles'. To remedy this parlous situation, Keufer called firstly for the mutual respect and toleration of competing opinions within the CGT, repeating his argument that practice and experience demonstrated better than theory the best means to defend the professional interests of the proletariat. Secondly, by excluding all divisive doctrines the CGT was to seek to rally all the workers to its cause. Finally, as a symbol of its independence, the *bourses du travail* were in the future to reject any financial support from local municipalities or the State. In effect, he argued, the CGT, had a choice between the tactics of revolutionary transformation and the attainment of its final goal through reforms and a gradualist strategy. His fear, as he was candid enough to admit, was that 'our divisions will cease only at the moment when French syndicalist organisations are exhausted and that the battle will only come to an end for lack of combattants'[12]. What Keufer clearly did not anticipate was the change of tactics effected by the CGT in the years before the First World War.

Louis Niel did not participate in *Le Mouvement socialiste*'s 'enquête' but whilst general-secretary of the CGT he made his position clear. 'We must', he wrote, 'devote our best efforts to the struggle for attainable improvements. This will have a threefold result: it will situate syndicalism in its correct position, unite and bring us together, and attract to us a large number of hesitant workers who will join us as swiftly as the results of our daily actions become more numerous'[13]. After his resignation, Niel adopted a less conciliatory tone. In a series of articles published in *La Démocratie sociale* Niel charged that the CGT should be renamed the POA, 'le Parti Ouvrier Anarchiste'. The CGT, he argued, had encroached upon the ground properly occupied by the political party; it was no longer 'travailliste', the distinction between citizen and producer had been abandoned. The syndicalist movement, he predicted, would eventually split into two[14]. Little was heard of Niel after these remarks. He remained in Paris for several years before taking up permanent employment as agent for the *Société des auteurs et compositeurs dramatiques* in Toulouse. Between 1935 and 1940 he was employed in the town hall of this southern city. He died in August, 1952 in Corsica.

A more perceptive, and ultimately more significant, analysis of recent events came from Alphonse Merrheim. Syndicalism, he argued, was not suffering from a domestic crisis but from what he referred to as 'a crisis of domestication'. The CGT, as a result of governmental pressure and persuasion, was being integrated into the political system. A year later he spoke critically of attempts to secure 'la parlementarisation du syndicalisme'[15]. But the real cause of the crisis, according to Merrheim, lay in the excessive preoccupation with theory displayed by the majority of syndicalist militants and their apparent lack of interest in what Merrheim termed 'positive realities'. 'Instead of drawing inspiration slavishly from the past', Merrheim commented, 'working class militants should learn to appreciate the contingency of theory and the necessities of practice'[16]. Over the next few years Merrheim was to work out the implications of this view in considerable detail.

Amongst the 'nouvelle école', as we have already seen, the crisis of syndicalism evoked an altogether different response. Sorel and Berth abruptly distanced themselves from syndicalism whilst Lagardelle progressively adopted a position of detachment. 'Socialism', Pierre Monatte cites Lagardelle as saying 'has taken everything from me: my illusions, my fortune and even my wife'[17]. Neither Sorel nor Berth made any effort to explain their disenchantment in the syndicalist press but Sorel did at least publish one article which offered an explanation of the difficulties being experienced by the syndicalist movement[18]. The moment was opportune, he commented, for syndicalism to 'rid itself of democratic humbug'. If it had managed to keep politicians out of strikes, it had yet to free itself from the bourgeois illusions that had penetrated the world of the working class. 'I speak here', Sorel wrote, 'of all the errors which tend to weaken, mislead or even completely corrupt the class struggle, by removing the characteristics which make it a genuine war'. Amongst these bourgeois intrusions were the belief that the proletariat needed leaders to think for it, imitations of democratic demogogy, and, worst of all, a faith in pacific demonstrations which, in Sorel's words, had 'cost so much workers' blood'. For syndicalism to overcome its present problems, Sorel argued, the proletariat must not sacrifice its long-term goal for immediate advantages and, to that end, it needed to see democratic principles for the self-interested sham they were. What was essential, he commented, 'resided in the will of men', and at this stage Sorel appeared to believe that the proletariat possessed sufficient conviction of purpose to defeat its democratic enemies. Shortly afterwards he concluded otherwise and the road leading to eventual collaboration with Jean Variot's *L'Indépendance* lay open.

In his response, Hubert Lagardelle self-consciously placed himself in the role of dispassionate 'outsider', locating his explanation of the crisis within the general framework of the history of syndicalism in France[19]. With the Congress of Amiens, he argued, the formation of syndicalism was complete but its famous Charter was more what he termed 'an historical anticipation than a reflection of the present'[20]. It looked to the future, illuminating an uncertain path and the task had remained of putting into practice the theoretical postulates it embodied. The syndicalist movement, however, quickly ran into trouble. The State proved unrelenting whilst the employers, 'surprised at first', organised their defense. The anarchists and parliamentary socialists, momentarily beaten, went back upon the offensive and 'the struggle between factions, the personal quarrels and inevitable errors' added internal to external difficulties. All too often the syndicalist movement appeared like 'a rudderless ship (*un bateau ivre*)' and after 1908 the gap between theory and practice became manifest. Writing in 1912 Lagardelle had little comfort to offer the CGT, his only advice being that 'syndicalism should be itself', and by way of conclusion he drew attention to a further problem looming upon the horizon: 'La grave question du fonctionnarisme syndical'. This, as we shall see, was to be a much discussed issue in the years before the First World War.

After his release from prison at the end of 1908 Emile Pouget did not return to his duties either within the CGT or at *La Voix du peuple* but under his aegis the revolutionaries launched a new daily paper in February 1909. Badly financed and organised *La Révolution* ceased publication at the end of March, leaving Pouget bitterly disillusioned and from this point onwards he effectively ceased to participate in the syndicalist movement. Age, ill-health, and straightforward exhaustion have been cited as possible explanations for this premature retirement but it also seems probable that it was partly the result of a growing personal antipathy towards Griffuelhes who could on occasions be arrogant and autocratic. Pierre Monatte for one got the impression that 'Pouget in quitting *La Voix du peuple* had perhaps wished to leave Griffuelhes and escape from his domination'; Pouget certainly reacted unfavourably to the suggestion that Griffuelhes could give editorial assistance to his new publishing venture.[21] Pouget did not vanish totally from view. At the end of 1909 he re-appeared as a regular columnist in Gustave Hervé's insurrectionist *La Guerre sociale*, continuing his attacks upon the parliamentary system, 'le régime fécal', and pursuing the same themes, in particular the defense of sabotage and the general strike, with equal vigour and the same colourful prose. 'When', he asked in 1911, 'would the *Fédération du livre* vomit up its Keufer?'.[22] Pouget remained with *La Guerre sociale* (renamed *La Victoire* in 1916) until after the outbreak of the First World War whilst from 1913 he figured as the author of several serial stories in *L'Humanité*. This collaboration also continued after 1914 and led to the publication of a 'feuilleton' entitled significantly *La Vieille Alsace*.

Pouget was not the only CGT militant in these years to distance himself from active participation in the syndicalist movement. From the beginning of 1907 Paul Delesalle began to devote an increasing proportion of his time to the running of a second-hand bookshop he had established in the Rue Monsieur-le-Prince in Paris and although he took over Yvetot's functions during the latter's ten months' imprisonment beginning in June 1907 Delesalle announced his resignation from the post of assistant-secretary of the *Fédération des Bourses du travail* at the Congress of Marseilles in 1908. If this marked something of a change of direction for a man who had entered the world of anarchism at the age of 20, it did not represent a complete rupture with his past. 'A militant he was', Jean Maitron has written, 'and a militant he remained and would remain'.[23] Delesalle's bookshop was to be no ordinary one. Its catalogue, *La Publication sociale*, was to be devoted almost entirely to the sale of literature relating either directly or indirectly to the working class and its struggle for emancipation. For Delesalle his bookshop was not primarily a commercial enterprise but an educational service, an aid to syndicalist propaganda. Moreover, Delesalle was not content to remain a bookseller. For 25 years until the closure of his business in 1932 Delesalle published a not inconsiderable quantity of pamphlets and books, amongst which were to be a reprint of Jouhaux's speech at the funeral of Jaurès in 1914, Max Ascoli's study of Georges Sorel, and a brochure, published in 1931 entitled *Emile Pouget: Ad Memoriam*, bringing together the obituary notices devoted to the recently deceased 'Père Peinard'. Delesalle's cramped shop performed another function: by intention, it became a meeting place for militants, journalists and intellectuals. Its most famous *habitué* was Georges Sorel who, after his acrimonious quarrel with Charles Péguy in 1912 and his consequent banishment from the offices of *Les Cahiers de la Quinzaine*, simply transferred his allegiance from the Rue de la Sorbonne to a less prestigious but more sympathetic environment. Until the outbreak of the First World War Sorel now spent every Thursday afternoon in the company of Delesalle and his wife, holding forth to anyone who was prepared to listen. What that relationship meant to Sorel is best illustrated by the fact that *Matériaux d'une théorie du prolétariat*, published in 1919, was dedicated to both Paul and Leona Delesalle. Delesalle's view of Sorel, with whom he continued to correspond until shortly before the latter's death in 1922, was summarised in the last sentence of the obituary he published in *L'Humanité*. 'Proletarians', Delesalle wrote, 'believe me, it your most lucid and greatest defenders who has just passed away'.[24]

The rapid demise of Pouget's *La Révolution* coincided with the effective closure of *Pages libres* (it was taken over by *La Grande revue*) and the internal crisis afflicting *Le Mouvement socialiste*. Guieysse's periodical, whilst it had always existed on the margins of the syndicalist movement, had nevertheless lent its tacit support to revolutionary syndicalism and Guieysse himself had been one of the first to appreciate its significance.[25] The possible loss of *Le Mouvement socialiste* represented an ever greater blow to the cause of the revolutionaries. In this situation there appeared to be room for a new review. On 5 October, 1909 it appeared: its title was *La Vie ouvrière* and its founder was Pierre Monatte.

Born in Monlet (Haute-Loire) in January 1881 of working-class parents, Pierre Monatte was first employed as an assistant schoolmaster. At an early age he became familiar with left-wing, and in particular anarchist, literature and it was not long before he found the restrictions imposed on him at work intolerable. School, he later commented, appeared to be more like a barracks. In 1902 he resigned and made his way to Paris. There he quickly gained employment in the offices of *Pages libres* and was soon to be found as a regular contributor to *Le Libertaire* and *Les Temps nouveaux*. In 1904 he left *Pages libres* to take up employment as a typesetter and in the same year, thanks to Pouget, he joined the federal committee of the CGT. 1905 was spent almost entirely in the Pas-de-Calais: Benoit Broutchoux, leader of the anti-guesdist 'jeune syndicat' of miners, chose Monatte to replace him during a period of imprisonment.[26] After this Monatte played a significant, but discreet, role within the CGT. His articles were to be found alongside those of other revolutionary syndicalists in *La Voix du peuple* and *L'Action directe* and in 1907 he presented the key speech (opposing Malatesta) on the relationship between syndicalism and anarchism at the international anarchist congress in Amsterdam. Following the shootings at Villeneuve-Saint-Georges, under the threat of arrest Monatte fled to Switzerland.

It was, Monatte informed Jean Maitron, as a result of reading Pelloutier's *Histoire des bourses du travail* and the influence of *Pages libres* that he moved away from pure anarchism to syndicalism.[27] Monatte's early articles, for example those commenting upon the mining disaster at Courrières in 1906 and the imaginary 'conspiracy' between syndicalists and bonapartists in which the government attempted to implicate him, concentrated upon drawing the lesson that the working class could only rely upon its own efforts to secure emancipation.[28] 'We have seen', he wrote, 'all the Dreyfusard journals of the past which not so long ago were calling for the overturning of the world in order to secure the release of Dreyfus appear the most eager to direct without a shred of evidence the worst slanders at the revolutionary militants'.[29] This theme was pursued in his remarks both before and after the Congress of Amiens.[30] It was, however, at Amsterdam that Monatte provided the clearest and most succinct expression of his views. At the very moment, he argued, that Guesdism had degenerated into verbalism and electoralism, Jaurèsian socialism had turned into ministerialism and anarchism had retreated into the ivory tower of philosophical speculation, syndicalism had re-awakened the revolutionary spirit. 'For the first time since anarchist dynamite became silent', Monatte declared, 'the bourgeoisie has trembled with fear'.[31]

From the outset, Monatte intended that *La Vie ouvrière* should be different from the syndicalist reviews that had preceded it. Unlike *La Révolution*, it was to be established upon a sound financial base, the greater proportion of the capital coming from Guieysse and James Guillaume, Bakunin's former associate in the First International and the founder of the anarchist *Fédération jurassiene*. Published twice monthly, 'à couverture grise', with a standard 64 pages of text Monatte calculated that to be viable he would need 1200 subscribers. As *Le Mouvement socialiste* had never obtained more than 700 this seemed an unrealistic target and at the end of 1909 the figure stood at only 550 but by 1911 the requisite number of sales was achieved and in March of that year the subscriptions were marginally in excess of 2600. The name of the review was intended unambiguously to locate its position within the libertarian tradition of syndicalism and was taken from the title of the book by Fernand and Maurice Pelloutier. *La Vie ouvrière*, as stated in the first appeal to its possible subscribers, was to be 'une revue d'action'. It had 'no catechism or sermon to offer' but was designed to help militants in their struggles by supplying them with detailed information of relevance to their working lives, thus enabling proletarian action to gain 'in intensity and volume'. *La Vie ouvrière* therefore provided a regular diet of reports on strikes, accounts of capitalist abuses (for example, child labour) and studies of the workings of the economic system (many of the latter being provided by the controversial figure of Francis Delaisi). Nor was the international dimension to these issues ignored: Tom Mann was, for example, a frequent contributor on the British labour movement. Theory and practice were to be united by the provision of facts.

Monatte's aim was to develop a different type of relationship with his audience. Not only were the readers of *La Vie ouvrière* to be regularly informed of its financial situation and incited to find new subscribers but they were also to be invited to participate and collaborate in writing its content. Each issue, for example, contained a section entitled 'Entre nous' in which information and opinions could be exchanged. Moreover, dialogue was not restricted to letters alone: a permanent meeting place for readers was organised.

If Monatte was the initiator of the project, *La Vie ouvrière* was built around a group or *'noyau'* of regular contributors. In the first instance this was composed amongst others of James Guillaume, Merrheim, Griffuelhes, Yvetot (the last two were quickly to depart) and trade union leaders such as Georges Dumoulin of the miners and Maurice Dubois of the teachers. To this list was added in 1911 that of Alfred Rosmer. Born André Alfred Griot in Philadelphia in 1877 Rosmer, like Monatte, not only came to syndicalism via anarchism but also enjoyed a career of over 50 years as a political activist which, in his case, took him from Zimmerwald to the Third International in Moscow and on into the world of Left Opposition and Trotskyism. Further it was Rosmer who between 1911 and 1927 was arguably to be Monatte's closest associate.[32] One notable absentee from the pages of *La Vie ouvrière* was Georges Sorel. On the basis of the fact that Monatte had received limited funds from Maurice Kahn, a colleague of Guieysse's at *Pages libres*, Sorel concluded that *La Vie ouvrière* was financed by Jews (which, in effect, for Sorel meant Dreyfusards) whilst for his part Monatte seemed eager to avoid the intrusion of artificial divisions arising from an excess of theory.[33] In 1913

Monatte omitted all Sorel's books from a list of what he regarded to be essential reading for syndicalists, commenting: 'If *L'Avenir socialiste des syndicats* had been republished I would have included it without hesitation amongst this list of the first books to be read by a militant worker, but as for *Réflexions sur la violence* I am convinced that it would have disappointed more than one reader in the same way that it disappointed me'.[34]

The 'noyau' was itself a loosely-formed, heterogeneous group of friends and acquaintances who would meet two or three times a month to discuss current events and the manner in which they were to be treated in the review. The members were bound together by the desire to extricate syndicalism from a crisis which, in their view, had been brought about by a lapse into reformism and a general loss of direction. 'Never', Monatte stated, 'have I experienced such a painful sensation as that caused by the Congress of Toulouse'.[35] Niel, he remarked, had been content to dissect syndicalism as if it were a dead body. The 'urgent task' was to put an end to 'the agony of reformism' by defeating 'the supporters of the peaceful, practical and conservative method' and by ensuring that the direction of syndicalism was in the hands of 'les minorités agissantes'.[36] Equally, however, *La Vie ouvrière* campaigned to prevent revolutionary syndicalism from degenerating into pure verbalism. Monatte, for example, wanted to see CGT conferences better organised, a new headquarters built where syndicalists would be 'at home', and active campaigns undertaken to reduce the working day and against the rise in the cost of living.[37] He talked of the need for a 'new effort at propaganda and organisation directed towards a concrete and immediate goal'.[38] Above all, by taking up where Pelloutier's *L'Ouvrier des deux mondes* left off *La Vie ouvrière* recognised that there were no short cuts to the goal of proletarian emancipation and that it could only be obtained after a long and patient process of self-education. 'In order that syndicalism should be sufficient to itself', an editorial commented, 'it is imperative that in the first place it should be capable of forming its own militants'.[39]

The desire to prevent syndicalism from descending into revolutionary verbiage also took the form of opposition to the pursuit of such secondary, but widely popular, side-issues as anti-clericalism and 'Neo-Malthusianism'. Rosmer, for example, argued against the campaign in favour of the systematic use of contraception on the double grounds that it was highly unlikely that a decrease in surplus labour would raise salaries and because, given the state of medical knowledge, contraception entailed considerable physical risks. Each couple, he acknowledged, should be free to limit the number of their children if they so chose but to imagine, as its proponents on the Left claimed, that this practice would hasten the demise of the capitalist system was positively puerile and had only been taken seriously, in Rosmer's view, because it 'coincided with individual egoism and appeared to simple minds as a panacea'.[40]

Another form of irrelevant distraction for the working class was provided by 'le Cas Bonnot'. Bonnot and his celebrated group of bandits had
in some quarters been seen as descendants from Ravachol but according
to Rosmer they practised 'methodical burglary and murder'. Whereas
Ravachol had committed his crimes from disinterested motives, Bonnot
had no other desire than to live like a member of the bourgeoisie in idle
luxury. Bonnot's daring deeds were, in other words, a manifestation of
the spirit of capitalist greed and were part of the same world which had
seen the pursuit of profits lead to the sinking of the Titanic and the
emergence of the new 'sport' of aeroplane racing which demanded that
'whatever the weather, the pilot must set out'. The potential mistake,
therefore, was to endorse what amounted to banditry as a form of revolutionary illegalism, an error made even more culpable by the fact that
these crimes provided an excuse for wholesale repression by the authorities.[41] Bonnot, moreover, was not the only form of revolutionary deviation
to be opposed by *La Vie ouvrière*.

A key member of the 'noyau' was Alphonse Merrheim and in the years
which preceded the First World War he too was to add a distinctive voice
to the pages of *La Vie ouvrière*.[42] Merrheim first came to Paris in 1904
when he was appointed secretary of the *Fédération des métallurgistes*. A
provincial militant from the Nord, Merrheim first met Monatte at the
offices of *Pages libres* and soon afterwards he was to make the acquaintance of Emile Pouget. There followed a steady rise through the ranks of
the CGT. In 1905 he began contributing to *Le Mouvement socialiste* and,
as we have already seen, was to become a participant at the monthly
gatherings that took place at Lagardelle's apartment. He situated himself,
therefore, upon the revolutionary wing of the syndicalist movement and
in 1909 was to be among the bitterest of Louis Niel's opponents.

Throughout his career Merrheim was a controversial man, capable of
evoking intense animosity. He made and broke many friendships (including that with Monatte which came to an end after the First World War)
and for all his dedication to his professional duties, his own branch of the
metalworkers' union for the Seine region expelled him in 1913. There
were those who questioned whether Merrheim had written all the articles
that appeared under his name (charging that they had been written by
middle-class intellectuals such as Francis Delaisi and Maxime Leroy) and
still others who claimed that Merrheim was in the pay of the *Comité des
Forges*, the powerful employers' federation in the iron and steel industry.
Nevertheless, Merrheim made a significant and original contribution to
syndicalist thought.

Merrheim's first articles for *Le Mouvement socialiste* were composed of
detailed and lengthy studies of strikes within the iron and steel industry
in France. It was to be from these enquiries that he sought self-consciously
to draw certain conclusions for syndicalist practice. 'Monographs of great

strikes,' he wrote, 'are worth more than the most conscientious theoretical studies. They allow us to perceive from life the salient episodes of the long drama constituted by the class struggle'.[43] What these strikes taught Merrheim was that in any dispute the workers would face the combined opposition and superior forces represented by the State and increasingly well-organised employers' federations. Commenting upon the defeat of a strike at Longwy in Lorraine in 1905, for example, Merrheim remarked that 'the strikers succumbed to the most formidable governmental, military and international police pressure that one has ever met in a strike'.[44] At the time Merrheim concluded that from this experience few workers would feel constrained to restrict themselves in their future struggles to peaceful methods — 'the fire smoulders beneath the cinders: the conflagration slumbers', he announced — but he quickly came to realise that the employers and their powerful allies in government would not be beaten by the tactics of revolutionary élan and instinctive combat. 'To act', he wrote in 1908, 'is to live. To live means to struggle'.[45] This was especially so, he maintained, for the worker who was obliged to fight for everything he possessed or achieved; but to be liberated from 'servitude and misery . . . courage, energy and will power are not enough. The worker must be well-informed'. The principal weakness of proletarian action, Merrheim now argued, derived from the failure of the workers to comprehend their employers' mode of action: 'consequently, if metalworkers want to fight their employer on equal terms, they must first understand him'. In effect, to Pelloutier's maxim that the worker must educate himself to a level where the proletariat would be capable of running industry was to be added the requirement that the workers should understand their adversary, the capitalist class.

To that end from 1906 onwards, and with the assistance of Delaisi, Merrheim was to undertake the most thorough examination of the workings of the capitalist system to be carried out by either a theorist or militant within the syndicalist movement. Concentrating upon iron and steel and the nascent automobile industry, this enquiry culminated in the publication of a brochure entitled *L'Organisation patronale: syndicats, comités régionaux, ententes et comptoirs, assurances contre les grèves* in 1908, a series of articles under the general rubric 'L'Organisation patronale en France' published between July 1908 and December 1909 in *Le Mouvement socialiste* and a comprehensive study drawing upon these earlier pieces, *La Métallurgie, son origine et son developpement. Les forces motrices*, published in 1913. To these must also be added *L'Affaire de l'Ouenza*, published in 1910, in which Merrheim highlighted the manner in which the steel owners' cartel, the *Comité des Forges*, had extracted mining and railway concessions in Algeria, thus demonstrating the complicity between parliament, steel barons and the French State. The *Comité des Forges*, Merrheim commented, exercised 'a hidden, formidable power'.[46] What these studies revealed to Merrheim was not only the burgeoning power and complexity of a capitalist system which was being dramatically transformed by the application of scientific advances to production methods but also the extent of the domestic and international co-operation that existed between the owners, such that 'the industrialists could at one and the same time fleece the consumer and bear upon the wage-earners with all their strength in order to weaken them'.[47] In short, for Merrheim the workers faced a formidable, well-organised capitalist class, confident of its strength, which would not be easily or quickly brushed aside.

If, therefore, in 1909 Merrheim was to be found at the side of Monatte it was because he accepted that there was no parliamentary route to proletarian emancipation — parliament, as the Ouenza affair revealed, was controlled by the bosses — but rooted in his analysis of capitalism was a new prognosis for syndicalist practice: in order to defeat its opponents, the syndicalist movement would need to match their organisational strength and structure. The de-centralist traditions of the CGT would have to be overturned. It was this line which was to be pursued by Merrheim in the years before the First World War. Ultimately it provided him with a justification for siding with the reformists.

The success of *La Vie ouvrière* brought with it another attempt to create a daily paper committed to revolutionary syndicalism. On 27 April 1911 Griffuelhes launched *La Bataille syndicaliste* with, in addition to himself and Léon Jouhaux, the majority of Monatte's 'noyau' as members of its editorial committee. Unfortunately Griffuelhes had failed to learn from Pouget's disastrous experience with *La Révolution* and the paper, for all its actual survival, existed in a state of permanent financial crisis. Sales were never to exceed 15 000, of which the greater proportion were in the Paris region.[48] Quickly discouraged, Griffuelhes sought to bring the publication of *La Bataille syndicaliste* to a speedy end, only to be thwarted by the determination of Monatte to keep the paper afloat. Griffuelhes' resignation was followed by Monatte's own departure at the end of 1912 to concentrate his efforts upon *La Vie ouvrière* (Rosmer meanwhile had joined the staff of *La Bataille syndicaliste* in February of that year) but the lasting significance of this quarrel was that it brought about a rupture in relations between Griffuelhes and Jouhaux on the one side and Monatte and his colleagues on the other: Monatte even went so far as to suggest that Griffuelhes and Jouhaux tried to organise a boycott of *La Vie ouvrière*.

The election of Léon Jouhaux to the post of general-secretary of the CGT after Louis Niel's short but catastrophic period of office meant that once again the key post within the syndicalist movement was in the hands of someone who belonged within the tradition of anarcho-syndicalism. It was upon Griffuelhes' initiative that Jouhaux was nominated for the post (they even shared an apartment) and from the outset Jouhaux loudly proclaimed the principles of syndicalist autonomy and direct action. Only a matter of weeks after his election he published an article entitled 'De l'utilité de la grève générale' in *La Voix du peuple*[49] and in the following year he could be found remarking that 'in the face of illegality, we will respond by illegality, in the face of legal violence, we will oppose revolutionary violence'.[50] In 1911 in a speech in Brussels (published that year and again in 1913[51]) he presented what amounted to a classic restatement of the revolutionary position, replete with an endorsement of anti-statism, anti-militarism, anti-patriotism, sabotage and strikes as a form of 'gymnastique nécessaire et indispensable'. Further, prior to the CGT's conference in Le Havre in 1912 Jouhaux's name appeared as the lead signature on a statement, known subsequently as the 'Encyclique syndicaliste', which stated categorically that the position of syndicalism was one of 'absolute and total independence from parties and sects, complete liberty in the choice of tactics' and which, in its second instalment, proclaimed that the CGT had as its 'sole objective the interests of the working class alone of which it is the natural representative'.[52] Following the conference, which re-affirmed its support for the Charter of Amiens by 1028 votes to 34, Jouhaux celebrated the restatement of 'the independence and the autonomy of the syndicalist movement'.[53] However, neither the position of the CGT nor that of Jouhaux himself were as unequivocally revolutionary as this would imply and nor, for that matter, did harmony suddenly break out amongst the syndicalists.

Jacques Julliard, in *Clémenceau, briseur des grèves*,[54] argues that the revolutionary wing of the syndicalist movement around 1910 can be divided into two groups: the *violents* and the *politiques*. For the *politiques* such as Griffuelhes and Jouhaux, revolutionary rhetoric was combined with a cautious awareness of the limitation of proletarian action. Jouhaux, for example, did not dismiss the possibility of a general strike but he did recognise that to be successful it would require a very particular set of conditions and circumstances which, at present, did not exist.[55] For this reason, therefore, while he lent his support to strikes he also campaigned vigorously to secure improvements in the living standards and conditions of the working class through the attainment of, for example, a reduction in the working week. 'Supporters of the class struggle', Jouhaux wrote, 'we are for energetic, sometimes violent action; but we are for action which extends the conscience of man, strengthens his will, by making him useful to his comrades'.[56] From this perspective, halfday working on Saturdays — 'la semaine anglaise' — was deemed to be beneficial because it permitted the physical, and therefore mental, reinvigoration of the worker and would make possible the moral elevation of his life. Saturday afternoons could be devoted to sport (the *syndicat* needed fit men) or self-education whilst Sundays could be spent *en famille* enjoying the benefits of the fresh country air.

For the *violents* — Yvetot is a primary example but to this can be added the name of Raymond Péricat who was to rise to prominence in the years immediately before the First World War[57] — the emphasis of their activity fell upon a constant call for agitation and action in an attempt to keep up the revolutionary momentum of the syndicalist movement. Yvetot's articles in *La Voix du peuple* throughout this period concentrated almost solely upon reminding the working class of the centrality of the general strike and of violence in the revolutionary process. It was Péricat who during 1913 was to be the principal proponent of the general strike as a means of responding to the government's plans to extend military service to three years.

Further, the *violents* were not to be the only firebrands that Jouhaux as general-secretary of the CGT had to contend with. In addition, there was firstly Gustave Hervé, editor of *La Guerre sociale* and member of the socialist party, whose special mixture of verbal violence, anti-patriotism and insurrectionism exercised considerable attraction and influence upon many syndicalists in these years. For example, for all his opposition to Hervé's Blanquism, Georges Sorel could argue that Hervé's 'useful role' was to disorganise the 'government' that Griffuelhes — 'the Napoleon of the proletariat' — was seeking to create within the CGT. By going against Hervé, Sorel counselled Lagardelle in 1908, 'you are working to ruin everything which can prevent syndicalism from descending into governmental demagogy, you are working for Jaurès, Combes and Briand'.[58] Secondly, in parallel to Valois' attempt to lure Sorel and Berth into the monarchist camp, the CGT had to withstand another royalist offensive — 'the low road' in Paul Mazgaj's phrase — as Maurras' *Action française* made a determined effort to establish a foothold amongst the working class. As demonstrated by *Si le coup de force est possible*,[59] the response of Maurras and Dutroit-Crozon to *Comment nous ferons la révolution*, the monarchists saw sufficient similarities between their own tactics and those of the CGT to lead them to believe that the syndicalist movement could be used to their own advantage. Monarchist initiatives received a remarkably favourable response in certain quarters, most notably from Emile Janvion. A former anarchist and member of the CGT's federal committee, Janvion had one quick and ready explanation of the crisis being experienced by syndicalism: it was the result of infiltration by freemasons. At the end of May 1908 Janvion published in the official organ of the CGT, *La Voix du peuple*, an article entitled 'Le Péril maçonique dans le syndicalisme' in which he argued that the aim of the freemasons was to take over the CGT in order to direct it in the interests of the bourgeoisie.[60] This theme was continued by Janvion in Hervé's *La Guerre sociale* and from November 1909 onwards in his own journal, *La Terre libre*. Anti-freemasonary was, however, only a thinly disguised form of anti-Semitism. The opening editorial of *La Terre libre* argued that its intention was to prevent syndicalism from becoming 'the prey of politicians, parties and occult sects' but it quickly became evident that its real target was 'la bourgeoisie judéo-républicaine', the Dreyfusard alliance which, in Janvion's eyes, now reigned supreme. 'We say and we repeat', Janvion wrote, 'that freemasonry is a front for Jewish capitalism'. The real master of France was the 'yid', *le youtre*, and it was for this reason, Janvion argued, that many revolutionaries now recognised the foresight of Edouard Drumont, author of *La France juive*.[61] These sentiments were given graphic illustration by the publication in March 1911 of an open letter by none other than Emile Pataud (Pouget's co-author of *Comment nous ferons la révolution*) which, in attacking the Baron Edouard de Rothschild for his supposed part in defeating the recent railwayman's strike, concluded with a parody of Gambetta's famous jibe at clerics in the form of 'Le Juif, voilà l'ennemi'.[62]

This is not the place to examine in any detail the undoubted collaboration that existed between Janvion and the royalists of *Action française:* the point is that in the form of men such as Hervé and Janvion there existed on the margins of the CGT those who opposed any compromise whatsoever with the Republican régime and who to that end and for a variety of, sometimes dubious, motives advocated a strategy of belligerence and instransigence that at times amounted to little more than dictatorial posturing. Moreover, given their undoubted skills as publicists (*La Guerre sociale* sold 60 000 copies to *La Voix du peuple*'s 9000), the CGT had to respond.

The various aspects of the controversies that had wracked the CGT since 1909 came to a head in 1913 and with this the disagreements amongst members of the revolutionary wing of the movement finally came out into the open. Conscious of the organisational weakness of the CGT Jouhaux, with Merrheim's support, was able to secure approval for a radical reform of its structure at the Congress of Le Havre in 1912. The changes proposed amounted to a break with the anarchist tradition of decentralisation and the model now became by implication that of Merrheim's *Fédération des métaux*, a union which sought to represent all metalworkers, irrespective of their different trades. It was Griffuelhes from his position of 'semi-retirement' who voiced the opposition to these innovations and who argued that they represented a fundamental revision of syndicalism's conception of itself. Writing in *La Bataille syndicaliste* at the beginning of 1913 Griffuelhes began his critique by observing that 'in the syndicalist world there exists a deplorable state of mind, a profound ignorance of the necessities of action'. To rectify that situation what was needed was less, not more, bureaucratic control of the base. What, he asked, was syndicalism if not a 'movement of offense'? Its object was not to resist attacks or to conserve what already existed but to augment the position of the worker. To that end, *syndicats* based on trades, not industries, in which local unions, not federations, would hold the initiative, were the appropriate form of organisation. 'With an aggregation of trades lacking direct links', he commented, 'the defensive alone is possible'. Centrally-run, industry-based *syndicats*, in other words, were not able to engender the action required to sustain syndicalism as a revolutionary movement. In effect, Griffuelhes was accusing Merrheim in particular of being mesmerised by cartels such as the *Comité des Forges*. 'If', he wrote, 'we recognise around us an industrial concentration — which we must not confuse with employer concentration — we must prevent ourselves from being hypnotised by it and from giving it an exaggerated importance capable of weakening our enthusiasm and our faith'.[63]

Merrheim's response concentrated for the most part upon the details of Griffuelhes' case. In an industry as complex as iron and steel, he argued, unions based upon trades would eventually produce *syndicats* for individual factories. Secondly, employer concentration did actually exist and therefore, unless 'revolutionary syndicalism' wished to 'consist solely of hollow phrases', it had to adapt to the new circumstances. Merrheim's overall point came in his final rejoinder to Griffuelhes. 'Far from denying the utility of active minorities', he wrote, 'I only ask of them that their actions should be clear-sighted and not blind . . . I ask them to live in realities and not dreams'.[64]

The government's decision in 1913 to extend compulsory military service to three years forced these disagreements further into the open. The CGT responded by organising protest demonstrations (sometimes in collaboration with the socialists) but no clear-cut strategy emerged. For Griffuelhes and Yvetot the proposed new law provided the opportunity for renewed calls to action — 'the hour of final repose has not sounded', Griffuelhes commented — whilst Péricat, long a supporter of a campaign to encourage the troops to desert, was the leading advocate of a twenty-four hour general strike. At a special conference in July, Péricat's proposal for an all-out stoppage in September to coincide with what would normally have been the release of the previous year's conscripts was rejected and in its stead an anodine motion proposed by Jouhaux calling vaguely upon workers to protest against the 'extension of the military spirit' was accepted. The CGT appeared to acknowledge that it was powerless to prevent the implementation of the new measure. In the face of criticism and controversy Jouhaux quickly responded by arguing that the CGT had not changed direction and this was backed up by a joint declaration signed by, amongst others, Jouhaux, Dumoulin, Merrheim and Monatte and published on 27 August. Recalling the Charter of Amiens the signatories denied that the recent decision entailed approval of the 'reformist method' and countered by asserting that 'today, as yesterday, syndicalism should not shelter behind the bureaucratic mechanism of the State but should destroy it and establish by its own efforts, through autonomous action, the society of the future'. But alongside this restatement of faith was the call for syndicalists to recognise the need for 'positive action' and to accept the modification of tactics necessitated by developments in the industrial environment. The document concluded by stating boldly that 'a movement which does not take account of the transformation occurring around it and which solidifies into an unchangeable attitude would be a movement without life, without influence, without a future'.[65]

The significance of the CGT's decision not to call a general strike was not lost upon the participants in our debate. At the end of July Merrheim announced prophetically that syndicalism was at a turning point in its history. It could either accept that the revolution involved more than taking the Champs-Elysées by storm and therefore that it needed to undertake a serious effort at recruitment and organisation or else 'within ten years' become nothing more than a discussion group, a resting place for 'discontents' and 'buffoons'. The CGT needed 'to rectify its aim'.[66]

The implications of this argument were spelt out a week later by Monatte in *La Vie ouvrière*.[67] For too long, he asserted, syndicalism had 'remained silent before the insurrectionary uproar of *La Guerre sociale*, and with dire consequences. The fact of the matter was that, contrary to the opinion of Hervé and his anarchist friends, a revolutionary situation did not exist. Syndicalist organisations were 'tired and weak' and the poor response to past calls for action showed that the people were not 'ready to throw themselves into a revolution'. Further, to give the government two months prior notice of a general strike was to invite defeat. Thus the decision of the CGT not to call a general strike did not imply a betrayal of principles. 'It has not repudiated', Monatte stated, 'any of the revolutionary ideals or methods of syndicalism. What it has repudiated are the impulsive acts of insurrectionism'. A 'truly' revolutionary situation, in Monatte's opinion, would only exist when the CGT had built up its numerical strength, when it had constructed strong organisations capable of sustained struggle and when, finally, the 'old Internationai' had been resurrected in Europe. In the meantime, the CGT was well-advised to resist 'pieces of ultra-revolutionary magniloquence'.

A more jaundiced view came from Pouget in the pages of *La Guerre sociale*. In January Pouget had sided with Griffuelhes in his dispute with Merrheim, arguing that the CGT needed to retain a flexible structure capable of adapting to the incessant changes of the industrial environment but his key point was that the controversy indicated 'a lack of camaraderie . . . of fraternal communion amongst militants'. A similar sentiment was evident in his response to the decision not to call a general strike. Whilst he did not deny that syndicalism needed more substance than mere 'verbal proclamations' and that the CGT should 'pursue its job of organisation, consolidation and recruitment', the clear implication of his comments was that the heart had now gone out of the CGT. 'There is', he wrote, 'a decline in idealism'. The task of revolutionary preparation was being neglected and the long-term goal, the final general strike, was being forgotten. Reflecting upon the disappointments of 1913 he concluded that if the CGT was to survive, defensive action was not sufficient: 'there must be offensive, there must be creative, exuberant action'.[68]

One observer who could scarcely contain his sense of self-satisfaction at the outcome of recent events was Auguste Keufer. Keufer had watched with pleasure the gradual evolution of the CGT's position under Jouhaux's leadership[69] and in his view there was no disguising the fact, despite the protestations of 'the principal leaders of the CGT', that the decisions taken in July 1913 denoted a fundamental shift in the orientation of the syndicalist movement. They showed, above all, 'the willingness to modify not the ends but the means of action, to take into account contingencies, to be no longer the blind instruments of individualists, of irresponsible insurrectionalists'. In short, the CGT had discreetly repudiated the methods that he himself had forcefully criticised in the past and it was now, he reported with considerable pleasure, the turn of Jouhaux and his colleagues to endure the charge of treason.[70]

What is beyond dispute is that Hervéism was being used as a catch-all phrase to denote adventurist tactics from which the CGT leadership, as it moved towards a more realistic appraisal of the possibilities of syndicalism, now wished to dissociate itself. Old-style revolutionary *jusqu'au boutisme* was being replaced by a more careful and considered approach to the problems of working-class emancipation and the CGT itself, with Jouhaux the former anarchist at its head, was being transformed into the reformist and centralised body that would fully emerge only after the First World War. As Madeleine Rebérioux has indicated, it was in this period that syndicalist hostility toward the State began to decline significantly and it was not to be long before the key notion of workers' control in industry was being challenged by the idea of nationalisation.[71] The syndicalist vision was being progressively undermined.

A further, and simultaneous, threat to that vision came from the introduction into France (most notably at the Renault plant at Boulogne-Billancourt) of the industrial management techniques known as Taylorism. To argue thus is not necessarily to accept the description of revolutionary syndicalism as the ideological expression of an artisan-based working class but it is to recognise the crucial place allotted to labour as man's supreme creative activity in much syndicalist theory. If production were to become a repetitious, rigidly controlled and rationally organised process with no room for individual self-expression on the part of the worker (as was envisaged by Taylor's schemes to increase productive efficiency), then the factory could no longer be perceived as the possible location of a morally elevating and aesthetically liberating experience and it made little sense to talk of the superiority of the producer over the citizen. Work, even in a socialist society (as Lenin's later support of Taylorism demonstrated) became solely the means to achieve greater material prosperity.

It was Merrheim who led the syndicalist attack on Taylorism, followed closely by Pouget. As *Le Mouvement socialiste*'s 1908 *enquête* on apprenticeship had revealed syndicalists were intimately aware of the potentially deleterious impact of advances in machine technology. 'What the boss demands of the worker he employs', Delesalle had commented, 'is more the quantitative value of work that he can supply than its qualitative value'. Nevertheless, Delesalle had insisted, following Sorel's conception of the factory of the future, that mechanisation need not necessarily diminish the technical proficiency and capacity for skill and initiative of industrial labour.[72]

Merrheim had taken a more sombre view. 'Modern machinism', he stated, 'requires not the "apprenticeship" but the "specialisation" of the worker'. Men were reduced to performing and repeating 'the same unvarying movement', the machine thought for the worker and imposed upon him a 'brutal discipline'.[73]

Taylorism, in Merrheim's view, was nothing less than the machinism raised to the highest levels of sophistication and exploitation.[74] It was, he proclaimed, 'the most ferocious, the most barbarous method of work conceived by a human mind'. The personality, intelligence, even the desires of the worker were subjugated to the imperatives of efficient production whilst his every movement was meticulously observed and controlled. 'The worker', Merrheim argued, 'must become, he has become an automaton regulated by the automatic movement of the machine'.[75] Merrheim was in no doubt as to the consequences of the implementation of Taylor's schemes of 'scientific' management. Rapidly, fatally, they would produce the physical and mental exhaustion of the workers. Healthy, vigorous men would be reduced to old age by the time they were forty. 'Thus', Merrheim commented, 'the Taylor method has resolved the issue of worker's retirement.' But this was not its only serious consequence. Machinism had destroyed the love of work felt by the worker and had engendered in him a hatred of the factory and the workshop and with this, in Merrheim's opinion, had come a general degradation in the behaviour and sentiments of the proletariat. 'Capitalism', he wrote, 'has perverted and rotted the worker's conscience. It is capitalism . . . which has suffocated the morality of the immense majority of the proletariat'.[76] Here, Merrheim conceded, was the real source of the weakness of revolutionary syndicalism. He might also have added that with this admission of the parlous state of working-class morals the syndicalist vision truly entered the realm of myth.

Merrheim's negative appraisal of Taylorism was not shared unanimously by his fellow syndicalists. If for Pouget Taylorism was nothing less than 'l'organisation du surmenage', institutionalised overwork inevitably inflicting debilitating damage upon the labour force, for Yvetot the enemy was not Taylorism but the capitalists who misused and exploited it.[77] 'To measure human effort', Yvetot wrote, 'is not in itself a detestable method, especially in the way that Taylor himself recommends his system'. But the most coherent defence of Taylorism came from former anarchist Jules Raveté. Responding specifically to Merrheim's critique Raveté argued that the 'scientific organisation of work' made possible increased production, saved worker's energy and thus, when utilised correctly, avoided the exhaustion associated with large-scale industry. Overlaid upon this was a Comtean rhetoric which glorified a system which at last had put paid to the 'king of economic chaos' and the reign of 'chance'. No longer would human energy be wasted and it remained only to ensure that the full fruits of this advance were shared equitably amongst 'humanity'.[78]

Merrheim's own response to these points was itself revealing. He readily admitted that a new level of industrial development had been reached which necessitated new methods of production and of work and that the merit of Taylor was that he had recognised this. There appeared, in other words, upon Merrheim's own admission, to be no alternative to radical changes in work practices.[79] In 1908, for example, he had commented that 'in order to revive apprenticeship it would be necessary to resuscitate the small workshop, the artisan of the past. This is impossible'.[80] The only option available to the syndicalist movement, therefore, was to defend the worker from the abuses and ferocious exploitation inherent in this new stage of capitalism but on this view, despite Merrheim's protestations to the contrary, there appeared to be little possibility of re-establishing the dignity and skills of labour. Further, Merrheim had already made it clear that the advances of machinism made a reduction in the working week top priority. 'The worker, having become a productive machine', he commented, 'needs rest' and only if it were forthcoming would he have the strength to act, to live and to produce.[81] This view, and the re-assessment of the place of work in the life of the proletariat it entailed, was the very antithesis of the Proudhonian-Sorelian vision of man, *homo-faber*, engaged in a ceaseless, all-consuming passion of productive activity. At this stage in the argument men were deemed to require leisure-time in order to recoup their energies but in the future leisure was seen to be an end in itself. It was this mentality, not the austere verities of the productivist ethic, which allowed the introduction of *congés payés*, paid holidays, by Léon Blum's Popular Front government with Jouhaux's support to be seen as a great triumph.

II

'Emperors of Germany and of Austro-Hungary, Prussian landowners and Austrian nobles, who through a hatred of democracy have wished this war', Jouhaux declared at the graveside of the assassinated Jean Jaurès on 4 August 1914, 'we commit ourselves to sounding the death-knell of your reign'.[82] With this statement Jouhaux indicated in unambiguous terms that the CGT had no intention of disrupting the nation's war effort. Further, by the end of the month, Jouhaux had accepted the honorific title of 'delegate to the nation' with special responsibility for explaining the government's actions to the workers. On 3 September, as German troops advanced on the capital, Jouhaux with other syndicalist leaders including Griffuelhes left Paris for Bordeaux in the privileged company of the representatives of the French State. The desire to maintain an ideological and economic gulf between the working class and the rest of the nation had vanished and the CGT's endorsement of the *union sacrée* appeared to be complete.

Despite the fact that the likelihood of war had been a constant topic of discussion amongst syndicalists — in 1911 Merrheim had even published an article entitled 'L'Approche de la guerre' in *La Vie ouvrière* — the actual outbreak of hostilities seems to have taken the CGT leadership by surprise. In the letters of Rosmer to Monatte dated the end of July 1914, for example, there is no real sense of the imminence of war[83] whilst in *La Voix du peuple* the lead story continued to be the Couriau affair as the CGT prepared for its Grenoble conference. To the sense of shock was also added that of fear. The existence of the *Carnet B*, a government compiled list of the names of approximately 3 000 people to be arrested in the event of anti-war demonstrations or strikes, was widely known, as was the desire (reported in *La Bataille syndicaliste* on 29 July) of certain government ministers to employ the guillotine to deal with recalcitrants. In addition, as Merrheim was later to observe, to have opposed the war at the very moment that France was engulfed in a wave of nationalism would have been to run the risk not only of being shot by the State but also by the people themselves. The response of the CGT leadership to the events of August 1914 was thus predominantly one of disarray and resignation and the personal testimonies of such men as Monatte, Dumoulin and Péricat, all of whom were called up into the army, are sufficient to indicate the feeling of powerlessness experienced by those opposed from the outset to the war. The real disagreement, given the CGT's admission that it had been 'submerged by events', centred not upon whether the war could have been stopped but upon whether Germany alone or all the belligerent nations were responsible for its occurrence.

The CGT's official line evolved with alarming speed. On 29 July it committed itself to participation in the anti-war demonstration planned for 9 August but on the same day issued a manifesto tacitly holding Austria responsible for the possibility of war. By 3 August the blame had been unequivocally attributed to Germany. 'Having officially declared war on Russia', an editorial in *La Bataille syndicaliste* announced, 'Germany, without announcement, without warning, without notification, without delay, launched an attack against France . . . the desire of Germany for war is thus demonstrated'.[84] The same editorial disclosed what was to be the central justification for the CGT's actions. In the face of German militarism, it went on, the democratic and republican traditions of France needed to be safeguarded. France, as Jouhaux repeatedly made clear during the first weeks of the war, was fighting not a war of conquest but a war of defence against German imperialism and despotism; it was a war for civilisation, progress and liberty and against barbarism, 'a war of revolution and not reaction, truly in the tradition of 1792'.[85] Revolutionary patriotism was thus combined with Germanophobia and in tune with this *La Bataille syndicaliste* (the CGT's sole remaining paper after the declaration of war) chose to reprint Bakunin's near racist diatribes against Germans, letters and articles by Kropotkin supporting the war, cartoons attacking the anti-war stance of Romain Rolland and numerous studies analysing the supposedly authoritarian German mentality. Such sentiments received broad approval amongst syndicalists, often from surprising quarters. In a letter to Monatte, James Guillaume announced that he supported the war on the grounds that it could 'destroy the two great plagues of the world: German imperialism and German social-democracy'.[86]

Amongst the first of the syndicalists to display his approval of Jouhaux's determination to back the war-effort was Victor Griffuelhes. As late as August 1916 Griffuelhes was still arguing that the central issue posed by the war was 'the opposition between two ways of thinking, two forms of life'. The sense of liberty, the hostility to moral and intellectual servitude, did not exist beyond the Rhine.[87] This conviction was backed up by reference to Griffuelhes' residual distaste for the German labour movement. For German socialists, he maintained, 'the individual does not exist, he is part of the State'.[88] But the major theme of Griffuelhes' journalism during the war was the continuation of his earlier preoccupation with the weakness of French capitalism. On 12 August 1914 Jouhaux launched the idea of industrial mobilisation as a means not only of securing military victory but also of solving unemployment and of strengthening the syndicalist movement in readiness for the post-war era.[89] This argument was taken up immediately by Griffuelhes.[90] Dramatic measures, he argued, need to be taken to utilise the human and physical resources of the nation. In order to defend France industrial production had to be maximised, even if it meant the violation of an individual's rights. One recurring aspect of this argument was an unfavourable comparison of the sluggishness of

French economic activity to the industrial vigour and might of Germany. 'By the side of the Germans who from the first moment put into effect all the active forces of their country', Griffuelhes wrote, 'we appear as the eternal speechifiers'.[91] If the German was by nature a manufacturer, the Frenchman was a usurer. The same sentiment led Griffuelhes to oppose the naval blockade of Germany on the grounds that it would reduce competition, disadvantage the French consumer, and encourage industrial lethargy. France, he argued, would not be strengthened by weakening Germany.[92] In similar fashion, Griffuelhes challenged the desirability of artisanal production. 'I have known,' he wrote in an article significantly entitled 'La Liberté avec le bien-être',[93] 'good proletarians, artists of their trade. They work in their room making exquisite shoes, exercising a skill . . . but they create products for the upper bourgeoisie who alone are capable of paying the right price for them. The factory worker who makes shoes for the people, for the general public, is the object of their scorn'. Such a pattern of manufacture was both economically and morally reprehensible. The purpose of work was not to achieve personal satisfaction but to perform a function that would contribute to the embellishment of the life of the collectivity and it was the modern 'airy' factory with its advanced, automated machinery rather than the small workshop which was most conducive to the efficient attainment of that end. Again, for Griffuelhes German industry offered the model that France was to follow. Throughout Griffuelhes was fearful that with the end of the war France would return to her earlier outworn practices and habits.[94] Further, his preoccupation with the necessity of raising levels of industrial production was such that with the revolution of February 1917 his sole piece of advice for the Russians was that they should recognise that material well-being was 'the brother of liberty'.[95] After the events of October his thoughts turned to other issues.

If Griffuelhes' rally to the nation was at least partly explicable in terms of an open and long-standing antipathy towards Germans,[96] then in the case of Auguste Keufer it was positivism that supplied a rationale for the defence of France. In 1913 he supported the extension of compulsory military service, arguing that 'it would be reckless and dangerous to neglect the strength of our military organisation'[97] and in 1914, shortly before the war, he restated his faith that it was the duty of every individual and of every people as servants of Humanity to defend their country 'against imperialism or invasion'. With the advent of war Keufer was in no doubt that its cause lay in 'the criminal ambition of two Emperors and their military and aristocratic underlings' and that enormous sacrifices would be needed to chase the enemy from the frontiers of France and of 'courageous Belgium'.[98] Throughout the war Keufer remained opposed to the renewal of international contacts with his German counterparts on the grounds that the word of German labour leaders was not to be trusted and that they were collaborators with Prussian militarism.[99] In March 1918, as France suffered the crippling effects of military and economic exhaustion, he again endorsed the Republic and rebuked its critics. 'After the present atrocious tragedy', he argued, 'to wish to substitute another régime would be to deliver up our land to the most frightful civil war.' The Republic, he believed, was now recognised by the majority as France's 'definitive political régime' and what was required was greater moral probity amongst its politicians rather than its destruction.[100] As a trade unionist, however, Keufer's primary concern was to ensure that the economic rights and interests of working people (including those at the front) were not violated or abused as a consequence of the exceptional circumstances created by the war. The *union sacrée* did not mean, therefore, that the syndicalist movement should cease to be vigilant. Moreover, the sacrifices made by the proletariat would ensure that with the end of the war the CGT would play a central role in the task of social and economic reconstruction.[101]

One unexpected supporter of the war whose past pronouncements gave no indication whatsoever of the position he was now to adopt was Emile Pouget. From the end of July 1914 Pouget's regular mouthpiece, Hervé's *La Guerre sociale*, underwent a dramatic metamorphosis and the evidence suggests that Pouget participated in its astonishing *volte-face*. On 29 July, in an editorial entitled 'Ni grève générale ni insurrection', the anti-patriot Hervé announced that he would not be sabotaging the defence of the nation. In the following two days the paper's line on the impending war was enunciated for its readers. 'The country of Revolution', Hervé declared, 'is in danger' and the revolutionary patriotism of its people, witnessed in 1789, 1792, 1830, 1848 and 1871, was to be its 'supreme safeguard'. For all its faults, the Republic was to be defended for the germs of intellectual liberty and social justice contained within it.[102]

Pouget immediately began producing a regular column entitled 'La Rue', intended to catch the mood of the populace in the streets.[103] 'There is,' he wrote, 'heroism in the air. The atmosphere is saturated with it'. The people, Pouget reported, were sustained by an unshakeable faith in the rightness of their cause. They were fighting to defend liberty and civilisation from German barbarism. He too compared 1914 to 1792.

Pouget's articles came to an unexplained end on 6 September (perhaps he too fled from Paris before the advancing enemy) but the following year his name was to be found in the pages of *L'Humanité*[104] as that of the author of a daily serial entitled 'Vieille Alsace'. The story's moral was a simple patriotic one and concerned the lives of those French people living under German occupation since 1870. 'I have submitted to the annexation', one of the principal characters remarks, 'I have considered it a duty to stay so as not to leave the way clear for our conquerors. But not for a day, not for a minute . . . have I accepted the right of conquest, anymore than I have admitted that there could exist an affinity between a German and myself'. One of the highpoints of the tale relates to an incident in which on the anniversary of the birthday of Bismarck and under cover of darkness German street signs were replaced by those bearing the original French names. Those who witnessed this protest felt their old Alsatian hearts stir. The story ends with the hope that 'les Boches', released from their militarism, would have the good sense 'to behead' their Kaiser.

The most immediate problem faced by those opposed to the war was how best to organise their dissent, a job made especially difficult due to the limited means at their disposal, the general dislocation of the labour movement, and the government's policy of where possible despatching militants to the front. To this was added the problems posed by strict press censorship.[105] With the outbreak of the war Pierre Monatte immediately ceased publication of *La Vie ouvrière* and returned to his native Auvergne. Rosmer departed for Perpignan, spending the autumn working on the grape harvest, whilst Merrheim, critical of Jouhaux's flight to Bordeaux, stayed on in Paris where he immediately set about using the power base provided by the *Fédération des métallurgistes* as a vehicle for opposition to the dominant pro-war sentiment within the CGT. After their return to the capital both Rosmer (for two short periods) and Monatte were called up into the army, the latter facing the difficult decision when called upon to fight of whether to disobey his orders and face summary execution, a dilemma resolved only by the advice of his friends that such action would be a pointless sacrifice.[106] In these almost impossible circumstances the capacity to sustain an anti-war campaign was limited and certainly prior to the international anti-war conference held at Zimmerwald in September 1915 little success was gained in challenging the pro-war consensus. It was, however, in this period that what was left of Monatte's *La Vie ouvrière* group first made contact with the Russian exiles Martov and Leon Trotsky.[107]

The first overt public demonstration of the minority position within the syndicalist movement came with Monatte's resignation in December 1914 from the CGT's *comité confédéral*. Monatte's decision was made in protest at the CGT's unwillingness to respond to the invitation to attend a conference in Copenhagen planned to facilitate contacts between labour leaders from the warring nations; to accompany his gesture he printed his letter of resignation and circulated it to leading syndicalist activists.[108] The following year saw a series of similar undertakings including the publication of a special May Day anti-war issue of *L'Union des Métaux*, produced by Merrheim and Rosmer to challenge the CGT's official celebratory (and self-justificatory) edition of *La Voix du peuple*,[109] and culminating in November in the printing of the first of the *Lettres aux abonnés de la Vie ouvrière*.[110]

The anti-war group concentrated firstly upon denouncing what they saw as the betrayal of the working class by the CGT leadership. That the masses could have accepted the government's declarations as articles of faith, Monatte announced in 'Pourquoi je démissionne du Comité confédéral', was in part understandable but 'that the leaders of syndicalism could not show more clear-sightedness, that they could not bring more critical judgement to the examination of government allegations, that they could have allowed themselves to be caught up by the fever of national vanity, that they could forget the principles which until now have guided their actions, that is the saddest sight'. The *union sacrée* was the negation of socialism and by supporting it syndicalism was not only consolidating the capitalist régime but also abandoning the proletariat at its gravest moment. Secondly, Monatte and his colleagues refused to accept any of the pious justifications proferred as a defence of the war. 'When', the editorial of the special issue of *L'Union des Métaux* stated, 'they claimed that the war would lead to the disappearance of militarism, we replied that this was to trap the working class because inevitably militarism would survive the war'. An equally uncompromising response was meted out to talk of a war against barbarism, for civilisation, against the teutonic race and so on. One persistent theme, especially after the expulsion of Trotsky from France in October 1916 by a government which contained socialist ministers, was the contradiction between fighting a war in the name of liberty and the constant internal threats to individual freedoms. 'The press is muzzled in France, people are imprisoned in Italy', the third of Rosmer's *Lettres aux abonnés . . .* stated.[111]

Crucially, an alternative account of the causes of the war was offered. 'This war', Monatte declared, 'has its real roots in the economic dual between England and Germany and in German-Slav rivalry'. The assassination at Sarajevo was only a pretext for war and if the Kaiser bore the heaviest responsibility then the governments of France, England and Russia were also to blame. The war, in short, had its source in the economic system and specifically in the clash between what Rosmer in 1915 referred to as 'competing imperialisms'. Imperialism, he argued, 'is the economic struggle that the great powers are engaged in for the conquest of outlets, for the acquisition of zones of influence in non-industrial countries where they can sell off their products, obtain concessions, exercise a sort of protectorate. It is at the heart of all modern wars'.[112] Consequently, military victory was not a pre-requisite for the end of hostilities. Peace was to be declared on the basis of the *status quo ante bellum*; there were to be no annexations and the political and economic independence of each nation was to be guaranteed. For the proletariat, the war was not its war.

It was these sentiments that found their way into the two principal declarations emanating from the Zimmerwald conference in 1915.[113] After Zimmerwald, where Merrheim represented the anti-war minority within the CGT, it was decided to establish the *Comité d'Action Internationale* as a grouping for all those — including socialists and anarchists — who supported the pro-peace movement. In February the CAI changed its name to that of the *Comité pour la Reprise des Relations Internationales* (with Merrheim as its secretary) and this in turn was sub-divided into two groups, of which the *Comité de Défense Syndicaliste* became henceforth the focal point of syndicalist opposition to the CGT leadership.[114]

Discord quickly surfaced amongst those who had supported the Zimmerwald initiative. At the conference Merrheim had for the first time met Lenin and there, upon his own testimony, he had been subjected to the latter's call for a complete break with the reformist practices and leaders of the past, the creation of a new socialist Third International, and an immediate general strike in protest at the war.[115] Lenin's views had been unable to obtain majority support from the delegates but in France they quickly gained ground amongst those opposed to any deviation from what they saw as the syndicalist commitment to the revolutionary overthrow of the capitalist system. Merrheim, by contrast, sought only an end to the war and believed that it could be achieved by international arbitration and without a prior social revolution. He was therefore to be amongst the first to rally to Woodrow Wilson's peace proposals and during 1917 effected a partial reconciliation with Jouhaux. Merrheim, Marie Guillot wrote to Monatte by way of explanation, 'does not have the temperament of a revolutionary'.[116] Monatte's own judgement was to be even harsher. Citing Ernest Renan's *Vie de Jésus*, he was to comment at the CGT's 1919 Lyons Congress that as with Judas so in Merrheim the administrator had killed the apostle.[117]

These differences became manifest in conflicting responses to events in Russia. Merrheim, partly due to a personal antipathy towards Lenin and Trotsky, quickly resolved to oppose the Bolsheviks whilst many within the anti-war minority, including Rosmer and Monatte, gave the October Revolution their immediate and unqualified support. Here in embryo was the source of new divisions and new alliances, symbolised for syndicalism in the post-war choice between the rival Internationals of Amsterdam and Moscow and in the years of internal crisis which preceded the scission of 1921. For Merrheim this was to mean collaboration not only with Jouhaux but also with his former opponent Auguste Keufer whilst for Rosmer and Monatte it was to entail membership and then expulsion from the communist party. Writing in 1917 Monatte was to argue that in the past the CGT had mistakenly believed that its membership had been one of quality, if not quantity. In truth, it had been neither. The pressing task in the post-war era, therefore, would be to create 'une minorité clairvoyante'. Only then would it again be possible to talk of 'une minorité agissante'.[118] Briefly for Monatte in the early 1920s it was to appear that such a minority had come into existence.

III

In July 1918 the CGT held its first national congress since the beginning of the war. Coinciding with the German offensive on the Marne, for the most part discussion centred upon the war-time activities of the CGT with Jouhaux in particular being called upon to provide an impassioned defence of his actions.[119] Merrheim, Bourderon (the former's associate at Zimmerwald) and the anti-war Dumoulin, despite their criticisms of Jouhaux's leadership, gave their support to the motion of the majority defending the policies of the previous four years. The same congress approved a revision of the CGT's statutes, intended to facilitate the modernisation and centralisation of the syndicalist movement's structure. Shortly afterwards Jouhaux unveiled the CGT's 'minimum programme'.[120]

Taken as a whole the minimum programme amounted to a strategy for the CGT in the post-war era. The spirit of the document was summarised in a statement contained in its preamble. 'We must', it declared, 'turn our efforts towards positive action and be capable not merely of rioting in the streets but of taking in hand the direction of production'. From now on the CGT was to adopt what Jouhaux termed 'la politique de présence': the workers were to be represented everywhere that their interests were being discussed.

The specific details of the programme included an endorsement of Woodrow Wilson's peace proposals and the creation of the League of Nations, a defence of civil and political liberties, and a list of desired reforms including the implementation of the eight-hour day. But its most innovative aspects related to the CGT's proposals for the reconstruction of the French economy. In order to secure the 'return to the nation of the national wealth' the CGT called for the establishment of a *Conseil économique national* and the collective ownership of the means of production. By these means the intention was to secure the rational and planned use of resources.

The proposed economic council, for example, was designed to direct industrial output and the use of labour. The link with the CGT's past was disclosed in the resolve that the CEN was to be a purely economic body and the determination that it should not fall foul of what Jouhaux described as 'bureaucratic methods and control by the State'. It was, however, the would-be composition of the council that illustrated the distance that separated the CGT from its pre-war position. Not only were its delegates to be drawn from government and various consumer groups but the definition of producer was to be stretched to include all those involved either directly or indirectly with the productive process (thereby taking in managers and technicians). The formula for collective ownership was to be *nationalisation industrialisée*, a programme framed explicitly to avoid the charge of *étatisation* but again amounting to a renunciation of the former belief in the hegemony of the producer. To hand over industry exclusively to the control of the workers, Jouhaux argued, would be to return to the corporatism of the *ancien régime* and to facilitate the exploitation of the consumer. Nationalisation, in the form of a *régie coopérative autonome* run jointly by the producers, consumers and representatives of the State, would ensure that output was organised in the 'general interests of the collectivity'.

The minimum programme, according to Jouhaux, corresponded to the 'immediate aspirations of the masses' whilst holding out the possibility of the definitive transformation of the economic order. What was being offered, in effect, was a gradualist strategy, positing peaceful change, in which the workers would progressively enter and then dismantle the bastions of the capitalist economy. As if to further symbolise its abandonment of the revolutionary course, at the Congress of Amsterdam in the summer of 1919 the CGT gave its blessing to the reconstitution of the reformist trade union International which in 1914 had failed so singularly to avert the outbreak of war.[121]

At the CGT's Paris Congress of 1918 Jouhaux had been able to secure a relatively easy victory but with the end of the war and the demobilisation of syndicalist activists organised opposition to the leadership and the policies being pursued by the CGT began to take shape. In the spring of 1919 the Bolsheviks announced the formation of the Third (Communist) International or Comintern and in May of that year the centre of the minority's activities, the *Comité pour la Reprise des Relations Internationales*, was renamed the *Comité pour l'adhésion à la IIIe Internationale*. In April Monatte relaunched *La Vie ouvrière*, this time as a weekly and with a reconstituted 'noyau' that was to include Robert Louzon, Maurice Chambelland (the future leading light behind the *Ligue syndicaliste*) and Gaston Monmousseau who was to take over as its editor in January 1922.[122] 'We were revolutionary syndicalists before the war', its first circular announced, 'and we remain so. The trial of the war has only hardened our convictions'.[123] To demonstrate the continuity *La Vie ouvrière* printed extracts from the pre-war writings of Pelloutier, Griffuelhes, Pouget and Delesalle, and new articles by Sorel, described as 'le vieil original de Boulogne', supporting the Russian Revolution. Also to be included amongst the contributors were Bukharin, Gorky and Trotsky. During the summer of 1919 industrial unrest intensified, with massive unofficial strikes and calls for a general strike, none of which elicited sustained support from the CGT leadership. At the Lyons Congress in September Monatte led the assault on Jouhaux, mercilessly castigating him for the betrayals of the war years, the class collaboration implied by the minimum programme, and the failure to support the strikes of the previous months.[124]

Immediately after the Lyons Congress the minority further consolidated its position by forming what from the end of the year were known as

Comités de syndicalistes révolutionnaires. During the next three years of bitter and sometimes violent debate, mirrored in the divisions amongst socialists which saw the birth of the French communist party at the Congress of Tours in 1920, the minority steadily gained in strength and to such an extent that by the time of the CGT's Lille Congress in July 1921 it was only narrowly defeated in the main motion by 1556 votes to 1348. Faced with an almost certain loss of control the CGT's national committee, in an attempt to stifle internal opposition, ordered the dissolution of the CSR. Opinion amongst the *minoritaires* was divided about what course of action to pursue. Monatte, in line with the position consistently adopted by *La Vie ouvrière*, was determined to preserve unity — 'the French syndicalist movement', he wrote, 'is too weak to afford the luxury of a schism'[125] — but at a special conference called by the minority in December 1921 the mood of the delegates favoured the creation of a new organisation. Six months later at St Etienne the *Confédération Générale du Travail Unitaire* (CGTU) held its first congress. The same congress voted overwhelmingly for the CGTU's membership of Moscow's Red Trade Union International, the Profintern. The syndicalist movement was now officially split into two.

According to Keufer the divisions within the CGT were between those, the *majoritaires*, who had had 'the good sense and courage' to recognise that with the declaration of war the interests of the proletariat could not be separated from the interests of France and those for whom every violation of the 'sacrosanct principle of class struggle' was a sign of weakness.[126] Later he transcribed this division into a struggle between the 'reformists' and 'les syndicalistes bolchevistes', the supporters of the 'abominable manoeuvres of the sinister dictators, Lenin, Trotsky and Zinoviev'.[127] In effect, what was being witnessed was a re-run — 'history', Keufer wrote, 'is a perpetual circle' — of the quarrels that had dominated the CGT's congresses at Bourges in 1904 and Amiens in 1906. The proponents of revolutionary verbalism, replete with their habitual malicious insults, were once again seeking to deflect syndicalism from the path of constructive and practical change.

It was upon this latter task that Keufer wished to see the CGT concentrate its efforts in the post-war years. In his view, the present condition of both the economy and the working class ruled out the possibility of the total transformation of the social order — 'it is sufficient', he wrote in 1918, 'to underline how the proletariat is still in a state of enormous intellectual and scientific inferiority, lacking the experience required to realise the suppression of the *patronat*, of property'[128] — and therefore the syndicalist movement would have to limit itself to facilitating and contributing towards the rebuilding of the war-damaged economy and the restoration of 'normal national life'. To that end Keufer openly advocated, in the spirit of the 'communal life of the trenches', the co-operation between workers and their employers. 'Faced with the gravity of the economic situation in which the war has placed us', he argued, 'I believe that instead of proclaiming the class struggle it is far more important and necessary to affirm the urgent necessity of *class collaboration*'.[129] Class war, Keufer believed, would only further aggravate the already precarious condition of France, whilst the policy of collaboration would secure not only increased industrial production and prosperity but would also enable the proletariat to effect a more equitable and just distribution of the nation's wealth. The workers would occupy their rightful place as integral members of society.

Keufer's fullest statement of this position came in his government-sponsored document *Rapport sur l'organisation des relations entre patrons et ouvriers*.[130] The entire emphasis of this long document fell upon the need for a change of attitude on both sides of industry away from division and hostility towards reciprocity and co-operation combined with a series of practical proposals for institutional reform — arbitration procedures, joint worker-management committees and so on — designed to aid the avoidance of conflict.

From this perspective Keufer was able to give the policies of the former anarchist Jouhaux his cautious support but even here he was critical that by its talk of the proposed national economic council as a general panacea the 'minimum programme' might have unduly raised the expectations of the workers and thus in part have been responsible for the labour disturbances of 1919 and 1920. 'A great experiment in economic transformation is being attempted', Keufer stated: 'we need to follow it attentively in order to assess carefully its diverse phases and social consequences'.[131] As for the programme of nationalisation he was not opposed *in principle* to the nationalisation of such industries as mining and the railways but he remained implacably opposed to strikes in public services. Yet overall Keufer stayed true to the positivist conviction that the task of social and economic transformation was a slow one and that the primary precondition for change was 'a courageous work of education' in which every individual would come to recognise the notions of duty, responsibility and justice and how 'intellectual and moral pleasures play a noble role in the happiness of Humanity'.[132]

A less qualified support for Jouhaux came from Merrheim. By the end of the war, if not before, Merrheim had ceased to be the leader of the minority and, as his pamphlet *La Révolution économique* revealed, he quickly showed his enthusiastic approval for the CGT's new post-war orientation. Merrheim began *La Révolution économique* with a restatement of the traditional syndicalist goal. 'Our ideal', he asserted, 'is the disappearance of the category of wage-earner' but he equally set himself against violent revolution as a means of achieving that end. 'Can one establish', Merrheim asked, 'a parallel between the circumstances which after the Russian Revolution brought about the German Revolution and the situation of our country? Immediately, I answer no'.[133] What was required was an economic revolution and this he defined in terms of increased production — 'an economic revolution', he wrote, 'draws its strength from work' — and the process by which the working class, through increased penetration, gradually took control of the economy. Rather than by frontal assault, capitalism was to be undermined from within.

The 'minimum programme' was a point of transition towards the attainment of that final goal and Merrheim therefore found little difficulty in defending what he took to be its specific proposals. Firstly, 'action for peace', which in essence meant support for Woodrow Wilson's plans for a post-war settlement and by unstated implication a rejection of the call, voiced specifically by the supporters of the Bolsheviks, to turn the war into a general European Revolution. Secondly, in addition to a shorter and *where possible* eight-hour day Merrheim demanded a formal recognition of the rights of the *syndicats* to negotiate directly with the employers on issues of pay and conditions of work. Consultation rather than confrontation was to be the practice of the future. Finally, Merrheim revealed the extent of his, and the CGT's, post-war preoccupation with production when he argued that one of the major goals of the minimum programme was to achieve 'the maximum production in the minimum of time for the maximum salary'. To achieve that end Merrheim accepted that this would require the application of 'scientific discoveries', that is the once-loathed Taylorism, to the activity of labour.[134]

In his conclusion to *La Révolution économique* Merrheim argued that 'the minimum programme is not class collaboration but the basis of action for the liberation of work and the complete emancipation of the workers'. That, as a former member of Lagardelle's circle and of the 'noyau' of *La Vie ouvrière*, he should have believed this to be the case and have argued it with such conviction is testimony to the manner in which Merrheim had progressively reached the conclusion that in France all genuine revolutionary endeavour was impractical. For Merrheim, as he was to argue at the Congress of Lyons in 1918, the sad reality was that if a revolutionary situation existed the workers themselves were not in a position to take advantage of it.

It was during the spring and summer of 1919 that Merrheim's own union members graphically illustrated the distance that now separated him from the 'minority'. In a wave of unofficial strikes metalworkers throughout France demonstrated that they, if not their leaders, had been inspired by the example of the Russian Revolution. Not only did Merrheim fail to support these strikes, condemning them for what he regarded as their political goals, but as the minority gained in strength (the *Fédération des métallurgistes* itself split into two in 1921) he devoted himself to an almost obsessive campaign against the Russian Revolution, Bolshevism and their supporters in France.[135]

At the heart of Merrheim's invective was a denunciation of the methods of Bolshevism. He spoke, for example, of the 'sarcastic and satanic dialectic of Lenin' and condemned him for his willingness to 'employ tricks, deceit and lies'. Merrheim was against membership of the Third International partly because of the insistence that all its member organisations should be prepared to use violence and resort to illegal acts.[136] Further, by 1920 Merrheim had appreciated that what was being established in Russia was not a dictatorship of the proletariat but a dictatorship by the party *over* the proletariat. Lenin he described as 'the red Czar',[137] whilst Bolshevism was a doctrine of 'a restricted, prussianised, militarised political party led by an élite'. The less numerous the party the more easily could the dictatorship of the leaders be exercised. In post-revolutionary Russia centralisation and 'bureaucratisation' had reached their apogee. The soviets and co-operatives had been crushed, reduced to appendages of the State and the *syndicats*, in line with Bolshevik doctrine, had been subordinated to the party, 'bowed beneath the dictatorship of a handful of communist functionaries'.[138] Of Trotsky's plans for the militarisation of labour Merrheim remarked: 'to dictatorship, he adds tyranny and thereby turns Russia into an immense industrial barracks where the worker is treated like a farm animal'.[139] For Merrheim, if not for the members of the *Vie ouvrière* group who appeared to accept the word of Trotsky, Radek and Victor Serge that the rebellion was led by counter-revolutionaries,[140] the nature of the Bolshevik dictatorship was symbolised by the revolt at Kronstadt and the manner in which it was ruthlessly put down.[141] Kronstadt, he argued, was a protest against State terrorism. No one could believe that it was anything other than 'criminal and odious to see a supposedly worker and communist government crush the insurrection with machine-gun fire, flame-throwers and cannon and at the same time seek to vilify and slander the rebels'.

For Merrheim, the failure of Bolshevism was amply demonstrated by the changes of economic strategy that led ultimately to the imposition of the New Economic Policy.[142] NEP, he argued, meant the capitulation of Bolshevism before capitalism, the restoration of the bourgeoisie and of private property. What it showed — and this for Merrheim was the crucial objection to the Russian experience — was that the Bolsheviks had failed to solve the 'problem of production'. Bolshevism was a destructive, not a constructive, doctrine; it had destroyed all the 'sources of activity, life, production and experience' and had brought only poverty and misery. The people, he believed, had almost come to regret the passing of the Czarist régime.

Merrheim's purpose in subjecting the Bolsheviks to this ferocious assault was to discredit the Russian experience in the eyes of the French proletariat and thus defeat those within the CGT who, in his view, were intent upon dividing the syndicalist movement by establishing the supremacy of the communist party.[143] 'It is syndicalism', he wrote, 'which is at stake, its independence and above all its doctrine and if we succumb it is not only syndicalism but the CGT which is finished'.[144] Part of that argument for Merrheim took the form of asserting the contrast between the violent and destructive character of Bolshevism and what he saw as the nature of syndicalism as a *constructive* doctrine which drew not upon feelings of hatred but upon the sentiments of personal dignity, morality and justice and which, by leaving intact the material base of society, would create the future of equality and joy through 'an abundance of production'.[145] But above all Merrheim wanted to establish that it was the opponents of Bolshevism and not their supporters who continued the tradition of the autonomy of the *syndicat* established by the Charter of Amiens.[146] If the communists were to win, he argued, 'perhaps we, who have always been at the forefront of the workers' movement, will become the most backward in the whole of Europe'.[147]

Writing in 1949 Pierre Monatte argued that it was a mistake to believe, as was often claimed, that in 1919 Jouhaux and Merrheim had saved the French working class from totalitarianism: at that date Russian totalitarianism did not exist. 'What existed', Monatte wrote, 'was the Russian Revolution which could have known another outcome if the German Revolution had succeeded in its second stage, if the Italian Revolution had experienced its first . . . then it would have been the European Revolution'. It was because of the failure of this revolution to materialise, Monatte argued, that totalitarianism in Russia had arisen.[148] Monatte himself from 1925 onwards was to be one of the most perceptive commentators upon that process and he was to be amongst the first to equate Stalinism with State-capitalism, with fascism and with counter-revolution. But Monatte, in contrast to such former supporters of the Bolsheviks as Boris Souvarine, was never to identify or confuse Stalinism with communism. The crushing of the hopes he had placed in the Russian Revolution was to remain the great drama and tragedy of his life.

Shortly after the first congress of the CGTU in 1922 Maurice Chambelland was led to ask whether it was 'mysticism' which explained support for the Russian Revolution with what he described as its 'errors and crimes'. His answer was in the negative. 'It is', he wrote, 'a reasoned admiration for a magnificent proletarian and revolutionary struggle that we have been incapable of in this country. This is the explanation of our attitude'.[149] Monatte shared these sentiments and felt an intense enthusiasm for what he saw as the heroic efforts not only of the Bolshevik leadership but of the Russian people as a whole. Writing to Trotsky in 1920, he remarked: 'You are fighting for yourselves and for us. We are fighting for you and for ourselves, ashamed of not having done more and of still being so weak. Your triumph prepares and announces ours'.[150] The Russian Revolution, it seemed, would soon spread to Europe, in the process bringing about the resurrection of socialism and if, therefore, Moscow had not provided a model that was to be followed slavishly it had furnished an example of what genuine revolutionary commitment could achieve. Moreover, at this early stage support for the Bolsheviks did not imply commitment to a fixed and codified doctrine. Thus Monatte could argue that the much-discussed 21 conditions imposed by the Bolsheviks for membership of the Comintern amounted solely to the imperative that its members should be revolutionaries. 'They only ask of sincere revolutionaries', he wrote, 'fidelity to the revolution and an examination of the conditions in which in the twentieth century a revolution is possible'.[151] Faced, therefore, with a choice between Wilsonian democracy which for all its liberal rhetoric was on the side of reaction and counter-revolution and support for the revolution in Russia there was no dilemma. 'We side with Moscow', Monatte wrote in September 1920, 'because as the statutes of the CGT and all our conference resolutions proclaim, we side with the social revolution'.[152] Nor did Monatte believe that this commitment should be lightly relinquished. 'True revolutionaries', he commented in September 1922, 'do not repudiate the revolution when it experiences difficult times'.[153]

A second aspect of the support for the Russian Revolution derived from the apparent compatibility of syndicalism and Bolshevism, a sentiment facilitated by the earlier collaborative endeavours of Rosmer, Monatte, Lenin and Trotsky in the Zimmerwald movement. The circular relaunching *La Vie ouvrière*, for example, remarked: 'What therefore is the Russian Revolution if not a revolution of a syndicalist character?'.[154] The journal itself was to carry numerous articles exploring the parallels between the *syndicats* and the soviets and the manner in which power had been turned over exclusively to the producers, its location transferred from the State to the factory. Robert Louzon went so far as to characterise Pelloutier as 'le père du soviétisme' and to argue that events in Russia confirmed the views of Sorel and Lagardelle on the nature of revolution.[155] Monatte wrote that Pelloutier, were he still alive, would say: 'mes enfants, vous êtes dans la bonne voie'.[156]

Less obviously the Bolshevik Revolution and the subsequent creation in France of a communist party made possible the acceptance amongst the syndicalists of the *Vie ouvrière* group of the legitimacy and role of the political party. Colette Chambelland has argued that when assessing the adherence of syndicalists — including Rosmer and Monatte — to the communist party it is necessary to distinguish between the 'circumstantial' and the 'fundamental' objections posed by syndicalists to political parties. 'The communist party', she writes, 'purged between 1920 and 1923 of its non-worker elements, appeared to them as an authentic workers' party, totally rid of its social-democratic dross, and capable of working on equal terms with the *syndicats*'.[157] In short, the antipathy towards parties was dispelled because it appeared that there existed a party which would escape the perils of bourgeois control and class collaboration. Thus shortly after the Congress of Tours Monatte could write that whilst he was not a member of the party he nevertheless took pleasure from observing its efforts to re-establish its revolutionary character. 'It is not yet', he commented, 'a revolutionary party in the image of the Russian communist party but it has begun the process of becoming one'.[158] After joining the party he argued that all the decisions taken since the Congress of Tours had served to enlarge its 'proletarian esprit', distancing it from electoralism, and therefore diminishing the 'points of friction' between party and *syndicat*.[159]

In addition, it was also the case that Monatte and his colleagues at *La Vie ouvrière* appeared to accept that there might possibly be occasions where the party, not the *syndicat*, would fulfil the role of revolutionary leadership. Certainly this had been the case in Russia and this implied that a revision in tactics was necessary. Responding to the charge that he had suggested that the Charter of Amiens was 'finished', Monatte countered by stating that his intention had been simply to argue that it 'does not answer all the problems that are present today'.[160] The war had shown that the State was 'infinitely stronger and more terrible' than had been imagined whilst the revolution in Russia had shown that 'a revolution will not involve a week's struggle but a struggle lasting years, that it demands the sacrifice of a whole generation'. In short, the actual reality of a revolution, with its massive organisational problems, civil war and foreign intervention, had demonstrated beyond doubt that the revolution would not occur in the easy manner envisaged by syndicalist theory.

What this meant — for all Monatte's re-assertion of the 'primordial role which belongs to the *syndicat* in the destructive phase of the revolution as well as in the constructive phase of social reorganisation' — was that, faced with a new brutal stage of capitalism, the State could not be abolished immediately. Here Monatte, like other syndicalists, drew inspiration from Lenin's *State and Revolution*, published in France in 1921, with its model of the proletarian State taken, via Marx, from the Paris Commune and in line with this he conceded that the revolution itself would 'render indispensable the establishment of a provisional dictatorship of the proletariat and the institution of our own red army'. Implicit within this argument was the admission that there were certain difficult tasks in the revolutionary process that the *syndicats* as presently constituted appeared ill-equipped to perform. 'Who will exercise this dictatorship?', Monatte asked: 'those who merit it, as in Russia. Will it be us, the syndicalists, through the CGT? Will it be the party? History will say'.[161] Monatte's point was that in Russia it was the party which constituted the revolutionary *avant-garde* of the proletariat and that it merited this status because of its past labour, struggles and sacrifice.[162]

For all this Monatte's view remained that in France 'the revolutionary spirit will have its refuge, its seat, in the purely class organisation that is syndicalism'.[163] In a country 'rotten from one hundred years of democracy' he believed it to be highly unlikely that a political party could become truly proletarian and therefore what he envisaged was not the subordination of the *syndicats* to the party but rather a relationship of close co-operation with the party, ultimately the disposable structure, in the role of auxiliary.

The most dramatic illustration of this perspective came with the controversy that surrounded the first congress of the Profintern in July 1921.[164] The Bolshevik stance on the correct relationship between party and unions was clearly set out by Trotsky in a letter to Monatte.[165] 'Is it possible,' Trotsky asked, 'that in 1921 we have to return to the positions of 1906 and to 'reconstruct' pre-war syndicalism? . . . This position is spineless, it is conservative, it runs the risk of being reactionary'. In Trotsky's view, revolutionary syndicalism was to be seen as the embryo of the new communist party — like many other Bolsheviks he had no difficulty equating the 'minorité agissante' with the élite constituted by the party — and therefore the ideal solution was the 'total fusion' of revolutionary syndicalists and communists in a 'single party'. It is not a question, Trotsky wrote, 'of subordinating the *syndicats* to the party but of unity'. Nevertheless, the Bolshevik leadership readily recognised that in order to pacify supporters of the syndicalist position — 'there is', Trotsky conceded to Monatte, 'a certain psychological difficulty in crossing the threshold of a party after a long revolutionary career outside one' — it would be necessary to establish a separate trade union International to run in parallel to that for political parties, the Comintern. At the first congress of the Profintern debate centred almost exclusively upon the relationship between the two Internationals and, by extension, upon the relationship between the *syndicats* and their national communist parties, with the final communiqué, approved by Rosmer amongst others, referring to the desirability of 'a real and tight liaison' and 'an organic and technical relationship' between the nominally distinct organisations. The response in France, in the shape of the CDS, was swift and hostile, with the publication in *La Vie ouvrière* of a declaration, signed by Monatte, repudiating the actions of its own delegates at the congress and denouncing the notion of 'an organic relationship' as a means likely to turn the *syndicat* from 'un groupement de classe' into 'un groupment de tendance'. Monatte went further in an article entitled 'Arrêt? Non! Simple halte'.[166] Whilst paying due respect to Moscow as 'the home of the first social revolution' he pointed out that those who spoke of anarchist and syndicalist prejudices were themselves the victim of 'social democratic prejudices'. In France, he affirmed, the party and the *syndicats* might well operate side by side but the party would never lead the *syndicats* into action.

On this vital issue the *Vie ouvrière* group were never able to reach either a complete or durable agreement with the leaders of the communist movement. In October 1922, following the communist party's calamitous Paris congress, Monatte's withdrawal from the editorial board of *L'Humanité* was accompanied by a declaration, signed also by Louzon and Maurice Chambelland, which affirmed that as revolutionary syndicalists 'we attribute to the *syndicat* the key role in the revolutionary struggle for the emancipation of the proletariat and we give to the party an auxiliary and not a directing role'.[167] Six months later Trotsky and Louzon crossed swords over what the former referred to as 'le prejugé anarcho-syndicaliste'.[168] The pages of *L'Humanité*, *Le Bulletin communiste*, and *La Vie ourvrière* testify to the frequency with which the subject was raised. But in 1919 this rancorous dispute was for the future. To support the Russian Revolution was to re-assert the virtue of revolutionary activism, and to do so, initially at least, involved for Monatte and the 'noyau' at *La Vie ouvrière* neither doctrinal conversion nor a complete rupture with past practices.[169]

With the relaunch of *La Vie ouvrière* Monatte was able once again to absorb himself in the affairs of the syndicalist movement. Rosmer, by contrast, quickly departed for Moscow where on a series of lengthy visits between 1920 and 1924 he was to be intimately involved in the early operations of the Communist International and in the establishment of the Profintern.[170] Monatte's efforts were directed primarily into three campaigns, none of which were aided by his imprisonment on a charge of conspiracy against the State between May 1920 and March 1921. Not surprisingly, he attempted to persuade syndicalists that their 'greatest preoccupation' and 'primary duty' should be to secure the victory of the Russian Revolution, preferably by contributing to the revolution in Europe.[171] At CGT congresses and in articles such as 'La Faute des masses?'[172] he continued to criticise and castigate the CGT leadership for its past errors and present mistakes. Finally, as the effective leader of the minority he fought to strengthen its position within the syndicalist movement whilst simultaneously seeking to avoid a split, a strategy which led him into conflict with the so-called 'pure' syndicalists led by Pierre Besnard and which by December 1921 had resulted in defeat and his own resignation from *La Vie ouvrière*.

Although Monatte did not formally join the communist party until May 1923 (becoming a member of the central committee only eight months later) he began writing for the now communist controlled *L'Humanité* in March 1922 when he was given special responsibility for its 'vie sociale' section. In the following two years his actions were to a great extent determined by the party's internal factional disputes and by the vicissitudes of communist policy at both an international and domestic level. 1922 brought Zinoviev's platform of the 'united front' with the once-loathed reformist parties, a policy which Monatte supported at the level of the syndicalist movement on the familiar grounds that a *syndicat*, as a grouping of people of similar economic interests, should embrace all workers irrespective of their doctrines.[173] 1924 saw the death of Lenin, the struggle for the succession in Moscow, the commencement of the battle against Trotsky and what became known as 'Trotskyism', and the strategy of the 'bolshevisation' of the world's communist parties.[174]

One central aspect of the process of bolshevisation was the complete structural reorganisation of the party. To enhance its proletarian base sections representing geographical areas were to be replaced by factory cells as the primary unit of membership. The policies and perspectives embodied in this upheaval were, however, inextricably enmeshed in the broader ideological and factional disputes that were increasingly in evidence within the Communist International and specifically its French section. As Danielle Tartakovsky has argued, bolshevisation itself was merely the pretext for purging dissident elements within the party in the name of an orthodoxy which came to define the content of Leninism solely by reference to the internal dispute within the Russian party.

At a meeting of the party's central committee on 18 March 1924 Monatte, Rosmer and Boris Souvarine (soon himself to be expelled from the party for indiscipline) were alone to oppose the party's policy statement endorsing bolshevisation. In the course of the debate Monatte was to condemn what he termed 'le centralisme mécanique' that dominated the party's decision-making process.[175] At the end of March Albert Treint, general-secretary of the party, published a lead article in *Le Bulletin communiste* (the party's theoretical journal) entitled 'Dans la voie tracée par Lénine' in which in defending bolshevisation he cast Monatte, Rosmer and Souvarine as right-wing critics of the party's policy.[176] He continued this line with the publication on 18 April of 'Contre la Droite internationale', a virulent attack categorising all three men as allies of Trotsky and the opposition in Russia. 'Our opposition', Treint wrote, in a statement typical of what was to become communist party rhetoric, 'is truly an opposition of the right, of liquidationism, of pessimism and of reactionary defeatism . . . A party, to fight effectively against the bourgeoisie, must reduce to impotence those in its ranks who discourage and weaken it'.[177] Four days later Monatte withdrew for the final time from *L'Humanité*, informing its editor that 'as a simple member of the party I will have a free hand to defend my point of view'. On 23 April other members of the so-called 'right', including Rosmer and Chambelland, acted likewise. In their collective letter of resignation they complained that members of the party who came from revolutionary syndicalism were being treated as 'carriers of the plague' and went on to express their determination to preserve 'a communist party where the workers themselves would not be mere extras but the real driving force of the whole organism'.[178] Monatte quickly turned his words into deeds, producing two articles in reply to Treint's allegations.[179] In both he supported efforts to extend the proletarian base of the party (the stated goal of bolshevisation) but disputed the effectiveness and sincerity of the leadership's proposals for reorganisation. 'It is not necessary', Monatte wrote, 'for the French party to copy exactly the structure and working methods of the Russian party'. To the charge that he belonged to the Right Monatte responded by suggesting that if he belonged anywhere it was in 'the little corner' reserved for 'la Gauche ouvrière'.

Treint's assault was followed by condemnation at the Fifth Congress of the Comintern held in Moscow during June and after this the campaign of vilification against Monatte and his associates was intensified further. On 5 October Monatte, Rosmer and Victor Delagarde of the *Fédération des métaux* responded by sending the central committee a letter in which they denied the charges of disloyalty levelled against them. 'How', they asked, 'have we shown a desire to harm the party?'[180] In the absence of any response (and in self-conscious imitation of the war-time letters to the subscribers of *La Vie ouvrière*) on 22 November they took the irrevocable step of publishing and circulating an open letter to the members of the party, and with inevitable consequences. Again they denied that they had acted against the interests of the party but upon this occasion the tone was less conciliatory. To the accusation that they had aided the opposition in Russia they replied by condemning the party leadership in France for their efforts to restrict access to Trotsky's writings and speeches. 'We will say more', they went on, 'we think that at the present time it is Trotsky who is really thinking and acting in the spirit of Lenin and not those who are now pursuing him with their attacks whilst draping themselves in the cloak of Leninism'. Turning to the internal affairs of the party, Treint was rebuked for his autocratic and bureaucratic methods. 'From the top to the bottom of the party', the letter stated, 'a cascade of instructions is being constructed that without understanding one must obey'.[181]

Party members were instructed to return all copies of the open letter unread to the party secretariat. On 5 December, after Rosmer had restated their position, a special conference expelled Monatte, Rosmer and Delagarde from the party by a unanimous vote for their part in 'the antiproletarian and anti-communist offensive led by the combined forces of demagogic fascism and the fascistic *Bloc des Gauches*'.[182] Unrepentant, in January 1925 the three dissidents published a résumé of their 'irreconcilable' disagreements with the party leadership. 'Leninism without Lenin', they remarked in a devastating phrase, 'frightens us'.[183] An important moment in the history of revolutionary syndicalism was over.

IV

In September 1920 Amadée Dunois, soon to be a member of the communist party's central committee, published an interview with Griffuelhes, Delesalle, Yvetot and Pouget in *L'Humanité*. The chosen topic of conversation was the current state of the syndicalist movement, and of the former leaders of the CGT, it was Griffuelhes who dominated the proceedings. 'What is truly criminal', he declared, 'what, in my view, constitutes a swindle worthy of the politicians whom formerly we fought so bitterly, is that people persist in misinterpreting and emasculating a text as clear and as straightforward as the Charter of Amiens'.[184] Just over a year later Pierre Monatte received a letter from his old friend Fritz Brupbacher (then residing in Moscow) in which the Swiss anarchist commented: 'You know that Griffuelhes was here. Reading between the lines I understand that he supports Trotsky's position and that he is being encouraged. Trotsky thinks that he will again play a part in the movement, that if you do not change your attitude you will have him as an adversary, and that perhaps it will be him who will be the instrument of communism in France and in the *syndicats*'.[185] Griffuelhes had clearly come a long way since his support of the *union sacrée* in 1914.

The first evidence of this evolution can be seen in Griffuelhes' articles in *La Feuille*. Writing in November 1917, while his knowledge of events in Russia was at best partial, he remarked that since the first days of the revolution 'I have placed great hopes in the soviets. Their composition, the authority they have acquired, corresponds exactly with my wishes, my conceptions'.[186] Subsequently he was to stress the parallels between the soviets and the *syndicats*.[187] From this perspective, and not without a hint of malice, Griffuelhes quickly went on to attack what he saw as 'le nouveau Millerandisme' of the CGT leadership and the stupidity of the policy of nationalisation. Writing in Charles Rappoport's *La Revue communiste* he commented that only the 'sovietism' being practised in Russia could threaten a capitalism strengthened by the war.[188] In part, Griffuelhes' views were a reflection of a sense of personal resentment that he undoubtedly felt towards a syndicalist movement that chose to see him as a man of the past but what gave his outbursts particular significance was that he did actually go to Russia and there he was to meet Lenin, Trotsky and Zinoviev.

Griffuelhes' account of that visit was published in *La Bataille*, the first article appearing on 4 May 1922.[189] Griffuelhes' death in July meant that the projected description of contemporary Russia and his examination of the nature of Bolshevism was never to be completed (the last article appearing on 17 August) but the weekly instalments that were published nevertheless convey a clear impression of his preoccupation and determination to make sense of events since 1917. By what standards were the actions of the Bolsheviks to be assessed? What was Bolshevism? Who was Lenin? These were the central questions posed by Griffuelhes. In reply he concluded that Bolshevism was a mixture of Guesdism, Blanquism and syndicalism. From the first it had taken the idea of the indispensability of the seizure of State power, from the second a belief in audacious action and the dictatorship of the proletariat, whilst from syndicalism came the notion that the factories and fields were to be the location of popular representation. Bolshevism, in short, was to be interpreted in terms of a vocabulary taken from French politics. On the achievements of the Revolution and its probable future Griffuelhes readily acknowledged the existence of economic chaos, saw the logic behind NEP, and concluded that the Russian people were capable of surviving the suffering associated with the birth of a new society that would itself take years to create. As for Lenin, Griffuelhes clearly shared the fascination felt by many French syndicalists for this previously unknown figure. What Griffuelhes saw was a man who did not fully belong to Europe. 'He is', Griffuelhes wrote, 'Western in what he likes, Eastern in what he does'. And it was the latter element that accounted for his success as a revolutionary.

Griffuelhes did not succeed in regaining what he saw as his rightful place amongst the leadership of the syndicalist movement,[190] although after his death he did receive dutiful praise from his former colleagues. 'Despite everything', Yvetot wrote, 'it is to Griffuelhes that syndicalism should return in order to be what it should be'.[191] Moreover, with his perception of Lenin as an oriental genius he had hit upon a theme that once again brought him close to the position adopted by Georges Sorel and Edouard Berth.

From the moment that Sorel first heard news of the Revolution he was an enthusiastic supporter of Lenin and the Bolsheviks but his assessment of the significance of events in Russia was unconventional to say the least. As Maria Malatesta has argued, Sorel's diagnosis of the 'crisis' of syndicalism also brought with it a rejection of France and as a consequence he turned his attention towards the proletariats of other nations.[192] Faced with the outbreak and then the horrors of the First World War Sorel's public position was one of silence but his private correspondence makes clear his immediate opposition to the war efforts of the allied powers. 'The entire Roman-Christian world of the past', he wrote in September 1914,' is collapsing and we are entering an era of plutocratic civilisation'.[193] In his view the primary motive behind the war was the desire of international financiers, the 'swindlers of the stock exchange' who had replaced the heroic capitalists of old, to destroy German economic power. Thus the intention was to foster a resurgence of usury capitalism — 'I am more and more convinced', Sorel wrote, 'that this war is a battle of the bourgeoisie against work' — and the actual outcome had been to accentuate the economic dominance of the modern embodiment of usury, the

American trust system. Beneath Sorel's cynicism lay the conviction that an allied victory would only further push Europe towards a new phase of economic decline with moral decadence as its inevitable corollary. 1918 was analogous to the victory of Carthage over Rome.

From this perspective Sorel had little difficulty in voicing his sympathy for Germany. 'What one calls German culture', he wrote, 'is at bottom very Roman'. It was culture which scorned the 'elegance' of the Alexandrian Greeks, respected the family and which posited military discipline as the principle governing all social relations. Germany was the most hard working nation in Europe. It was also, with the collapse of Catholicism as a serious movement, the 'home of true Christianity'. In brief, Germany, more than any other nation, had preserved the solid virtues of Europe's Roman and Christian past and its defeat would mark a further victory for the vulgar, demagogic and materialistic values of plutocracy.[194] It is interesting to note, therefore, that in 1920 Sorel disputed the veracity of the nationalist reading of Proudhon, highlighting his anti-chauvinism and his internationalism and in the process stressing his admiration for German protestantism and philosophy.[195]

With the end of the war Sorel's antipathy towards France intensified further. 'France', he wrote in 1920, 'is not the intellectual leader of Europe'.[196] It was 'the rock of reaction', a leading partner in the coalition of western plutocracy against the proletariats of eastern and central Europe.[197] The socialist and syndicalist movements were in crisis as the policy of national unity, forged during the war, was continued by an increasingly bureaucratised and reformist CGT. It would need an 'external force', Sorel believed, to re-awaken the energies of the French proletariat and that force, he concluded, would in all probability be Bolshevism.[198] Henceforth he saw the Russian Revolution primarily as a means of establishing a class war across Europe.

Events in Russia, Sorel argued, had once again given reality to the idea of revolution. Everywhere the masses, if not their leaders, recognised that the 'republic of the soviets' defended the interests of their class and that the efforts of the Western powers to suppress the Revolution proved that there existed on irreducible opposition between democracy and the mission of the proletariat. Thus, if a 'new truly revolutionary philosophy' was to be outlined all socialist doctrine had to be re-interpreted in the light of this experience.

For Sorel the Russian Revolution now became the model of the proletarian revolution, the revolt of the producers against politicians, intellectuals and the bourgeoisie. A new form of proletarian State had been created which in the tradition of the Paris Commune had established a dictatorship of the proletariat by reserving political rights for the workers alone. The break with parliamentary democracy was complete. Further, the soviets represented the new institutional expression of working-class autonomy, the location not only of a productivist ethic that would in turn create an economy as progressive as anything associated with capitalism but also of a new juridical code prefiguring the values operative in the new society. The ethos of the Revolution, Sorel repeatedly proclaimed, was Proudhonian rather than Marxist. Equally, the special strength of Bolshevism derived from the fact that it was resolutely Muscovite and Asiatic in character. Lenin, Sorel argued, had to be judged by the standards of Russian history, as 'one of the great Czars and not as a President of the United States'. By this criterion, the defence of the Revolution justified 'the most terrifying severities'.[199] Moreover, the Bolsheviks as 'new Mongols' despised the decadent values of the West, were intent upon destroying them by violence and hence appeared capable of providing the foundations of a new civilisation. Sorel's hope, therefore, was that the Russia of the soviets would provide a new myth capable of inspiring the proletariat in Europe and especially in Germany and Italy where for cultural and economic reasons — Italy, Sorel believed, was 'naturally' proletarian — the possibility of challenging the plutocratic order was at its greatest. Less obviously, Sorel also believed that the Bolsheviks could provide an example for revolutionary forces outside Europe.

Sorel's analysis of the Russian Revolution as a revolution of the producers which in the soviets had given institutional reality to the autonomy of the working class led him to give his unconditional support to the factory council movement associated with Gramsci's *Ordine nuovo* group. 'What is happening in the Fiat factories', Sorel wrote, 'is more important than all the writings published in *Die Neue Zeit*'.[200] The Italian proletariat had 'a marvellous occasion to prove its maturity'.[201] This enthusiasm was in part a reflection of the high esteem in which Sorel held the Italian socialist movement. Ever an attentive observer of Italian affairs, the neutralism of the socialist party during the war had convinced him that it was destined to play a leading role in the European Left. Italy, like Germany, was a victim of Europe's plutocratic powers in the post-war settlement at Versailles and this, when combined with the support of the Italian working class for Lenin, indicated that it now embodied what Sorel termed 'the proletarian Weltgeist'.[202]

What this should serve to prove is that Sorel had no sympathy whatsoever for either Mussolini or the fascist movement.[203] The only evidence to the contrary is provided by Jean Variot's accounts of his conversations with Sorel published after the latter's death and, as Michel Charzat has argued, Variot's 'lack of seriousness' is demonstrated in his preface to *Propos de Georges Sorel*, published in 1935, where the year of Sorel's death is incorrectly stated to be 1924. Similar factual errors are also to be found in Variot's article 'Georges Sorel et la révolution nationale'. Sorel's alleged comparison 'around 1912' of Mussolini to a *conditierre* of the fifteenth century, published by Variot in *L'Eclair* in September 1922, did not figure in the volume of 1935 supposedly because, as Variot explained to Pierre Andreu in 1953, it had been forgotten. The authenticity of Variot's 'conversations' with Sorel has therefore to be questioned, especially as there is nothing in either Sorel's published writings or private correspondence which gives credence to Variot's picture.[204] Indeed, the numerous articles published by Sorel in a succession of Italian journals and his letters to friends in Italy such as Croce, Mario Missiroli and Guglielmo Ferrero indicate only disapproval of the fascist movement and increasing concern at its success. To Croce on 11 March 1921 he remarked that 'Italy moves more and more towards a régime which resembles Ireland: the fascists operate like the Black and Tans'. Despite his opposition to ministerialism, with the resignation of Giolitti in June 1921 Sorel called for socialist participation in government in order 'to defend proletarian institutions against the fascists'. Further direct evidence confirming Sorel's antipathy to fascism can be easily found but one personal detail adequately indicates his position. On being informed by Pareto that Missiroli's paper *Il Resto del Carlino* had been taken over by the fascists Sorel immediately ceased his collaboration, thereby forfeiting his major source of income.

Sorel's preoccupation with the fate of Germany and Italy at the hands of the victorious Entente was matched by a less readily understood interest in the fortunes of Egypt.[205] Long the subject of Anglo-French rivalry Egypt had become a British protectorate. Taking the liberal democracies at their word many Egyptian nationalists had presumed that the right of national self-determination proclaimed as one of the guiding principles of the Paris peace conference would necessarily include a recognition of full independence for Egypt. They were to be disappointed but the presence of an Egyptian delegation in Paris acted as a catalyst for a concerted campaign asserting the legitimacy of Egypt's claims. Intellectuals of the stature of Anatole France — for whom Egypt was 'the great victim of the peace' — flocked to the cause. A key figure in the movement was novelist Victor Margueritte whose journal *L'Egypte* published three articles by Sorel. In these pieces and in two others dealing with the same issue Sorel was able to provide a clear statement of what he took to be the relationship between the colonial and socialist revolutions.[206]

The ambiguity inherent in the socialist response to colonialism went back to Marx himself but amongst French socialists it was particularly evident. Rebérioux in her study of the journals *La Guerre sociale* and *Le Mouvement socialiste*[207] has shown that these key periodicals treated colonialism as an issue of secondary importance. A detailed and coherent analysis of the nature of colonialist exploitation is absent from their pages. Likewise, Fernand Pelloutier paid scant attention to colonialism, his only article on the subject being anti-militarist rather than anti-colonialist in sentiment.[208] The French Left in general seemed content to criticise the excesses of colonial rule while preserving a naive faith in its progressive and civilising impact. Sorel, with his vision of a degenerate Western capitalism and a decaying bourgeois civilisation, was led to take a less optimistic view.

'It is evident', Sorel wrote, 'that we have entered a period dominated by the desire of old States to enrich themselves at the expense of poorer and lesser populations'.[209] British policy in Egypt fitted into this framework. Traditionally, he argued, British diplomacy had been 'moderate' in character but 'the enormous transformation of English morals' that had occurred had produced a more aggressive colonial policy. 'Today', observed Sorel, 'the decisive influence in England belongs to a class of adventurers whose brazen cynicism equals that of our worst demagogues'.[210] Using their power and prestige to control the press and corrupt the political process an imperial policy had been devised that openly furthered their interests and which placed the population of Egypt in an economic stranglehold.

If Sorel was alarmed by the economic character and consequences of British colonialism in Egypt he was even more concerned by its potentially deleterious effects upon the morals of its native people. Sorel had only scorn for those rulers of nineteenth-century Egypt who had sought 'to transform Cairo into an imitation of Montmartre' and for those Egyptian intellectuals who 'in their passion for Parisianism' had sacrificed the future of their country. The imitation of European morals not only involved the destruction of the indigenous (and valuable) national culture but also ensured the permanent servitude of the colonised.

Yet for Sorel the key to the Egyptian question lay in the *lack* of cultural assimilation that had taken place. Here he drew upon a common misconception of the differences between British and French colonial policy. The French policy of assimilation, in Sorel's opinion, would only have succeeded in imposing a culture of 'stupidity, bourgeois sophistry and servility' upon the Egyptian people. British rule, while it might have been 'harsh, rapacious and humiliating', had the advantage that it had left Egyptian culture intact. The Egyptian people had been allowed to preserve their genius and originality. It was these very qualities — a distinct moral and intellectual code and an absence of corruption — that Sorel had formerly ascribed to the syndicalist movement. Sorel himself saw the parallel: 'we are allowed to hope', he wrote, 'that British domination will provide the Egyptian proletarians with an intellectual and moral preparation appropriate to the needs of the dictatorship of the proletariat'. Once the Egyptians realised their own strength, like the Russians they could, with the aid of 'strong-willed socialists', set up a soviet-style government and free Egypt from foreign domination. Nor was this entirely fanciful. 1919 had seen widespread unrest, violence and sabotage throughout Egypt. The rural villages, long regarded as the embodiment of passivity, joined the rebellion. And, as the culmination of the protest against

British policy, a general strike was called which effectively paralysed the country.

Sorel's advice to the Egyptians was therefore clear enough. Do not rely upon the efforts of Western diplomacy or 'les gens de lettres de Paris'; rather than adopt European manners, preserve Egyptian culture as a means of maintaining the 'barriers' that separated Egyptians from their British masters. Nor did Sorel believe that the Egyptians could necessarily expect support from the British proletariat. The tactic, then, needed to be one of 'Egyptianisme intransigent'. And this for Sorel implied the use of violence. Citing the advice of Proudhon, he argued that the foreign 'aristocracy' that governed Egypt could only be 'exterminated', not reformed. But it was, above all, in the strike that Sorel saw Egypt's means of national liberation. 'It is through strikes', he wrote, 'that they can hope to impose the acknowledgement of their independence upon the English'.

In Sorel's pre-war syndicalist writings the proletariat was portrayed as a class which possessed its own values, its own institutions, that had not been corrupted by bourgeois society and in particular by the bourgeois ideal of social peace. With the demise of syndicalism Sorel believed that the proletariat in France had been absorbed into a shallow, materialistic and alien culture and this conclusion was confirmed in 1914. The French proletariat had lost its revolutionary potential. After a period of intense disillusionment, Sorel concluded that the establishment of a new civilisation could only be achieved, if at all, by groups which existed outside a corrupt and decaying European society. Sorel found these groups in Russia, Italy and Egypt. The location of revolutionary potential shifted but it was only the *location* that changed. The actual specification of the qualities of the revolutionary class remained unaltered, so too did the tactics to be employed. Even the language used by Sorel continued to be that of his earlier writings: intransigence, division, conflict and moral purity were the key themes. Sorel's final public pronouncement, an interview with Bernard Lacache in *L'Humanité* on 9 March 1922, amounted to a passionate call to defend the Russian Revolution. An old man, not far from death, Sorel's last writings show him still a restless spirit, committed to the cause of the proletariat and in search of a force that would destroy the decadent bourgeois society that he despised so totally. In line with this, for the conclusion to the 1922 edition of *Les Illusions du progrès* Sorel chose to reprint the final sentences of his *Insegnamenti sociali della economia contemporanea*, published originally in 1907. 'Early Christianity', the concluding lines read, 'could very probably have obtained toleration . . . but it sought to isolate itself . . . There was no lack of wise men who treated Tertullian and all those who refused to accept any conciliation as madmen. Today we see that it was thanks to these madmen that Christianity was able to form its ideas and become master of the world when its hour had come'.[211] Immediately after his death, Edouard

Berth did not hesitate to describe Sorel himself as 'le Tertullian du socialisme'.[212]

Berth's own analysis of the post-war epoch, culminating in the publication of *Guerre des états ou guerre des classes* in 1924,[213] gave greater depth and detail to the position outlined by Sorel. If Berth did not join the communist party, he was certainly an enthusiastic supporter of it, writing several articles in *L'Humanité* during 1922–23 and fulsome homilies in praise of Lenin in Henri Barbusse's *Clarté*.[214] *Les Nouveaux aspects du socialisme* was republished as *Les Derniers aspects du socialisme* with a new preface drawing the parallels between syndicalism and Bolshevism in which the opponents of the Bolsheviks were lectured on their lack of 'any true understanding of the realities of a revolution'.[215] Like Sorel, but only in retrospect, Berth saw the First World War as an enormous trick, 'une horrible mystification', perpetrated upon the working class by a plutocratic bourgeoisie intent upon destroying the industrial power of Germany.[216] 'I see only corruption, meanness, sloppiness, prostitution and gambling', Berth wrote.[217] The actual outcome of the war had not been to reinvigorate civilisation but to produce 'two new historical forces', fascism and communism. Fascism, Berth believed, was 'the last spiritual arm' of a bourgeoisie intent upon protecting itself from the revolutionary proletariat, a final effort to 'slow down its inevitable fall' by positing devotion to the nation as 'the essential and cardinal virtue'.[218] 'Fascism', he wrote, 'is violence in the interests of the bourgeoisie, communism is violence in the interests of the proletariat'.[219] The two movements were separate and distinct. The choice before Europe, therefore, was between war and revolution, nationalism or communism, a bourgeois peace or a proletarian peace, Maurras or Lenin. We had to decide which date, 2 August 1914 or 27 October 1917, was the start of a new era.

Berth's own choice was unequivocal. 1914 was only an 'accident' in history: 1917 signalled the beginning of the dissolution of an ignoble civilisation. Yet for all his protestation to Georges Guy-Grand that no serious reader of *Réflexions sur la violence* could 'confuse Sorelian violence with the exploits of the fascists', he was nevertheless conscious that he himself, because of his pre-war links with *Action française* and Georges Valois in the *Cercle Proudhon*, could be accused of 'fascisme avant la lettre'. 'I owe the public', he conceded, 'an explanation'.[220]

Recalling *Les Méfaits des intellectuels* and his suggestion that Sorel and Maurras were destined to play parallel and complementary roles, Berth recognised that before the war he had believed in the restoration of the monarchy as a means of *neutralising* the State and that to that end he had no qualms in allying himself with those from the Right intent upon waging 'a stubborn and categorical war against democratic conceptions'. *Action française* had appeared 'new and audacious', its conservatism seemed not to be 'shabbily bourgeois' but to be in 'the grand style'. However, the willingness of Maurras and his associates to rally to the defense of the nation and of Valois to denounce the class struggle as 'a German invention' indicated, as Berth put it, that 'since August 1914 *Action française* had ceased morally to exist'.[221] Maurras represented nothing else but a bastard-ised combination of the old and the new régimes, 'un ancien régime bourgeoisifié', he was the 'soul of reaction', not Apollo to Sorel's Dion-ysus, but 'a false Apollo', the embodiment of a sterile rationalism. The monarchy of Maurras, Berth now argued, was not the monarchy of Henri IV but the monarchy of Catherine de Medici.

Berth's overall point was that bourgeois morality as a whole in France had lost all sense of the 'sublime'. The bourgeoisie had been concerned solely to secure the impossible goal of destroying Germany and in order to achieve that unworthy end war itself had been 'de-poetised', the 'countries of work' had been subordinated to 'the countries of capital', leaving only an amorphous, obscene and materialistic France and a Europe effectively under English control. The victory of the Entente had been the victory of John Bull.[222]

Henceforth, Berth argued, it was impossible to be under any illusions about the character of *Action française* and far from wishing to see a conflation of nationalism and socialism he predicted that the central con-flict of the future would be between those who saw the nation and those who saw classes as the primary motive force behind human progress. In Berth's view, the recent experience of the war demonstrated incontroverti-bly that the struggle between nations was incapable of producing anything but ethical and material decline and therefore that it was to the proletariat that fell the task of constructing the new European order. Class war alone retained an epic quality and was alone capable of inspiring the masses. Berth was thus able to rehearse several familiar themes: the Russian Revolution was the start of a new era, a sceptical and materialistic West was to be awoken from torpor by an instinctive and mystical breath of life from the East, as their differences rested upon 'a scission of a meta-physical order' no compromise was possible between the proletariat and the bourgeoisie. But to this was added a new refrain that owed much to a Sorelian perception of the balance of international power in post-war Europe. If Europe, and more generally civilisation, was not to fall under English control, the proletariats of Russia, Germany, Italy and France needed to combine their forces. 'In order to save the world', Berth wrote, 'it is necessary that the Germany of Marx, the Russia of Lenin, and the France of Proudhon and Sorel (and Italy has the right to claim Sorel as much, if not more, than France) should unite in a proletarian *holy alliance* to declare a War of Independence against the tyrant of the world, anglo-saxon plutocracy'.[223] Proletarian imperialism was to challenge bourgeois imperialism.

Berth's settling of accounts with his own past had a further dimension:

in 1923 he ceased to avail himself of the religious rites of the Roman Catholic Church. This did not mean, however, that his concern to analyse the relationship between socialism and Christianity, begun in *Dialogues socialistes*, had come to an end nor that his newly-found scorn for Maurras was echoed in distaste for another of his former allegiances. Berth's view, like that of Sorel who in *Le Système historique de Renan* published in 1906 produced his definitive statement of this position, was that socialism and religion need no more be competitors than science and religion. Each dealt with a separate domain of man's existence. If Catholicism was to re-establish its rightful place in the world, Berth now argued, it needed to give up any idea of reconstituting the 'Christian State' and, more importantly, 'to deepen the supernatural and appropriately mystical aspects of the Christian idea'.[224] To that end, in the same manner that the Russia of the soviets sought to restore 'the revolutionary spiritual unity' of Europe, the task of the Papacy was to restore its 'Christian spiritual unity'. And in Berth's opinion it was precisely the Russian Revolution that facilitated the attainment of that objective. By making possible the unification of Europe it made possible the overcoming of 'religious nationalism' and, secondly, a lethargic Roman Catholicism would be invigorated by the infusion of the 'ardently evangelical spirit' of Russian Christianity. 'Who knows', Berth therefore asked in a question that fully revealed his determination to reconcile Catholic faith with his faith in Lenin, 'if this Bolshevik Russia, which seems so impious and irreligious, is not destined in effect to assure a new life to a rejuvenated Catholicism?'[225] If Berth's reverence for the Soviet Union was to be quickly dispelled, the passion to locate an authentic spiritual force was, as we shall see, to remain with him to the end of his life.

6 Diverging Paths

Victor Griffuelhes died on 30 July 1922. Sorel's death followed a few weeks later at the end of August. For all their earlier, and in Sorel's case later, notoriety both spent their final months in relative isolation and obscurity. A sadder fate befell Alphonse Merrheim. In June 1923 his articles attacking Bolshevism came to a sudden and unexplained end. He had, in fact, been committed to an asylum, the victim of a mental break-down from which he was not to recover. He died in October 1925. As for Auguste Keufer, after 36 years as its effective leader he finally retired from the *Fédération du livre* in 1920. At his death in 1924 he remained president of the *Cercle des Prolétaires positivistes* and vice-president of the *Société positiviste internationale*. Cautious to the last, one of his final public acts was to argue against the alteration of the positivist calendar on the grounds that 'on this issue it is preferable to leave intact the work of Auguste Comte'.[1]

Of the three remaining members of the CGT's pre-war leadership inter-viewed by Dunois in 1920 none was to regain or seek a position of eminence. Emile Pouget lived quietly with his wife on the southern out-skirts of Paris, earning a modest living compiling artists' catalogues. Shortly before his death in 1931 he was asked by Maurice Chambelland to write an account of his early life as an activist but to no avail. In his obituary for his former colleague Georges Yvetot correctly observed that 'le Père Peinard died before Pouget himself'.[2]

Yvetot's own life, by contrast, was to end in controversy. Recognising that his anti-militarist propaganda had come to nothing, in 1914 Yvetot resigned his union posts and took up employment in the favourite trade of syndicalist militants, that of typographer. Shortly afterwards he was appointed director of an association helping war orphans, a position which took him to Montenegro and Serbia during 1915. What is certain is that he took no part in the anti-war campaign organised by the 'minority' within the CGT. After the war he adopted a similarly low profile and little, if anything, was heard from him during the 1920s. In 1931 he re-appeared in anarchist circles as a columnist in *La Voix libertaire* and subsequently as a contributor to Sebastien Faure's monumental *Encyclopédie anarchiste*. His obsessions remained anti-militarism and anti-patriot-ism, although for Faure he produced a series of entries dealing with such diverse topics as socialisation and sabotage as well as (significantly in view of later events) sincerity and the renegade or turn-coat.[3] On the eve of the Second World War, and as Hitler trampled the Munich Agreement underfoot, Yvetot's name appeared alongside that of 30 other left-wing pacifists including those of the writer Alain and future collaborators Félicien Challaye, Marcel Déat and Georges Dumoulin (himself about to finish a tortuous journey from revolutionary syndicalist to supporter of the Vichy régime) on what was the most important anti-war document of the day, the manifesto 'Paix immédiate'. Three years later he was persuaded to become president of the *Comité ouvrier de secours immédiats*, an organisation intended to aid the victims of the British bombing but in reality a vehicle for pro-German propaganda. In that capacity in April 1942 he gave an interview to Jacques Doriot's collaborationist paper *Le Cri du peuple*. Asked if he considered himself to be a traitor Yvetot replied: 'As long as there are workers to defend one must struggle without letting oneself be stopped by the judgement of others'. He was, he believed, under a duty to help those workers who suffered in the changed circumstances brought about by the war. In the same interview he also admitted that he was not offended when he saw 'well-off Jews' being dispossessed of their wealth.[4] The following month Yvetot's funeral was attended by the German ambassador in Paris, Von Gissenberg, who, *Le Cri du peuple* reported, expressed his sympathy to the family.[5]

Like Yvetot, Paul Delesalle played no part in the anti-war movement. Indeed, the most reliable indication of his position comes in the form of his decision to publish Jouhaux's controversial hommage to Jean Jaurès and the reticence expressed by Rosmer towards utilising Delesalle's *La Publication sociale* as a means of printing Romain Rolland's anti-war articles.[6] After the war Delesalle's forays into public debate were spasmodic and limited, especially during his long enforced retirement from 1932 until his death in 1948. The primary focus of his activities continued to be his bookshop and to this was added a long-term project of research on the Paris Commune.[7] His most revealing articles were the obituaries he was called upon to write for former comrades, steeped as they were in his own experiences as an activist, but arguably his most significant achievement in these years was the arduous compilation of the 'Bibliographie Sorélienne' published in 1939 by the *International Review of Social History*.[8]

Delesalle did not distance himself completely from political realities. He too initially shared the 'joy and enthusiasm' aroused by the Russian Revolution, although by February 1922 he can be found arguing against the tactics of the 'united front' on the grounds that to the workers it would appear like old-fashioned 'political manoeuvring' and complaining about Jules Humbert-Droz's characterisation of anarchists as counter-revolutionaries in *Le Bulletin communiste*.[9] After this he became increasingly sceptical about the régime in Russia and the tactics of the communist party in France, although as late as 1928 he was a member of *Les Amis de l'Union Soviétique* and he continued to have links with the communists during the 1930s. Delesalle's own private papers not only reveal his continued contact with old friends such as Lagardelle and Monatte but that in 1932 he was a member of the ardently Republican *Ligue française pour la Défense des Droits de l'Homme et du Citoyen* and that, despite criticisms of the socialists only slightly earlier in *Les Temps nouveaux*, he joined the socialist party in 1935. His last party card is for the year 1944. Thus in the course of his long life Delesalle was to move from anarchism to revolutionary syndicalism and on to support for the communist party and finally the SFIO. He was throughout a model of intellectual and personal probity.

Of the members of the original group who form the core of this study we are therefore left with Edouard Berth, Hubert Lagardelle and Pierre Monatte. Each, from similar premises rooted in the syndicalist experience of the first decade of the twentieth century but taking markedly different routes, still had much to say.

I

From 1924 until his death in 1939 two themes are predominant in the writings of Edouard Berth. The first consists of a persistent attempt to preserve and protect the memory of Georges Sorel. Thus, for example, Berth republished some of Sorel's earliest essays from *L'Ere nouvelle* as *'D'Aristote à Marx* in 1935, repeatedly denied the legitimacy of categorising Sorel as 'the spiritual father of fascism' and, where necessary, even defended Sorel's reputation as a socialist.[10] The second theme is not unrelated to this obsession and derives in part from Berth's belief that Marx, to be correctly understood, had to be read through the eyes of Sorel. As the traumatic years of the inter-war period unfolded Berth quickly concluded that what was needed was what in 1931 he termed a 'metaphysics of liberty'.[11]

Berth's analysis of the state of European civilisation and the prospects for the future was an almost unremittingly pessimistic one and became, if anything, gloomier with each passing year. In 1927 he published a volume of essays (the majority of which had first appeared in Barbusse's *Clarté*) entitled *La Fin d'une culture* as the summation of an attack upon what in *L'Humanité* he had earlier referred to as 'la stupide': the degenerate and plutocratic culture characteristic of bourgeois France since the *coup d'état* of Napoleon III in 1851. Ernest Renan, Anatole France, Maurras, Barrès and Paul Bourget were all dismissed as the representatives of a world nearing dissolution and ruin, as the embodiment of an intellectual senility that bore no resemblance to the great bourgeois culture of eighteenth-century France.[12] To this was later added the vision of a bourgeoisie which in a state of moral and political bankruptcy had abandoned all its liberal principles by submitting itself to fascist dictatorship across Europe.[13]

Berth initially greeted this process of progressive decadence as the signal for the dawn of a new proletarian epoch and while his faith in the Russian

Revolution held this remained his view: as that consoling vision itself disintegrated so too vanished a belief in the probability of proletarian victory. Berth's line on the Soviet Union was, in short, subject to a gradual, yet fundamental, change. In *Du 'Capital' aux 'Réflexions sur la violence'* published in 1932, for example, he republished his essay of 1924 'Lénine, qui est-ce?' primarily as a means of demonstrating the 'sincerity' of the enthusiasm and sympathy once aroused by the Russian Revolution. The passing of time, he acknowledged, had made possible an objective assessment. In the same volume he also went out of his way to correct his earlier statement to the effect that the dictatorship of the proletariat in Russia was only a temporary expedient designed to secure economic modernisation. That dictatorship, he now conceded, resorted to 'the most brutal and disagreeable' methods. Certainly, by 1925 Berth's hope that the twentieth century would be the Russian century was on the decline and he appeared already to accept that the revolution had been betrayed by a party bureaucracy determined to preserve its privileged status. Stalinism he saw as a 'Russian deviation' of Marxism, the turning inwards of the revolution as it adapted to the existence of Russia's rural masses and the external threat of capitalism.[14]

Furthermore, by slavishly copying the Russian model the sympathisers of the Bolsheviks in the West had, in Berth's view, committed a fundamental error and with dire consequences. Berth readily recognised that contrary to his expectations the Russian Revolution had been unable to re-awaken the revolutionary spirit in Europe but to this was added an awareness that the process of bolshevisation had effectively killed any independence or autonomy within the working-class movement. In France, the CGTU had been transformed into an 'appendage of a party of NCO's and mercenaries' whilst publications such as the now 'unreadable' *L'Humanité* induced passivity in the proletariat. Berth's overall point was that the tactic of regimentation and control, whilst it might have a rationale in the context of a backward Soviet economy in desperate need of rapid transformation, was singularly inappropriate in Europe. 'The problem for us', Berth wrote, 'is not in effect that of establishing a dictatorship but on the contrary of acquiring complete liberty'.[15] By pursuing the wrong course the only group capable of overthrowing plutocracy, the working class, had been transformed into a lumpenproletariat, lacking in dignity and personality, 'inferior to its destiny'.[16] Translated into prosaic language, Berth had no difficulty in accepting that 'for the moment we are witnessing the — temporary — failure of Marxism, Sorelianism and even of Leninism'.[17]

How, if at all, was this situation to be rectified? At an organisational level Berth continued to argue that 'salvation' lay in the return of the working class to the principles and practices of revolutionary syndicalism and this, as we will see, was a line which he consistently repeated from

1925 onwards. At an abstract level (and it was here that he deployed most of his energies) he concluded that what was required was 'a new metaphysics', a 'less mechanistic philosophy'.

The foundations of this new metaphysics were not surprisingly to be found in the 'new materialism' that had provided the backbone of Berth's earliest syndicalist writings and once again what was to be offered was an attempted fusion of the philosophies of Marx and Bergson.[18] Berth's renewed interest in this endeavour can first be discerned in his preface to the 1925 German edition of Sorel's *Réflexions sur la violence* and it remained his central preoccupation for the next decade, culminating in the long introduction to his edition of Sorel's *D'Aristote à Marx* published three years after the appearance of Bergson's *Les Deux sources de la morale et de la religion*.

At the heart of Berth's new metaphysics was a familiar Sorelian reading of Marx stipulating that historical materialism was not to be confused with either the 'abstract materialism' of the eighteenth century or a rigid economic determinism and an interpretation of Bergson which by drawing heavily upon the description of *homo faber* in *L'Evolution créatrice* emphasised what was seen as Bergson's desire to locate spiritual values in a precisely defined material setting. Perceived in this light, the philosophies of Marx and Bergson had 'definite affinities' and could, quite properly, be reconciled. 'To the extent that the new spiritualism emanates from Bergsonism', Berth wrote, 'its originality is to have seen that the body exists on a path which leads to the life of the spirit and that it is necessary to tie the spiritual life to its material conditions, as opposed to detaching it from them and running the risk of making it appear as a simple mirage: the *Marxist postulate* is thus at the base of the new spiritualism'.[19] The significance of this portrayal of Bergson with a 'Marxist accent' was that implicit to the whole thrust of Berth's argument was the conviction that the two doctrines, when combined, could undermine the philosophical basis — the 'old metaphysics' — sustaining the purely instrumentalist conception of socialism that was then in the ascendent.

The argument here is at several levels and its tortuous logic is not always easy to discern. Socialism, Berth wanted to emphasise, was fundamentally a revolt of the spirit against a world in which man had been reduced to the status of an automaton, a world in which man was threatened by 'a monstrous moral and metaphysical materialism'. Hence the great merit of Marx was to have perceived that the industrial civilisation which at present enslaved the worker could become an instrument of liberation.[20] Bergsonian philosophy, in Berth's interpretation, strengthened this message, giving it a new dimension. Like Marx, Bergson saw the immense industrial structure created by modern capitalism as the means for man to establish his own autonomy through the transcendence of his animal instincts. Liberty is here equated with personality. But, Berth argued, for Bergson the creation of this artificial milieu had not been matched by 'an equivalent development of the soul' and as a consequence man was subject to a 'profound spiritual disarray'. Stated this way the philosophies of Marx and Bergson demonstrated that it was only when industrial production was taken to be an end in itself that it precluded the existence of those spiritual values commensurate with and constitutive of human liberty. To reverse this process of suffocation there was a need for 'an extension of the soul (*un supplément d'âme*)', which Berth in turn identified with the advent of socialism.[21] The working class, Berth wrote, needed 'to raise itself to the level of a moral person, to be master of itself and of its destiny'.[22]

The second part of the argument drew more heavily upon Bergson and in particular upon *Les Deux sources de la morale et de la religion* with its conception of 'open' and 'closed' societies and moralities. Berth's 'new materialism', it must be remembered, had taken as its central concept the idea of reality as a process of movement and becoming. To this was now added the notion of a dynamic, expansive 'open' culture as both the projected expression of human liberation and a characterisation of the future proletarian society. By replacing the image of an immobile Eternity with the concept of Time as the 'very stuff of reality' life itself becomes synonymous with perpetual invention and incessant creation. The 'old metaphysics' resting upon the 'Platonic mirage' is surpassed; man breaks out from stultifying routine and reaches for the sublime; and, Berth assures us, the machine becomes our servant.

What in effect Berth is offering here is syndicalism's final philosophical onslaught upon what were seen as the premises of both bourgeois thought and orthodox Marxism. Man the producer, the inventor inspired by poetic intuition, the creator of an artificial milieu, is posited as the embodiment of socialism as liberty, socialism as 'a living ethics', and as the antithesis of the constrained, instinct and habit-bound worker of capitalist industry and Soviet five year plans. But this was not all that Berth was offering.

If the academic purpose of Bergson's *Les Deux sources de la morale et de la religion* was to demonstrate that anthropological investigations of religion were not necessarily incompatible with a religious or spiritual outlook (thus dismissing Durkheim's *Les Formes élémentaires de la vie religieuse*), at a private level it was a reflection of a personal evolution towards Catholicism. According to Bergsons' family only his desire not to betray his fellow Jews at a time of rising anti-semitism prevented his formal conversion. Thus, as Berth recognised, *Les Deux sources* . . . appeared to justify his and Sorel's much earlier assertion that the primary significance of Bergsonism was as a religious philosophy. Further, with the obvious demise of his expectation that a Bolshevik-led unified Europe would bring about a rejuvenation of Catholicism, *Les Deux sources* . . . appeared to provide another opportunity for Berth to effect a reconciliation between Christianity and socialism.

Bergson's concept of an 'open', dynamic religion drawing inspiration from the visions of the great mystics was perceived by Berth to be a form of the new metaphysics. For Bergson, Berth wrote, 'the Christian *mystique* . . . is not a purely contemplative and renunciating *mystique*; it is a *mystique* of action, a social and not an individualistic *mystique*, a dynamic and not a static *mystique*'.[23] The religion of an abstract, immutable Being, of Eternity, was replaced by that of Time and Becoming, of the 'Soul in motion (*l'Ame mobile*)'.[24] Life itself became an act of the spirit. Berth's point was that such a religion, shorn as it was of scholasticism and rationalism, could not be used to induce submission on the part of the workers but would act only as a force of inspiration, as a means of enhancing the non-materialistic dimension of our existence.

In truth, it is hard to know what form of religion this would be. At the end of his introduction to *D'Aristote à Marx* Berth himself compares it to music, an 'art of movement and becoming', and contrasts it with sculpture and this neatly expresses the dismissal of substance that is at the heart of Bergsonian metaphysics. If God can be said to exist it is in the world, within the process of lived Time and change, and He is known, it seems, through the very act of intuitive creation that defines our relationship with the finite objects of the artificial milieu in which we live. Religion, Berth wrote, 'will not be the religion of the Father, nor that of the Son, but that of the Holy Ghost'.[25] What is certain is that Berth was talking about a religion of sorts and it requires something like the severe rationalist criticism directed by Julien Benda against Bergson himself to dispute its legitimacy as an authentically religious vision.

After Berth's withdrawal from *Clarté* in 1925 he quickly found a home with Pierre Monatte's new journal *La Révolution prolétarienne*, and this remained his principal mouthpiece until 1938.[26] Disenchanted with the CGT which he saw as little more than 'an academy of pseudo-proletarian ideas' and with the communist-controlled CGTU he now came to regard the 'small group' associated with Monatte as the representatives of the authentic tradition of revolutionary syndicalism.[27]

Beyond this tiny minority seeking to keep alive the autonomy of the working class — 'Le Syndicalisme revolutionnaire, est-il encore possible?'[28] was the title of one of his best essays in this period — Berth saw only 'impotence and sterility', neo-Millerandism and neo-Guesdism. There was no genuinely revolutionary culture, only a divided proletarian movement whose 'lamentable deficiencies' had contributed to the rise of fascism, nor anyone to match the pre-war leadership of Griffuelhes, Pouget, Yvetot and Delesalle. In 1931 he condemned the 'deplorable scission' that divided socialists and communists but not even the Popular Front managed to raise Berth's spirits. After the right-wing riots of February 1934 he argued that the choice facing France was between 'caesarism' and 'anarchy', the creation of a 'free order', and in this context the Popular Front

figured only as 'a new hoax', an 'old-style democratic formation' resting
upon the mystique of universal suffrage.[29] For Berth the widespread factory occupations of 1936 were a spontaneous expression of a new syndicalist tactic, the logical extension of the right to strike to the right of occupation, and therefore the desire of the socialist premier Léon Blum and
the communist party leader Maurice Thorez to bring these occupations to
an end betrayed their true position. If the goal of fascism was to take
away liberty of movement from the working class, Berth argued, then the
Popular Front was an example of *'fascisme de gauche'*.[30] As for the Civil
War in Spain, Berth recognised that on its outcome depended the future
destiny of Europe. The defeat of the Spanish working class, following on
so quickly from the defeats already suffered by the working classes in
Germany, Austria and Italy, would in all probability be the prelude to
the defeat of the French proletariat. Europe, already in the grip of
recession, would fall to the 'new barbarians'. A 'new Middle Ages' would
commence, replete with the 'persecution of Jews, book-burning and the
violence of roaming gangs'.[31]

As early as 1931 Berth realised that if nothing was done to prevent the
rise of what he referred to as the 'Hitlerian wave' the result would be 'an
atrocious and purely destructive war'. He also recognised that little could
be expected from the Soviet Union to prevent this possibility. Bolshevism,
he wrote in 1933, was 'the twin brother' of fascism and in 1937 he went
so far as to equate Stalin's Russia with 'counter-revolution' and to dub
Stalinism itself as 'asiatic caesarism'.[32] Nor, as their non-intervention in
Spain demonstrated, were the 'so-called democratic States', Britain and
France, prepared to stand up and fight. In a biting article entitled 'Clan
des Ya? Clan des Da?',[33] published in 1938, Berth argued that for the
proletariat there was nothing to choose between the 'pluto-democratic
imperialism' of the Paris-London axis and the 'military and totalitarian
imperialism' of the Rome-Berlin axis. Both had shown themselves determined to bring down the Spanish Republic in order to preserve capitalism.
Equally Berth set himself against any attempts to reconstitute the *union
sacrée* of 1914 (even under the guise of defending the Soviet Union) and
it was for this reason that in 1935 he lent his support to the plan of the
Révolution prolétarienne group to launch another Zimmerwald movement.[34] Throughout the 1930s therefore Berth consistently argued that
only a European Revolution could defeat Hitler and Mussolini. 'The real
way to rid ourselves of these two accomplices', he wrote in 1937, 'is to
undermine the social foundations beneath their feet and to give to the
proletariats of Germany and Italy an example of a truly revolutionary
stance in both word and deed'.[35]

There was, however, one final twist to Berth's story. Shortly after the
signing of the Munich Agreement by Hitler, Mussolini, Chamberlain and
Daladier in 1938 Berth submitted an article commenting upon its signifi-

cance to the anti-war *La Révolution prolétarienné*. The article was rejected
by Monatte and subsequently appeared in Georges Valois' *Nouvel âge* in
three parts at the end of December. Since their days together in the *Cercle
Proudhon* before the war Berth and Valois had taken markedly different
paths. Berth's return to the fold of revolutionary syndicalism had been
matched in the 1920s by Valois' departure from *Action française* and his
formation in 1925 of the *Faisceau* with Valois himself cast in the role of
the French Mussolini.[36] In 1928 Valois shifted position again, turning
leftwards, first with the *Cahiers bleus* as the organ of the *Parti Républicain
Syndicaliste*, and then with the anti-fascist and anti-Stalinist *Nouvel âge*.[37]

Summarising his friend's career to date, Berth concluded in 1931 that
Valois, despite his 'astounding and unexpected' changes of direction, had
never varied in his determination to 'safeguard work and the intellect
from the clutches of plutocracy'.[38] In 1935, amidst the controversy caused
by the so-called 'cas Valois', he was again called upon to state this view.
The *Révolution prolétarienne* group, for all the welcome it had accorded to
Berth, had shown itself less willing to excuse the earlier *Cercle Proudhon*
episode;[39] when therefore Valois, who in the 1920s had gone on to commit
even greater outrages, put himself forward for membership of the anti-
war committee which Monatte and his friends had been instrumental in
setting up the response was one of outright condemnation of the man and
his past.[40] Berth rallied to Valois' defence, testifying to his honesty and
sincerity but also pointing out that he had advised Valois to be content
with a less conspicuous role in the anti-war movement. *La Révolution
prolétarienne* refused to print Berth's letter of support and thus it was that
in March 1936 it duly appeared in Valois' *Nouvel âge*.[41] Berth's name
again figured in the pages of *Nouvel âge* two years later when both he
and Valois responded to deny the accusation, voiced by Anne Darbois,
that Sorel's concept of violence led to fascism and the guillotine.[42] When
La Revolution prolétarienne refused publication of Berth's article on the
Munich Agreement it was, therefore, not entirely out of the ordinary that
it should be seen in *Nouvel âge*.

Nor is it difficult to discern why Monatte was disconcerted by 'L'Accord
de Munich'.[43] For the most part it drew upon Berth's earlier analysis
of the complicity between the Paris-London and the Rome-Berlin axes,
contending that Munich demonstrated incontrovertibly that there existed
no 'essential opposition' between the 'demo-plutocratic' and 'totalitarian
States'. So too Berth restated his view that it was impossible any longer
for the Left to look upon Moscow as the capital of revolutionary Europe.
'For the moment', he wrote, 'the Revolution is crushed'. But beneath this
seemed to lay a sense of unease, even a sense of shame and regret, at
this final refusal to accept the challenge thrown down by Hitler. When
Berth asked who would take up the revolutionary mantle bequeathed by
the Soviet Union he knew that it would not be a France which wished for

nothing else but to 'live quietly behind the Maginot line' with its 40-hour week and its paid holidays. 'War', he wrote, 'has been avoided and that is good: but at a price and in lamentable circumstances and that is serious, very serious, for the future not only of France but above all of the Revolution'.

II

For Hubert Lagardelle the end of the First World War brought with it the termination of his posting with the *Comité d'Action Economique* and the decision to concentrate his efforts upon the family estate near Toulouse. There appeared to be no intention of either a return to Paris or the re-establishment of contacts with his pre-war acquaintances. In 1920, however, Lagardelle was asked by the minister of commerce, Etienne Clémental, to create and direct the institutional structures required for the new *Région Economique de Toulouse et des Pyrénées* and this gave him a further and unexpected opportunity to display his publishing and journalistic skills. In 1921 he launched a periodical entitled *La Région de Toulouse et des Pyrénées*, which itself opened up the possibility of subsequent participation in *L'Information régionale* and the influential *Sud-Ouest Economique* of Bordeaux. In 1929, as the culmination of the regionalist phase of his career, Lagardelle published a volume entitled *Sud-Ouest: une région française*.[44]

The numerous articles that appeared under Lagardelle's name during the 1920s touched upon a multitude of topics that bore directly upon the life of the Midi-Pyrénées — the need for rural schools, the restoration of the Canal du Midi, hydro-electric power, problems of Italian immigration, improved road and rail links to Spain, and so on — but the limited number of underlying themes that bind them together represent, in essence, a continuation of his pre-war concern to overturn the democratic and republican preference for the abstract over the concrete. Writing in *L'Humanité* in 1913 Lagardelle had commented of syndicalism that 'for the old society in two parts, the individual and the State, it substitutes the new society in three parts: the individual, the State and the group'.[45] Over a decade later this formula was repeated in almost identical fashion. 'The society prescribed by the twentieth century', Lagardelle wrote, 'cannot resemble the anarchic society of the nineteenth. It can no longer be a society based upon two abstract parts, the State and the individual, but a balanced society, resting upon a third part which expresses social reality: the group'.[46] Whereas in the first formulation, however, the group was defined primarily in terms of occupation, in its post-war guise equal prominence was given to the locality, the area in which work itself actually took place. The region was put alongside the *syndicat* as a further manifestation of the 'associationist tendency' that Lagardelle himself had drawn attention to in 1912.[47]

Faced with the post-war need for economic reconstruction, Lagardelle argued, organisation at a regional level was a 'necessity'. His own studies of the south-west revealed a region of immense potential economic wealth whose possibilities were being vastly under-exploited. The land suffered from depopulation as human and financial resources were increasingly drawn to Paris, producing what Lagardelle termed 'a sickly body beneath an enormous head'. Whilst Lagardelle was at pains to emphasise that this argument was not to be seen as part of a holy war against the capital — 'Paris is, and should remain, the co-ordinating centre of French life', he wrote[48] — he did, nevertheless, contend that excessive centralisation entailed not only the impoverishment of the provinces but also incompetence and inefficiency. The State — 'our congested State' as Lagardelle frequently referred to it — was breaking under the strain.[49] By contrast, an element of decentralisation appeared to offer the opportunity for a flexible, informed and co-ordinated response to a region's needs, thus unleashing previously dormant energies and making possible the maximum utilisation of the nation's productive forces.

It was when Lagardelle came to consider the institutional implications of this position that not only the radical elements but also the points of continuity in his argument became evident, for in his view an endorsement of regionalism also brought with it a requirement for 'the complete restructuring of the State'.[50] What Lagardelle chose to stress was that the demand for decision-making at a regional level derived not from abstract principles but from the lessons of practical experience. Powers 'usurped' by the State to everyone's disadvantage were to be given back to the 'spontaneous institutions of life', the 'living forces' constituted by a region's producers and professions. More specifically, the essential task was to group together a 'conscious élite', a 'minority of qualified men', in an *Assemblée Régionale Professionnelle*.

The defining characteristic of this institution was that its members were to be chosen upon the basis of technical competence rather than political affiliation, their authority deriving not from the ballot box but from their ability 'to express the aspirations of the masses they represent'. The clear assumption, made explicit in all of Lagardelle's articles dealing with this topic, was that politics, the affairs of the citizen, would not figure in their deliberations; rather they would place themselves upon the 'neutral terrain' formed by a region's 'common interests'. 'Of little importance', Lagardelle wrote, in a phrase that bore the hallmark of his syndicalist past, 'are the divergent political or philosophical conceptions of men who produce. A real solidarity unites them . . . the solidarity of producers'.[51] Hence, all farmers, 'whether they be from the left, the centre, or the right', shared the same concerns.[52] To this was added the observation that *geographical proximity*, life in a particular physical environment with its attendant shared economic concerns, also played its part in fostering a homogeneous and shared existence.

In this way, Lagardelle argued, the disequilibrium that had been introduced into French society by the Revolution of 1789 and its legacy, 'the absolutist State', would be rectified. The absurd and irrational conception of a national parliament as the 'sole master' of a country's destiny would be abandoned and with this would come the 'disqualification of the régime of intermediaries, of eloquence and of bureaucracy'. A voice would again be given to the productive forces upon whom the economic life of the nation depended. '*L'homme réel*', Lagardelle wrote, 'takes his revenge'.[53]

The orthodox response to the regionalist dimension Lagardelle had given to syndicalism was voiced in a review of *Sud-Ouest* that appeared in Monatte's *La Révolution prolétarienne*. 'For us', A. Richard wrote, 'from the moment that it hides conflict between classes, geographical solidarity . . . is only a fiction'. It was of no greater validity than another concept which had deluded the workers for so long, that of the general interest. *La Révolution prolétarienne* was, however, to be more intrigued by the next stage of Lagardelle's career.[54]

On the basis of slender, indirect evidence Zeev Sternhell has suggested that in the mid–1920s Lagardelle was to be found amongst the supporters of Georges Valois' *Faisceau*.[55] Given Valois' preoccupation with economic regionalism this is not entirely improbable and it was indeed the Librairie Valois that published *Sud-Ouest*, although by 1929 Valois had disbanded the *Faisceau*, turning again towards syndicalism. More accurately, it seems that if Lagardelle was attracted to a movement it was Ernest Mercier's *Le Redressement Français*.[56] Founded in 1925 after Mercier's visit to the United States, the programme of *Le Redressement Français* was broadly technocratic, concentrating its demands upon the need for economic rationalisation, the overhaul of the State, and a greater say for the producers in the running of the economy. At its height between 1926–28 *Le Redressement Français* attracted considerable support and attention but Poincaré's successful stabilisation of the French franc (and thus the apparent avoidance of economic catastrophe) meant that by 1929 it was effectively finished. However, the Great Crash and the subsequent slump that hit France from the early 1930s onwards meant that Mercier was not to be the last to propose radical alternatives to liberal economics and bourgeois democracy.

Much has been written about the so-called 'spirit of the 1930s' and the (predominantly) young intellectuals who through journals like *Esprit* and *L'Ordre Nouveau* sought to respond to the challenge posed by what they saw as not merely an economic crisis but a total crisis of civilisation.[57] Youth alone was deemed capable of forging the spiritual renaissance required to break with the established order, to liberate the human personality from the twin perils posed by the chaos of capitalism and the threat of Bolshevik oppression. It was into this world that at the behest of Philippe Lamour the not-so-young Hubert Lagardelle stepped when in 1930 he returned to Paris.[58]

Without doubt one of the vogue ideas of the 1930s was planning: few organisations or journals failed to come up with proposals for the rational and controlled management of the economy along with an outline of the appropriate *dirigiste* institutional apparatus.[59] *Planisme* also had a philosophical dimension, which all too often expressed itself in the imprecise sentiment that new institutions and a new ethic needed to be created that were appropriate to the demands of the twentieth century. Lamour's journal, *Plans*, was very much in this mould.[60]

In addition to the collaboration of Lagardelle, *Plans* was also able to call upon the formidable talents of François de Pierrefeu, Jean Picart le Doux, Arthur Honegger, Fernand Léger as well as Le Corbusier and occasionally René Clair. It was here, for example, that Le Corbusier outlined his proposals for 'la cité radieuse' and the scope of the journal was intentionally set to cover all aspects of modern culture from sport to aesthetics. Lagardelle's own contribution was decisive in shaping the orientation of the review but in essence what he offered was yet another reworking of his favourite themes and concepts, this time within the context of what was for him a new endorsement of '*l'économie dirigée*'.

Lagardelle's first article in *Plans* was entitled '*De l'homme abstrait à l'homme réel*' and this set the tone for all his following pieces.[61] 'The crisis of democracy', he wrote, 'is an expression of the powerlessness of an individualistic society to adapt itself to the conditions of modern life'.[62] These conditions were, in Lagardelle's opinion, ones in which the individual, the citizen, was being increasingly absorbed by the collective, the group, and in which a culture based upon leisure and consumption — the culture that ancient civilisation had passed on to democracy — was being superceded by one which drew inspiration from the machine and the activity of work. It represented, Lagardelle stated with no great novelty, 'the end of abstract man and the birth of real man'.[63] Once again, therefore, Lagardelle was able to assault the democratic State bequeathed by 1789 for its imposition of the artificial world of politics upon the concrete world of the economy whilst at the same time re-asserting the fundamental premise of his thought, namely that both 'physically and morally, man is fashioned by his occupation'.[64]

Writing to Paul Delesalle at the beginning of 1932 Lagardelle was to comment that if the principal ideas which had issued from the syndicalist movement between 1900 and 1908 were to a certain extent outdated 'those which were the soul of the movement remained a light and a guide'.[65] In line with this, Lagardelle's articles in *Plans* continued to give pride of place to the *syndicat* as the institutional expression of the victory of the concrete over the abstract and as 'the primary organ in any coherent system of production and exchange'.[66] To this was then added the region as 'the second natural level of collective life'.[67] The third level was to be the State, a 'non-political' State, 'reduced to its functions of control, administration and accountancy'. That State, it appears, was largely to be responsible for the harmonisation of production and consumption, a function which, as the economic depression had amply illustrated, capitalism itself had been incapable of performing. Lagardelle, as we know, had, ever since the publication of 'La Démocratie en France' in 1912, found a place for the State in his modified version of syndicalism but it is only at this point that the corporatist direction his thought was soon to take becomes evident. Unlike many of the enthusiasts for *planisme*, Lagardelle was of the opinion that capitalism could not be reformed, that a new economic order needed to be created, and that this would depend upon 'the seizure by the producers of the means of production'. Yet it is transparently clear that what was being contemplated was not necessarily the seizure of the means of production by the working class — reference is always to the producers, never to the proletariat — but rather the creation of an economy characterised not by class antagonisms and competition but by co-operation with the State acting as the co-ordinator of economic activity. What was being offered was a vision of a society shorn of politics in which, in an unspecified way, production was to dominate capital. Lagardelle was soon to have first hand knowledge of a country which claimed to embody precisely this vision.

Lagardelle's last article in *Plans*, 'Sources du syndicalisme', appeared in February 1932. The journal itself ceased publication shortly afterwards. Lagardelle then again returned to Toulouse but in October of that year attended an international conference in Rome where, as a letter to Robert Louzon makes clear, he found many of his former Italian acquaintances from the syndicalist movement working for Mussolini's government, convinced that they remained 'true to their past'. Such a seemingly paradoxical phenomenon, Lagardelle commented, 'needs to be studied on the spot if it is to be understood'.[68] Three months later Lagardelle found himself to have just such an opportunity: he was called to the French Embassy in Rome, where he remained until 1940.

Lagardelle was sent to Italy by the French government in an attempt to facilitate better relations at a moment of rising international tension. In 1932, along with Sorel and Péguy, he had been cited by Mussolini as one of the intellectual forbears of fascist doctrine and it was correctly assumed, therefore, that Lagardelle would be accorded privileged access to the Italian leader. What might not have been expected, however, was Lagardelle's own enthusiastic endorsement of the fascist régime in an article published in volume x of the *Encyclopaedie Française* in 1935.[69]

As befitted its place of publication, 'Le fascisme: doctrine, institutions'

provided a straightforward, comprehensive account of recent developments in Italy that was relatively free from polemic. Each of the various
aspects of the fascist régime were examined in turn and it is only in
the concluding paragraphs of the article that Lagardelle's own personal
sympathy for fascism becomes visible. In those concluding paragraphs not
only did Lagardelle acknowledge what he took to be the affinity of fascism
and syndicalism — 'it is to the syndicalism of the turn of the century that
fascism owes the most', he wrote — but he also again revealed his capacity
to use old formulas to support new causes. Like *planisme*, for example,
fascism was seen in terms of the need to construct institutions that confor-
med to the requirements of their time but more significantly it was now
the turn of fascism, after syndicalism and then regionalism, to be described
as a manifestation of the new ascendency of *l'homme réel* and the group.
'In a world which is being renewed and which has only known a society
in two parts: the individual and the State', Lagardelle wrote, without a
hint of weariness at his own monotony, 'it [fascism] is organising a society
in three parts: the individual, the group and the State'.

What Lagardelle found in fascism was the same opposition to parliamentary democracy and the same preference for the producer over the citizen,
quality over quantity, the conscious minority over the passive majority,
that had formerly constituted the strength of syndicalism. Fascism's innovation was to reabsorb classes into the nation — 'the nation', Lagardelle
recognised, 'is the beginning and end of fascism' — and to dismiss as
'historical memories' the series of syndicalist 'myths' relating to the revolutionary proletariat and the catastrophic collapse of capitalism. This was
made possible, Lagardelle believed, through the corporation, the professional association designed to group together all those — especially
employers and workers — engaged in a common economic activity and
fascism's distinctive contribution to the ordering of the economy. 'Under
capitalism', Lagardelle wrote, 'capital serves the private interest; under
the corporation, it serves the collective interest'. Fascism, in short,
denounced the exploitation of the masses by capitalism and through the
corporation sought to bring this abuse to an end. To the corporation then
went the task of ordering the diverse aspects of production in the economy,
leaving a purified State, as with *planisme*, in the overseeing role of 'arbiter
and guardian of the general interest'.

Lagardelle's own later account of his stay in Rome, written and published during the 1950s,[70] makes clear that his principal preoccupation was
to prevent Mussolini from being drawn into Hitler's orbit and it remained
his opinion that only a modicum of sympathy on the part of the British
and French governments for Italy's predicament and ambitions would
have been sufficient to secure that goal. In other words, there was in
Lagardelle's view no natural sympathy between Hitler and Mussolini at
either the level of national interest (witness their competing claims over

Austrian territory) or, more specifically, ideology. Italian fascism was not German nazism. If the former exalted the nation, the latter exalted the race and, as Lagardelle pointed out, Mussolini had only contempt for Hitler's racial theories.[71] Moreover, if fascism posited the *syndicat* and the corporation as mediating institutions placing workers and employers in a position of equality, the *syndicats* 'were brutally suppressed by Hitler and every economic enterprise became a military style organisation with its own führer and subordinate hierarchy'.[72] Did this therefore mean that Mussolini's Italy had lived up to the high ideals of Lagardelle's 1935 account? In 1936, Lagardelle tells us, Mussolini announced that Italy's key industries were to be directly controlled by the State and with this the corporate economy was substituted by the war economy. The State ceased to be merely the juridical expression of the nation and became an economic agent, thus blotting out the corporations at birth and opening up the way for dictatorship and a brand of 'personalism' that ultimately was to be Mussolini's undoing.[73] If, however, this was to be Lagardelle's position from the perspective of the 1950s it appears that at the end of his stay in Rome he had not lost all his illusions.

The summer of 1940 brought not just the complete military defeat of France but also the end of the Third Republic. The hexagon was divided into two, with the unoccupied zone covering approximately the southern half of France being administered in theory from the spa town of Vichy under the leadership of the First World War victor of Verdun, Marshal Pétain. The Vichy régime, with its *Etat Français* under the banner of 'family, country and work' and its projected National Revolution, has usually been seen as being both right-wing and backward-looking — it was, René Rémond wrote in his classic study of the French Right, 'conservatism triumphant, reaction in its pure state: a mixture of paternalism, moralism, clericalism and militarism'[74] — but in truth for all its abject failure it was in part an attempt to renovate France. Thus the renewed reverence for such institutions as the family, the Army and the Roman Catholic Church — 'the new régime', Pétain proclaimed, 'will be a social hierarchy'[75] — and the heavy emphasis placed upon the land and the peasant was matched by an interest in economic management and recovery that continued the 1930s preoccupation with modernisation. Equally, the support initially enjoyed by the Vichy régime was nothing if not heterogeneous. Anti-semites, crooks, and defeatists were joined by members of *Action française*, traditional conservatives, pre-war fascists, technocrats from the planning movement, as well as the forces of big business. So too endorsement for the new order came from elements amongst the syndicalist movement and in general on the Left. Indeed, at the outset the Vichy régime seems to have received the assent of the vast majority of the population.

Those on the left who rallied to Pétain — for example, René Belin who in 1940 quit the CGT to become Minister of Industrial Production and Labour[76] — did so for a variety of reasons and motives:[77] the desire to protect French interests and in particular French workers, pacifism (here the person of Jean Jaurès as a symbol of franco-german *rapprochement* was of great utility), virulent anti-communism, even disillusionment with the masses after the disappointments of the Popular Front. But Vichy held out another attraction for the French Left. The rejection of liberal capitalism as being somehow un-French coupled with the desire to re-structure industrial life seemed to suggest for some at least that the con-struction of a just and equitable order that accorded broadly with, for example, their syndicalist principles was a genuine possibility.

Vichy's National Revolution was to entail not just the reform of the State, the administration and education but also a broader project for a corporatist society.[78] At its heart was the *Charte du Travail*. The basic goal was to put an end to unbridled individualism by first abolishing all existing trade unions and employers' federations — Vichy shared the pre-war obsession with the power of anonymous trusts — and then by institut-ing corporations for each occupational group with compulsory membership for both labour and management. Class conflict was to be overcome through enhanced loyalty to the *métier* and 'the organised profession'. Work was no longer to be the pursuit of self-interest but a duty performed for the good of the whole community. In truth, as an attempt to dissolve the mechanisms of capitalism the *Charte du Travail*, introduced in the autumn of 1941 only after lengthy and acrimonious discussion, was always something of a hopeless case. Ignored by the employers, the supposedly autonomous corporations were, in effect, bureaucratic instruments of State control designed primarily to restrict the demands of the working class and guarantee social order. Yet during the time of its formulation and for some time afterwards there were syndicalists who continued to believe that, perhaps if only with their support, the *Charte du Travail* could provide the basis not only of an *économie associée* but also of an *économie humaine*.[79] If by April 1942 René Belin had despaired of this possibility, this was not true of Hubert Lagardelle. In that month with the return of Pierre Laval to power he replaced Belin as Minister of Labour.

Amongst the private papers of Lagardelle that remain is to be found a dossier of newspaper cuttings which catalogues the sabotage of his efforts to implement the *Charte du Travail*. Those papers also contain a note which reveals just how far Lagardelle had travelled since his days as editor of *Le Mouvement socialiste*. 'The problem', the note reads, 'is less to establish a society without classes than a society without clans: oligarchies = corruption of power'.[80] Lagardelle's speeches and articles also make clear that in his view the *Charte du Travail* was an integral part of the total social and political transformation required for France. The choice facing the country, he remarked, was a simple one: 'either change or perish'.[81] As such the *Charte du Travail* was not only the most efficient means of fostering 'French unity' but by creating a 'new climate' in which mediation and concessions replaced 'irreducible antagonisms' it presaged 'the disappearance of the proletarian condition'.[82] It represented the first component in the creation of a community of work, 'the organic union of all the elements that participate in the cycle of production'.[83] Indeed, for Lagardelle the comparison was always between the 'inorganic individualism', the 'inorganic society', of liberal capitalism (and by extension of parliamentary democracy) and the opportunity the *Charte du Travail* provided through the 'syndicat unique' for the 'organic incorporation' of employers, technicians and workers into 'the collective life' of the nation.

Interviewed by Jean Rivain in June 1942 Lagardelle was to comment: 'what interests me is not the past form of my thought; it is the permanence of my past thought in today's form'.[84] By this criterion, and by the manifest sincerity with which he set about his task ('I cannot hide', he commented in October 1943, 'the emotion I felt when eighteen months ago I was called by a logical but unforeseen destiny to the Ministry of Labour'[85]) it is evident that Lagardelle found little difficulty in reconciling his efforts to implement the *Charte du Travail* with his own earlier pronouncements. The *Charte du Travail*, he believed, drew upon 'the great French syndicalist tradition' and at one point he went so far as to state that 'the *Charte* will be syndicalist or it will not be'. Nor for that matter did Lagardelle seem to think that the prospects held out for the future by the *Charte du Travail* differed significantly from those endorsed by syndicalist theory. 'We are offering', he announced, 'the formation of a world liberated from money and from the oppression of economic forces, liberated by work and through work'.[86]

Lagardelle resigned from the Ministry of Labour in November 1943 only to re-appear two months later on the editorial board of Georges Daudet's collaborationist paper *La France socialiste*. In that capacity he continued to champion the complete and immediate application of the *Charte du Travail* and remained committed to this position until shortly before the liberation of Paris in August 1944. Indeed, some five weeks after the Allied invasion of Normandy Lagardelle still felt able to write that 'if 1789 starts a critical period, 1944 heralds an organic period' and to talk of 'the conquest of a world without capitalism and without the proletariat'.[87] Further, Lagardelle's articles in *La France socialiste* also served to reveal the extent of his attachment to Pétain and the National Revolution. Pétain himself was described as 'the symbol of national unity', the embodiment of national strength and of French honour whilst the National Revolution was accredited with having turned the French State into a 'social State'.[88] 'It has placed work', Lagardelle proclaimed, 'at the head of the national device; it has sought to integrate the proletariat into the new social order and to give to it pride of place in its institutions'. So too Lagardelle displayed an equal loathing for the Soviet Union and the United States. Both were seen as harbingers of a new barbarism, the representatives of 'a brutal world, the world of money and of material force'.[89] On the subject of nazism and the need or otherwise for collaboration with Germany Lagardelle remained silent, although he did offer one further defence of Italy's corporate economy.[90]

Beyond this, Lagardelle provided a final statement of what he now referred to as 'le syndicalisme institutionnel' or 'le syndicalisme construtif'.[91] With the *syndicat*, the antithesis of the bourgeois State, at its base and as the primary 'modality' of economic and professional life the new 'national community', the community of labour, was to be built around the existing diverse 'natural' communities which formed the structure of the country: the commune (described by Lagardelle as 'a gathering of families in a permanent local setting' and as an expression of common 'interests, manners and customs),[92] the region, and (now) the sports association, the study group and the arts society.[93] At the summit was to be a 'strong State', a State which did not absorb all the functions of the nation's life but which left to 'real' institutions the tasks for which they were suited. 'The new State', Lagardelle wrote, 'will be the co-ordinator of the groups which will protect the individual'.[94] In this way the producer would replace the citizen, power would reside in 'conscious minorities', the 'abstract' would make way for the 'real'. And, of course, a collective life built around the 'individual, the group and the State' would finally demolish the democratic 'fiction' of the 'allegorical individual' and the 'theoretical man'.[95]

With the end of the war Lagardelle was arrested and subsequently sentenced to hard labour for life. In addition to a general support of Pétain and the Vichy régime his specific crime as Minister of Labour was adjudged to have been the deployment of the French workforce for the sole profit of the enemy. Lagardelle was, however, released on grounds of ill health long before his death at the age of 84 in 1958, thus providing him with the opportunity of publishing *Mission à Rome* in 1955. Unfortunately, he was never able to complete his final project, the publication, almost half a century after their acrimonious dispute, of *Un bourgeois révolutionnaire: Georges Sorel et son époque*. Lagardelle had, in fact, throughout his episodic career been obsessed by his break with Sorel in 1909, continuously collecting material relevant to its causes, significance and consequences. In 1933, for example, he had published an edited version of the 94 letters he had received from Sorel between 1898 and 1910 whilst in May 1942 an interview with Raymond Racouly in *Gringoire* was given over largely to a discussion of their relationship.[96] What this inability to free himself from Sorel's presence illustrates above all is Lagardelle's constant preoccupation to demonstrate the continuity of his own thought and the compatibility of the successive positions he had adopted.

So in 1933 after having reflected upon Sorel's own hopes and disappointments he could conclude: 'Ideas move towards their triumph by unexpected routes. They never preserve the purity of their morning and in mixing
with the day follow the rhythm of life. But in their new form subsists
hidden their original essence. The pessimism deriving from action does
not lead to discouragement but gives us a sense of the relative. The
search for an absolute is a myth'.[97] Thus for Lagardelle syndicalism never
represented (as he believed it did for Sorel) a fixed system, an absolute
to be rigidly adhered to, but a series of insights and practices that required
constantly to be adapted to historical necessities. And, therefore, by way
of explanation for his own support of the *Charte du Travail* he felt able
in October 1943 to quote his own earlier comment (published originally
in 1911 as part of the Preface to Jean Gaumont's *L'Etat contre la nation*)
to the effect that: 'as for myself, I have never seen syndicalism as a new
school, with its own dogmatic and inflexible series of formulas. It has
appeared to me more as a movement suggestive of new ideas . . . provok-
ing reflections which are necessarily various and always revisable'.[98]
Indeed, even a superficial reading of Lagardelle's writings quickly reveals
that it was only between 1904–08 that he was fully committed to the
position of revolutionary syndicalism: certainly by the eve of the First
World War the concessions towards the existence of the State necessary
to facilitate his later evolution from regionalism through to support for
the *Charte du travail* had been made. Thus, what syndicalism symbolised
for Lagardelle was the revolt of economic society against political society,
the insurrection of the producer against incompetence, parasitism and the
bogus oratory of parliament and the citizen. But as such it could be
wedded to what Lagardelle, with little difficulty and no sense of self-
betrayal, came to regard as further manifestations of the victory of the
real over the abstract. This was made possible in Lagardelle's particular
case because unlike Sorel, whose syndicalism was deeply imbued with
Marxist notions, his condemnation of capitalism was not grounded in an
analysis of the process of production and hence it became possible to
contemplate the existence of a new economic order, a 'civilisation of work'
without the exploitation of the proletariat, which nevertheless rested upon
the same property relations. What mattered was that '*l'homme réel*' should
reign supreme and this, in theory, could be achieved in a variety of ways.
Hence from the turn of the century until 1944 Lagardelle was able to
repeat and rework a limited number of themes in the defence of what in
conventional terms were widely differing political practices. What this
categorically does not demonstrate, however, is that the voyage from
revolutionary syndicalism to fascism and corporatism is a necessary logical
transition. It is not, as the life of Pierre Monatte amply demonstrates.

III

In January 1925, only weeks after his expulsion from the communist party, Pierre Monatte launched *La Révolution prolétarienne*, taking for its sub-title, 'revue syndicaliste-communiste'.[99] The intention, Monatte commented in the first issue, was 'to continue, excluded from the party, that which we were doing when we were in the party'.[100] A month later the review's goals were more narrowly defined. 'We wish', the *Entre nous* column stated, 'to study the problems raised by the Russian experience for the Revolution and to work for the reconstitution of syndicalist unity, at a national and international level'.[101] In short, in both content and style *La Révolution prolétarienne* was to continue the traditions established by *La Vie ouvrière*. Built around a 'noyau' of regular contributors it was conceived as an 'intellectual co-operative' and delighted in what in 1929 it described as 'notre éclectisme incohérent'. Monatte, under the rubric 'Le Carnet du Sauvage', was to provide a commentary upon current events, Robert Louzon a column on economic issues, whilst Maurice Chambelland was to deal with what even he himself at times acknowledged to be a misnomer, 'la renaissance du syndicalisme'. Prior to 1929, when he departed to join the ranks of the Trotskyist Left Opposition, Alfred Rosmer was again to play a significant role alongside Monatte and, as we have already seen, Edouard Berth was to figure amongst the leading contributors until shortly before his death. During the 1930s new names, for example those of Simone Weil, Daniel Guérin and Victor Serge, were to be found in its pages. Prominence was also to be given — and this for a syndicalist journal was an innovation — to the analysis of colonial issues and movements of national liberation.

The priority in 1925, however, was to define the relationship of *La Révolution prolétarienne* to the communist movement and, specifically, developments within the Russian party. The first issue, therefore, reprinted the second letter of Monatte, Rosmer and Delagarde to the members of the French communist party, cataloguing their differences with the party leadership. The conception of the party held by Treint and his colleagues, they argued, denoted contempt for the masses and was itself a reflection of their own petit-bourgeois origins. The revolution would be prepared by developing the class-consciousness of the proletariat, not by producing reciters of a catechism. Thus, if they had supported the Communist International it was because with 'Lenin alive' it had seemed large enough to embrace Trotsky, 'so-called Trotskyism', the Workers' Opposition in Russia as well as elements from revolutionary syndicalism. Without Lenin, the movement was subject to regression and disintegration.[102] A month later Rosmer denied that they were Trotskyists on the simple grounds that in his opinion Trotskyism was a heresy invented by the party bureaucracy. 'Whoever resists', Rosmer wrote, 'is immediately classifed as right-wing, menchevik, petit-bourgeois, (objectively) counter-revolutionary, etc. But where in this is communism?'.[103] Perhaps surprisingly Trotsky did not welcome this support and in October 1925 argued that the content of *La Révolution prolétarienne* justified the exclusion of Rosmer and Monatte from the party: its 'interior logic', he suggested, would lead them 'to the other side of the barricade'. Trotsky's advice was that Monatte and Rosmer should close down their review and apply to the executive of the Comintern to have their case reconsidered. The response was equally to the point: 'Since one cannot speak either in the party or in the International, it is necessary to be able to speak outside, because there are things that need to be said, not out of the desire for a pointless polemic but in the interests of the working class. *La Révolution prolétarienne* is a refuge for the sincere revolutionaries who can no longer endure the suffocating atmosphere of the party, a defence against the sabotage of the movement'.[104] The message, then, was that it was they, not the supporters of 'bolshevisation', who were the 'true communists' and that it was not *La Révolution prolétarienne* but their opponents who were betraying the working class and the hopes aroused in 1917. Moreover, it is no exaggeration to say that it was the analysis of the nature and consequences of this betrayal, both in the Soviet Union and elsewhere, which became the abiding preoccupation of Monatte and *La Révolution prolétarienne* in the years up to 1939. 'To defend the Russian Revolution', Monatte wrote in 1929, 'is to defend it against itself'.[105]

The immediate and pressing need, therefore, was to follow the evolution of the situation inside Russia, to understand the reality of the Soviet Union. Monatte's diaries[106] show that in the years from 1925 until the outbreak of the Second World War he was an avid reader of books on Marxism and the Bolsheviks. Trotsky's account of the Russian Revolution, for example, was supplemented by a reading of Max Eastman, Krupskaia's *Souvenirs de Lénine* as well as Boris Souvarine's *Staline* and Gide's *Retour d'URSS*. In 1926 *La Révolution prolétarienne* published Lenin's *Testament* with its critical account of Stalin's personality. To this was added regular correspondence with dissidents within the Soviet Union and close contacts with exiles such as Guiheneuf-Yvon and Victor Serge (both of whom were to make a major contribution to *La Révolution prolétarienne* during the 1930s). The Soviet press, debates within the party (for example about NEP and socialism in one country), the decisions of the Comintern, Five Year Plans and collectivisation, and so on, were all followed with meticulous, almost obsessive, detail.

The picture that emerged — at the very moment when many on the Left in Europe were prepared to see a paradise of social justice — was one in which a party machine, then a State bureaucracy, and finally a dictator, Stalin, progressively withdrew power from the proletariat in order to concentrate it in their own hands, crushing all opponents and autonomous institutions, including the soviets, in the process. Certainly by the end of 1926 Rosmer, having withheld judgement, spoke of the Russian Revolution 'turning its back on communism'[107] but the decisive moment, when all illusions were finally dispelled, appears to have come the following year with the expulsion of Trotsky from the Executive of the Comintern. In rapid succession, first Monatte with 'Le Phare, va-t-il s'éteindre?', then Louzon with 'Staline, premier consul' and finally Rosmer with 'La Dictature stalinienne et la liquidation du communisme'[108] charted the rise of Stalin's 'personal dictatorship' and the degeneration of the Soviet Union into a virtual police State run by the GPU. From this point onwards it was a case of unremitting condemnation as 'la vérité sur l'URSS' became ever more manifest. *La Révolution prolétarienne*'s campaign, for example, to secure the liberation of Victor Serge, imprisoned in Russia first in 1928 and then again between 1933 and 1936, gave Monatte ample opportunity for insight into what Serge himself was to describe as 'the Stalinist nightmare'.[109] So too did the Moscow show trials. At one level Monatte was simply perplexed by these judicial charades. How could the confessions of Zinoviev, Radek, and others, be explained if not by the desire to make their final sacrifice to the party? 'In libelling themselves', Monatte commented, 'they are libelling the entire revolutionary movement'. Yet he was in no doubt as to the significance of the trials. Stalin was expressing the 'will of the dominant stratum, the bureaucracy of the Russian State' and in so doing not only was he seeking to destroy all possible centres of revolutionary opposition but he was also showing that the Soviet legal system was worse than anything offered either by the bourgeoisie or even Hitler.[110] Equally, *La Révolution prolétarienne* was quick to highlight what it saw as the disastrous consequences for the international communist movement of Stalinist rule. From the outset a critic of the disruptive and damaging process of bolshevisation it went on to condemn the tactic of imposing one form of action upon all communist parties irrespective of their particular situation — in 1930 Monatte spoke explicitly of the 'Vatican communiste'[111] — and to this was added a recognition that the strategy of the Comintern was determined primarily by the foreign policy requirements of the Soviet Union, that, as Monatte put it in 1935, 'the bureaucracy of the Third International' was the 'interpreter of Russian patriotism'.[112]

Disabused of his faith in the Russian experience where then was Monatte to turn? Certainly he was not prepared to follow Rosmer into the Trotskyist movement. Commenting upon his time as a member of the communist party he was to remark that 'I there again found the eternal opponents of syndicalism . . . the decor changes, the personalities also, but it is always the same comedy, the same drama, which is being played out'[113] and this conclusion seems to have been decisive in shaping his hostility to Trotsky's plans to create what Monatte referred to as a 'parti communiste idéal'. 'We did perhaps commit an act of folly in 1919', Monatte remarked, 'but in 1929 this would constitute a grave mistake'.[114] So, placing himself amongst the admirers but not disciples of Trotsky, Monatte was prepared to support the latter in his fight against Stalin whilst all the time acknowledging that upon central points of doctrine — the role of the party, the autonomy of the *syndicats*, the dangers of Statism — the two were in substantial disagreement. Indeed, in 1932 Monatte's diary talks of a style common to both Trotsky and Stalin which has its source in their similar (bolshevik) conceptions of party organisation.

In short, Monatte returned — 'seuls contre tous' as he described the position of *La Révolution prolétarienne* in 1927 — to the syndicalism of the Charter of Amiens, to an advocacy of the autonomy of the *syndicat* as the sole strategy capable of defending and furthering the permanent interests of the proletariat as a distinct class. In article after article, and usually in response to the criticisms of Trotsky, he argued that this was neither an out-dated nor dangerous position: on the contrary, it was 'a formula rejuvenated by experience and the only one which should allow the syndicalist movement to get out of the mire'.[115]

To that end, the first requirement, proclaimed as one of *La Révolution prolétarienne*'s main campaigning issues from its inception, was the recon-stitution of syndicalist unity, the merger of the communist-controlled CGTU and Jouhaux's CGT. From Monatte's perspective, this process was to be one of fusion rather than the takeover of one rival organisation by the other. Syndicalism would simultaneously disengage itself from communist party 'colonisation' and the reformist tactics of class collaboration and the *union sacrée*. At no point, however, did Monatte underestimate the obstacles that needed to be overcome to secure that goal; but only then, he believed, would the syndicalist movement cease to be a 'syndicalisme de secte' and become again a 'syndicalisme de masse', only then would the bourgeoisie have something to fear as the proletariat, united in a 'genuine class organisation', accomplished the first phase in its preparation for a revolutionary role.[116]

The opening initiative in this endeavour was the creation of the *Ligue syndicaliste*. The suggestion for such an organisation first appeared in the pages of *La Révolution prolétarienne* during the late spring of 1925 and was formally endorsed by Maurice Chambelland in October of that year.[117] At first sceptical about the idea — 'our sole ambition', Monatte wrote, 'is to see clearly in the confusion' — by May 1926 he was to be found amongst its supporters: two months later 'Ce qu'est, ce que veut la Ligue syndicaliste' was published.[118] If the espoused aim was to put an end to the schism that had wracked the French trade union since the early 1920s, then the flavour of the document was undoubtedly that of pre-war revol-utionary syndicalism. The *Ligue*, it stated, 'does not wish to direct the syndicalist movement: it wants the syndicalist movement to relearn to direct itself'. On 4 December 1929, Maurice Chambelland, Daniel Guérin, Monatte and Louzon, this time under the guise of the *Comité pour l'indépendance du syndicalisme*, launched the weekly *Le Cri du peuple*, again with the intention of galvanising support for the reunification and autonomy of the syndicalist movement; and it was, in part, out of this experience that came the 'Manifeste des 22', published on 9 November 1930. Unity, it proclaimed, would be built around 'the practice of class struggle and the independence of the syndicalist movement, beyond all interference by political parties, factions or sects, as well as governments'.[119]

The 'Manifeste des 22', signed by Monatte, Chambelland, and twenty others, including Georges Dumoulin, drawn from the CGT, CGTU and various non-affiliated organisations, evoked an echo of support from wide sections of the Left but after a year's campaigning the *Comité des 22*, renamed the *Comité de propagande pour l'unité syndicale*, met with crushing defeats, first at the CGT's conference in September (securing only 132 votes out of over 2200) and then at the congress of the CGTU only two months later. Unity seemed further away than ever and shortly afterwards *Le Cri du peuple*, plagued by debts, closed. As for Monatte, having written the obituary of the *Comité des 22*, he lapsed into relative silence, leaving much of the day-to-day running of *La Révolution prolétarienne* to Maurice Chambelland.[120] It would take the explosion of 1936 to bring him back fully to life.

'Like unity of action', Monatte wrote, 'syndicalist unity is the fruit of 6 February. It is the result of the fascist menace. The Popular Front is another'.[121] He was not mistaken. The right-wing riots of 6 February 1934 induced not only a sentiment of 'republican defence' but when combined with the rise of Hitler to power led directly to an anti-fascist counter-attack. Organisations such as the *Comité de Vigilance des Intellectuels Antifascistes* (which Monatte joined) were mirrored in wider co-operation between the socialist and communist parties and, after over eighteen months of negotiation, in the formal merger of the CGT and CGTU at the Congress of Toulouse in March 1936. Two months later Léon Blum led a broad left-wing coalition to victory in parliamentary elections and immediately afterwards France came to a virtual standstill as workers throughout the country occupied their factories in a series of spontaneous strikes. On June 5, two days after Blum was installed as France's first socialist prime minister, the Matignon agreements were signed, granting workers substantial wage increases, paid holidays, a 40 hour week and greater shop-floor union representation.

Initially *La Revolution prolétarienne* was critical of moves towards the establishment of a Popular Front — it represented, Louzon wrote, the negation of the class struggle and was a possible prelude to another *union sacrée*[122] — whilst Monatte himself was in no doubt about what had made possible the ending of the schism begun at Tours in 1920: a change in tactics in Moscow as Stalin finally appreciated the seriousness of the fascist threat. Nevertheless, he concluded, if 'syndicalist unity is not made according to our recipe . . . we can only rejoice in it and without reservation'. Any extension of working-class strength, he argued, no matter how it was achieved, would lead to 'a renewal of the revolutionary spirit'.[123]

This analysis appeared to be confirmed by the dramatic events of May-June 1936. What Monatte saw in the 'marvellous wave of strikes' was a situation in which the proletariat had 'regained confidence in itself'.[124] In addition to the remarkable concessions secured from a stunned *patronat* — *La Révolution prolétarienne* in general placed great stress upon the introduction of 'délégués d'atelier'[125] — the French trade union movement had rekindled its enthusiasm, introduced new tactics, experienced an astonishing increase in membership; and it would, Monatte believed, be foolish to deny that these gains were the result of a Popular Front strategy that reflected the desire of the masses, if not their leaders, for unity of action. Monatte's question was: could that impetus be sustained; or would the Popular Front be deflected from its original purpose and objectives?

The answer, of course, was that Blum's government, and with it the Popular Front, progressively disintegrated under the weight of domestic and international problems that were simply beyond its control.[126] By November 1936 Monatte was warning of a new counter-offensive from the employers, arguing that the workers must not allow them 'to win the second round', and six months later he was openly denouncing the 'sectarianism' of the communists as once again they blatantly put the interests of their party before those of the working class.[127] Certainly, by the end of 1938, if not long before, the optimistic excitement of the summer of 1936 had been replaced by deep foreboding as the impending defeat of Republican forces in Spain and the threat of general European war accompanied the end of the Popular Front experiment. Less than two years later, on 10 September 1939, *La Révolution prolétarienne* was to close: it was not until 1947 that it recommenced publication.

As we have already seen, with the signing of the Munich Agreement *La Révolution prolétarienne* refused to publish an article by Edouard Berth which, for all its expression of pleasure at the avoidance of war, nevertheless conveyed the strong impression that something shameful had taken place.[128] By contrast, the editorial policy of *La Révolution prolétarienne* was one of undisguised support for Munich — little, if any sympathy, was voiced for the Czech government — whilst moves to enhance national defence were met with resolute opposition. More controversially still, after the fall of France the members of the 'noyau', though they continued to meet, played no active part in the resistance movement, preferring, like Jean-Paul Sartre, not to co-operate with either the Gaullists or the communists.

The roots of this position clearly go back to a belief in the internationalism of the working-class movement and specifically to the anti-war stance of Monatte and his associates in 1914. Thus, for example, in the 1930s efforts were made to launch a second Zimmerwald movement (Maurice Chambelland was to try again in 1952) and extreme vigilance was shown towards any initiatives which might prefigure renewed moves towards class collaboration or a national war effort.[129] Yet to this were added a series of other considerations which very much had their origin in the complex political picture of the inter-war period. For all *La Révolution prolétarienne*'s undoubted hatred of Hitler and fascism, it was nevertheless the case that it frequently recognised the legitimacy of many of the demands that Hitler was making on behalf of the German nation. 'Hitler', Monatte wrote, 'is a product of the Treaty of Versailles' and it was, therefore, this treaty and subsequent attempts by the other European powers to encircle Germany that had to be opposed. It was also the case that throughout the 1930s articles in *La Révolution prolétarienne* repeatedly disparaged the claims to political superiority of the so-called parliamentary democracies. So, for example, in an article attacking Roosevelt's New Deal Daniel Guérin felt able to compare 'the corporate American State' to the Third Reich; and Robert Louzon, in the wake of Daladier's return to power in 1938, talked of 'the fascistisation of the French State'. But without doubt the decisive factor in determining the position of Monatte and his collaborators at *La Révolution prolétarienne* was their categorical and vehement repudiation of the status of the Soviet Union as a revolutionary force. In 1935 Stalin signed the Franco-Soviet pact of mutual assistance, thus obliging French communists to recognise that they could not sabotage the defence of France without simultaneously weakening the position of the Soviet Union.[130] Further evidence of 'communist treason' was then graphically provided by what was seen as Soviet complicity in the destruction of the forces of proletarian revolution in Spain and, finally, by the Nazi-Soviet pact. Stalin, in short, was playing the same infernal game as Hitler, Mussolini and the rest of the capitalist powers, with war as the inevitable end result. In 1939, as in 1914, there was no virtue in choosing between competing imperialisms. Moreover, after the Second World War the avoidance of such a path was to remain Monatte's principal concern.

Monatte's seven-year silence was finally broken in 1946 with the appearance of *Où va la CGT?*[131] and the following year, after an absence of 91 months, *La Révolution prolétarienne* resumed publication with a *noyau* built again around Monatte, Chambelland, Rosmer and Louzon. All the indications are, however, that from the outset the task of sustaining anew *La Révolution prolétarienne*, with its small number of readers and contributors, was to prove a difficult one. Monatte himself was to be employed as a typographer on *France-Soir* until his retirement in 1952 and this, when combined with persistent ill-health and increasing age — Monatte was 70 in 1951 — meant that his participation in the day-to-day running of the journal was of necessity limited. His diaries — always the best source of information on his activities and ideas in the years preceding his death in 1960 — also show that serious disagreements were quickly to surface amongst the members of the reconstituted *noyau*.

The signing of the Nazi-Soviet pact had meant that once again the trade union movement in France was split into two but upon this occasion the schism was quickly brought to an end with the signing of the Perreux accords in 1943. However, as in 1936 so in the immediate post-war period, unity was less the outcome of genuine agreement between the rival factions that made up the CGT than a reflection of broader domestic and international considerations that made possible the co-operation of socialists, communists and left-wing catholics in the spirit of national reconstruction. Likewise, the exclusion of communist ministers from the government of Paul Ramadier in May 1947, coinciding with the adoption of a harder line in Moscow, meant that the communist party, through the CGT, unleashed a series of violent and overtly politically motivated strikes at the end of 1947, leading in early 1948 to the resignation of Jouhaux and other reformists and their creation of a second organisation, the *Confédération générale du travail – Force ouvrière*. In short, the CGT's third split since 1921 was the direct result of the growing tension between East and West characteristic of the beginning of the Cold War. France itself, a country in turmoil which in October 1947 saw the right-wing and seemingly anti-republican Gaullist party secure almost 40 per cent of the vote in municipal elections, appeared to be on the verge of becoming either a Russian or American satellite.

Monatte's war-time diaries show that he held Stalin largely responsible for the outbreak of war in 1939 — if Stalin had not signed the pact with Hitler war would simply have been impossible — and as a consequence Monatte's hostility towards the official communist movement, in contrast to many members of France's intellectual élite, hardened during the period of Nazi occupation. Equally, if by 1944 Monatte was haunted by the idea of the triumph of Stalinism in Eastern Europe, so too he feared that under de Gaulle France would soon be subject to military government. Was this 'intelligent general', Monatte wrote on the day Paris was liberated, about to become another Boulanger? Thus the period of post-war provisional government found Monatte in a mood of irreducible opposition to what he described as 'red' and 'white fascism'.[132] Fascism, he commented, 'is a compound of strident nationalism and false socialism: all things that can be re-found in Gaullism'.[133] Behind de Gaulle Monatte saw only the spirit of reaction and the grip of the employers. His politics of grandeur was totally inappropriate for a France bedevilled by food shortages and inflation. This was still to be Monatte's view in 1958 when with the support of the army de Gaulle seized power.[134] Monatte's description of the 'red fascism' he associated with Stalinism followed similar lines: the 'Russian régime', he commented, 'with its nationalism, its statism, its cult of the leader, resembles characteristic by characteristic Italian fascism and nazism'.[135] Russia was no more the country of socialism than the France of Napoleon had been the country of revolution.

Monatte for one certainly believed that a Russian invasion of Western Europe was a definite possibility — 'after German aggression, Russian aggression', he noted in June 1950 — and consequently the analysis of Stalinism and the 'totalitarian' State was to figure prominently in the pages of *La Révolution prolétarienne*. Once more Monatte and Rosmer, especialy after the publication of the latter's *Moscou sous Lénine* in 1953, were to reflect upon the relationship between bolshevism and Stalin's dictatorship. At what point had the revolution been deflected from its original path? Both, if with a difference of emphasis, now accepted that the decline had begun while Lenin was still alive: for Monatte the turning point was as early as the suppression of the Kronstadt rebellion. Similarly *La Révolution prolétarienne* viewed with increasing alarm the gradual emergence of the Soviet bloc in Eastern Europe, welcoming first Tito's break with Stalin in 1948 and then the opposition to Russian domination in East Berlin and Hungary. Stalin's death was greeted with positive pleasure. 'Czar Stalin is dead' the cover of the April 1953 issue announced and Monatte, having the previous year said of Stalin that he made Hitler and Mussolini look like 'little boys', now wished the Russian leader not his hero's funeral but the same ignominious fate as had befallen the Italian dictator.[136] Did this mean that Stalinism was at an end and that Stalin's successors would dismantle his repressive régime? For Monatte the execution of Beria the following year indicated that the answer was in the negative. Nevertheless, Khrushchev's speech to the 20th Congress of the Soviet Communist Party condemning Stalin provided Monatte and his closest associates with one last opportunity to pillory communist orthodoxy. Their 'Lettre aux membres du parti communiste français' contended that it was not enough simply to denounce the personality cult: the faults of the system were structural and lay primarily in the party and State apparatus. 'The social ownership of the means of production and of exchange', they argued, 'does not suffice as a definition of socialism. It cannot ensure that the exploitation of the workers will disappear'.[137]

Monatte's hostility to Stalinism clearly extended to its representatives or 'flunkeys' in France, the 'so-called communists' like Thorez and Duclos who were in reality, he believed, the 'agents of counter-revolution'. Their sole goal, as the 'Molotov strikes' of 1947–48 proved, was to destabilise France in order to extend the domain of 'Russian statism, Russian red fascism'.[138] It was thus largely in the hope of seeing broken the monopoly of control exercised by the 'Stalinists' over the French working class that Monatte initially lent his support to Jouhaux's break-away *Force ouvrière*.

A 'loyal and temporary' compromise with the reformists was necessary given the possibility of creating a non-bureaucratic and independent organisation 'capable of guiding the working class towards its genuine emancipation'.[139] Sadly for Monatte not only did his own union, the *Fédération du livre*, vote against affiliation to *Force ouvrière* but he too quickly came to appreciate that his hopes were not to be realised. Another opportunity to resuscitate syndicalism had been missed.

Yet for Monatte the decision to support *Force ouvrière* was only one part of the complicated dilemma posed by the existence of Stalinism. If in 1947 Monatte recognised that France faced the twin internal threats of either a Gaullist or Stalinist take-over, he also acknowledged that the post-war world could fall victim to the rivalry between American and Russian imperialism. 'Europe, we are told, has no choice', Monatte observed: 'either the knout or the iron-heel'.[140] Monatte's own view was that history offered other options, that the spirit of working-class internationalism provided a possible alternative to Russian or American domination. At one level this meant that Monatte continued to believe in the possibility (however remote) that one day the Russian and American proletariats would remove their oppressors;[141] at another that he followed with intense interest organisations such as the *Rassemblement Démocratique Révolutionnaire* (in which both Sartre and Camus were leading participants) designed to rally non-Communist Party left intellectuals to the idea of Europe as a mediating force between the two competing power blocs. 'Neither Washington nor Moscow', Monatte wrote in 1949 summarising his position, 'but the international revolutionary action of peoples. Then Zimmerwald! Zimmerwald, which was the preface to the Russian Revolution. Zimmerwald 49, which will be the preface to the European Revoluiton'.[142] The intention, then, was to follow a course that involved support for neither the Russian nor American camps.

However, while Monatte was always insistent that his own anti-Stalinism had to be distinguished from 'bourgeois anti-communism',[143] it is also clear that he had no hesitation in identifying Russian expansionism as the greatest threat to world peace and therefore in categorising Stalinism as 'the number one enemy'.[144] So, in January 1949 Monatte could comment in his diary: 'for us Stalinism is not the only problem but the principal problem which alters all the others'. This meant, for example, that Monatte saw the signing of the Atlantic pact as a 'natural', if belated, response to the 'militarisation' of Russia and 'her vassals', and that at the end of the 1950s he could believe that Khrushchev intended to attack the West via the Middle East. The same perspective also brought Monatte into conflict with Sartre and Merleau-Ponty for their refusal in the January 1950 edition of *Les Temps modernes* to condemn the existence of Soviet labour camps on the grounds that the USSR was on the side of the forces fighting to end exploitation. Has Sartre not seen, Monatte asked, 'that for the past 30 years the entire soviet system in Russia has completely disappeared in order to make way for an increasingly visible and odious fascist system?'. Sartre, Monatte suggested, would have been an anti-Dreyfusard.[145] Several months later Monatte and Rosmer were again to criticise *Les Temps modernes* but this time for their publication of Daniel Guérin's unreservedly hostile account of life in the United States. The logic inherent in Monatte's position was forcibly spelt out in a letter to André Spire in 1953. Writing at the time of the Slansky purge trial in Prague after which 11 of the defendants were executed and the controversial prosecution in the USA of Julius and Ethel Rosenberg as Soviet spies, he remarked: 'I have no more admiration for American capitalism than I have for the French bourgeoisie but I cannot put on the same level the eleven people who have been hanged in Prague and the two American prisoners, I cannot put on the same level the American bourgeois régime and the Czechoslovakian totalitarian régime'.[146] There was for Monatte, it seems, a difference in kind between the two forms of oppression.

This, without doubt, was a view shared by several other members of *La Révolution prolétarienne*'s editorial board, most notably Robert Louzon and Roger Hagnauer, and it was not therefore entirely surprising to find them arguing, when with the outbreak of the Korean War many believed that a Russian invasion of Europe was imminent, that France could not be neutral, that it had to side with America. The choice, Louzon wrote, was either 'to accept the régime of slavery and forced labour or fight it with armed force'. To seek to avoid this dilemma, he believed, was sheer folly.[147] This, somewhat disingenuously, was a judgement that Monatte was never prepared to make.

The first signs of the internecine quarrel that plunged *La Révolution prolétarienne* into deep crisis, leading first to Maurice Chambelland's departure in 1951 and then Monatte's own virtual withdrawal for the last decade of his life, appeared after the publication of Louzon's *L'Ere de l'impérialisme* in 1948. In 1949 Monatte's diary talks of Louzon's 'fatalism' and by January the following year he noted with specific reference to Louzon: 'we are not members of the American party: we are members of the internationalist party'. For the most part the dispute was kept out of the pages of *La Révolution prolétarienne*, its most immediate manifestation (apart from the sudden cessation of Monatte's *Carnet du Sauvage* column) being the creation in December 1951 of the *Cercle Zimmerwald*, headed by Monatte, Rosmer and chambelland, and then the following April, the *Cercle Pelloutier*. Both, if formally designed to provide a forum for discussion and propaganda activities, were so set up as to exclude Louzon — 'Two "blocs" confront each other', the declaration of the *Cercle Zimmerwald* stated: 'we support neither' — without breaking all contacts. It was, however, the publication in October 1953 of Louzon's article 'A propos de l'"indépendance française" ' that finally brought the issue fully into the open.[148] Louzon's call for a recognition that, when faced with a system based on 'despotism' and one based on 'relative liberty', *La Révolution prolétarienne* should place itself on the side of the 'American party' evoked a withering reply from Monatte in the shape of 'Parti américain? Non! Parti internationaliste'.[149] Tangled within, around and between the Russian and American empires, Monatte remarked, lay the working class and to ignore this was to side with American support for repressive régimes in Iran, Indo-China and Spain. 'The *RP*', he concluded, 'cannot become, without denying and ridiculing itself, an organ of the American party. With difficulty but by its own resources it was created, has existed for 30 years, to preserve, in spite of everything, faith in working-class internationalism and proletarian revolution. To renounce its *raison d'être* would be equivalent to committing suicide'.

After this Monatte's contribution to *La Révoluiton prolétarienne* declined dramatically. Seven months later he lambasted its generous tribute to the recently deceased former head of the CGT, Léon Jouhaux, and from then on restricted himself almost entirely to memoirs and reminiscences about his own and the syndicalist movement's past: the life of Pelloutier, Monatte's own arrival in Paris as a young man, the famous congresses in Montpellier and Amiens, and the foundation of *La Vie ouvrière* were all re-examined as Monatte reflected upon his experience of over 60 years as a militant. Remarkably, despite his age and increasing physical isolation, Monatte continued as best he could to keep abreast of affairs, reading Koestler, Djilas and Gramsci for the first time, maintaining contacts with Camus, and vainly attempting to keep alive the *Cercle Zimmerwald* and the *Cercle Pelloutier*. Even here, amongst the small group that sought to preserve the values of internationalism, class struggle and working-class independence, disagreements were not slow to emerge — 'the crisis at the RP', Monatte noted, 'now becomes complicated with a sub-crisis within our own current' — and he himself readily admitted that they had succeeded in creating not a movement but a *club de faubourg*. The *Cercle Zimmerwald* produced one issue of its review (reprinting Khrushchev's denunciation of Stalin) but to little, if any, effect; and the experience of Monatte and his divided group was one of progressive marginalisation.

In April 1947 Pierre Monatte recorded that he paid a quick visit to a hat-seller, with the result that he bought a hat that was too small. 'I am truly a pathetic character', he remarked of himself: 'I want to make a revolution and I cannot even defend myself against a shopkeeper'. The same person also knew that throughout his life, before 1914, after 1919, after 1924, after 1936, and even after 1946, he had idealised the syndicalist movement and that both he and the militants of his generation, having failed to prevent two world wars and experienced numerous defeats, had accomplished virtually nothing. By the mid–1950s he, probably better than most, could see that the tradition of working-class autonomy was all but extinguished, crushed by the twin forces of Stalinism and reformism. The member of the *syndicat* was more often than not 'apathetic', the movement itself, split into competing confederations, both morally and materially weakened. As proof, in 1958 General de Gaulle was accorded a rapturous return to power. 'Decidedly', Monatte commented in his diary, 'the bulk of the French people are more reactionary, chauvinistic and drawn towards one man than I had believed'. Did this therefore mean that revolutionary syndicalism, with its conceptions of direct action and the general strike, was finally dead and that the believer in this original variety of syndicalism should despair?

Monatte's answer, for all the difficulties he experienced as he neared the end of his life, never varied. The discouragement and disarray, he believed, derived primarily from three sources: the schisms of 1921, 1939 and 1947; a feeling of 'physical exhaustion' and 'impotence' after decades of tyranny and carnage; and the deception engendered by the caricature of socialism foisted upon the world by a revolution that had been betrayed. But none of this meant, as many argued, that with the advance of industrialism the workers had been reduced to robots or that the revolutionary will of the proletariat no longer existed. Despite defeat upon defeat, Monatte believed, the working class continued to move slowly and with difficulty towards its emancipation, having fallen to the bottom of the ravine for a second or third time it would again reclimb the slope. Therefore for Monatte the first task was not always to do one's duty but, as he never tired of repeating, to see clearly. That maxim told him that the greatest danger for the future lay in the working class's loss of confidence in itself, the abandonment of its faith in its own destiny and capacity to lead civilisation; and equally that the function of syndicalism in the 1950s was to reverse this, that its role still remained that laid down by Pelloutier: to prepare the moral, administrative and technical education required for a society of free men. 'The defeat of the revolutionary workers' movement', Monatte wrote, 'has been above all a defeat of intelligence and character'.[150]

7 Conclusion

Pierre Monatte died in 1960, Alfred Rosmer in 1963, Maurice Chambelland in 1966. *La Révolution prolétarienne*, albeit in much-diminished form, continues to this day and still proclaims its allegiance to the tradition of Pelloutier.[1] As for the broader trade union movement in France, it remains divided into three major and at least two minor confederations, and has yet to escape from the traditional problems of low membership and lack of funds. The Communist Party, despite its own dramatically reduced strength, retains its grip over the CGT and for all the dramatic events of May 1968, the subsequent vogue for *autogestion*, and economic recession there appears little room for a renaissance of direct action syndicalism in the epoch of François Mitterrand and *l'ouverture* towards the political centre.[2] As Sorel once said of Marxism, the doctrine of syndicalist autonomy seems ready to join 'the necropolis of the departed gods'.

Thus of late it has largely been as a subject of interest to the historian, not the militant, that the activities and writings of the pre-First World War leadership of the CGT and Sorel's *nouvelle école* has figured. One of those historians, Jean Maitron, died in 1988. Another, Zeev Sternhell, has succeeded in shrouding the whole subject in controversy.[3] Sternhell's overall thesis — that it is in France more than any other country that the Platonic 'idea' or 'ideal type' of fascism was realised[4] — is a challenging and much-contested one and if this is not the place to consider at length the detailed methodological and interpretive criticism that has been levelled against it the argument certainly merits our attention to the extent that it directly touches upon the subjects and individuals examined in this book.[5] For Sternhell, central to the appearance of a full-blown fascist ideology was the simultaneous rejection (on both the Left and the Right) of liberalism and Marxism. Specifically, it was out of a revision of Marxism and an undermining of its rationalist, Hegelian foundations that emerged an anti-materialism and anti-positivism which 'made possible a socialism without a proletariat'. All that was then required was to replace the idea of the proletariat with that of the nation. Furthermore, according to Sternhell, this synthesis of socialism and the nation preceded the First World War and found its first expression in the meeting of the followers of Sorel and Maurras constituted by the *Cercle Proudhon*.[6] 'The logical transition from revolutionary syndicalism to national socialism', Sternhell has written, 'took place quite naturally'.[7]

At an immediate level one can question Sternhell's assertion that the emergence of fascism as an ideology was completed prior to the events of 1914–18. What sense, for example, does it make to describe Sorel's pre-First World War writings as 'openly fascist'[8] and Edouard Berth's 'Satellites de la ploutocratie', published in 1912, as 'a classic work of national socialism'[9] when, as we know, the hopes and disappointments engendered by the First World War (not to mention the impact of post-war economic depression and the fears aroused by communism) had such an input into both the style and content of fascism? More seriously, Sternhell effectively categorises all anti-liberal and 'irrational' thought as fascist. If this is most clearly mistaken in the case of someone like Emmanuel Mounier, editor of *Esprit*, the same point applies equally to the likes of Pouget and Griffuelhes.[10] That the attacks of the revolutionary syndicalists upon democracy and the parliamentary régime found an echo in the themes of the extreme Right does not serve to negate their resolute hostility to any attempt to extend State power or eradicate the class struggle — both of which, presumably, must be counted as constitutive elements of fascist ideology. But Sternhell's basic error is to regard Sorel's brief interest in *Action française* between 1909 and 1912 and Berth's participation in the activities of the *Cercle Proudhon* as sufficient grounds for classifying the general tenor and pattern of development of a whole body of ideas. Symptomatic of this process is the elevation to a position of centrality of two figures marginal to the history of syndicalism, Emile Janvion and Gustave Hervé, and the total neglect accorded to Alphonse Merrheim (cited only three times) and Pierre Monatte (cited only once!). The point is that the synthesis of socialism and nationalism leading to fascism was no 'logical transition' accomplished universally by the pre-war leadership of the CGT and the theoreticians of the *nouvelle école* but one possible *choice* amongst many. If that choice was made by Lagardelle in the 1930s it was categorically not made by Sorel (who, it must be remembered, rallied to Lenin, not Mussolini) nor Berth (who ended his life ashamed of the Munich Agreement); and it did not preclude a range of other options. Merrheim, like the CGT as a whole, moved towards reformism. Griffuelhes and Delesalle supported the Russian Revolution. Yvetot, after a return to anarchism and renewed anti-war agitation, seemed content in a minor way to aid the efforts of the German authorities in occupied Paris. In Pouget's case, the option was silence; whilst for Monatte there remained a life dedicated to the tradition of working-class internationalism and autonomy, dominated for over 30 years by anti-Stalinism. Faced with the need to come to terms with and understand the novel and frightening conditions before them it is variety, and not homogeneity, that character-ises their responses and it is this very diversity that escapes Sternhell in his headlong search for traces of fascism in French culture.

A more fruitful approach is to see the emergence of a distinct syndicalist vision at the end of the nineteenth century as one aspect of what is sometimes referred to as '*la deuxième gauche*'.[11] The dominant tradition on the French Left, supreme in both the modern communist and socialist parties, has been that of Jacobinism. Descended from the eighteenth century and the French Revolution, it has not sought to disguise its affection for the State, Paris, and the centralisation of power. Its chosen field of action has been politics; its leaders: intellectuals; and its means: parliamentarism and, at times, insurrectionalism. Philosophically, it has been rationalist and monist. Only rarely, for example during the Second Empire, has this tradition been dislodged from its position of dominance. The second, newer tradition finds its roots in a rejection of this Jacobin experience. Described as anti-State and sometimes as anarchist, it has emphasised the importance of civil, as opposed to political, society, has counternanced decentralisation (even going so far as to accept the virtues of regionalism), and has seen merit in the free association of autonomous (usually economic) groups. Furthermore, it has always been an ambiguous tradition. Never wholly secular, it has tended to see progress in terms of the realisation of certain ethical values, doubting at times either the attainability or wisdom of material plenty. Frequently, it has been associated with the defence of certain vested (normally artisanal) interests and a hostility towards (Parisian) modernity. Was it not after all Proudhon who expressed the desire to be both the most revolutionary and the most conservative thinker of his day? More recently this perspective has found expression in the *Confédération Française Démocratique du Travail* (CFDT), Catholic in origin and now a vociferous supporter of Poland's *Solidarity* movement.

It is here, within this second and often subterranean strand of the French Left, that can properly be located Pelloutier and those of his admirers who found their way to Lagardelle's apartment in the Avenue Reille or Monatte's *La Vie ouvrière*. Workers' control, the assertion of the primacy of labour and its elevation into a philosophy of *ouvriérisme*, the self-emancipation of the proletariat through direct action, the challenge to Guesdism and later Stalinism, Sorel's hostility to the notion of the Rousseauian 'general will' and the *raison d'être* of State force, Lagardelle's scorn for the abstract citizen of democratic theory, and even Berth's expression of profound distaste for the mercantile culture of modern city-life: all find a place as components of this anti-political vision. Equally, as a tradition that is open-ended and without fixed parameters it allows not only for internal diversity but for those who draw inspiration from it to change sides without necessarily realising the distance they have covered. Lagardelle, with apparent complete sincerity, continued to proclaim his fidelity to the ideas of Pelloutier even as the Vichy régime and his role in it came to a close. Thus if intellectual rigidity of the kind that has had such a deadening impact upon the French Communist Party has been avoided it has been in part at a price of confusion and betrayal. Whether this or basic tactical and conceptual deficiencies accounts for the failure of the supporters of syndicalist autonomy to achieve a position of hegemony within the French labour movement for all but a few years in the first decade of the twentieth century is an altogether different and unanswerable question. The fact of the matter is, however, that in men such as Pelloutier and Monatte and the theoreticians of the *nouvelle école* socialism finds its most eloquent proponents of a society composed of free and equal producers. And it is for this that they should primarily be remembered.

List of Abbreviations

The following abbreviations are used for periodicals in the footnotes.

AO	*L'Action ouvrière*
BS	*La Bataille syndicaliste*
EE	*L'Ecole émancipée*
GS	*La Guerre sociale*
IOS	*Information ouvrière et sociale*
IR	*L'Information régionale*
JduP	*Le Journal du peuple*
MS	*Le Mouvement socialiste*
Rev. mét.	*La Revue de métaphysique et de morale*
RO	*La Revue occidentale*
RP	*La Révolution prolétarienne*
RPI	*La Revue positiviste internationale*
RS	*La Revue socialiste*
SOE	*Sud-Ouest Economique*
TN	*Les Temps nouveaux*
VduP	*La Voix du peuple*
VO	*La Vie ouvrière*

Notes

Notes to Chapter 1

1. See Fonds Delesalle (14 AS 53bis), *Institut français d'histoire sociale*; 'Lettere di Georges Sorel a Roberto Michels', *Nouvi studi di diritto, economia e politica*, II, 1929, p. 288; and S. Sand, *L'illusion du politique: Georges Sorel et le débat intellectuel 1900* (Paris: 1985), pp. 12–14.

2. E. Dolléans, *Histoire du mouvement ouvrier (1871–1936)* (Paris: 1939), p. 126.

3. 'Patriotisme national et luttes de classes', *Libres entretiens*, 2nd series, 11 March 1906, pp. 389–436.

4. 'Lettere di Giorgio Sorel a Uberto Lagardelle', *Educazione fascista*, XI, 1933, p. 962.

5. G. Sorel, 'Préface' to V. Griffuelhes and L. Niel, *Les Objectifs de nos luttes de classe* (Paris: 1909).

6. A. Lebey, 'M. Griffuelhes juge la Barricade', *La Démocratie sociale*, 15 January, 1910.

7. K. Kautsky, 'Le Socialisme et les carrières libérales', *Le Devenir social*, I, 1895, pp. 105–19, 264–74.

8. C. Chambelland, 'Monatte, lecteur de Sorel', *Cahiers Georges Sorel*, 4, 1986, p. 140.

9. H. Lagardelle, 'Intellectuels et syndicalisme', *L'Avant-garde*, 3 September 1905; see also H. Lagardelle, *Les Intellectuels devant le socialisme* (Paris: 1900) and R. Louzon, 'Les Intellectuels', *VO*, 116, 1914, pp. 84–94.

10. 'Lettres de Georges Sorel à Edouard Berth: Troisième partie 1911–1917', *Cahiers Georges Sorel*, 5, 1987, pp. 174–5.

11. For the text of the Charter of Amiens see J. Julliard, *Autonomie ouvrière: Etudes sur le syndicalisme d'action directe* (Paris: 1988), p. 222.

12. P. Monatte, 'Paris, 1902', *Témoins*, 8, 1955, pp. 6–15.

13. M. Prat, 'Georges Sorel et le monde des revues', *Cahiers Georges Sorel*, 5, 1987, pp. 11–14.

14. See G. Pirou, 'A propos du syndicalisme révolutionnaire: théoriciens et militants', *Revue politique et parlementaire*, LXX, 1911, pp. 130–42 and R. Goetz-Girey, *La Pensée syndicale française: militants et théoriciens* (Paris: 1948).

15. Nor, of course, is this to assert that Sorel had no influence whatsoever upon the syndicalist movement. See a letter from C. Reynier to Paul Delesalle, dated 5 August 1938, which as 'the modest testimony of a pre-war syndicalist' attests to the contrary: Fonds Delesalle (14 AS 53ter), *Institut français d'histoire sociale*.

16. See J. Julliard, 'Le monde des revues au début du siècle', *Cahiers Georges Sorel*, 5, 1987, pp. 3–9.

17. E. Berth, 'Marchands, Intellectuels et Politiciens', *MS*, XXII, 1907, p. 389.

18. Z. Sternhell, *La Droite révolutionnaire 1885–1914* (Paris: 1978) and *Ni droite ni gauche* (Paris: 1983).

19. J. Julliard, *Autonomie ouvrière: Etudes sur le syndicalisme d'action directe*, p. 23.

20. See E. Weber, *Peasants into Frenchmen* (London: 1977).

21. C. Charle, *Les Elites de la République* (Paris: 1988).

22. J. Julliard, *Autonomie ouvrière*, p. 28.

23. W. H. Sewell, *Work and Revolution in France* (Cambridge: 1980) and B. H. Moss, *The Origins of the French Labor Movement* (Berkeley and Los Angeles: 1976).

24. T. Judt, *Marxism and the French Left* (Oxford: 1986), p. 86.

25. M. Perrot, *Workers on Strike: France 1871–1890* (Leamington Spa: 1987), p. 232.

26. See M. Branciard, *Syndicats et partis: Vol. I 1879–1947* (Paris: 1982) and J. Guesde, H. Lagardelle and E. Vaillant, *Le Parti socialiste et la confédération générale du travail* (Paris: 1908).

27. See R. Brécy, *La Grève générale en France* (Paris: 1969).

28. See F. Pelloutier, *Histoire des bourses du travail* (Paris: 1902); P. Delesalle, *Les bourses du travail et la CGT* (Paris: 1910); C. Franck, *Les bourses du travail et la confédération générale du travail* (Paris: 1910) and L. de Seilhac, *Les bourses du travail* (Reims: 1906).

29. See E. Shorter and C. Tilly, *Strikes in France: 1830–1968* (Cambridge: 1974).

30. For a discussion of the Charter of Amiens see J. Julliard, *Autonomie ouvrière*, pp. 199–219.

31. A prevailing Marxist explanation, of course, has been to see 'anarcho-syndicalism' in terms of the supposed backwardness of the French working class.

32. For a selection of the literature on this issue see G. Pirou, *Proudhonisme et syndicalisme révolutionnaire* (Paris: 1910); A. Kriegel, *Le Pain et les roses* (Paris: 1968), pp. 33–50; K. S. Vincent, *Pierre-Joseph Proudhon and the Rise of French Republican Socialism* (New York: 1984) and M. Fitzpatrick, 'Proudhon and the French Labour Movement: the Problem of Proudhon's Prominence', *European History Quarterley*, 15, 1985, pp. 407–30.

33. See 'Patriotisme national et luttes de classe', *Libres entretiens*, pp. 419–24; S. Lukes, *Emile Durkheim* (Harmondsworth: 1973), pp. 542–6 and J. E. S. Hayward, 'Solidarist Syndicalism: Durkheim and Duguit', *Sociological Review*, 8, 1960, pp. 17–36, 185–202.

34. J. Jaurès, *Etudes socialistes* (Paris: 1902), pp. 97–121: see also R. Trempé and J. Julliard, 'Jaurès et les grèves', *Jaurès et la classe ouvrière* (Paris: 1981), pp. 101–23.

35. J. Grave, *Le Syndicalisme dans l'évolution sociale* (Paris: 1908); P. Bietry, *Rouges et jaunes* (Paris: 1908); M. Rigaux, *Syndicalisme et religion* (Paris: 1913); and E. Quillent, *Le Sabotage et l'action directe* (Paris: n.d.).

36. On Michels see A. Mitzman, *Sociology and Estrangement* (New York: 1973); D. Beetham, 'Robert Michels — From Socialism to Fascism', *Political Studies*, 25, 1977, pp. 3–24, 161–81; J-L. Pouthier, 'Roberto Michels et la fatalité de la classe politique', *Intervention*, 12, 1985, pp. 21–5 and 'Roberto Michels et les syndicalistes révolutionnaires français', *Cahiers Georges Sorel*, 4, 1986, pp. 39–60.

37. E. Berth, 'Prolétariat et bourgeoisie dans le mouvement socialiste italien', *MS*, xx, 1906, pp. 164–70 and R. Michels, 'Controverse socialiste', *MS*, 1907, pp. 278–88.

38. H. Lagardelle, *MS*, xxxii, 1912, pp. 136–9 and R. Michels 'L'Oligarchie et l'immunité des syndicats', *MS*, xxxiii, 1913, pp. 90–6.

39. P. Schöttler, *Naissance des bourses du travail* (Paris: 1985): see also J.

Julliard 'A propos d'un livre de Peter Schöttler', *Cahiers Georges Sorel*, 4, 1986, pp. 147–58 and P. Schöttler, 'Bourses du travail, "subventionnisme" et sciences sociales', *Cahiers Georges Sorel*, 5, 1987, pp. 205–12.

40. P. Stearns, *Revolutionary Syndicalism and French Labor* (New Brunswick: 1971).

Notes to Chapter 2

1. P. Monatte, 'Fernand Pelloutier et Aristide Briand', *RP*, 308, August–September, 1947, p. 129.
2. C. Chambelland, 'La grève générale, thème de la pensée de F. Pelloutier et d' A. Briand', *L'Actualité de l'histoire*, 18, May 1957, pp. 18–27 and 19, October 1957, pp. 1–12; P. Delesalle, 'Fernand Pelloutier', *TN* 23 March 1901, pp. 1–2.; E. Dolléans, 'Fernand Pelloutier' *L'Homme réel*, 19 July 1935, pp. 36–42; F. Foulon, *Fernand Pelloutier* (Paris: 1967); J. Julliard, *Fernand Pelloutier et les origines du syndicalisme d'action directe* (Paris: 1971); P. Monatte, review of Maurice Pelloutier, *Fernand Pelloutier*, *VO*, 59–60, March 1911, pp. 449–52; P. Monatte, 'Fernand Pelloutier et Aristide Briand', *RP*, August–September, 1947, pp. 129–37; P. Monatte, 'La jeunesse de Pelloutier', *RP*, 475, September 1962, pp. 13–18; A. Spitzer, 'Anarchy and Culture: Fernand Pelloutier and the Dilemma of Revolutionary Syndicalism', *International Review of Social History*, 8, 1963, pp. 379–88; G. Yvetot, 'Fernand Pelloutier' *VO*, 40, May 1911, pp. 577–93 and 41, June 1911, pp. 641–58. The work by Julliard contains both a commentary on Pelloutier's work and an extensive selection of his writings. Where possible references to Pelloutier's writings will cite the Julliard edition as this is the most easily available source. Julliard's book, *without* the texts by Pelloutier, was republished in 1985.
3. 'Evolution et Révolution: lettre ouverte au docteur Pioger', *La Question sociale*, December, 1894, in Julliard, p. 390. See also 'L'Argent', *La Démocratie de l'Ouest*, 24 June 1892.
4. 'L'Organisation corporative et l'anarchie', *L'Art social*, October 1896, p. 98.
5. Ibid., p. 98.
6. Ibid., p. 101.
7. 'Qu'est-ce que la question sociale?', *L'Art social*, January 1894, in Julliard, p. 386.
8. 'L'Organisation corporative et l'anarchie', pp. 100–1.
9. Ibid., p. 100.
10. Ibid., p. 100.
11. 'Dans quatre ans', *La Démocratie de l'Ouest*, 8 June 1892, in Julliard, p. 273.
12. See for example, 'L'Affaire de Panama', *La Démocratie de l'Ouest*, 18 November 1892; 'En Droit et en Fait', *La Démocratie de l'Ouest*, 31 August 1892.
13. 'Le Mois politique et social', *L'Art social*, July 1896, p. 29.
14. 'Le Suffrage', *TN*, 28 September 1895.
15. 'L'Oeuvre de 1789', *La Démocratie de l'Ouest*, 24 August 1892.
16. 'La Tare parlementaire', *Le Journal du peuple*, 20 February 1899; *La Vie ouvrière en France* (Paris: 1900), p. 22; *Histoire des bourses du travail* (Paris: 1902), p. 54.

17. 'Qu'est-ce que la question sociale?', *L'Art social*, January 1894, in Julliard, pp. 383–4; 'La conquête du pouvoir politique et l'Internationale', *TN*, 3 August 1895; 'Les congrès ouvriers de Toulouse', *L'Ouvrier des deux mondes*, November 1897, p. 147; 'La loi sur les accidents du travail', *Le Monde ouvrier*, February 1899, pp. 17–18, March 1899, pp. 33–9; *La Vie ouvrière en France*, p. 126; *Histoire des bourses du travail*, p. 53.

18. 'Morale', *La Démocratie de l'Ouest*, 27 November 1892; 'Les congrès ouvriers de Toulouse', p. 147; *La Vie ouvrière en France*, p. 276; *Histoire des bourses du travail*, p. 53.

19. 'La conquête du pouvoir politique et l'Internationale'; 'La conquête du pouvoir politique et les partis ouvriers', *TN* 24 August 1895; 'L'anarchisme et les syndicats ouvriers', *TN*, 2 November 1895; 'Les congrès ouvriers de Toulouse', p. 147; *Histoire des bourses du travail*, pp. 49–56.

20. 'La tactique nouvelle', *La Démocratie de l'Ouest*, 28 October 1892, in Julliard, pp. 315–17; 'La conquête du pouvoir politique et les partis ouvriers'; 'Centralisation et Gouvernement', *Almanach de la question sociale pour 1897*, pp. 102–03, in Julliard, pp. 397–9; 'Les deux congrès', *Le Journal du peuple*, 10 April 1899, in Julliard, p. 352; *La Vie ouvrière en France*, pp. 52–3.

21. 'Lettre ouverte au citoyen Jules Guesde', *La Démocratie de l'Ouest*, 5 October 1892; 'La tactique nouvelle' (au citoyen Jules Guesde)', and J. Guesde, 'Réponse ouverte', in *Le Socialiste*, 16 October 1892 and *La Démocratie de l'Ouest*, 25 October 1892. All three articles can be found in Julliard, pp. 312–17.

22. 'De la révolution par la grève générale' (unedited manuscript, 1892) in Julliard, pp. 291–5; 'La motion de Tours', *La Démocratie de l'Ouest*, 9 September 1892, in Julliard, pp. 306–7; 'Réplique au 'Temps', *La Démocratie de l'Ouest*, 11 September 1982, in Julliard, pp. 307–8; 'La semaine politique et sociale', *L'Avenir social*, 19 November 1893; *Qu'est-ce que la grève générale?* (Paris: 1895), in Julliard, p. 326; 'L'action populaire, ses raisons, ses ressources', *L'Ouvrier des deux mondes*, 15 May 1898, in Julliard, p. 340.

23. 'Souvarine', *La Démocratie de l'Ouest*, 20 December 1892, in Julliard, pp. 275–7; 'La semaine politique et sociale', *L'Avenir social*, 19 November 1893.

24. 'Qu'est-ce que la grève générale?', in Julliard, pp. 319–33.

25. Whilst the greater part of this text was not published, some of it did appear in an article signed by Pelloutier, entitled 'L'Oeuvre de 1789', *La Démocratie de l'Ouest*, 24 August 1892.

26. 'Qu-'est-ce que la grève générale?', in Julliard, p. 322; 'Motion de la Fédération des bourses', *Le Radical*, 10 September 1895, in Julliard, pp. 333–5; 'Les congrès ouvriers de Toulouse', *L'Ouvrier des deux mondes*, 1 November 1897, pp. 146–7; 'Réponse à A. D. Bancil, "Loi d'Airain des Salaires", *L'Ouvrier des deux mondes*, 1 February 1898, pp. 194–7; *La Vie ouvrière en France*, pp. 80–4.

27. 'La semaine politique et sociale', *L'Avenir social*, 19 November 1893; 'Qu'est-ce que la grève générale?', in Julliard, pp. 327–8.

28. Ibid., pp. 330–1; 'Le Trade-Unionisme en Angleterre', *L'Ouvrier des deux mondes*, 1 February 1897, p. 13.

29. 'Qu'est-ce que la grève générale?', in Julliard, pp. 325–7.

30. Ibid., p. 329.

31. Ibid., p. 327.

32. L'Organisation corporative et l'anarchie', p. 103.
33. Ibid., p. 103.
34. 'L'action populaire, see raisons, ses ressources', in Julliard, p. 339.
35. In January 1899 the paper became *Le Monde ouvrier*. See J. Julliard, 'L'Ouvrier des deux mondes', *Cahiers Georges Sorel*, 5, 1987, pp. 3–9.
36. 'Rapport moral', *L'Ouvrier des deux mondes*, 1 August 1898, p. 280.
37. 'L'enseignement social: le Musée du travail', *L'Ouvrier des deux mondes*, 1 April 1898, in Julliard, p. 497.
38. *La Vie ouvrière en France* was composed largely of articles previously published in *La Société nouvelle, L'Ouvrier des deux mondes, La Revue socialiste* and *Almanach de la question sociale*.
39. *La Vie ouvrière en France*, p. 315.
40. Ibid., p. 239.
41. 'L'enseignement social: le Musée du travail', in Julliard, pp. 497–501; 'Le Musée du travail', *Le Journal du peuple*, 21 March 1899; *Histoire des bourses du travail*, pp. 113–15.
42. *L'Art et la révolte* (Paris: 1896), reprinted in Julliard, pp. 502–18.
43. *De la colère, de l'amour, de la haine* (Paris: 1898). *L'Art et la révolte* was reprinted as a preface to this volume.
44. 'Amour Libre', *L'Ouvrier des deux mondes*, 1 February 1898, p. 197. A free translation might be:

They walked together in the splendour
of the evening, tenderly, talking of many
things, those sweet nothings which bring an
added blush to the cheeks, looking at each
other as if into a mirror.

Tormented by a melancholy of which I did not
know the cause I followed them, beguiled by
the fragile hope that their happiness would
bring respite to those morose thoughts which
obsessed my spirit and sapped my will.

Now I saw them stretch out, together, on the
moss, near to me in a full and sweet ecstasy
which made my heart more calm and my cares
less heavy.

Of their free expression, of their free
embraces, I, whose being loathed all
constraints, I thought this is truly
the real, the only love.

45. 'L'enseignement en société libertaire', *La Question sociale*, August 1895, in Julliard, pp. 492–7.
46. *Histoire des bourses du travail*, pp. 120–1.
47. Ibid., p. 111.
48. Ibid., p. 85. The following outline of the functions of the *bourses du travail* is taken from ibid., pp. 85–148.
49. Ibid., pp. 143–8. See also 'La Verrerie ouvrière de Carmaux', *TN*, 18

January 1896; 'La Verrerie ouvrière', *L'Ouvrier des deux mondes*, 1 February 1897, pp. 9–11.

50. See Yvetot, op. cit., p. 586.
51. 'Les congrès ouvriers de Toulouse', *L'Ouvrier des deux mondes*, 1 November 1897, p. 149.
52. *Histoire des bourses du travail*, p. 160.
53. 'Les congrès ouvriers de Toulouse', pp. 152–3.
54. 'Du rôle des bourses du travail dans la société future', Report presented to the 5th congress of the *Fédération des bourses*, 9–12 September 1896, in Julliard, pp. 412–14.
55. 'Centralisation et Gouverment', in Julliard, pp. 403–5.
56. Ibid., p. 398.
57. 'L'anarchisme et les syndicats ouvriers', *TN*, 2 November 1895, in Julliard, pp. 399–405; 'Lettre aux anarchistes', Préface to *Le congrès général du parti socialiste français* (Paris: 1900), pp. III–IX, in Julliard, pp. 415–19.
58. Ibid., p. 418.
59. 'L'organisation corporative et l'anarchie', p. 101.
60. 'Lettre aux anarchistes', p. 418.
61. 'L'Art et la révolte', p. 512.
62. See J. Maitron, *Le Mouvement anarchiste en France* (Paris: 1975), I, pp. 206–61.
63. E. Pouget, 'A roublard, roublard et demi', in R. Langlois (ed.), *Le Père Peinard* (Paris: 1976), pp. 34–41.
64. F. Pelloutier, 'L'Anarchisme et les syndicats ouvriers', *TN*, 2 November 1895.
65. See, for example, the numerous articles on this issue in *Le Libertaire* from 1899 onwards and see especially L. Grandidier, 'Anarchistes et syndicalistes', 5 November 1899; M. Pélerin, 'Syndicats et anarchistes', 14 March 1900; G. Yvetot, 'Syndicats et anarchistes', 18 March 1900.
66. A. Lorulot, 'Anarchistes ou syndicalistes', in A. Lorulot and G. Yvetot, *Le Syndicalisme et la transformation sociale* (Paris: 1909). This text contains a series of articles by Lorulot and Yvetot which outline their contrasting views on this issue. The articles were first published in *Le Libertaire* at the end of 1905.
67. Ibid., p. 10.
68. Ibid., p. 9.
69. For a discussion of these groups see J. Maitron, *Le Mouvement anarchiste*, I, pp. 122–30.
70. M. Pélerin, 'Syndicats et anarchistes'.
71. E. Girault, 'Les Sans-travail', *Le Libertaire*, 3 June 1897.
72. ESRI, *Les Anarchistes et les syndicats* (Paris: 1898).
73. Ibid., p. 14.
74. For a discussion of Pouget's life and ideas before 1901 see E. P. Fitzgerald, *Emile Pouget, the Anarchist Movement and the origins of revolutionary trade-unionism in France* (Yale University Ph.D. thesis, 1973).
75. E. Pouget, 'A roublard, roublard et demi', p. 37.
76. For a critique of the *'groupe d'affinité'* see E. Pouget, *Le Syndicat* (Paris: 1905), p. 9.
77. E. Pouget, 'Action corporative et duperie politique', in R. Langlois (ed.) pp. 145–52.
78. P. Delesalle, *L'Action syndicale et les anarchistes* (Paris: 1900).
79. Ibid., p. 14.

80. G. Yvetot, 'Syndicats et anarchistes'.
81. P. Delesalle, 'Réponse à 'Une Remarque'', *TN*, 1 November 1902.
82. P. Delesalle, 'A Propos du congrès corporatif', *TN*, 16 October 1897. See also G. Yvetot, 'Causerie ouvrière', *Le Libertaire*, 12 July 1902.
83. See, for example, P. Delesalle, 'Le Congrès de Londres', *TN*, 27 June 1896 and 15 August 1896.
84. P. Delesalle, 'Réponse à 'Une Remarque''.
85. P. Delesalle, 'Le Congrès corporatif de Rennes', *TN*, 29 October 1898.
86. E. Pouget, 'Le Congrès de Rennes', *Le Père Peinard*, 9 October 1898.
87. See P. Delesalle, *La Confédération Générale du Travail* (Paris: 1907), pp. 16–19; P. Delesalle, *Les bourses du travail et la CGT* (Paris: 1909), p. 45.
88. P. Delesalle, 'Encore l'unité', *VduP*, 1 June 1902. Delesalle and Niel produced a series of articles exploring this issue in *La Voix du peuple* during May and June 1902. Pouget was of the view that unity had not destroyed the federalist structure of the syndicalist movement; see E. Pouget, 'Le Congrès syndical de Bourges', *MS*, xiv, 1904, pp. 38–41.
89. P. Delesalle, *La Confédération Générale du Travail*, p. 16.
90. E. Pouget, *Le Syndicat*, pp. 10–13. See also P. Delesalle, *La Confédération Générale du Travail*, pp. 19–20 and G. Yvetot, *ABC syndicaliste* (Paris: 1908), pp. 26–7.
91. See P. Delesalle, *Les bourses du travail et la CGT*, pp. 45–50; P. Delesalle, 'Les bourses du travail et leurs difficultés actuelles', *MS*, xxiii, 1908, pp. 161–70; G. Yvetot, 'Fernand Pelloutier', *VO*, 40, 1911, p. 586. For the view of Griffuelhes see V. Griffuelhes, 'L'Acte de contrition d'un repenti', *L'Action directe*, 29 January 1908.
92. G. Yvetot, 'Causerie ouvrière', *Le Libertaire*, 22 February 1903.
93. V. Griffuelhes, *'L'Action syndicaliste* (Paris: 1908), p. 3.
94. For a discussion of this process see E. Pouget, 'Notes pour une double conférence sur le syndicalisme', manuscript held at the *Institut Français d'Histoire Sociale*.
95. E. Dolléans, *Histoire du mouvement ouvrier* (Paris: 1948), ii, p. 118.
96. P. H. Hutton, *The Cult of the Revolutionary Tradition: The Blanquists in French Politics 1864–1893* (Berkeley and Los Angeles: 1981).
97. See V. Griffuelhes, *L'Action syndicaliste*, pp. 14–18.
98. V. Griffuelhes, 'Les Grèves et le syndicalisme français', *MS*, xix, 1906, pp. 249–55.
99. V. Griffuelhes, 'Des Chiffres', *VduP*, 29 October 1905.
100. V. Griffuelhes, 'Les Caractères du syndicalisme français', in H. Lagardelle (ed.), *Syndicalisme et socialisme* (Paris: 1908), pp. 55–8; V. Griffuelhes, 'Sur une délégation', *VduP*, 4 February 1906. Michels wrote regularly for *Le Mouvement socialiste* but see R. Michels, 'Le syndicalisme et le socialisme en Allemagne', in H. Lagardelle (ed.), *Syndicalisme et socialisme*, pp. 21–8 and 'Lettre de Victor Griffuelhes à Roberto Michels', *Cahiers Georges Sorel*, 4, 1986, p. 60.
101. V. Griffuelhes, 'Les Caractères du syndicalisme français', p. 57.
102. P. Delesalle, 'Le Vie militante d'Emile Pouget', *Le Cri du peuple*, 5 August 1931.
103. P. Delesalle, *Aux travailleurs — la grève* (Paris: 1900), pp. 3–9.
104. E. Pouget, *Le Syndicat*, pp. 1–5.
105. V. Griffuelhes, *L'Action syndicaliste*, p. 11. See also V. Griffuelhes, 'Le Chômage et son remède', *VduP*, 8 December 1901; 'Pour la vie humaine', *VduP*, 26 January 1902; 'Constatations', *VduP*, 9 March 1902.

106. The phrase 'disappearance of the wage-earner and employer' was frequently used to describe the goal of the syndicalist movement. See for example P. Delesalle, *La Confédération Générale du Travail*, p. 22 and P. Delesalle, *Les Deux Méthodes du syndicalisme* (Paris: 1903), p. 2.

107. For a discussion of Merrheim's views see N. Papayanis, *Alphonse Merrheim: The Emergence of Reformism in Revolutionary Syndicalism 1871–1925* (Dordrecht: 1985), pp. 59–70 and C. Gras, 'Merrheim et le capitalisme', *Le Mouvement social*, 63, 1968, pp. 143–63.

108. See especially E. Pouget, *Le Parti du travail* (Paris: 1905).

109. P. Delesalle, *La Confédération Générale du Travail*, p. 22.

110. E. Pouget, *Le Parti du travail*, p. 2.

111. P. Delesalle, *L'Action syndicale et les anarchistes*, p. 6.

112. G. Yvetot, *Le Syndicalisme, les intellectuels et la CGT* (Paris: n.d.), p. 3.

113. E. Pouget, *Le Parti du travail*, pp. 3–4.

114. V. Griffuelhes, 'Des Professions libérales', *VduP*, 29 December 1907. See also P. Monatte, 'Syndicats de médecins', *VduP*, 22 December 1907 and R. Louzon, 'L'Etat et l'enseignement de médecine', *MS*, xxv, 1909, pp. 130–50. Doctors, Louzon argued, 'do not constitute a class'. For Louis Niel the issue was not as clear-cut; see 'Mouvement social', *TN*, 25 January 1908.

115. E. Pouget, *Le Parti du travail*, p. 3.

116. E. Pouget, 'A Propos du congrès socialiste', *VduP*, 2 June 1901.

117. E. Pouget, 'Pas de politique', *VduP*, 15 June 1902 and E. Pouget, *Les Bases du syndicalisme* (Paris: 1905), pp. 1–2.

118. E. Pouget, *L'Action directe* (Paris: 1910), p. 1. See also E. Pouget, 'L'Unité', *JduP*, 22 July 1899.

119. G. Yvetot, 'Causerie ouvrière', *Le Libertaire*, 4 October 1903.

120. G. Yvetot, 'Mouvement ouvrier', *Le Libertaire*, 3 January 1902.

121. See *XIV Congrès national corporatif* (Bourges: 1904), pp. 144–90.

122. E. Pouget, 'Le Congrès syndical de Bourges', *MS*, xiv, 1904, p. 62. See also P. Delesalle, 'Le Congrès de Bourges', *TN*, 24 September 1904 and V. Griffuelhes, 'Le Congrès de Bourges', *Almanach de la révolution pour 1905* (Paris: 1905), pp. 30–33.

123. E. Pouget, 'L'Unité'.

124. P. Delesalle, 'Le Scrutin de dimanche', *TN* 19 May 1900.

125. G. Yvetot, 'Mouvement ouvrier', *Le Libertaire*, 1 February 1902.

126. See for example A. Bourchet, 'Rapport sur l'organisation de la société au lendemain de la grève générale', *XIII Congrès national corporatif* (Montpellier: 1902), p. 223 and Comité de Propagande de la grève générale, 'Réponse à Jaurès, *VduP*, 22 September 1901. Bourchet spoke of 'la masse moutonnante', whilst the 'Réponse à Jaurès' argued that 'les majorités sont moutonnières'. Pouget, in *Les Bases du syndicalisme*, spoke of 'des majorités moutonnières'.

127. E. Pouget, 'Le Congrès syndical de Bourges', pp. 45–6.

128. Ibid., p. 45. Elsewhere Pouget spoke of the 'minorité désintéressée et tolérante'.

129. E. Pouget, *L'Action directe*, pp. 22–3.

130. E. Pouget, 'Marianne la salope', in P. Langlois (ed.), *Le Père Peinard*, pp. 194–6.

131. See E. Pouget, 'Le Roi des grinches' and 'Rothschild-Roussin' in P. Langlois (ed.), *Le Père Peinard*, pp. 119–23 and 124–7.

132. E. Pouget, 'Action corporative et duperie politique', p. 149.

133. E. Pouget, *Variations guesdistes* (Paris: 1896).

134. Ibid., p. 4.
135. E. Pouget, 'Contre le suffrage universal', in P. Langlois (ed.), *Le Père Peinard*, p. 176.
136. See J. Maitron, *Le Mouvement anarchiste*, I, pp. 331–42.
137. E. Pouget, 'Soyons nous-mêmes: ni dreyfusiens ni esterhaziens', *Le Père Peinard*, 16 January 1898 and 23 January 1898.
138. E. Pouget, 'Une Ecole de révolte', *JduP*, 31 August 1899.
139. E. Pouget, 'Où allons-nous', *JduP*, 10 September 1899.
140. E. Pouget, 'Le Triomphe du sabre', *JduP*, 11 September 1899 and 'Dreyfus gracié', *JduP*, 21 September 1899. Pouget described the pardon granted to Dreyfus after the retrial at Rennes as 'l'hypocrisie de la justice'.
141. E. Pouget, 'L'Oeuvre à accomplir', *JduP*, 12 September 1899.
142. P. Delesalle, 'A Propos des lois scélérates', *TN* 31 December 1898. Pouget echoed this concern; see E. Pouget, 'La Banqueroute de la République', *JduP*, 5 July 1899.
143. Quoted in J. Maitron, *Paul Delesalle* (Paris: 1985), p. 107.
144. P. Delesalle, 'L'Auteur de la condamnation', *JduP*, 16 September 1899; 'Gens de caserne', *JduP*, 18 September 1899; 'Gens de caserne', *JduP*, 19 September 1899.
145. P. Delesalle, 'C'est dans l'ordre', *TN*, 28 January 1899.
146. P. Delesalle, 'Millerand et Cie', *TN*, 22 July 1899.
147. Ibid. and P. Delesalle, 'Le Mouvement social', *TN*, 30 December 1899.
148. E. Pouget, 'Esclaves du capital', *VduP*, 10 February 1901.
149. P. Delesalle, 'La Loi de 10 heures et ses conséquences', *TN*, 17 December 1904.
150. See for example P. Delesalle, 'Quelle tactique?', *TN*, 30 August 1902 and 'Les Réformes de M. Millerand', *TN*, 25 June 1904.
151. E. Pouget, 'L'Etranglement de grèves, *VduP*, 30 December 1900, 6 January 1901 and 17 March 1901.
152. P. Delesalle, 'Les Réformes de M. Millerand'.
153. G. Yvetot, 'Après l'émeute', *Le Libertaire*, 27 April 1902.
154. V. Griffuelhes, 'Le fond et la forme', *VduP*, 29 March 1903.
155. V. Griffuelhes, 'Monarchie et République', *VduP*, 26 July 1903. Pouget made the identical point in 'Réformes légales', *VduP*, 10 September 1905.
156. E. Pouget, 'L'Agonie du 14 juillet', in R. Langlois (ed.), *Le Père Peinard*, p. 48.
157. E. Pouget, 'A Montceau-les-Mines', *VduP*, 3 February 1901.
158. P. Delesalle, 'Assez de massacres', *VduP*, 10 October 1905. See also P. Delesalle, 'A Longwy. A bas l'armée', *L'Avant-garde*, 17 September 1905.
159. A. Merrheim, 'Un grand conflit social: la grève d'Hennebont', *MS*, xx, 1906, pp. 194–218, 347–79.
160. Ibid., pp. 378–9.
161. See *VduP*, 30 June 1907.
162. See *VduP*, 2 August 1908.
163. See *VduP*, special issue 'L'Appel de la classe', September 1908.
164. E. Pouget, 'Césarion garde-chiourme', *VduP*, 12 January 1908.
165. V. Griffuelhes, 'Veut-on encore du sang', *La Révolution*, 12 March 1909.
166. G. Yvetot, 'Causerie ouvrière', *Le Libertaire*, 17 August 1902.
167. G. Yvetot, 'Causerie ouvrière', *Le Libertaire*, 23 August 1902.
168. Ibid.
169. See J. Julliard, 'La CGT devant la guerre (1900–1914)', *Le Mouvement social*, 49, 1964, pp. 47–62.

170. See for example E. Pouget, 'Justification', *VduP*, 15 October 1905.

171. G. Yvetot, 'Causerie ouvrière', *Le Libertaire*, 1 February 1903.

172. E. Pouget, 'La Conscription', *VduP*, special issue, January 1904.

173. G. Yvetot, *Le Nouveau manuel du soldat* (Paris: 1903); reference to (Paris, 1908), p. 10.

174. See especially 'Enquête sur l'idée de patrie et la classe ouvrière', *MS*, XVI, 1905, pp. 433–70 and XVII, 1905, pp. 36–71 and 202–31.

175. Ibid., XVI, p. 443.

176. Ibid., p. 466.

177. Ibid., XVII, p. 203.

178. G. Yvetot, *Ma Pensée libre* (Paris: 1913), p. 19.

179. See in particular the 'L'Appel de la classe' issues of *La Voix du peuple*.

180. G. Yvetot, *Le Nouveau manuel du soldat*, pp. 29–30.

181. P. Delesalle, 'La Moralisation par l'armée', *TN*, 18 July 1896.

182. This was the view of the majority of those who responded to Lagardelle's 'Enquête' in *Le Mouvement socialiste*.

183. See G. Yvetot, 'Ce que fut la grève générale de 24 heures à Paris', *VduP*, 29 December 1912.

184. G. Yvetot, 'Enquête sur l'idée de patrie', *MS* XVI, 1905, p. 468.

185. C. Guieysse, 'Action patriotique et action révolutionnaire', *Pages libres*, X, 1905, p. 302. See also C. Guieysse, 'Patriotisme démocratique et patriotisme capitaliste', *MS*, XVII, 1905, pp. 129–59.

186. G. Yvetot, 'Causerie ouvrière', *Le Libertaire*, 5 April 1903.

187. Hubert Lagardelle neatly summarised the problem faced by the syndicalists. 'What use', he writes, 'are power, guns, barricades and bombs when the disorganised and unconscious masses do not have the first idea of their role'; H. Lagardelle, 'La Réforme d'enseignement', *La Révolution*, 6 March 1909.

188. E. Pouget, 'Le Congrès syndical de Bourges, p. 42.

189. V. Griffuelhes, *Voyage révolutionnaire* (Paris: 1910) and V. Griffuelhes, *La Grève des délaineurs de Mazzamet* (Paris: 1909).

190. Ibid., p. 7.

191. For a discussion of this issue see M. Ferre, *Histoire du mouvement syndicaliste révolutionnaire chez les instituteurs (des origines à 1922)* (Paris: 1955).

192. For a succinct expression of these views see M. T. Laurin, 'L'Enseignement primaire et le prolétariat', *MS*, XIX, 1906, pp. 212–27; M. T. Laurin, 'Les Ecoles syndicales', *MS*, XXV, 1909, pp. 40–8; L. Jouhaux, 'Le Monopole de l'enseignement et le socialisme', *MS*, XXVII, 1910, pp. 66–70 and H. Lagardelle, 'L'Ecole et le prolétariat', *MS*, XX, 1906, pp. 185–8.

193. See M. T. Laurin, *Les Instituteurs et le syndicalisme* (Paris: 1908).

194. See P. Delesalle, 'Les Instituteurs et les syndicats', *TN*, 23 December 1905; C. Guieysse, 'Syndicats de fonctionnaires', *Pages libres*, X, 1905, pp. 465–8; M. T. Laurin, 'Les Instituteurs et les Bourses du travail', *MS*, XXXIII, 1908, pp. 120–4; M. T. Laurin, 'La Faillite de l'enseignement primaire', *MS*, XXXIV, 1908, pp. 374–7; Un groupe d'instituteurs, 'Ce que nous voulons', *VduP*, 17 March 1907. The journal *L'Ecole émancipée*, first published in October 1910, provided a forum for the discussion of these ideas.

195. The issue of education was debated at the Marseille congress of the *bourses du travail* in 1908; see *XVI Congrès national corporatif* (Marseille: 1908), pp. 311–27.

196. G. Yvetot, 'L'Ecole syndicale', *L'Ecole émancipée*, I, 28 January 1911, p. 1.

197. Ibid., pp. 1–2; E. Pataud and E. Pouget, *Comment nous ferons la révolution*

(Paris, 1909), pp. 224–30. Part of Yvetot's article consisted of a reprint of his contribution to the 1908 debate at Marseille. For a more complete discussion of syndicalist educational principles see the articles contributed by Albert Thierry to *La Vie ouvrière* in 1912. These articles were reprinted in A. Thierry, *Réflexions sur l'éducation* (Paris: 1923), pp. 3–135.

198. For the development of this argument see R. Louzon, 'L'Ouvriérisme dans les mathématiques supérieures', *VO*, iv, 1912, pp. 320–5.

199. G. Yvetot, 'L'Ecole syndicale', *L'Ecole émancipée*, i, 1 October 1910, pp. 4–5. See also M. T. Laurin, 'Les Ecoles syndicales', *MS*, xxv, 1909, pp. 40–8 and H. Lagardelle, 'Les Ecoles syndicales', *La Révolution*, 18 February 1909.

200. P. Delesalle, 'La Crise de l'apprentissage', *MS*, xxiii, 1908, pp. 245–6. For a more extensive discussion of this issue see the 'Enquête ouvrière sur la crise de l'apprentissage', *MS*, xxiii, 1908, pp. 241–67, 321–40, 401–17; xxiv, 1908, pp. 96–8, 278–84; xxv, 1909, pp. 100–7, 290–9.

201. P. Delesalle, *Les Bourses du travail et la CGT*.

202. P. Delesalle, 'Mouvement social', *TN*, 12 January 1901 and 26 January 1901.

203. E. Pouget, 'Les Paysans et la révolution', *Almanach de la révolution pour 1906* (Paris: 1906), pp. 23–5. See also V. Griffuelhes, 'L'Agitation rurale', *VduP*, 13 September 1903 and E. Pouget, 'La Jacquerie', *VduP*, 14 February 1904 and 'Le Sens du mouvement', *VduP*, 30 June 1907.

204. J. Julliard, 'Le Syndicalisme révolutionnaire et les grèves', *Le Mouvement social*, 65, 1968, pp. 55–69.

205. E. Pouget, 'Action directe', in V. Griffuelhes and L. Jouhaux (eds), *Encyclopaedie du mouvement syndicaliste* (Paris: 1912), p. 13. See also E. Pouget, *L'Action directe*. Two journals created by syndicalist militants bore the title *L'Action directe*.

206. Griffuelhes made explicit the connection between a rejection of the idea of God and the advocacy of direct action in V. Griffuelhes and L. Niel, *Les Objectifs de nos luttes de classe* (Paris: 1909). Griffuelhes' contribution to this volume covered pp. 11–40. It was printed separately under the title *Le Syndicalisme révolutionnaire* (Paris: 1909).

207. For an outline of the various forms of direct action see V. Griffuelhes and L. Niel, pp. 21–36 and G. Yvetot, *ABC syndicaliste*, pp. 38–56.

208. See G. Yvetot, 'L'Illégalité par la force non par l'abjection', *VduP*, 6 November 1910.

209. *Boycottage et Sabotage: Rapport de la Commission du Boycottage au Congrès Corporatif tenu à Toulouse en septembre 1897* (Paris: 1897).

210. E. Pouget, 'Le Sabotage', *La Sociale*, 26 July 1896; E. Pouget, 'Le Sabottage', *Le Père Peinard*, 19 September 1896; E. Pouget, *Le Sabotage* (Paris: 1910).

211. G. Yvetot, *ABC syndicaliste*, pp. 41–5; A. Luquet, 'Le Sabotage', *L'Avantgarde*, 3 September 1905; A. Bousquet, 'Il faut sabotter', *VduP*, 21 May 1905; D. Sieurin, 'Sabotage', *VduP*, 10 December 1905; V. Griffuelhes and L. Niel, pp. 29–32.

212. H. Lagardelle, 'La Formation du syndicalisme en France', *MS*, xxx 1911, p. 163 and G. Sorel, 'Le Syndicalisme révolutionnaire', *MS*, xvii, 1905, pp. 276–7.

213. E. Pouget, *Le Sabotage* (Paris: 1910), p. 16.

214. See G. Yvetot, 'Le Sabotage n'est pas une légende', *VduP*, 28 September 1913.

215. G. Yvetot, 'Causerie ouvrière', *Le Libertaire*, 18 October 1902.

216. E. Pouget, *Le Sabotage* (Paris: 1910), pp. 64–8.

217. P. Delesalle, *Aux travailleurs – la grève*, pp. 13–15.

218. P. Delesalle, 'Etatisme et organisation ouvrière', *TN*, 19 September 1903.

219. See E. Pouget, 'Tactique de grève' *VduP*, 28 May 1907 and V. Griffuelhes, 'Quelques extraits', *L'Action directe*, 30 April 1906.

220. V. Griffuelhes and L. Niel, pp. 21–9.

221. V. Griffuelhes, 'Romantisme révolutionnaire', *L'Action directe*, 23 April 1908. This article was reprinted in *MS*, xxiv, 1908, pp. 293–5.

222. E. Pouget, *L'Action directe*, pp. 9–20.

223. V. Griffuelhes, 'Romantisme révolutionnaire', *MS*, p. 295. Griffuelhes reiterated these sentiments in *Les Objectifs de nos luttes de classe*, p. 35 and 'Quelques réflexions sur l'idée de grève', *L'Action directe*, 15 April 1908.

224. E. Pouget, 'Réformes et révolution', *VduP*, 16 August 1903.

225. P. Delesalle, *Les Deux Méthodes du syndicalisme*, p. 9.

226. See *XIV Congrès national corporatif*, pp. 204–20.

227. E. Pouget, 'La Conquête de la journée de huit heures', *MS*, xv, 1905, pp. 357–80; 'Les Résultats du mouvement du premier mai', *MS*, xix, 1906, pp. 269–88; 'En attendant la révolution', *VduP*, 20 August 1906; 'L'Agitation pour les huits heures', *L'Avant-garde*, 23 April 1905.

228. P. Delesalle, 'La Journée de huit heures et les salaires' *VduP*, 19 March 1905.

229. See for example Comité Confédéral, 'Nous voulons la journée de 8 heures', *VduP*, 29 January 1905 and the special editions of *La Voix du peuple* devoted to this issue on 1 May 1905 and 1 May 1906. See also three CGT pamphlets: *La Journée de huit heures* (Paris: n.d.); *En Avant pour les huit heures* (Paris: n.d.) and *La Journée de huit heures dans le bâtiment* (Paris: n.d.).

230. E. Pouget, *L'Action directe*, pp. 20–1.

231. V. Griffuelhes, *L'Action syndicaliste*, p. 32.

232. Ibid., p. 33.

233. G. Yvetot, *ABC syndicaliste*, p. 52.

234. G. Yvetot, 'Réflexions d'actualité', *VduP*, 22 August 1909; 'La Tragédie de l'Espagne', *VduP*, 22 August 1909; 'Sur la grève de Suède', *VduP*, 12 September 1909; 'La Fin d'une grande grève', *VduP*, 28 November 1909.

235. E. Pouget, 'Les Caractères de l'action directe', *Almanach de la révolution pour 1909* (Paris: 1909), p. 37.

236. G. Yvetot, 'La Force', *VduP*, 2 April 1911.

237. G. Yvetot, 'La Fin d'une grande grève'.

238. E. Pouget, 'Les Caractères de l'action directe', p. 38.

239. P. Delesalle, *La Confédération Générale du Travail*, pp. 27–8.

240. V. Griffuelhes, *L'Action syndicaliste*, p. 34.

241. Ibid., p. 32.

242. V. Griffuelhes, 'Conditions de lutte', *L'Action directe*, 6 May 1908.

243. V. Griffuelhes, *L'Action syndicaliste*, p. 33.

244. V. Griffuelhes and L. Niel, p. 34.

245. See E. Pouget, 'La Grève russe', *VduP*, 12 November 1905 and 'Nouvelle étape', *VduP*, 5 December 1905.

246. G. Yvetot, 'La Mort d'une utopie', *VduP*, 27 August 1911.

247. V. Griffuelhes, 'A Propos d'un livre', *VO*, i, 1909, pp. 274–5 and E. Pouget, 'L'élève Pouget au prof. Jaurès', *GS*, 1 December 1909.

248. E. Pataud and E. Pouget, *Comment nous ferons la révolution*, pp. 1–132.

249. V. Griffuelhes and L. Niel, p. 39.
250. See 'Enquête sur la grève générale', *VduP*, 27 July 1902. The 'enquête' was signed by Griffuelhes in his capacity as secretary of the CGT.
251. See *XIII Congrès national corporatif*, pp. 223–31; *VduP*, 7 December 1902 and 14 December 1902; and *Au Lendemain de la grève générale* (Montpellier: 1902).
252. E. Pouget, 'Faramineuse consultation sur l'avenir', *Almanach du Père Peinard* (Paris: 1896), pp. 22–34.
253. E. Pataud and E. Pouget, p. 141.
254. Ibid., pp. 140–84.
255. Ibid., p. 188.
256. Ibid., pp. 188–9.
257. Ibid., pp. 190–1.
258. Proudhon held similar views on punishment: see A. Ritter, 'Godwin, Proudhon and the Anarchist Justification of Punishment', *Political Theory*, 3, 1975, pp. 69–87.
259. E. Pataud and E. Pouget, p. 293.
260. Ibid., pp. 243–61.
261. Ibid., pp. 294–5. Sorel, in particular, was to take up this theme; see pp. 69–71.
262. See also E. Pouget, *Les Bases du syndicalisme*, pp. 10–13.
263. M. Leroy, *La Coutume ouvrière* (Paris: 1913).
264. Ibid., pp. 190–293.
265. For a syndicalist view of administration see R. Lenoir, 'Administration', in V. Griffuelhes and L. Jouhaux, *Encyclopédie du mouvement syndicaliste*, pp. 21–2.
266. For a discussion of these issues see A. Ritter, *Anarchism: A Theoretical Analysis* (Cambridge: 1980).

Notes to Chapter 3

1. G. Sorel, 'Le Socialisme en Belgique', *L'Ouvrier des deux mondes*, 1 June 1898, pp. 244–7; 'l'Histoire du trade unionisme anglais', 1 December 1898, pp. 337–40; 'La Fédération américaine du travail', 1 June 1899, pp. 82–3.
2. G. Sorel, 'Préface', to F. Pelloutier, *Histoire des bourses du travail*, p. 1.
3. 'Une lettre de Boris Souvarine', *Cahiers Georges Sorel*, 2, 1984, pp. 187–8.
4. Several bibliographies of Sorel's work are available but the best is to be found in J. Julliard and S. Sand (eds), *Georges Sorel en son temps* (Paris: 1985), pp. 425–67.
5. G. Sorel, 'Préface', to S. Merlino, *Formes et essence du socialisme* (Paris: 1898), p. xlii.
6. G. Sorel, 'L'Ethique du socialisme', *Rév. mét.*, VII, 1899, pp. 280–301.
7. G. Sorel, 'Morale et socialisme', *MS*, I, 1899, p. 208.
8. Ibid., p. 209.
9. On Sorel's reading of Vico see my 'Sorel, Vico and Marx', in G. Tagliacozzo (ed.), *Vico and Marx* (Atlantic Highlands, New Jersey: 1983), pp. 326–41.
10. See especially G. Sorel, *Le Procès de Socrate* (Paris: 1899) and 'Essai sur la philosophie de Proudhon', *Revue philosophique*, XXXIII, 1892, pp. 622–38 and XXXIV, 1892, pp. 41–68.
11. G. Sorel, 'Socialismes nationaux', *Cahiers de la Quinzaine*, 14th cahier of the 3rd series, 1902, p. 52. See G. Sorel, 'Les Aspects juridiques du socialisme', *RS*, XXXII, 1900, pp. 385–415, 558–85 and S. Sand, 'Lutte de classes

et conscience juridique dans la pensée de Georges Sorel', in J. Julliard and S. Sand, pp. 225–45.

12. G. Sorel, *L'Avenir socialiste des syndicats* (Paris: 1898), p. 10. This section was not reprinted in the later editions.

13. G. Sorel, 'L'Avenir socialiste des syndicats', in G. Sorel, *Matériaux d'une théorie du prolétariat* (Paris: 1919), p. 127.

14. G. Sorel, 'L'Ethique du socialisme', p. 295.

15. G. Sorel, 'Les divers types de sociétés coopératives', *La Science sociale*, XXVIII, 1899, p. 188. See also G. Sorel, *Les Illusions du progrès* (Paris: 1908), pp. 276–86.

16. G. Sorel, 'Les Dissensions de la social démocratie en Allemagne', *Revue politique et parlementaire*, xxv, 1900, pp. 33–66.

17. Ibid., p. 42.

18. G. Sorel, 'L'Avenir socialiste des syndicats', p. 98.

19. Ibid., p. 98, n. 1.

20. Ibid., p. 118.

21. G. Sorel, 'Les Dissensions de la social démocratie', p. 49.

22. See specifically 'L'Eglise et l'Etat', *RS*, xxxiv, 1901, pp. 129–54, 325–42, 402–20.

23. G. Sorel, 'L'Avenir socialiste des syndicats', p. 123.

24. G. Sorel, 'Mes Raisons du syndicalisme', in *Matériaux d'une théorie du prolétariat*, p. 248.

25. G. Sorel, 'Les Dissensions de la social démocratie', p. 61.

26. Ibid., p. 54.

27. G. Sorel, 'L'Avenir socialiste des syndicats', p. 132.

28. G. Sorel, 'Les Dissensions de la social démocratie', p. 63.

29. G. Sorel, 'Le Socialisme en Belgique'.

30. Ibid., p. 245.

31. G. Sorel, 'La Fédération américaine du travail'.

32. G. Sorel, 'Les divers types de sociétés coopératives' and 'Les Grèves', *La Science sociale*, xxx, 1900, pp. 311–32 and 417–36.

33. G. Sorel, 'L'Avenir socialiste des syndicats', pp. 107–8.

34. Ibid., pp. 118–9.

35. Ibid., pp. 101–2 and 'Les Grèves', pp. 428–36.

36. G. Sorel, 'Les divers types de sociétés coopératives', p. 188.

37. Ibid., p. 188.

38. Ibid., p. 189.

39. Ibid., p. 200.

40. Ibid., p. 179–83, 186–9, 192–4.

41. Ibid., pp. 195–9. See also 'Socialismes nationaux'; 'Economie et agriculture', *RS*, xxxiii, 1901, pp. 289–301, 421–41; and *Introduction à l'économie moderne* (Paris: 1903).

42. G. Sorel, 'Les Grèves', p. 332.

43. G. Sorel, 'Les Dissensions de la social démocratie', p. 49.

44. G. Sorel, 'L'Avenir socialiste des syndicats', p. 125.

45. G. Sorel, 'L'Ethique du socialisme', p. 298.

46. See G. Sorel, 'Préface', to F. Pelloutier, *Histoire des bourses du travail*, pp. 1–32 and P. Schöttler, ' "La Commune ouvrière en formation"? Georges Sorel et les Bourses du travail', in J. Julliard and S. Sand (eds), pp. 53–74.

47. G. Sorel, 'Préface' to F. Pelloutier, p. 26.

48. Ibid., p. 27.

49. Ibid., p. 27.

50. Ibid., p. 32.
51. G. Sorel, 'Qu'est-ce qu'un syndicat?' *Pages libres*, 116, 21 March 1903, pp. 241–57.
52. Ibid., p. 247.
53. G. Sorel, 'Préface' to S. Merlino, p. xix.
54. G. Sorel, 'L'Eglise et l'Etat', p. 418.
55. G. Sorel, *La Révolution dreyfusienne* (Paris: 1909).
56. G. Sorel, *Réflexions sur la violence* (Paris: 1908). The first edition appeared as a series of articles in *Le Mouvement socialiste*, beginning in January 1906.
57. Ibid., p. 99.
58. Ibid., p. 187.
59. Ibid., p. 225.
60. Ibid., p. 194.
61. Ibid., p. 161.
62. Ibid., p. 163.
63. Ibid., p. 164.
64. Ibid., p. 169.
65. Ibid., p. 330.
66. Ibid., p. 273.
67. Ibid., pp. 210–11.
68. Ibid., p. 331.
69. Ibid., pp. 281–331.
70. G. Sorel, *Les Illusions du progrès* (Paris: 1908), p. 276.
71. Ibid., p. 274.
72. G. Sorel, *Réflexions sur la violence*, p. 184.
73. Ibid., p. 149.
74. G. Sorel, *Saggi di critica del marxismo* (Milan-Palermo-Naples: 1903), p. 15.
75. G. Sorel, *La Décomposition du marxisme* (Paris: 1908), p. 58.
76. G. Sorel, *Réflexions sur la violence*, p. 153.
77. Ibid., p. 153.
78. Ibid., p. 312.
79. G. Sorel, 'Eglise, Evangile et Socialisme', (1899), in G. Sorel, *La Ruine du monde antique* (Paris: 1902), p. 311.
80. Ibid., p. 311.
81. M. Rebérioux, 'La place de Georges Sorel dans le socialisme au tournant du siècle', in J. Julliard and S. Sand (eds), p. 48. Pierre Monatte made a similar point: see C. Chambelland, 'Monatte, lecteur de Sorel', *Cahiers Georges Sorel*, 4, 1986, p. 141.
82. For details of Berth's life and an incomplete bibliography see P. Andreu, 'Bibliographie d'Edouard Berth', *Bulletin of the International Institute of Social History*, 8, 1953, pp. 196–204, and P. Andreu, Introduction to 'Lettres de Georges Sorel à Edouard Berth', *Cahiers Georges Sorel*, 3, 1985, pp. 77–100.
83. E. Berth, 'Avant-Propos', to G. Sorel, *D'Aristote à Marx* (Paris: 1935), p. 8.
84. See G. Sorel, 'La crise de la pensée catholique', *Revue de métaphysique et de morale*, x, 1902, pp. 523–57 and E. Berth, 'La crise de la pensée catholique', *MS*, xii, 1904, pp. 188–94.
85. *Dialogues socialistes* (Paris: 1901).
86. Subsequently Berth was to use the pseudonym Jean Darville.
87. *Dialogues socialistes*, p. 31.

88. Ibid., p. 37.
89. Ibid., p. 52.
90. Ibid., pp. 70–71.
91. Ibid., p. 73.
92. Ibid., p. 127.
93. Ibid., p. 175.
94. Ibid., p. 278.
95. Ibid., p. 243.
96. Ibid., p. 265.
97. Ibid., p. 266.
98. Ibid., p. 271–2.
99. See, in particular, 'Les Revues socialistes allemandes', *MS*, xv, 1905, pp. 66–72 and 'Le Centenaire de Proudhon', *MS*, xxv, 1909, pp. 49–55.
100. *Dialogues socialistes*, p. 313.
101. Ibid., p. 314.
102. 'A Propos de la Lutte de classe', *MS*, iii, 1900, pp. 23–31.
103. 'De l'Utopie à la science', *RS*, 33, 1901, pp. 398–420. Berth derived this point from Sorel's 'L'Ethique du socialisme', *Rév. mét.*, vii, 1899, pp. 280–301.
104. 'De l'Utopie à la science', p. 412.
105. Ibid., p. 402.
106. Ibid., p. 411.
107. Ibid., p. 411.
108. Ibid., p. 412.
109. 'Classiques ou modernes?', *RS*, 1902, p. 658; 'Marchands, Intellectuels et Politiciens', *MS*, xxiii, 1908, pp. 210–11.
110. Ibid., pp. 213–14.
111. 'De l'Utopie à la science', p. 411.
112. Ibid., p. 412.
113. 'Classiques ou modernes?' pp. 656–7.
114. 'Marchands, Intellectuels et Politiciens', *MS*, xxii, 1907, pp. 302–4; *MS*, xxiii, 1908, p. 215. These ideas were to be explored in greater detail in Berth's preface to Sorel's *D'Aristote à Marx*.
115. 'Les "Considérations Inactuelles" de Nietzsche', *MS*, xxiv, 1908, p. 53.
116. 'Marchands, Intellectuels et Politiciens', *MS*, xxiii, 1908, p. 215; *Les Nouveaux aspects du socialisme* (Paris: 1908) pp. 48–9.
117. 'De l'Utopie à la science', pp. 401, 413–20.
118. 'Les "Discours" de Jaurès', *MS*, xiv, 1904, pp. 213–23, 302–19.
119. 'Anarchisme individualiste, Marxisme orthodoxe, Syndicalisme révolution- naire', *MS*, xvi, 1905, pp. 5–35. The argument of this article was restated in a different form in *Les Nouveaux aspects du socialisme*.
120. 'Anarchisme individualiste . . .', p. 9.
121. Ibid., p. 20.
122. *Les Nouveaux aspects du socialisme*, p. 42.
123. 'Les "Considérations Inactuelles" de Nietzsche', p. 56.
124. 'Anarchisme individualiste . . .', pp. 14–16.
125. Ibid., p. 21.
126. Ibid., p. 31.
127. Ibid., p. 32.
128. 'Marchands, Intellectuels et Politiciens', *MS*, xxii, 1907, pp. 1–12, 302–16, 384–98, xxiii, 1908, pp. 202–22.
129. 'Socialisme ou étatisme?', *MS*, ix, 1903, pp. 1–17.

130. 'La Politique anticléricale et le socialisme', *RS*, 36, 1902, pp. 513–39.
131. 'De l'Utopie . . .' p. 406.
132. 'La Politique anticléricale . . .', p. 514.
133. Ibid., p. 514.
134. Ibid., p. 539.
135. 'Catholicisme social et socialisme', *MS*, xi, 1903, pp. 321–50.
136. G. Sorel, 'Idées socialistes et faits économiques', *RS*, xxxv, 1902, pp. 294–318, 385–410, 519–544.
137. 'Catholicisme social et socialisme', p. 344.
138. 'Esprit démocratique et esprit socialiste', *Pages libres*, 9 April 1904, vii, pp. 281–93. The editors of the journal felt compelled to remark that many of their readers would be 'extremely surprised' by the contents of Berth's article. It was normal, they commented, to see 'socialism as the end of democracy, socialist ideas as an extension of democratic ideas'.
139. G. Sorel, *Introduction à l'économie moderne* (Paris: 1903).
140. 'Esprit démocratique . . .', p. 284.
141. Ibid., p. 286.
142. 'Marchands, Intellectuals et Politiciens', p. 7.
143. Ibid., p. 6.
144. Ibid., p. 7.
145. Ibid., p. 206.
146. 'La Politique anticléricale', p. 514.
147. Ibid., p. 527.
148. 'Classiques ou modernes?', p. 655.
149. 'Socialisme ou étatisme?', p. 3.
150. 'De l'Utopie . . .', p. 415.
151. Ibid., pp. 407–8, 412–15.
152. 'Politique et socialisme', *MS*, xii, 1904, pp. 5–37.
153. Ibid., p. 30.
154. Ibid., pp. 28–30. See also 'Les Revues socialistes allemandes', *MS*, xv, 1905, pp. 71–2.
155. 'Révolution sociale ou évolution juridique', *MS*, xvii, 1904, pp. 121–39.
156. See G. Sorel, 'Taine devant l'Académie', *La Jeunesse socialiste*, i, 1895, pp. 100–104; 'L'hypocrisie du devoir', *La Jeunesse socialiste*, i, 1895, pp. 138–41; 'Education bourgeoise', *La Jeunesse socialiste*, i, 1895, pp. 169–72; 'Faillite de la science bourgeoise', *La Jeunesse socialiste*, i, 1895, pp. 209–11; 'Les procédés historiques de M. Tarde', *La Jeunesse socialiste*, i, 1895, pp. 254–8; 'Sémites et cléricaux', *La Jeunesse socialiste*, i, 1895, pp. 325–8.
157. See H. Lagardelle, 'Lettere di Giorgio Sorel a Uberto Lagardelle', *Educazione fascista*, xi, 1933, pp. 229–43, 320–34, 506–18, 760–783, 956–75; A. Riosa, 'La correspondance Sorel-Lagardelle: la découverte de l'original', *Cahiers Georges Sorel*, 2, 1984, pp. 130–6. Alceo Riosa intends to publish the complete correspondence in the near future.
158. Surprisingly little has been written on Lagardelle but see M. Dachary de Flers, *Lagardelle et l'Equipe du Mouvement socialiste*, Thèse de Doctorat du Troisième Cycle, Institut d'Etudes Politiques de Paris, 1982; G. A. P. Turko, *The Life and Ideas of Hubert Lagardelle* (Ph.D., London 1977).
159. H. Lagardelle, 'Nos Principes', *La Jeunesse socialiste*, i, 1895, pp. 57–66.
160. H. Lagardelle, 'La Question sociale et le socialisme', *Le Devenir social*, iv, 1898, pp. 270–84.
161. For a detailed discussion of the contents, contributors and readership of *Le Mouvement socialiste*, see de Flers, op. cit. See also M. de Flers, 'Le

Mouvement socialiste (1899–1914)', *Cahiers Georges Sorel*, 5, 1987, pp. 49–76.

162. See in particular H. Lagardelle, 'Le Socialisme et l'Affaire Dreyfus', *MS*, I, 1899, pp. 155–66, 285–99.

163. Ibid., p. 299.

164. 'Avant-Propos', *MS*, XIII, 1904, pp. 1–8.

165. Ibid., p. 3.

166. 'L'Amnistie et les Socialistes', *MS*, V, 1901, p. 5.

167. See in particular 'Concurrence patriotique', *MS*, VI, 1901, pp. 257–9; 'Le Tzar et la République', *MS*, VI, 1901, pp. 385–7.

168. 'Ministérialisme et socialisme', *MS*, VI, 1901, pp. 65–70; 'Ministérialisme et Socialisme', *MS*, VII, 1902, pp. 721–31.

169. 'Les Elections Cantonales', *MS*, VI, 1901, p. 131.

170. 'La Nouvelle Loi sur la Durée du Travail', *MS*, III, 1900, p. 451.

171. 'Les Elections municipales et le parti socialiste', *MS*, III, 1900, p. 579.

172. 'L'Amnistie et les Socialistes', p. 7.

173. 'Socialisme ou Démocratie', *MS*, VII, 1902, pp. 625–32, 673–87, 774–81, 889–97, 1009–16, 1081–88.

174. 'Karl Marx: Commémoration', *MS*, IX, 1903, p. 484.

175. 'Avant-Propos', *MS*, XIII, 1904, pp. 1–8; 'Le Socialisme Ouvrier', *MS*, XIV, 1904, pp. 1–8.

176. *L'Evolution des Syndicats Ouvriers en France: de l'interdiction à l'obligation* (Paris: Imprimerie l'Emancipatrice, 1901).

177. 'Le Mouvement Ouvrier', *MS*, VI, 1901, p. 323.

178. 'Le Congrès et le Socialisme ouvrier', *MS*, XIV, 1904, pp. 29–32.

179. 'Avant-Propos', p. 8.

180. 'Le Socialisme Ouvrier', p. 5.

181. 'La Logique des partis socialistes', *MS*, XIX, 1906, pp. 496–501.

182. 'Mannheim, Rome, Amiens', *MS*, XX, 1906, p. 262. See also 'Les Radicaux-Socialistes et le Programme de Saint-Mandé', *MS*, VI, 1901, pp. 1–5.

183. 'Révolutionnarisme électoral', *MS*, XVII, 1905, pp. 381–92.

184. 'Socialisme ou Démocratie', pp. 889–97, 1009–16, 1081–88.

185. Ibid., p. 891.

186. Ibid., pp. 1013–14.

187. Ibid., p. 1014.

188. Ibid., p. 1015.

189. *L'Evolution des Syndicats Ouvriers en France*, p. 313.

190. 'Socialisme ou Démocratie', p. 1014.

191. Ibid., p. 1087.

192. Ibid., p. 1016.

193. See in particular 'La Confédération du travail et le parti socialiste', *MS*, XXII, 1907, pp. 97–112, 283–7; 'Le Syndicalisme et la politique socialiste', *MS*, XXIV, 1908, pp. 447–68; 'Classe sociale et parti politique', *MS*, XXVI, 1909, pp. 5–25.

194. 'La Confédération du travail et le parti socialiste', p. 106.

195. 'Le Syndicalisme et la politique socialiste', p. 452.

196. 'La Confédération du travail et le parti socialiste', p. 105.

197. 'La Crise révolutionnaire du socialisme français', *MS*, XVII, 1905, p. 261.

198. *Les Intellectuels devant le socialisme* (Paris: 1901).

199. 'Les Intellectuels et le socialisme', *MS*, XXI, 1907, pp. 105–20, 217–32, 349–64, 409–20.

200. See in particular 'La France et la paix armée', *MS*, XVI, 1905, pp. 401–17;

'Antimilitarisme et syndicalisme', *MS*, xix, 1906, pp. 121–6; 'L'Idée de patrie et le socialisme', *MS*, xix, 1906, pp. 5–32, 329–40; xx, 1906, pp. 130–153.

201. 'La Confédération du travail et le parti socialiste', p. 112.
202. 'L'Idée de patrie et le socialisme', p. 15.
203. 'La France et la paix armée', p. 412.
204. Lagardelle's description of the 'protectionist' state drew heavily upon the analysis provided by Sorel in 'Idées socialistes et faits économiques', *RS*, xxxv, 1902, pp. 519–44.
205. 'L'Idée de patrie et le socialisme', p. 146.
206. Ibid., p. 146.
207. 'La France et la paix armée', p. 416.
208. See G. Sorel, 'Préface' to S. Merlino, *Formes et essence du socialisme*, (Paris: 1898), p. xiv, and H. Lagardelle, 'Les Caractères généraux du syndicalisme', *MS*, xxiii, 1908, p. 436.
209. 'Le Syndicalisme et le socialisme en France', in Lagardelle (ed.), *Syndicalisme et socialisme* (Paris: 1908), p. 45.
210. 'Le syndicalisme et la politique socialiste', p. 447.
211. 'Les Caractères généraux du syndicalisme', p. 434.
212. 'La Confédération du travail et le parti socialiste', p. 110.
213. *Le Socialisme ouvrier* (Paris: 1911).
214. G. Sorel, *Lettres à Paul Delesalle* (Paris: 1947), p. 109.
215. G. B. Furiozzi, 'Quattro lettere inedite di Sorel', *Pensiero politico*, x, 1977, pp. 419–424; G. Sorel, *Lettres à Paul Delesalle*, p. 109; G. Sorel, 'Lettere a Uberto Lagardelle', *Educazione fascista*, xi, 1933, p. 963.
216. For a detailed account of the 'Byzantine interactions' involved see P. Mazgaj, *The Action Française and Revolutionary Syndicalism* (Chapel Hill: 1979).
217. For Valois' own account of this episode see G. Valois, *D'un siècle à l'autre* (Paris: 1921). Having begun his career as an anarchist Valois had first met Pelloutier, Delesalle and Sorel before the turn of the century. He went on to become the founder of France's first overtly Fascist political party.
218. *La Révolution sociale ou le Roi* (Paris, 1907); *La Monarchie et la classe ouvrière* (Paris, 1909).
219. See G. Valois, 'Syndicalisme et démocratie, une note de M. Hubert Lagardelle', *Revue critique des idées et des livres*, xii, 1911, pp. 87–90.
220. See R. Louzon, in G. Valois, *La Monarchie et la classe ouvrière*, pp. 78–91.
221. G. Sorel, in ibid., pp. 67–77.
222. 'Lettres de Georges Sorel à Edouard Berth', *Cahiers Georges Sorel*,, 4, 1986, pp. 124–7.
223. A facsimile edition of the *Cahiers du Cercle Proudhon* has recently been issued: see P. Andreu (ed.), *Cahiers du Cercle Proudhon* (Paris: 1976).
224. G. Guy-Grand, 'Le Procès de la démocratie', *Revue de métaphysique et de morale*, xviii, 1910, pp. 102–35, 242–61, 356–96, 545–80, 694–710. Sorel used the expression 'guy-grandesque' as a term of contempt.
225. Ibid., p. 356.
226. E. Berth, 'Le procès de la Démocratie', *Revue critique des idées et des livres*, xiii, 1911, pp. 9–46.
227. Ibid., p. 26.
228. Ibid., p. 24.
229. Ibid., p. 28.

230. 'Déclarations du Cercle', *Cahiers du Cercle Proudhon*, 3–4, May-August, 1912, pp. 174–5.

231. G. Valois, 'Pourquoi nous rattachons nos travaux à l'esprit proudhonien', *Cahiers du Cercle Proudhon*, 1, January-February, 1912, p. 42.

232. A. Vincent, 'La Famille chez Proudhon et dans la Démocratie', *Cahiers du Cercle Proudhon*, 3–4, May-August, 1912, p. 149.

233. G. Valois, 'Pourquoi nous rattachons nos travaux à l'esprit proudhonien', p. 37.

234. J. Darville, 'Proudhon', *Cahiers du Cercle Proudhon*, 1, January-February, 1912, pp. 9–28.

235. J. Darville, 'Satellites de la ploutocratie', *Cahiers du Cercle Proudhon*, 5–6, 1913, pp. 177–211.

236. J. Darville, 'La Monarchie et la classe ouvrière', *Cahiers du Cercle Proudhon*, 2nd series, January-February, 1914, pp. 7–34.

237. Ibid., p. 15.

238. Ibid., p. 29.

239. Ibid., p. 34.

240. E. Berth, *Les méfaits des intellectuels* (Paris: 1914).

241. Ibid., 2nd edition (Paris: 1926), p. 85.

242. G. Sorel, 'La disfatta dei "mufles" ', *Il Divenire sociale*, v, 1909, pp. 177–81; 'Socialistes antiparlementaires', *Action française*, 22 August 1909.

243. G. Sorel, 'Le Réveil de l'âme française', *Action française*, 14 April 1910. This article was published on the same day in *La Voce*.

244. 'Lettres de Georges Sorel à Edouard Berth', *Cahiers Georges Sorel*, 5, 1987, p. 168.

245. H. Lagrange, 'L'Oeuvre de Sorel et le Cercle Proudhon', *Cahiers du Cercle Proudhon*, 3–4, May-August, 1912, p. 129.

246. P. Andreu, Introduction to 'Lettres de Georges Sorel à Edouard Berth', *Cahiers Georges Sorel*, 3, 1985, p. 81.

247. G. Sorel, 'Mes raisons du syndicalisme', reprinted in G. Sorel, *Matériaux d'une théorie du prolétariat* (Paris, 1919), p. 265.

248. G. Sorel, *Terre libre*, 15 July 1910. I thank Michel Prat for bringing this letter to my attention.

249. G. Sorel, 'Urbain Gohier', *L'Indépendance*, II, 1912, pp. 305–20.

250. Ibid., pp. 314–5.

251. G. Sorel, *La Révolution dreyfusienne* (Paris: 1908); reference to 2nd edition (Paris: 1911), p. 64.

252. G. Sorel, 'Urbain Gohier', p. 319.

253. G. Sorel, 'Urbain Gohier'; 'Quelques prétentions juives', *L'Indépendance*, III, 1912, pp. 217–36, 277–95, 317–36; 'Aux temps dreyfusiens', *L'Indépendance*, IV, 1912, pp. 29–56.

254. G. Sorel, 'Urbain Gohier', p. 315.

255. R. Louzon, 'La faillite du Dreyfusisme ou le triomphe du parti juif', *MS*, xx, 1906, pp. 192–9.

256. S. Sand, 'Sorel, les Juifs et l'antisémitisme', *Cahiers Georges Sorel*, 2, 1984, pp. 7–36. For a different view see D. Lindenberg, 'Mouvement prolétarien et révolution religieuse: Georges Sorel critique de Renan', in J. Julliard and S. Sand (eds) *Georges Sorel en son temps* (Paris: 1985), pp. 189–201.

257. G. Sorel, 'Urbain Gohier', p. 320.

258. G. Sorel, 'Quelques prétentions juives', p. 336.

259. G. Sorel, 'Modernismo nella religione e nel socialismo', *Il Divenire sociale*,

III, 1907, pp. 339–45; reprinted in the original French in *Revue critique des idées et des livres*, II, 1908, pp. 177–204.

260. 'Aux temps dreyfusiens', p. 51.
261. G. Sorel, 'Trois problèmes', *L'Indépendance*, II, 1911, pp. 221–40, 261–79.
262. 'Quelques prétentions juives', p. 284.
263. G. Sorel, 'Lyripipi sorbonici moralisationes', *L'Indépendance*, I, 1911, pp. 111–25; 'Si les dogmes évoluent', II, 1911, pp. 31–44; 'Une critique des sociologues', II, 1911, pp. 73–84.
264. G. Sorel, 'L'Evolution créatrice', *MS*, XXII, 1907, pp. 257–82, 478–94; *MS*, XXXIII, 1908, pp. 34–52, 184–94, 276–94.
265. See in particular G. Sorel, *De l'utilité du pragmatisme* (Paris: 1921), pp. 357–451. For a discussion of this issue see S. Sand, 'Quelques remarques sur Sorel critique de "l'Evolution créatrice". Quatre lettres inédites de Bergson à Sorel', *Cahiers Georges Sorel*, I, 1983, pp. 109–23.
266. G. Sorel, 'Vues sur les problèmes de la philosophie', *Rev. mét.*, XIX, 1911, p. 99.
267. Ibid., p. 68.
268. G. Sorel, 'Préface' to E. Berth, *Les méfaits des intellectuels*, p. xxxvii.
269. H. Lagardelle, *Le Socialisme ouvrier* (Paris: 1911) p. xiv.
270. See H. Lagardelle, 'La formation du syndicalisme en France', *MS*, XXX, 1911, pp. 161–86, 241–57; XXXI, 1912, pp. 134–146.
271. See in particular H. Lagardelle, review of G. Valois, La monarchie et la classe ouvriére, *MS*, XXVIII, 1910, pp. 239–40; 'La Critique syndicaliste de la démocratie', *MS*, XXIX, 1911, pp. 81–6; 'Nouveaux problèmes', *MS*, XXX, 1911, pp. 321–4; 'Proudhon et les Néo-Monarchistes', *MS*, XXXI, 1912, pp. 65–9; 'Les Ennemis de Rousseau', *MS*, XXXII, 1912, pp. 101–6.
272. H. Lagardelle, 'Monarchistes et syndicalistes', *MS*, XXIX, 1911, p. 54.
273. 'Proudhon et les Néo-Monarchistes', p. 66.
274. 'La Critique syndicaliste de la démocratie', p. 84.
275. H. Lagardelle, 'La Démocratie en France', *MS*, XXXIII, 1912, pp. 321–32; XXXIV, 1913, pp. 13–29. See also H. Lagardelle, 'Préface' to J. Gaumont, *L'Etat contre la nation* (Paris: 1911).
276. 'La Démocratie en France', pp. 324–5.
277. Ibid., pp. 330–2; see also H. Lagardelle, 'La Démocratie et les partis politiques', *MS*, XXXII, 1912, pp. 313–8.
278. 'La Démocratie en France', p. 22.
279. Ibid., p. 24.
280. Ibid., p. 27.
281. Ibid., p. 29.
282. For details of Lagardelle's life in this period see R. Recouly, 'Une entretien avec M. Lagardelle', *Gringoire*, 22 May 1942.
283. *Charles Maurras, poèmes, portraits, jugements* (Paris: 1919), pp. 143–4.
284. 'Lettres de Georges Sorel à Edouard Berth', *Cahiers Georges Sorel*, 5, 1987, p. 200.
285. G. Sorel, 'Lettres à Mario Missiroli', in G. Sorel, *Da Proudhon a Lenin e l'Europa sotto la tormenta* (Rome: 1974), p. 513.

Notes to Chapter 4

1. E. Berth, 'Un Marx inédit!', *MS*, XIV, 1904, pp. 99–100.
2. See P. A. Carcanagues, *Le Mouvement syndicaliste réformiste en France* (Paris: 1912); F. Challaye, *Syndicalisme révolutionnaire et syndicalisme*

réformiste (Paris: 1909) and the special issue of *Le Mouvement social*, 87, 1974 devoted to 'Réformismes et réformistes français'.

3. J. Michel, 'Syndicalisme minier et politique dans le Nord-Pas-de-Calais: le cas Basly (1880–1914)', ibid., pp. 9–33.

4. M. Rebérioux and P. Fridenson, 'Albert Thomas, pivot du réformisme français', ibid., pp. 85–97.

5. On Dumoulin see P. A. Arum, 'Du syndicalisme révolutionnaire au Reformisme: Georges Dumoulin (1903–1923)', ibid., pp. 35–62 and G. Dumoulin, *Carnets de route* (Lille, 1938).

6. A. Keufer, 'Réfutation nécessaire', *RPI*, VII, 1909, p. 65. This article was orginally published in *La Typographie française*, 1 June 1909.

7. R. Montélimard, 'La Politique du syndicalisme', *AO*, 15 August 1910 and A. Keufer, 'La Politique du syndicalisme', *AO*, 1 September 1910.

8. A. Keufer, 'Réponse nécessaire', *L'Humanité*, 4 January 1909.

9. G. Sorel, 'Lettres de Georges Sorel à Edouard Berth', *Cahiers Georges Sorel*, 4, 1986, p. 93.

10. The literature on Comte is vast but for an interesting recent analysis see R. Vernon, *Citizenship and Order* (Toronto: 1986), pp. 125–45. Much of the debate that has surrounded Comte has concentrated on the apparent gap between the first 'positivist' phase of his writings and the later 'religious' phase. It is significant therefore that the proletarian positivists, in opposition to Emile Littré, denied the existence of the break; see E. Littré, *Auguste Comte et la philosophie positive* (Paris: 1864) and E. Antoine, 'Aperçu sommaire de la vie et sur l'oeuvre de M. Pierre Laffitte', in P. Laffitte, *De la morale positive* (Paris: 1881), pp. 52–7.

11. See M. Sutton, *Nationalism, Positivism and Catholicism* (Cambridge: 1982).

12. Little has been written on positivism and the workers' movement but see M. Perrot, 'Note sur le positivisme ouvrier', *Romantisme*, 21–22, 1978, pp. 201–4 and P. Boivin, *Choix d'écrits* (Paris: 1938).

13. Magnin, Jacquemin, Belpaume, *Rapport à la société positiviste par la commission chargée d'examiner la question du travail* (Paris: 1848).

14. See F. Magnin, *Etudes sociales* (Paris: 1913).

15. See P. Sorlin, *Waldeck-Rousseau* (Paris: 1966), pp. 246–52.

16. E. Laporte, F. Magnin and I. Finance, *Le Positivisme au congrès ouvrier* (Paris: 1877).

17. Ibid., p. 13.

18. Ibid., p. 140.

19. Ibid., pp. 219–95.

20. Ibid., p. 58.

21. Ibid., p. 68.

22. Ibid., p. 102.

23. Ibid., p. 7.

24. Ibid., p. 17.

25. Ibid., p. 149.

26. P. Laffitte, 'Nécessité de l'intervention du positivisme dans l'ensemble des affaires humaines', *RO*, I, 1878, p. 21.

27. E. Laporte, F. Magnin, I. Finance, op. cit., p. 82.

28. P. Laffitte, op. cit., p. 18. For a more detailed exposition of Laffitte's views see P. Laffitte, *De la morale positive* (Paris: 1881).

29. See M. Rebérioux, *Les Ouvriers du livre et leur fédération* (Paris: 1981). For a critical assessment of Keufer's achievement see M. Harmel, 'Auguste Keufer', *Les Hommes du Jour*, 136, 27 August 1910.

30. A. Keufer, 'Le 107ᵉ Anniversaire de la naissance d'A. Comte', *RO*, xxxi, 1905, p. 279.
31. A. Keufer, 'Discours prononcé par M. Aug. Keufer sur le tombe de Fabien Magnin', *RPI*, iii, 1907, p. 266.
32. A. Keufer, 'Discours de M. Auguste Keufer', *RO*, xxvi, 1902, p. 47.
.33 A. Keufer, 'Discours de M. Keufer sur la tombe d'Auguste Comte', *RPI*, vii, 1909, p. 283.
34. Ibid., p. 289.
35. Ibid., p. 289.
36. A. Keufer, 'Discours de M. Auguste Keufer', *RO*, xxvi, 1902, p. 47.
37. A. Keufer, 'Singulières déclarations', *RPI*, ii, 1907, pp. 435–6. This article was first published in *VduP*, 14 April 1907 and 5 May, 1907.
38. A. Keufer,'Discours de M. Keufer sur la tombe d'Auguste Comte', *RPI*, vii, 1909, p. 289.
39. A. Keufer, 'Discours de M. Auguste Keufer', *RO*, xxvi, 1902, p. 49.
40. Ibid., p. 51.
41. A. Keufer, 'Hommage international à Auguste Comte', *RO*, xxi, 1900, p. 323.
42. A. Keufer, 'Discours de M. Auguste Keufer', *RO*, xxvi, 1902, p. 49.
43. Ibid., p. 50.
44. A. Keufer, 'Discours de M. Auguste Keufer sur la tombe d'Auguste Comte', p. 292.
45. A. Keufer, 'Discours de M. Auguste Keufer', *RO*, xxvi, 1902, p. 48.
46. A. Keufer, 'Discours de M. Auguste Keufer sur la tombe d'Auguste Comte', p. 295. See also A. Keufer, 'Discours de M. A. Keufer', *RO*, xvi, 1898, p. 227.
47. A. Keufer, 'Discours de M. Auguste Keufer', *RO*, xxvi, 1902, p. 50.
48. A. Keufer, *L'Education syndicale: exposé de la méthode organique* (Paris: 1910), p. 15. This text was first published as a series of articles in *La Typographie française* beginning 1 July 1909.
49. A. Keufer, 'Le syndicalisme réformiste', *MS*, xv, 1905, p. 21.
50. A. Keufer, *L'Education syndicale*, pp. 13–14.
51. Ibid., p. 6.
52. A. Keufer, 'Le syndicalisme réformiste', p. 41.
53. A. Keufer, *L'Education syndicale*, pp. 7–9.
54. A. Keufer, 'Le syndicalisme réformiste', p. 23.
55. A. Keufer, 'Hommage international à Auguste Comte', p. 325.
56. F. Fagnot, *Les Syndicats ouvriers en Angleterre* (Paris: 1890). For Fagnot's own view of the *syndicats* see F. Fagnot, *Les Attributions des syndicats ourvriers* (Paris: 1897). Keufer's preface was reprinted as 'L'Histoire du trade-unionisme en Angleterre', *RO*, xviii, 1899, pp. 350–8.
57. F. Fagnot, *Les Syndicats ouvriers en Angleterre*, p. 2.
58. A. Keufer, 'L'Histoire du trade-unionisme en Angleterre', p. 354.
59. The two most complete statements of his position are 'Le Syndicalisme réformiste' and *L'Education syndicale*.
60. A. Keufer, *L'Education syndicale*, p. 30.
61. A. Keufer, 'Discours de M. Keufer sur la tombe d'Auguste Comte', p. 295.
62. Ibid., p. 295.
63. A. Keufer, *L'Education syndicale*, p. 45.
64. A. Keufer, 'Discussion sur la réglementation légale du travail', *RO*, xxxi, 1905, p. 172.
65. A. Keufer, 'Singulières déclarations', p. 431.

66. A. Keufer, 'Ce qui est licite et illicite en cas de grève', in C. Gide (ed.), *Le Droit de grève* (Paris: 1909), pp. 73–99.
67. A. Keufer, 'Singulières déclarations', p. 438.
68. A. Keufer, *L'Education syndicale*, pp. 40–41.
69. A. Keufer, 'Ce qui est licite et illicite en cas de grève', p. 96.
70. Ibid., p. 89.
71. A. Keufer, *L'Education syndicale*, p. 47.
72. A. Keufer, 'Ce qui est licite et illicite en cas de grève, p. 74.
73. A. Keufer, 'Singulières déclarations', pp. 431–2.
74. V. Griffuelhes, 'Singulières déclarations', *VduP*, 24 March 1907. Keufer's interview was reprinted as a footnote to his 'Singulières déclarations' when it was published in the *Revue positiviste internationale*.
75. See A. Keufer,, 'Les minorités agissantes', *La Typographie française*, XXXI, 16 March 1912.
76. A. Keufer, *L'Education syndicale*, p. 61.
77. Ibid., pp. 58–77.
78. *XV Congrès national corporatif* (Amiens: 1906), pp. 155–6.
79. As Keufer himself acknowledged for the 'Enquête sur l'idée de patrie et la classe ouvrière' organised by *Le Mouvement socialiste* of the respondants he alone opposed anti-patriotism, see A. Keufer, *MS*, XVII, 1905, pp. 47–51.
80. A. Keufer, 'L'Anti-militarisme et les syndicats', *RPI*, IV, 1908, p. 99. This article was first published in *La Revue syndicaliste*, II, 1906, pp. 160–7.
81. A. Keufer, 'L'Anti-militarisme et les syndicats', p. 106.
82. P. Laffitte, *De la morale positive*, p. 184.
83. See A. Comte, *Catéchisme positiviste* (Paris, n.d.), pp. 305–6.
84. Ibid., p. 306.
85. A. Keufer, 'L'Anti-militarisme et les syndicats', p. 105.
86. A. Keufer, *MS*, XVII, 1905, p. 48.
87. A. Keufer, 'L'Anti-militarisme et les syndicats', pp. 107–8.
88. L. Niel, 'Réflexions sur l'évolution syndicaliste', *AO*, 1 October 1910, pp. 5–8.
89. L. Niel, 'Moutons de panurge', *VduP*, 9 December 1900.
90. See in particular L. Niel, 'L'Unité ouvrière', *VduP*, 14 July 1901.
91. L. Niel, *Les Syndicats et la révolution* (Paris: 1902).
92. L. Niel, 'L'Education ouvrière', *VduP*, 23 February 1902.
93. L. Niel, 'La Scission', *VduP*, 22 September 1901.
94. L. Niel, 'Le Système syndicaliste', *VduP*, 7 June 1903.
95. L. Niel, 'Grèves paysannes', *VduP*, 7 February 1903 and 'La Citadelle paysanne', *Almanach de la révolution pour 1904* (Paris: 1904), pp. 42–4.
96. See *XIV Congrès national corporatif* (Bourges: 1904), pp. 144–90.
97. Ibid., pp. 163–5.
98. L. Niel, *La Journée de 8 heures* (Paris: 1905).
99. L. Niel, 'La Journée de huit heures et les salaires', *VduP*, 26 March 1905.
100. L. Niel, 'Le Parfait syndicalisme', *VduP*, 24 September 1905.
101. L. Niel, 'Les Réformes révolutionnaires', *La Revue syndicaliste*, V, 1909, pp. 2–4.
102. See *XV Congrès national corporatif* (Amiens: 1906), pp. 142–9.
103. L. Niel, 'Quelle couleur?' *L'Humanité*, 24 January 1908.
104. See *XVI Congrès national corporatif* (Marseilles: 1908) p. 186.
105. L. Niel, 'L'Antimilitarisme', *La Revue syndicaliste*, II, 1906, pp. 157–60.
106. L. Niel, 'Gompers', *L'Humanité*, 6 July 1909.
107. See *XVI Congrès national corporatif*, p. 191.

108. L. Niel, 'Le Syndicalisme syndicaliste', *AO*, 15 December 1909.
109. L. Niel, 'Réflexions sur l'évolution syndicaliste', p. 8.
110. See pp. 138–9.
111. L. Niel, *La Valeur sociale du syndicalisme* (Paris: 1909).
112. Ibid., p. 16.
113. Ibid., p. 23.
114. L. Niel, *Deux principes de vie sociale*, p. 49.
115. Ibid., p. 77.
116. Ibid., p. 91.
117. L. Niel, 'Quel programme?', *L'Humanité*, 6 January 1910.
118. E. Pouget, 'Réformes et révolution', *VduP*, 5 April 1903, and A. Keufer, 'Réformes et révolution', *VduP*, 12 April 1903.
119. See *XIV Congrès national corporatif* (Bourges: 1904), pp. 92–190, 204–220.
120. See *XV Congrès national corporatif* (Amiens: 1906), pp. 130–72, 174–9.
121. 'Notre but', *La Revue syndicaliste*, I, 1906, pp. 3–5.
122. A. Keufer, 'Misérable comédie', *La Typographie française*, xxvii, 1 October 1908, and A. Keufer, 'Les Justiciers du syndicalisme', *La Typographie française*, xxvii, 1 August 1908.
123. A. Keufer, 'Réfutation nécessaire', p. 69.
124. See for example, L. Niel, 'Syndicalisme et corporatisme', *L'Humanité*, 6 July 1908; 'Vers le centre', *L'Humanité*, 28 August 1908; 'La Course à la mort', *L'Humanité*. 29 October 1908; 'Ni vertige, ni illusions', *L'Humanité*, 26 November 1908; 'L'Unité morale', 13 February 1909.
125. See *La Révolte du 17ᵉ* (Paris: 1907). For Griffuelhes' own assessment of the Charter of Amiens see V. Griffuelhes 'Amiens-Marseille', *L'Humanité*, 29 November 1908.
126. *XVI Congrès national corporatif* (Marseilles: 1908), pp. 175–212.
127. A. Keufer, 'L'Orientation de la CGT', *L'Humanité*, 13 April 1909. See also A. Keufer, 'L'Election de Niel à la CGT', *La Typographie française*, xxviii, 1 April 1909; A. Thomas, 'L'Election de Niel', *La Revue syndicaliste*, v, 1909, pp. 281–5 and V. Renard, 'Notre Vote à la CGT', *L'Humanité*, 12 March 1909.
128. E. Pouget, 'Victoire ministérielle', *La Révolution*, 25 February 1909. In *La Révolution* see also A. Merrheim, 'Candidat d'Union', 20 February 1909; A. Merrheim, 'Silence significatif', 28 February 1909; G. Yvetot, 'Tout va bien!', 1 March 1909; G. Yvetot, 'A l'oeuvre', 9 March 1909.
129. L. Niel, 'Discours de Lens', *Le Temps*, 18 May 1909.
130. A. Keufer, 'Le Mariage forcé', *L'Humanité*, 30 June 1909.
131. L. Niel, 'A l'oeuvre tous, pour les résultats', *VduP*, 21 March 1909 and R. Péricat, 'A l'oeuvre tous, pour la grève générale', *VduP*, 21 March 1909.
132. L. Niel, 'De l'Action pratique', *VduP*, 20 June 1909; A. Luquet, 'De l'Action pratique', *VduP*, 20 June 1909. See two later articles by Niel: 'Sur le minimum de salaire', *VduP*, 5 June 1910 and 'Idéalisme et réalisme', *VduP*, 19 June 1910.
133. A. Keufer, 'Parlementarisme ou dictature', *VduP*, 4 July 1909.
134. G. Yvetot, 'Pour la République', *VduP*, 11 July 1909.
135. *XVII Congrès national corporatif* (Toulouse: 1910), pp. 204–34.
136. Ibid., p. 226.

Notes to Chapter 5

1. P. Monatte, 'La Fondation de "La Vie ouvrière"', in C. Chambelland (ed.), *La Lutte syndicale* (Paris: 1976), pp. 62–119. Monatte's account of these years originally appeared in *La Révolution prolétarienne* at the end of 1959.

2. B. Georges and D. Tintant, *Léon Jouhaux, Cinquante Ans de Syndicalisme*, I, (Paris: 1962), p. 11.

3. E. Dolléans, 'Les Temps héroïques du syndicalisme', *L'Homme réel*, 41, 1937, pp. 7–23. For contemporary accounts see E. Poisson, 'La Crise syndicaliste', *RS*, LIV, 1911, pp. 289–301; J. Blois, 'A la CGT: Deux Hommes – Deux Thèses', *Le Correspondant*, 25 July 1910, pp. 242–63; and P. Louis, 'Y-a-t-il une crise du syndicalisme', *La Grande revue*, 1912, pp. 785–801.

4. See the responses of A. Merrheim, *MS*, XXVI, 1909, pp. 291–9; E. Klemczynski, *MS*, XXVI, 1909, pp. 299–304; G. Yvetot, *MS*, XXVII, 1910, pp. 57–62; Marty-Rollan, *MS*, XXVII, 1910, pp. 63–5; A. Keufer, *MS*, XXVII, 1910, pp. 262–75; and R. Lenoir, *MS*, XXVIII, 1910, pp. 116–23. *Le Mouvement socialiste* returned to this theme with a series of articles in 1913.

5. V. Griffuelhes, 'La Leçon du passé', *VO*, I, 1909, pp. 1–7.

6. V. Griffuelhes and L. Niel, *Les Objectifs de nos luttes de classe* (Paris: 1909), p. 13.

7. V. Griffuelhes, 'L'Infériorité des capitalistes français', *MS*, XXVIII, 1910, pp. 329–32; 'Stagnation capitaliste', *MS*, XXIX, 1911, pp. 34–7; and 'Utopisme petit-bourgeois', *MS*, XXXI, 1912, pp. 30–6. Griffuelhes also published several articles on this theme in *La Bataille syndicaliste*.

8. V. Griffuelhes, 'Utopisme petit-bourgeois', p. 34.

9. V. Griffuelhes, 'L'Infériorité des capitalistes français', p. 332.

10. G. Yvetot, 'La Crise syndicaliste', *MS*, XXVII, 1910, pp. 57–62.

11. A. Keufer, 'La Crise syndicaliste', *MS*, XXVII, 1910, pp. 262–75.

12. Ibid., p. 275.

13. L. Niel, 'A l'oeuvre, tous pour les résultats', *VduP*, 21 March 1909.

14. See in particular 'Autour du 1er Mai: POA', 30 April 1911; 'Qu'est-ce que le syndicalisme Ouvrier', 21 May 1911; 'Leur Bonne Foi', 18 June 1911; and 'La Révision de la constitution', 9 July 1911 and 23 July 1911.

15. A. Merrheim, 'La Parlementarisation du syndicalisme', *MS*, XXVII, 1910, pp. 241–7.

16. A. Merrheim, *MS*, XXVI, 1909, pp. 291–9.

17. P. Monatte, 'La Fondation de "La Vie ouvrière"', p. 70.

18. G. Sorel, 'La Leçon du malheur', *Almanach de la Révolution pour 1909*, pp. 9–13.

19. H. Lagardelle, 'La Formation du syndicalisme en France', *MS*, XXX, 1911, pp. 161–86, 241–56; XXXI, 1912, pp. 134–45; 'Les Difficultés du syndicalisme', *MS*, XXXII, 1912, pp. 161–4.

20. Ibid., p. 161.

21. P. Monatte, 'La Fondation de "La Vie ouvrière"', pp. 67–9.

22. F. Pouget, 'L'Orphelinal du livre', *La Guerre sociale*, 30 August 1911.

23. J. Maitron, *Paul Delesalle* (Paris: 1985), p. 166.

24. P. Delesalle, 'Georges Sorel', *L'Humanité*, 26 August 1922.

25. See for example C. Guieysse, 'Les Syndicalistes révolutionnaires', *Pages libres*, VIII, 1904, pp. 309–28.

26. On this episode see P. Monatte, 'Pas-de-Calais', in C. Chambelland (ed.), *La Lutte syndicale*, pp. 12–25 and J. Julliard, 'Jeune et vieux syndicat chez les mineurs de Pas-de-Calais', *Le Mouvement social*, 47, 1964, pp. 7–30.

27. J. Maitron, *Le Mouvement anarchiste en France*, I, (Paris: 1983), p. 325, n. 181.

28. See P. Monatte, 'Un Crime capitaliste', *TN*, 17 March 1906, in C. Chambelland (ed.), pp. 26–33 and 'Le Complot', *TN*, 16 June 1906, in C. Chambelland (ed.), pp. 34–9.

29. Ibid., p. 38.

30. See for example P. Monatte, 'Le Parti socialiste et la confédération'. *TN*, 11 August 1906; 'Parti socialiste et syndicats', *TN*, 18 August 1906; 'Le Parti socialiste et les syndicats', *TN*, 25 August 1906; and 'Le Congrès d'Amiens', *TN*, 27 October 1906, 3 November 1906, and 10 November 1906. 'Le Congrès d'Amiens' is reprinted in C. Chambelland (ed.), pp. 40–52.

31. Monatte's speech was reprinted as 'Syndicalisme et anarchisme', *VO*, 94, 1913, pp. 227–36 and in C. Chambelland (ed.), pp. 53–60.

32. On Rosmer see C. Gras, *Alfred Rosmer et le mouvement révolutionnaire international* (Paris: 1971).

33. See for example an editorial entitled 'Notre plan de travail pour 1912–1913' which stated that 'At the beginning of *La Vie Ouvrière* we accepted the rule of engaging in as little theory as possible'; *VO*, 73, 1912, pp. 1–6.

34. On the relationship between Sorel and Monatte see C. Chambelland, 'Monatte lecteur de Sorel', *Cahiers Georges Sorel*, 4, 1986, pp. 140–6.

35. P. Monatte, 'Le Congrès de Toulouse', *VO*, 26, 1910, p. 449.

36. Ibid, 28, 1910, pp. 697–9. See also P. Monatte, 'Les Cheminots en tutelle', *VO*, 27, 1910, pp. 545–7.

37. See, for example, P. Monatte, 'La Cherté des vivres', *VO*, 23, 1910, pp. 264–70.

38. P. Monatte, 'Le Premier mai', *VO*, 14, 1910, p. 461.

39. 'Notre plan de travail pour 1912–1913', p. 3.

40. A. Rosmer, 'A Propos du néo-malthusianisme', *VO*, 74, 1912, pp. 99–102.

41. A. Rosmer, 'Le Cas Bonnot', *VO*, 65, 1912, pp. 329–36. Left-wing papers devoted considerable column space to an analysis of the sinking of the Titanic and the deaths of aviators as examples of the consequences of capitalist exploitation. In the case of the Titanic much was made of the fact that the majority of survivors were first-class passengers.

42. On Merrheim see in particular N. Papayanis, *Alphonse Merrheim: The Emergence of Reformism in Revolutionary Syndicalism 1871–1925* (Dordrecht: 1985); C. Gras, 'Merrheim et le capitalisme', *Le Mouvement social*, 63, 1968, pp. 143–63 and 'La Fédération des Métaux en 1913–1914 et l'évolution du syndicalisme révolutionnaire français', *Le Mouvement social*, 77, 1971, pp. 85–111.

43. A. Merrheim, 'Un grand conflit social: La Grève d'Hennebont', *MS*, xx, 1906, p. 194.

44. A. Merrheim, 'Le Mouvement ouvrier dans le bassin de Longwy', *MS*, xvii, 1905, p. 480.

45. A. Merrheim, *L'Organisation patronale* (Paris: 1908), pp. 1–2.

46. A. Merrheim, *L'Affaire de l'Ouenza* (Paris: 1910), p. 24.

47. A. Merrheim, *L'Organisation patronale* (Paris: 1908).

48. P. Monatte, 'La Crise de la "Bataille Syndicaliste"', *VO*, 104, 1914, pp. 65–72.

49. L. Jouhaux, 'De l'Utilité de la grève générale', *VduP*, 15 August 1909.

50. L. Jouhaux, 'Ose-donc, traitre!', *VduP*, 13 November 1910.

51. L. Jouhaux, 'Le Syndicalisme français', in L. Jouhaux and J. Sassenbach,

Les Tendances syndicales (Brussels: 1911), pp. 5–27. See also L. Jouhaux, *Notre syndicalisme* (Paris: 1912).

52. L. Jouhaux, V. Griffuelhes, C. Volrin, et al., 'Notre position', *BS*, 20 August 1912 and 22 August 1912.

53. L. Jouhaux, 'Après Le Havre', *BS*, 29 September 1912.

54. J. Julliard, *Clémenceau, briseur des grèves* (Paris: 1965), pp. 70–1.

55. L. Jouhaux, 'L'Enseignements d'une grève: sa valeur sociale', *BS*, 3 May 1912.

56. See L. Jouhaux, 'Notre action', *BS*, 1 May 1912; 'Conquêtes positives', *BS*, 12 May 1912; 'La Semaine anglaise', *BS*, 26 January 1913; 'Sortie d'usine', *BS*, 16 February 1913.

57. R. Péricat, *Etre un homme* (Courbevoie: 1938).

58. G. Sorel, 'Lettere di Giorgio Sorel a Uberto Lagardelle', *Educazione fascista*, XI, 1933, p. 969.

59. C. Maurras and H. Dutroit-Crozon, *Si le coup de force est possible* (Paris: 1910).

60. E. Janvion, 'Le Péril maçonnique dans le syndicalisme', *VduP*, 31 May, 1908. This argument was taken sufficiently seriously for Sorel to suggest to Lagardelle that Janvion might rewrite his articles for *Le Mouvement socialiste*.

61. For a representative selection of *La Terre libre* see 'Pourquoi ce journal?', 15 November 1909; E. Janvion, 'Dans les coulisses de la politique', 15 June 1910; Argus, 'Le Syndicalisme maçonnique', 15 September 1910; 'Notre Programme et les événements', 1 November 1910; M. Riquier, 'La Race persécutée', 15 November 1910; E. Janvion, 'Les Juifs et Jaurès', 1 January 1911; E. Janvion, 'Devant les Hébreux . . .', 15 February 1911; E. Janvion, 'Le Youtre', 1 March 1911; E. Janvion, 'Aux Prolétaires juifs', 15 April 1911 and E. Janvion 'La Franc-Maçonnerie et la classe ouvrière', 15 April 1911.

62. On this whole incident see P. Mazgaj, *The Action Française and Revolutionary Syndicalism* (Chapel Hill: 1979), pp. 155–65.

63. V. Griffuelhes, 'Où va-t-on?', *BS*, 23 January 1913; 'Retour sur nous-mêmes', *BS*, 24 January 1913; 'Impuissance', *BS*, 27 January 1913; and 'Pour une fois', *BS*, 1 February 1913.

64. A. Merrheim, 'Contre l'impuissance, Pour l'action', *BS*, 28 January 1913; and 'Précisions', *BS*, 5 February 1913.

65. 'Déclaration à propos de l'action confédérale', *BS*, 27 August 1913.

66. A. Merrheim, 'Les Réacteurs se demasquent', *BS*, 30 July 1913.

67. P. Monatte, 'La CGT a-t-elle rectifié son tir?', *VO*, 93, 1913, pp. 129–39; reprinted in C. Chambelland (ed.), pp. 119–27.

68. See E. Pouget, 'Sur une controverse syndicale', *La Guerre sociale*, 28 January 1913; 'La Réponse de la CGT', 22 July 1913; 'L'Orientation de la CGT', 3 September 1913; and 'L'Année syndicaliste', 31 December 1913.

69. A. Keufer, 'Au Camarade Griffuelhes: simple réponse', *VduP*, 5 May 1912 and 'Un Positiviste à un libertaire', *VduP*, 9 February 1913.

70. A. Keufer, 'Changement de tactique', *La Typographie française*, XXXII, 1 October 1913; reprinted in *RPI*, XIII, 1913, pp. 446–53.

71. M. Rebérioux, 'Les tendances hostiles à l'Etat dans la SFIO (1905–1914)', *Le Mouvement social*, 65, 1968, pp. 21–37.

72. P. Delesalle, 'La Crise de l'apprentissage', *MS*, XXIII, 1908, pp. 241–6.

73. A. Merrheim, 'La Crise de l'apprentissage', *MS*, XXIII, 1908, pp. 327–38.

See also A. Merrheim, 'L'Invasion du machinisme', *VduP*, 12 April 1908 and 19 April 1908.

74. A. Merrheim, 'La Méthode Taylor', *VO*, 82, 1913, pp. 210–26; 83, 1913, pp. 298–309; 108, 1914, pp. 345–62; 109, 1914, pp. 385–98. See also A. Merrheim, 'Un retour vers la barbarie par la méfhode Taylor', *VduP*, 23 February 1913, 3 March 1913 and 14 March 1913.

75. A. Merrheim, 'La Méthode Taylor', p. 224.

76. Ibid., p. 306.

77. E. Pouget, *L'Organisation du surmenage* (Paris: 1914) and G. Yvetot, 'La Méthode Taylor', *BS*, 17 February 1913. See also the articles by Pouget on this issue in *La Guerre sociale* from February 1913 onwards.

78. J. Raveté, 'Une défense de la Méthode Taylor', *VO*, 107, 1914, pp. 257–67 and 'Brèves observations pour Merrheim', *VO*, 116, 1914, pp. 103–6.

79. A. Merrheim, 'Réponse de Merrheim', *VO*, 116, 1914, pp. 106–11.

80. A. Merrheim, 'La Crise de l'apprentissage', p. 333.

81. Ibid., pp. 337–8.

82. L. Jouhaux, *A Jean Jaurès* (Paris: 1914), p. 11.

83. C. Chambelland and J. Maitron (eds), *Syndicalisme révolutionnaire et communisme: les archives de Pierre Monatte 1914–1924* (Paris: 1968), pp. 18–22.

84. *BS*, 3 August 1914.

85. See in particular L. Jouhaux, 'Paroles de solidarité', *BS*, 23 August 1914; 'Le Prolétariat et la guerre: des raisons de notre attitude';, *BS*, 26 September 1914; 'Le Prolétariat et la guerre: l'alliance des peuples', *BS*, 27 September 1914; 'A l'Assaut de l'impérialisme allemand', *BS*, 10 October 1914.

86. C. Chambelland and J. Maitron (eds), p. 28.

87. V. Griffuelhes, 'Puisqu'il faut écrire', *La Feuille*, 3 August 1916.

88. V. Griffuelhes, 'Il faut un examen de conscience', *La Feuille*, 10 August 1916.

89. L. Jouhaux, 'Il faut du travail', *BS*, 12 August 1914 and 'Organisons la solidarité', *BS*, 13 August 1914.

90. V. Griffuelhes, 'Organisons l'assistance et la reprise du travail', *BS*, 22 August 1914; 'Pour remédier au chômage des mesures extraordinaires s'imposent', *BS*, 26 August 1914; 'Voilà des mesures', *BS*, 28 August 1914; and 'Par le Crédit foncier on pouvait agir', *BS*, 31 August 1914.

91. V. Griffuelhes, 'Voilà des mesures' and 'Démocratie et révolution', *La Feuille*, 7 September 1916.

92. V. Griffuelhes, 'Il faut une production concurrencée', *La Feuille*, 24 August 1916; 'Les Grandes Foires et l'essor humain', *La Feuille*, 5 October 1916.

93. V. Griffuelhes, 'La Liberté avec le bien-être', *La Feuille*, 11 January 1917.

94. V. Griffuelhes, 'Gare à demain', *La Feuille*, 23 November 1916; 'Presser les mêmes citrons ou en augmenter le nombre', 4 January 1917; and 'Mieux vaudrait appliquer', 5 April 1917.

95. V. Griffuelhes, 'Le Bien-Etre, frère de la liberté', *La Feuille*, 19 April 1917.

96. V. Griffuelhes, 'Il faut un examen de conscience'.

97. A. Keufer, 'Le Rapprochement franco-allemand', *RPI*, xiii, 1913, pp. 52–4 and 'La Patrie et l'Humanité', *RPI*, xvi, 1914, pp. 143–5.

98. A. Keufer, 'Les Conséquences de la guerre sur la main d'oeuvre', *La Typographie française*, xxxiv, 16 January 1915 and 'Les Conséquences de la guerre sur la vie syndicale', 16 May 1915. See also *La Bataille*, 26 December 1916.

99. A. Keufer, 'Discours de Keufer', *XIV Congrès Corporatif* (Paris: 1918), p.

259 and 'Le Congrès de la CGT et le problème économique, *La Clairière*, I, 1918, p. 972.

100. A. Keufer, 'La Réponse d'Auguste Keufer', *La Bataille*, 12 March 1918.
101. A. Keufer, 'Les Conséquences de la guerre sur la main d'oeuvre'; 'Commissions mixtes départementales', *La Typographie française*, XXXIV, 16 April 1915; and 'Les Conséquences de la guerre sur la vie syndicale'.
102. See 'Ni grève générale ni insurrection', *GS*, 29 July 1914; G. Hervé, 'Le Patriotisme révolutionnaire', *GS*, 30 July 1914; G. Hervé, 'Le Patrie en danger', 31 July 1914.
103. Pouget's 'La Rue' column ran in *GS* from 7 August 1914 to 6 September 1914.
104. E. Pouget, 'Vieille Alsace', *L'Humanité*, 14 May 1915 to 16 October 1915.
105. An invaluable source of documentary material on opposition to the war amongst syndicalists is to be found in Volume III, *L'Opposition syndicaliste*, and Volume VII, *Tracts et documents divers*, of *Le Mouvement ouvrier français contre la guerre* (Paris: 1985). See also 'Alphonse Merrheim et sa Correspondance confidentielle' in V. Daline, *Hommes et idées* (Moscow: 1970) and A. Rosmer, *Le Mouvement ouvrier pendant la guerre* (Paris: 1936).
106. See C. Chambelland and J. Maitron (eds), pp. 100, 134, 220 and 237–9.
107. P. Monatte, 'Préface' to F. Brupbacher, *Socialisme et liberté* (Paris: 1954), pp. 17–19.
108. P. Monatte, 'Pourquoi je démissionne du Comité confédéral', in C. Chambelland (ed.), *La Lutte syndicale*, pp. 128–32.
109. *L'Union des Métaux*, 1 May 1915 and *VduP*, 1 May 1915. The May Day issue of *La Voix du peuple* was the first issue since the beginning of the war and in addition to a reprint of Jouhaux's speech at Jaurès' graveside comprised a series of articles which attempted to justify the CGT's actions in 1914.
110. A. Rosmer, *Lettres aux abonnés de la Vie ouvrière: I* (Paris: 1915)
111. A. Rosmer, *Lettres aux abonnés de la Vie ouvrière: III L'expulsion de Léon Trotsky* (Paris: 1916), p. 8.
112. A. Rosmer, *Lettres aux abonnés de la Vie ouvrière: I*, p. 9.
113. See C. Chambelland and J. Maitron (eds), pp. 183–7.
114. See for example Comité de Défense Syndicaliste, *Aux Organisations syndicales françaises, à leurs militants* (Paris: 1916) which accused the majority of 'tearing up' the Charter of Amiens and *L'action de la majorité confédérale et la conférence de Leeds* (Paris: 1916) which declared that 'in our view, syndicalism ought not to adapt to circumstances'.
115. See *XIXe Congrès national corporatif* (Paris: 1918), pp. 210–12 and Merrheim's preface to M. Horschiller, *Le Mirage du soviétisme* (Paris: 1921), pp. 7–13.
116. C. Chambelland and J. Maitron (eds), p. 253.
117. P. Monatte, 'Discours au congrès de Lyon', in C. Chambelland (ed.), pp. 173–4.
118. P. Monatte, 'Réflexions sur l'avenir syndical', in C. Chambelland (ed.) pp. 133–50.
119. 'Discours de Jouhaux', *XIXe Congrès national corporatif* (Paris: 1918), pp. 221–39.
120. The text of the 'minimum programme' can be found in *IOS*, 28 November 1918; B. Georges and D. Tintant, *Léon Jouhaux*, I, pp. 461–6; and L. Jouhaux, *Le Syndicalisme et la CGT* (Paris: 1920), pp. 205–13.

121. See the numerous articles published by Jouhaux in *IOS* from the middle of 1919 onwards.

122. See P. Monatte, 'Préface' to F. Brupbacher, pp. 21–6.

123. 'Circulaire de lancement de "La Vie ouvrière" ', in C. Chambelland (ed.) p. 159.

124. P. Monatte, 'Discours au congrès de Lyon', ibid., pp. 160–74.

125. P. Monatte, 'Sauveurs ou Fossoyeurs', *VO*, 4 November 1921.

126. A. Keufer, 'Impressions du militant', *La Clairière*, I, 1918, pp. 597–603.

127. A. Keufer, 'Le Congrès d'Orléans', *La Revue du travail*, III, 1920, pp. 534–42.

128. A. Keufer, 'Collaboration des classes ou lutte de classes', *IOS*, 27 June 1918.

129. A. Keufer, 'L'Action sociale du prolétariat pendant et après la guerre', *IOS*, 23 May 1918.

130. A. Keufer, *Rapport sur l'organisation des relations entre patrons et ouvriers*, (Paris: 1920).

131. A. Keufer, 'Le Congrès d'Orléans', p. 537. See also A. Keufer, 'Les Evénements du 1er Mai', *La Revue du travail*, III, 1920, pp. 103–9.

132. A. Keufer, 'Le Congrès d'Orléans', p. 542 and 'L'Action sociale du prolétariat pendant et après la guerre'.

133. A. Merrheim, *La Révolution économique* (Paris: 1919), p. 25.

134. Ibid., p. 32. Keufer used exactly the same formula; see A. Keufer, *Rapport sur l'organisation des relations entre patrons et ouvriers*, p. 108.

135. See the numerous articles which Merrheim published in *IOS* and *L'Atelier*.

136. A. Merrheim, 'Parlons clair et net', *IOS*, 23 September 1920.

137. A. Merrheim, 'Une nouvelle maladie infantile de la bolchévisme russe', *IOS*, 23 February 1921.

138. A. Merrheim, 'Parlons clair et net', *IOS*, 30 September 1920.

139. A. Merrheim, 'La Dictature imposée aux syndicats', *IOS*, 29 August 1920.

140. L. Trotsky, 'Kronstadt et la Bourse', *VO*, 24 June 1921; K. Radek, 'Cronstadt', *VO*, 7 May 1921; V. Serge, 'Le Tragique d'une révolution', *VO*, 31 March 1922. See also V. Serge, 'Le Problème de la dictature', *VO*, 19 May 1922, where Serge argues 'it is necessary to impose the will of the revolution, to break the resistance of the counter-revolution'.

141. A. Merrheim, 'L'Insurrection contre la dictature', *IOS*, 13 March 1921; 'Les Maladies infantiles du communisme russe', 17 March 1921; and 'La Révolte de Cronstadt', 3 April 1921.

142. A. Merrheim, 'L'Opportunisme de Lénine', *IOS*, 12 December 1920, 6 January 1921, and 13 January 1921; 'La Capitulation définitive de Lénine devant les exigences capitalistes', *L'Atelier*, 21 January 1922 and 'Les Bolsheviks à genoux devant le capitalisme', 4 March 1922.

143. A. Merrheim, 'Nos futurs dictateurs', *IOS*, 23 January 1921 and 'Le Syndicalisme français en péril', *IOS*, 26 May 1921.

144. A. Merrheim, *Amsterdam ou Moscou?* (Paris: 1921), p. 5.

145. A. Merrheim, 'Préface' to M. Horschiller, *Le Mirage du soviétisme* (Paris: 1921), pp. 24–5.

146. Ibid., p. 23 and *Amsterdam ou Moscou?*, pp. 52–60.

147. Ibid., p. 60.

148. P. Monatte, 'Destin du syndicalisme' (1949), in P. Monatte, *Trois Scissions Syndicales* (Paris: 1958), p. 70. See also Monatte's preface to Brupbacher, p. 23, where Monatte writes: 'Up to 1923 we kept the hope that the German Revolution would relieve the Russian Revolution. This hope realised, the

destiny of the Russian Revolution would have been different, that of the world would have changed'.

149. M. Chambelland, 'Où nous en sommes', *VO*, 14 July 1922.
150. C. Chambelland and J. Maitron (eds), p. 267.
151. P. Monatte, 'L'Internationale de la Révolution', *VO*, 10 December 1920. During his period of imprisonment from May 1920 to March 1921 Monatte's articles in *VO* were published under the pseudonym of Pierre Lemont.
152. P. Monatte, 'Orléans, première étape', *VO*, 24 September 1920.
153. P. Monatte, 'Le Syndicalisme, est-il mort à Saint-Etienne', *Clarté*, 1922, p. 470.
154. 'Circulaire de lancement de la "Vie ouvrière" ', p. 159.
155. R. Louzon, 'Guesde, avait-il raison?', *VO*, 27 August 1919 and 'Le Régime des conseils', *VO*, 15 October 1919.
156. P. Monatte, 'Genève ou Moscou', *VO*, 20 August 1920.
157. C. Chambelland, 'La naissance de la Révolution prolétarienne', *Communisme*, 5, 1984, pp. 77–87.
158. P. Monatte, 'Le premier Congrès Communiste du PSU', *VO*, 31 December 1920.
159. P. Monatte, 'Les commissions syndicales', in C. Chambelland (ed.), p. 218.
160. P. Monatte, 'En revenant de Lille', *VO*, 19 August 1921.
161. P. Monatte, 'Faut-il entrer au parti', *VO*, 28 January 1921.
162. P. Monatte, 'Avec Moscou, sans conditions, et dans la CGT quand même', *VO*, 29 October 1920 and 'Syndicalisme et révolution russe', *L'Humanité*, 17 April 1922.
163. P. Monatte, 'Unis pour vaincre', *VO*, 2 December 1921.
164. C. Chambelland, 'Autour du premier Congrès de l'Internationale Syndicale Rouge', *Le Mouvement social*, 47, 1964, pp. 31–44.
165. C. Chambelland and J. Maitron (eds), pp. 295–7.
166. P. Monatte, 'Arrêt? Non! Simple Halte', *VO*, 22 July 1921.
167. See *Bulletin Communiste*, 3, 9 November 1922, pp. 847–8.
168. L. Trotsky, 'Une Explication nécessaire avec les syndicalistes communistes', *Bulletin Communiste*, 4, 12 April 1923, pp. 143–6; R. Louzon, 'Réponse à Trotsky', *Bulletin Communiste*, 4, 3 May 1923, pp. 211–12; and L. Trotsky, 'Encore une fois le préjugé anarcho-syndicaliste', *Bulletin Communiste*, 4, 31 May 1923, pp. 263–4.
169. See K. Amdur, 'Syndicalistes révolutionnaires et communistes', *Le Mouvement social*, 139, 1987, pp. 27–50.
170. See A. Rosmer, *Moscou sous Lénine* (Paris: 1953).
171. See, for example, P. Monatte, 'Notre plus grande préoccupation', *VO*, 28 May 1919.
172. P. Monatte, 'La Faute des masses?' *VO*, 23 July 1919.
173. See the numerous articles written by Monatte during 1922–23 in *L'Humanité*.
174. See A. Kriegel, *Aux origines du communisme français* (Paris: 1964); R. Wohl, *French Communism in the Making 1914–1924* (Stanford: 1966) and D. Tartakowsky, *Les premiers communistes français* (Paris: 1980).
175. P. Monatte, 'Déclarations de Monatte au Comité directeur du 18 mars 1924', *Bulletin Communiste*, 5, 4 April 1924, pp. 252–3.
176. A. Treint, 'Dans la voie tracée par Lénine', *Bulletin Communiste*, 5, 28 March 1924, pp. 321–2.
177. A. Treint, 'Contre la Droite Internationale', *Bulletin Communiste*, 5, 18 April 1924, pp. 385–91.

178. C. Chambelland and J. Maitron (eds), pp. 385–7.
179. P. Monatte, 'Réponse à Treint', *Bulletin Communiste*, 5, 9 May 1924, pp. 461–2 and 'Seconde Réponse à Treint', *Bulletin Communiste*, 5, 16 May 1924, pp. 484–5.
180. C. Chambelland and J. Maitron (eds), pp. 403–6.
181. Ibid., pp. 407–13.
182. Ibid., pp. 416–17.
183. A. Rosmer, P. Monatte, and V. Delagarde, 'La Réponse des trois exclus', *RP*, I, January 1925, p. 28.
184. A. Dunois, 'Une conversation sur la motion d'Amiens avec l'ancien Bureau confédéral', *L'Humanité*, 23 June 1920.
185. C. Chambelland and J. Maitron (eds), pp. 361–2.
186. V. Griffuelhes, 'Ici comme partout! . . .', *La Feuille*, 15 November 1917.
187. V. Griffuelhes, 'Une conférence de M. Victor Griffuelhes', *L'Information ouvrière et sociale*, 8 February 1920; V. Griffuelhes, 'La Conférence de Griffuelhes', *VO*, 13 February 1920.
188. V. Griffuelhes, 'Le nouveau Millerandisme', *La Revue communiste*, I, 1920, pp. 30–3; 'La lutte pour la nationalisation', *La Revue communiste*, I, 1920, pp. 357–60.
189. V. Griffuelhes, 'Ce que personne n'a jamais dit . . .', *La Bataille*, 4 May 1922.
190. See P. Besnard, *L'Ethique du syndicalisme* (Paris: 1938), pp. 127–9.
191. G. Yvetot, *La Bataille*, 6 July 1922.
192. M. Malatesta, 'Georges Sorel devant la guerre et le bolchévisme', in J. Julliard and S. Sand (eds), *Georges Sorel en son temps*, p. 101. See also S. Romano, 'Sorel et le système des relations internationales à la fin de la Première Guerre mondiale', *Cahiers Georges Sorel*, 3, 1985, pp. 39–50.
193. G. Sorel, 'Lettres a Mario Missiroli', in G. Sorel, *Da Proudhon a Lenin e L'Europa sotto la tormenta* (Rome: 1973), p. 513.
194. See G. Sorel, 'Lettres a Mario Missiroli'; 'Germanesimo e storicismo di Ernesto Renan', *La Critica*, XXIX, 1931, pp. 110–14, 199–207, 358–67, 430–44; *Matériaux d'une théorie du prolétariat* (Paris: 1919), p. 53.
195. G. Sorel, 'Exégèses proudhoniennes', *Matériaux d'une théorie du prolétariat*, (Paris: 1921), pp. 415–49.
196. G. Sorel, 'Ultime meditazioni', *Da Proudhon a Lenin e L'Europa sotto la tormenta*, pp. 413–34; reprinted as 'Aperçu sur les utopies, les soviets et le droit nouveau', *Les Cahiers de l'Institut de science économique appliquée*, V (121), 1962, p. 111.
197. G. Sorel, 'La rocca del reazione', *Da Proudhon a Lenin e L'Europa sooto la tormenta*, pp. 127–31.
198. G. Sorel, 'Aperçu sur les utopies, les soviets et le droit nouveau', p. 93.
199. G. Sorel, 'Pour Lénine', *Réflexions sur la violence* (Paris: 1919), pp. 385–7.
200. G. Sorel, 'Il massimalismo italiano', *Da Proudhon a Lenin*, pp. 172–3.
201. G. Sorel, 'Lettres a Mario Missiroli', p. 716.
202. G. Sorel, 'Aperçu sur les utopies, les soviets et le droit nouveau', p. 112.
203. See S. Sand, *L'Illusion du politique* (Paris: 1985), pp. 14–22; M. Charzat, 'Georges Sorel et le fascisme. Eléments d'explication d'une légende tenace', *Cahiers Georges Sorel*, 1, 1983, pp. 37–52; R. Vivarelli, 'Georges Sorel et le fascisme', in J. Julliard and S. Sand (eds), pp. 123–33.
204. See J. Variot (ed.), *Propos de Georges Sorel* (Paris: 1935); J. Variot, 'Quelques souvenirs: le père Sorel', *L'Eclair*, 11 September 1922; P. Andreu, *Georges Sorel: entre le noir et le rouge*, (Paris: 1982), p. 109, n. 1;

P. Andreu, Introduction to 'Lettres de Georges Sorel à Edouard Berth', *Cahiers Georges Sorel*, 3, 1985, pp. 79–80.

205. See G. Sorel, 'L'Indépendance Egyptienne', *L'Egypte*, ii, 2, 1920, pp. 3–6; 'Egypte et Impérialisme', *ibid*, ii, 4, 1920, pp. 3–8; 'Nouvelle position de la question Egyptienne', *ibid*, ii, 10, 1920, pp. 8–11; 'Le bolchevisme en Egypte', *La Revue communiste*, i, 1920, pp. 27–32; G. Sorel and L. Auriant, 'Jeremy Bentham et l'indépendance de l'Egypte', *Le Mercure de France*, clv, 1922, pp. 397–410. For an account of the collaboration between Sorel and the mysterious figure of L. Auriant see L. Auriant, *Fragments* (Brussels: 1942), pp. 9–16.

206. For a more detailed examination of this issue see my 'Georges Sorel and colonialism: the case of Egypt', *History of Political Thought*, viii, 1987, pp. 325–33.

207. M. Rebérioux, ' "La Guerre sociale" et "Le Mouvement socialiste", face au problème colonial', *Mouvement social*, 46, 1964, pp. 91–103.

208. F. Pelloutier, 'La Pétaudière coloniale', *Le Journal du peuple*, 14, 21, and 27 March 1899 and 3 April 1899.

209. G. Sorel, 'L'imperialismo', *Da Proudhon a Lenin*, pp. 42–7.

210. G. Sorel, 'L'Egypte et Impérialisme', p. 6.

211. G. Sorel, *Les Illusions du progrès* (Paris: 1921), pp. 385–6.

212. E. Berth, 'Georges Sorel', *Clarté*, i, 1922, pp. 495–6; 'Le Tertullien du Socialisme', *La Rivoluzione liberale*, 14 December 1922, pp. 139–40.

213. E. Berth, *Guerre des états ou guerre des classes* (Paris: 1924).

214. See for example the four articles written by Berth under the pseudonym of E. Darville for *L'Humanité*: 'On croit mourir pour sa patrie', 23 July 1922; 'Guerre ou révolution', 18 September 1922; 'Le "stupide" ', 14 October 1922; 'La "Tyrannie de Moscou" ', 2 April 1923; and 'Lénine, qui est-ce?', *Clarté*, 64, 1924, pp. 343–9; 65, 1924, pp. 383–6; 66, 1924, pp. 422–4.

215. E. Berth, *Les Derniers aspects du socialisme* (Paris: 1923).

216. E. Berth, 'On croit mourir pour sa patrie'.

217. E. Berth, 'Guerre ou révolution'.

218. E. Berth, 'La leçon du fascisme', *Clarté*, 26, 1922, pp. 43–6 and *Guerre des états ou guerre des classes*, p. 153, n. 1.

219. E. Berth, 'La "Tyrannie de Moscou" '.

220. E. Berth, *Guerre des états ou guerre des classes*, p. 19 and G. Guy-Grand, 'Violence, Fascisme et Bolchevisme', *Le Quotidien*, 17 December 1926.

221. E. Berth, *Guerre des états our guerre des classes*, p. 42.

222. *Ibid*, p. 86.

223. E. Berth, *Les Derniers aspects du socialisme*, p. 29.

224. E. Berth, *Guerre des états ou guerre des classes*, p. 263.

225. *Ibid*, p. 261.

Notes to Chapter 6

1. See 'Hommage à Keufer', *RPI* xxiii, 1920, pp. 102–5; 'Discours de M. Keufer', *RPI*, xxxi, 1924, pp. 115–20.

2. See M. Chambelland, 'Dernière visite au "Père Peinard" ', in P. Delesalle (ed.), *Emile Pouget: Ad Memoriam* (Paris: 1931), pp. 11–14; G. Yvetot, 'Les vieux s'en vont: ce que fut Emile Pouget — Le Père Peinard', *La Voix libertaire*, 19 September 1931.

3. Yvetot's articles appeared in *La Voix libertaire* throughout 1931 and 1932.

See S. Faure (ed.), *Encyclopédie anarchiste* (Paris: 1934–5), 4 vols. pp. 2203–4, 2227–33, 2281–4, 2338–9, 2344–5, 2359–60, 2364–7, 2491–4, 2584–5, 2621–22, 2624–31.

4. R. Courtois, 'Un pionnier du syndicalisme: Georges Yvetot', *Le Cri du peuple*, 28 April 1942.

5. *Le Cri du peuple*, 16 May 1942.

6. See B. Georges and D. Tintant, *Léon Jouhaux* (Paris: 1962), I, pp. 270–1 and C. Gras, *Alfred Rosmer et le mouvement internationale révolutionnaire* (Paris: 1971), pp. 125–6.

7. P. Delesalle, *Épisodes et vies révolutionnaires: Paris sous la Commune* (Paris: 1937).

8. P. Delesalle, 'Jules Guesde', *La Bataille*, 3 August 1922; 'Souvenirs d'un camarade de lutte: Griffuelhes', *L'Humanité*, 10 July 1922; 'La Vie militante d'Emile Pouget', *Le Cri du peuple*, 29 July 1931 and 5 August 1931; 'Bibliographie Sorélienne', *International Review of Social History*, IV, 1939, pp. 463–87.

9. P. Delesalle, 'Front unique et syndicalisme', *Bulletin communiste*, 3, 1922, pp. 132–3; 'Albin Villeval', *RP*, 146, 25 February 1933, pp. 63–5.

10. See for example E. Berth, 'Sorel . . . pas socialiste!', *RP*, 124, 15 February 1932, pp. 57–60; ' "La Révolte des masses" ', *RP*, 264, 10 February 1938, pp. 38–43; 'Georges Sorel ou . . . l'esprit déchu!', *RP*, 272, 10 June 1938, pp. 179–81.

11. E. Berth, *Du "Capital" aux "Réflexions sur la violence"* (Paris: 1932), p. 44.

12. E. Berth, *La Fin d'une culture* (Paris: 1927); see also E. Berth, *La France au milieu du monde* (Turin: 1924).

13. E. Berth, 'Enfin, nous avons Hitler! ou La fin de l'Europe libérale', *RP*, 161, 10 October 1933, pp. 371–6 and 162, 25 October 1933, pp. 391–4.

14. See for example *Du "Capital" au "Réflexions sur la violence"*, pp. 259–68 and E. Berth, 'Le Syndicalisme révolutionnaire, est-il encore possible?', *RP*, 105, 1 June 1930, pp. 165–71.

15. *Du "Capital" au "Réflexions sur la violence"*, p. 262.

16. Ibid., p. 42.

17. *La Fin d'une culture*, p. 201.

18. See pp. 77–9.

19. E. Berth, 'Préface' to G. Sorel, *D'Aristote à Marx*, p. 46. For Bergson's response to this argument see the letter he wrote to Berth dated 14 January 1936 in S. Sand, 'Quelques remarques sur Sorel, critique de *L'Evolution créatrice*', *Cahiers Georges Sorel*, 1, 1983, pp. 109–10.

20. E. Berth, 'Préface' to *D'Aristote à Marx*, p. 32.

21. Ibid., p. 51.

22. *Du "Capital" au "Réflexions sur la violence"*, p. 185.

23. E. Berth, 'Préface' to *D'Aristote à Marx*, p. 41.

24. Ibid., pp. 89–91.

25. Ibid., p. 63.

26. See also E. Berth, 'Variations sur quatre thèmes proudhoniens', *L'Homme réel*, I, September 1934, pp. 8–21 and 'La Propriété selon Proudhon', *L'Homme réel*, 4 Jan 1937, pp. 9–31.

27. *Du "Capital" au "Réflexions sur la violence"*, p. 7 and 'Le Syndicalisme révolutionnaire, est-il encore possible?', p. 168.

28. Ibid., pp. 165–71 and *RP*, 106, 15 June 1930, pp. 177–83.

29. E. Berth, 'Nous n'aurons pas "notre" Hitler!', *RP*, 174, 10 May 1934, pp.

163–8 and 'Vers une nouvelle mystification', *RP*, 210, 10 November 1935, pp. 345–8.

30. E. Berth, 'L'Occupation des usines', *RP*, 234, 10 November 1936, pp. 335–41 and 'Guerre des Etats ou guerre des classes?', *RP*, 243, 25 March 1937, p. 506, n. 1.

31. Ibid., pp. 501–6.

32. 'Enfin, nous avons Hitler!', p. 391 and 'Guerre des Etats ou guerre des classes', pp. 501–2.

33. E. Berth, 'Clan des Ya? Clan des Da?', *RP*, 277, 25 August 1938, pp. 257–9.

34. *RP*, 202, 10 July 1935, p. 223.

35. 'Guerre des Etats ou guerre des classes?', p. 505.

36. See R. Soucy, *French Fascism: the first wave* (Newhaven: 1986).

37. See Y. Guchet, *Georges Valois* (Paris: 1975), pp. 144–241.

38. *Du "Capital" aux "Réflexions sur la violence"*, p. 83, n. 1.

39. See the editorial note appended to Berth's 'Sorel . . . pas socialiste!', p. 60.

40. See 'La Conférence nationale de St-Denis', *RP*, 205, 25 August 1935, pp. 267–71 and P. Monatte, 'Les saboteurs du mouvement contre la guerre', *RP*, 207, 25 September 1935, pp. 302–3.

41. E. Berth, 'Lettre ouverte aux camarades de la RP à propos du "cas Valois" ', *Nouvel âge*, 5 March 1936.

42. G. Valois, 'Sorel, la violence, la guerre, notre action', *Nouvel âge*, 5 April 1938 and E. Berth, 'Réflexions à propos des "Réflexions sur la violence" ', *Nouvel âge*, 6 May 1938 and 10 May 1938.

43. E. Berth, 'L'Accord de Munich', *Nouvel âge*, 22 December 1938, 23 December 1938 and 24 December 1938. Valois himself was critical of the pacifism of the left: see 'La faute à ne pas commettre', *Nouvel âge*, 4 May 1938 and 'Devant Hitler', *Nouvel âge*, 5 May 1938.

44. H. Lagardelle, *Sud-Ouest: une région française* (Paris: 1929).

45. H. Lagardelle, 'La France vue par un Etranger', *L'Humanité*, 3 November 1913; see also 'L'Anarchisme', 1 October 1913.

46. H. Lagardelle, 'Pour l'Assemblée Régionale Professionnelle', *IR*, 27 March 1926.

47. Ibid., and *Sud-Ouest: une région française*, p. 164.

48. H. Lagardelle, 'Le Régionalisme', *IR*, 27 March 1926.

49. See especially H. Lagardelle, 'Pour l'Assemblée Régionale Professionnelle' and 'Aspects économiques de la région Toulousaine', *SOE*, 184, March 1929, p. 237.

50. H. Lagardelle, *Sud-Ouest: une région économique*, p. 166.

51. H. Lagardelle, 'L'Assemblée Régionale Professionnelle', *IR*, 13 March 1926. See also 'Pour la Région', *IR*, 9 January 1926; 'Pour l'Assemblée Régionale Professionnelle'; 'Organisons les compétences', *IR*, 10 July 1926; 'La Région Professionnelle' *IR*, 31 July 1926.

52. H. Lagardelle, 'Profession et politique', *IR*, 20 February 1927.

53. H. Lagardelle, *Sud-Ouest: une région française*, p. 167.

54. See *RP*, 102, 15 April 1930, p. 124 and *RP*, 125, 1 May 1932, p. 93.

55. See Z. Sternhell, *Ni droite ni gauche* (Paris: 1983), pp. 33, 67, 129 and 333.

56. See 'Le Redressement français', *IR*, 9 April 1927. On Mercier see R. F. Kuisel, *Ernest Mercier: French Technocrat* (Berkeley and Los Angeles: 1967). According to Kuisel, Lagardelle acted as an adviser to *Le Redressement Français* and became a close friend of Mercier's.

57. See specifically J. Touchard, 'L'Esprit des années 1930: une tentative de

renouvellement de la pensée politique française' in G. Michaud (ed.), *Tend-ances politiques dans la vie française depuis 1789* (Paris: 1960) and J-L Loubet del Bayle, *Les non-conformistes des années 30* (Paris: 1969).

58. Lamour himself published an article which set out many of the typical 1930s themes: see 'La Révolution et la jeunesse', *Nouvelle revue française*, XXIX, 1932, pp. 812–14. For a broader perspective see the series in which Lamour's article appeared, 'Cahier de revendications', *Nouvelle revue française*, XXIX, 1932, pp. 801–45. The contributors included Paul Nizan, Raymond Aron, Emmanuel Mounier and Thierry Maulnier.

59. On planning in the 1930s see J. Jackson, *The Politics of Depression* (Cambridge: 1986).

60. See for example the editorial for the first issue, 'La Ligne Générale', *Plans*, I, January 1931, pp. 7–9.

61. H. Lagardelle, 'De l'homme abstrait à l'homme réel', *Plans*, I, January 1931, pp. 24–32.

62. Ibid., p. 24.

63. Ibid., p. 32.

64. H. Lagardelle, 'L'Homme réel et le syndicalisme', *Plans*, 3, March 1931, pp. 11–17.

65. Fonds Delesalle, Institut Français d'Histoire Sociale, 14 AS 53bis.

66. H. Lagardelle, 'Supercapitalisme', *Plans*, 10, December 1931, pp. 7–12. See also 'Sources du syndicalisme', *Plans*, 12, February 1932, pp. 14–21.

67. H. Lagardelle, 'Supercapitalisme', p. 12.

68. Letter from Lagardelle to Robert Louzon, dated 31 December 1932; repro-duced in M. Dachary de Flers, *Lagardelle et l'équipe du Mouvement sociali-ste*, p. 313.

69. H. Lagardelle, 'Le fascisme: doctrine, institutions', *Encyclopaedie Françai-se*, X, (Paris: 1935), pp. 84, 5–84, 15.

70. H. Lagardelle, *Mission à Rome: Mussolini* (Paris: 1955).

71. Ibid., p. 60.

72. Ibid., p. 89.

73. Ibid., pp. 260–2.

74. R. Rémond, *Les Droites en France* (Paris: 1982), p. 236.

75. P. Pétain, *La France nouvelle* (Paris, n.d.), p. 78.

76. R. Belin, *Du Secrétariat de la CGT au Gouvernement de Vichy* (Paris: 1978).

77. See in particular J. Rancière, 'De Pelloutier à Hitler: syndicalisme et collab-oration', *Les Révoltes logiques*, 4, Winter 1977, pp. 23–61 and P. Ory, *Les collaborateurs 1940–1945* (Paris: 1976), pp. 128–45.

78. On Vichy economic policy see R. F. Kuisel, *Capitalism and the State in Modern France* (Cambridge: 1981), pp. 128–56.

79. See here two left-wing newspapers, *L'Atelier* and *Germinal*. The latter continued as late as July 1944 to demand 'the honest application' of the *Charte du Travail*.

80. These papers are to be found at the Institut d'Histoire Sociale (IHS).

81. H. Lagardelle, 'Principes de la Charte du travail', *La Politique Française*, 1, 1 October 1943, pp. 28–9.

82. H. Lagardelle, 'Allocution prononcée le 18 Avril 1943', IHS.

83. Ibid.

84. J. Rivain, 'Les Entretiens de Vichy: Anticipations par Hubert Lagardelle', *L'Unité française*, June 1942, pp. 131–40.

85. H. Lagardelle, 'Déclaration au Petit Parisien (4 October 1943)', IHS.

86. H. Lagardelle, 'Allocution prononcée à l'Ecole Supérieure d'Organisation Professionelle (20 January 1943)', IHS.

87. H. Lagardelle, 'Retours offensifs', *La France socialiste*, 13–14 July, 1944 and 'Tendances communes', 15–16 July, 1944.

88. H. Lagardelle, 'Le Maréchal est venu à Paris', *La France socialiste*, 27 April 1944; 'Retour', 10 May 1944; 'Deux Dates', 24–25 June 1944.

89. H. Lagardelle, 'Retour des barbares', *La France socialiste*, 5 April 1944 and 'Créations et destructions', 5 June 1944.

90. H. Lagardelle, 'Socialisations italiennes', *La France socialiste*, 1–2 April 1944.

91. H. Lagardelle, 'Le Socialisme nécessaire', *La France socialiste*, 31 January 1944; 'Syndicalisme construtif', 15 March 1944; 'Socialisme 1944', 18 May 1944.

92. H. Lagardelle, 'Communes et régions', *La France socialiste*, 12 April 1944.

93. H. Lagardelle, 'Sport et travail', *La France socialiste*, 3 May 1944.

94. H. Lagardelle, 'Individualisme', *La France socialiste*, 18–19 March 1944; 'Parlementarisme', 25–26 March 1944; 'Les Syndicats et l'Etat', 29 March 1944; 'Communes et régions'.

95. H. Lagardelle, 'Démocratie politique', *La France socialiste*, 22 March 1944.

96. H. Lagardelle, 'Lettere di Giorgio Sorel a Uberto Lagardelle', *Educazione fascista* XI, 1933, pp. 229–43, 320–34, 507–18, 760–83, 956–75 and R. Racouly, 'Un entretien avec M. Lagardelle', *Gringoire*, 22 May 1942.

97. 'Lettere di Giorgio Sorel a Uberto Lagardelle', p. 233.

98. H. Lagardelle, 'Préface' to J. Gaumont, *L'Etat contre la nation* (Paris: 1911), p. 2 and 'Déclaration au Petit Parisien (4 October 1943)'.

99. The sub-title was changed in 1930 to 'Revue bi-mensuelle syndicaliste révolutionnaire'.

100. P. Monatte, 'Carnet du Sauvage', *RP*, 1, January 1925, p. 7.

101. 'Entre nous', *RP*, 2 February 1925, p. 32.

102. 'La Réponse des trois exclus', *RP*, 1, January 1925, pp. 23–8.

103. A. Rosmer, 'La Légende du trotskyisme', *RP*, 2 February 1925, pp. 1–8.

104. 'La Réponse du "noyau" à deux demandes de Trotsky', *RP*, 10, October 1925, pp. 1–6.

105. P. Monatte, 'L'Exil de Trotsky', *RP*, 10, October 1925, p. 66.

106. The diaries of Pierre Monatte are in the personal possession of Colette Chambelland. I am indebted to her for allowing me to consult them.

107. A. Rosmer, 'Les Problèmes de la révolution russe', *RP*, 24, December 1926, pp. 16–20.

108. P. Monatte, 'Le Phare, va-t-il s'éteindre?', *RP*, 45, 1 November 1927, pp. 321–4; R. Louzon, 'Staline, premier consul', *RP*, 46, 15 November 1927, pp. 337–8; A. Rosmer, 'La Dictature stalinienne et la liquidation du communisme', *RP*, 47, 1 December 1927, pp. 357–61.

109. Serge made numerous contributions to *RP* during the 1930s but see 'La Profession de foi de Victor Serge', *RP*, 152, 25 May 1933, p. 193 and 'Une lettre de Victor Serge au Comité Central Exécutif des Soviets', *RP*, 153, 10 June 1953, pp. 210–11. See also Jean-Louis Panné, 'L'affaire Victor Serge et la gauche française', *Communisme*, 5, 1984, pp. 89–104.

110. M. Martinet, V. Serge, M. Yvon, P. Monatte, 'Le 30 juin de Staline', *RP*, 230, 10 September 1936, pp. 261–70 and P. Monatte, 'Le troisième acte de 30 juin de Staline', *RP*, 240, 10 February 1937, pp. 437–43.

111. P. Monatte, 'Carnet du Sauvage', *RP*, 100, 15 March 1930, p. 83–4.

112. P. Monatte, 'Remercions Staline', *RP*, 199, 25 May 1935, p. 173.

113. P. Monatte, 'Le Scandale de la direction unique', *RP*, 25, 1 January 1927, pp. 3–6.
114. P. Monatte, 'L'Autonomie syndicale, formule d'avenir', *RP*, 94, 15 December 1929, p. 373.
115. Monatte wrote numerous pieces on this theme but see in particular P. Monatte, 'L'Autonomie syndicale, formule d'avenir', *RP*, 91, 15 November 1929, pp. 341–4 and 94, 15 December 1929, pp. 369–74; 'Le Syndicalisme de 1906 ne peut pas mourir', *RP*, 242, 10 March 1937, pp. 493–5.
116. See for example P. Monatte, 'La Lutte pour l'unité syndicale', *RP*, 3, March 1925, pp. 1–3; 'Quand sonnera l'heure de l'unité', 13, Jan 1926, pp. 13–18, 14, Feb. 1926, pp. 15–18, 16, April 1926, pp. 1–4; 'Le Scandale la "direction unique"', 21, September 1926, pp. 1–4; 'La campagne pour l'unité', 113, 5 January 1931, pp. 1–3; 'La deuxième étape du mouvement pour l'unité', 114, 5 February 1931, pp. 42–4.
117. M. Chambelland, 'Une Ligue Syndicaliste', *RP*, 10, October 1925, p. 12.
118. 'Ce qu'est, ce que veut la Ligue Syndicaliste', *RP*, 19, July 1926, pp. 21–22. See also P. Monatte, 'La Ligue Syndicaliste doit se persévérer', *RP*, 98, 15 February 1930, pp. 61–2.
119. The text of the 'Manifeste de 22' can be found in *RP*, 112, 5 December 1930, p. 333 and *Le Cri du peuple*, 12 November 1930. See also P. Monatte, 'Le Réveil du syndicalisme' *RP*, 111, 5 November 1930, pp. 289–92 and 'La peur de l'unité syndicale', 112, 5 December 1930, pp. 321–4.
120. P. Monatte, 'La Vie et la mort du Comité des 22', *RP*, 122, 1 December 1931, pp. 292–302.
121. P. Monatte, 'La Classe ouvrière reprend confiance en elle', *RP*, 226, 10 July 1936, pp. 177–82; reprinted in C. Chambelland (ed.), *La Lutte syndicale*, pp. 222–36.
122. R. Louzon, 'Notes d'économie et de politique', *RP*, 202, 10 July 1935, pp. 217–18.
123. P. Monatte, 'L'unité nous donnera une CGT d'action', *RP*, 208, 10 October 1935, pp. 315–6.
124. P. Monatte, 'La Classe ouvrière reprend confiance en elle'.
125. See for example M. Chambelland, 'Les Délégués d'atelier', *RP*, 236, 10 December 1936, pp. 376–82.
126. On the Popular Front see J. Jackson. *The Popular Front in France: Defending Democracy, 1934–38* (Cambridge: 1988).
127. P. Monatte, 'La contre-offensive du patronat', *RP*, 234, 10 November 1936, pp. 344–6 and 'Le Syndicalisme de 1906 ne peut pas mourir'.
128. See pp. 198–200.
129. See for example 'Pour un nouveau Zimmerwald', *RP*, 200, 10 June 1935, p. 185 and 'Contre la guerre! contre l'union sacrée', *RP*, 203, 25 July 1935, pp. 233–4.
130. P. Monatte, 'Remercions Staline'.
131. P. Monatte, *Où va la CTG?*, reprinted in C. Chambelland (ed.), pp. 238–65.
132. P. Monatte, 'Le Carnet du Sauvage', *RP*, 309, November 1947, p. 225.
133. P. Monatte, 'Le Carnet du Sauvage', *RP*, 317, July 1948, p. 488.
134. P. Monatte, 'L'Antimilitarisme imbécile', *RP*, 439, May 1959, p. 97.
135. P. Monatte, 'Le Carnet du Sauvage', *RP*, 362, May 1952, p. 146.
136. P. Monatte, 'Le Carnet du Sauvage', *RP*, 372, April 1953, p. 111.
137. *Cercle Zimmerwald*, ɪ, July-September 1956, p. 11.
138. See here the articles reprinted in P. Monatte, *Trois scissions syndicales* (Paris: 1958), pp. 176–230.

139. P. Monatte, 'Le Carnet du Sauvage', *RP*, 311, Jan 1948, p. 291. See A. Bergounioux, *Force ouvrière* (Paris: 1975).
140. P. Monatte, 'Deuxième lettre d'un ancien à quelques jeunes syndiqués sans galons', in C. Chambelland (ed.), p. 278.
141. Ibid., p. 278 and 'La 3me unité syndicale', *RP*, 428, May 1958, p. 118.
142. P Monatte, 'Le Carnet du Sauvage', *RP*, 327, May 1949, pp. 132–4.
143. See C. Chambelland (ed.), p. 278 and *RP*, 406, June 1956, p. 117.
144. C. Chambelland (ed.), p. 278.
145. P. Monatte, 'Le Carnet du Sauvage', *RP*, 335, Jan 1950, pp. 5–7.
146. See Monatte's diary for 1953.
147. R. Louzon, 'La Répétition générale et le drame de demain', *RP*, 341, July 1950, pp. 193–6.
148. R. Louzon, 'A propos de l' "indépendance française" ', *RP*, 377, October 1953, pp. 257–60.
149. P. Monatte, 'Parti américain? Non! Parti internationaliste', *RP*, 378, November 1953, pp. 257–60. Monatte noted in his diary: 'Louzon has never been and is not a Zimmerwaldian'. Rosmer in particular was insensed by Louzon's comparison at one point of Trotsky and Lenin, the suppressors of the Kronstadt rebellion, with Thiers and Cavaignac, the suppressors of the Paris Commune.
150. P. Monatte, 'Préface', to F. Brupbacher, *Socialisme et liberté*, reprinted in *Trois scissions syndicales*, p. 255. See also ibid., pp. 5–17, 69–78, 133–7 and 'La 3me unité syndicale'.

Notes to Chapter 7

1. See J. Moreau, 'Le Syndicalisme hier et demain', *RP*, 674, 1986, p. 1.
2. For a discussion of the dilemma facing French trade unions see M. Rose, 'Economic nationalism and the unions: the decline of the solution *franco-française*', in J. Howorth and G. Ross, *Contemporary France*, II (London: 1988), pp. 157–83.
3. See in particular Z. Sternhell, *La Droite révolutionnaire: 1885–1914* (Paris: 1978); *Ni droite ni gauche* (Paris: 1983); 'The 'Anti-materialist' Revision of Marxism as an Aspect of the Rise of Fascist Ideology', *Journal of Contemporary History*, 22, 1987, pp. 379–400. For Sternhell's latest contribution see *Naissance de l'idéologie fasciste* (Paris: 1989).
4. *Ni droite ni gauche*, pp. 40–41.
5. For a selection of the literature on Sternhell's work see M. Winock, 'Fascisme à la française ou fascisme introuvable', *Le Débat*, 25 May 1983, pp. 35–44; S. Sand, 'L'idéologie fasciste en France', *L'Esprit*, 80–1, 1983, pp. 149–60; J. Julliard, 'Sur un fascisme imaginaire', in Julliard, *Autonomie ouvrière* (Paris: 1988), pp. 269–85; S. Berstein, 'La France des années trente allergique au fascisme', *Vingtième siècle*, 2, 1984, pp. 84–94; S. Romano, 'Sternhell lu d'Italie', *Vingtième siècle*, 6, 1985, pp. 75–81; A. C. Pinto, 'Fascist Ideology Revisited: Zeev Sternhell and His Critics', *European History Quaterley*, 16, 1986, pp. 465–83.
6. Sternhell here makes considerable use of Pierre Andreu's article 'Fascisme 1913' (published in the February 1936 issue of *Combat*) to support his case. He might equally have referred to Jean Variot's 'Georges Sorel et la Révolution nationale' (published in August 1941 in *La Revue universelle*). Unlike Andreu who implies that elements of a fascist atmosphere are to be

found in pre-First World War France, Variot states categorically that Sorel could not be considered as a 'guide' by those intent on implementing Vichy's 'national revolution'.

7. See Sternhell, 'The 'Anti-Materialist' Revision of Marxism . . .', p. 380 and *Ni droite ni gauche*, pp. 15–43.
8. Ibid., p. 35.
9. 'The "Anti-Materialist" Revision of Marxism . . .', p. 389.
10. Sternhell, *La Droite révolutionnaire*, pp. 318–47.
11. See Julliard, *Autonomie ouvrière*, pp. 242–7, 268; T. Judt, *Marxism and the French Left* (Oxford: 1986), pp. 1–11; H. Hamon and P. Rotman, *La Deuxième gauche* (Paris: 1982).

Index